THE CLAY SANSKRIT LIBRARY
FOUNDED BY JOHN & JENNIFER CLAY

WWW.CLAYSANSKRITLIBRARY.COM
WWW.NYUPRESS.ORG

First Edition 2006.

The Clay Sanskrit Library is co-published by
New York University Press
and the JJC Foundation.

Further information about this volume
and the rest of the Clay Sanskrit Library
is available on the following Websites:
www.claysanskritlibrary.com
www.nyupress.org.

ISBN-13: 978-0-8147-8295-8 (cloth : alk. paper)
ISBN-10: 0-8147-8295-7 (cloth : alk. paper)

Artwork by Robert Beer.
Typeset in Adobe Garamond at 10.25 : 12.3+pt.
XML-development by Stuart Brown.
Editorial input by Dániel Balogh, Tomoyuki Kono,
Eszter Somogyi & Péter Szántó.
Printed in Great Britain by St Edmundsbury Press Ltd,
Bury St Edmunds, Suffolk, on acid-free paper.
Bound by Hunter & Foulis Ltd, Edinburgh, Scotland.

RĀMA BEYOND PRICE
BY MURĀRI

EDITED AND TRANSLATED BY

JUDIT TÖRZSÖK

NEW YORK UNIVERSITY PRESS
JJC FOUNDATION
2006

Library of Congress Cataloging-in-Publication Data
Murāri
[Anargharāghava. English & Sanskrit]
Rama Beyond Price / by Murāri ;
edited and translated by Judit Törzsök. – 1st ed.
p. cm. – (The Clay Sanskrit library)
Play.
In English and Sanskrit (romanized) on facing pages;
Includes translation from Sanskrit.
Includes bibliographical references and index.
ISBN-13: 978-0-8147-8295-8 (cloth : alk. paper)
ISBN-10: 0-8147-8295-7 (cloth : alk. paper)
I. Törzsök, Judit. II. Title.
PK3798.M82A813 2006
892.2 '2–dc22
2006022414

CONTENTS

Sanskrit alphabetical order 7
CSL conventions 7

RAMA BEYOND PRICE

Introduction 13

Benediction 43
Prologue 47
Act I: The Discussion of the Sages 61
Prelude to Act II 103
Act II: Childhood Exploits 125
Prelude to Act III 173
Act III: The Breaking of Shiva's Bow 187
Prelude to Act IV 231
Act IV: Dasha·ratha is Tricked 257
Prelude to Act V 307
Act V: Sugríva's Consecration 325
Prelude to Act VI 369
Act VI: Rávana's Defeat 397
Prelude to Act VII: Indication of Events 449
Act VII: The Happiness of the Hero 453

Paraphrase of Prakrit *(chāyā)* 555
Notes 565
Index 615

A *sandhi* grid is printed on the inside of the back cover

SANSKRIT ALPHABETICAL ORDER

Vowels:	*a ā i ī u ū ṛ ṝ ḷ ḹ e ai o au ṃ ḥ*
Gutturals:	*k kh g gh ṅ*
Palatals:	*c ch j jh ñ*
Retroflex:	*ṭ ṭh ḍ ḍh ṇ*
Dentals:	*t th d dh n*
Labials:	*p ph b bh m*
Semivowels:	*y r l v*
Spirants:	*ś ṣ s h*

GUIDE TO SANSKRIT PRONUNCIATION

a	b*u*t
ā, â	f*a*ther
i	s*i*t
ī, î	f*ee*
u	p*u*t
ū, û	b*oo*
ṛ	vocalic *r*, American p*ur*dy or English p*re*tty
ṝ	lengthened *ṛ*
ḷ	vocalic *l*, ab*le*
e, ê, ē	m*a*de, esp. in Welsh pronunciation
ai	b*i*te
o, ô, ō	r*o*pe, esp. Welsh pronunciation; Italian s*o*lo
au	s*ou*nd
ṃ	*anusvāra* nasalizes the preceding vowel
ḥ	*visarga*, a voiceless aspiration (resembling English *h*), or like Scottish lo*ch*, or an aspiration with a faint echoing of the preceding vowel so that *taiḥ* is pronounced *taih[i]*
k	lu*ck*
kh	blo*ckh*ead
g	*g*o
gh	bi*gh*ead
ṅ	a*n*ger
c	*ch*ill
ch	mat*chh*ead
j	*j*og
jh	aspirated *j*, he*dgeh*og
ñ	ca*ny*on
ṭ	retroflex *t*, *t*ry (with the tip of tongue turned up to touch the hard palate)
ṭh	same as the preceding but aspirated
ḍ	retroflex *d* (with the tip of tongue turned up to touch the hard palate)
ḍh	same as the preceding but aspirated
ṇ	retroflex *n* (with the tip of tongue turned up to touch the hard palate)

t	French *t*out	*y*	*y*es
th	ten*t h*ook	*r*	trilled, resembling the Italian pronunciation of *r*
d	*d*inner	*l*	*l*inger
dh	guil*dh*all	*v*	*w*ord
n	*n*ow	*ś*	*sh*ore
p	*p*ill	*ṣ*	retroflex *sh* (with the tip of the tongue turned up to touch the hard palate)
ph	u*ph*eaval	*s*	hi*ss*
b	*b*efore	*h*	*h*ood
bh	a*bh*orrent		
m	*m*ind		

CSL PUNCTUATION OF ENGLISH

The acute accent on Sanskrit words when they occur outside of the Sanskrit text itself, marks stress, e.g. Ramáyana. It is not part of traditional Sanskrit orthography, transliteration or transcription, but we supply it here to guide readers in the pronunciation of these unfamiliar words. Since no Sanskrit word is accented on the last syllable it is not necessary to accent disyllables, e.g. Rama.

The second CSL innovation designed to assist the reader in the pronunciation of lengthy unfamiliar words is to insert an unobtrusive middle dot between semantic word breaks in compound names (provided the word break does not fall on a vowel resulting from the fusion of two vowels), e.g. Maha·bhárata, but Ramáyana (not Rama·áyana). Our dot echoes the punctuating middle dot (·) found in the oldest surviving forms of written Indic, the Ashokan inscriptions of the third century BCE.

The deep layering of Sanskrit narrative has also dictated that we use quotation marks only to announce the beginning and end of every direct speech, and not at the beginning of every paragraph.

CSL PUNCTUATION OF SANSKRIT

The Sanskrit text is also punctuated, in accordance with the punctuation of the English translation. In mid-verse, the punctuation will not alter the *sandhi* or the scansion. Proper names are capitalized. Most Sanskrit metres have four "feet" *(pāda):* where possible we print the common *śloka* metre on two lines. In the Sanskrit text, we use French *Guillemets* (e.g. *«kva saṃcicīrṣuḥ?»*) instead of English quotation marks (e.g. "Where are you off to?") to avoid confusion with the apostrophes used for vowel elision in *sandhi*.

Sanskrit presents the learner with a challenge: *sandhi* ("euphonic combination"). *Sandhi* means that when two words are joined in connected speech or writing (which in Sanskrit reflects speech), the last letter (or even letters) of the first word often changes; compare the way we pronounce "the" in "the beginning" and "the end."

In Sanskrit the first letter of the second word may also change; and if both the last letter of the first word and the first letter of the second are vowels, they may fuse. This has a parallel in English: a nasal consonant is inserted between two vowels that would otherwise coalesce: "a pear" and "an apple." Sanskrit vowel fusion may produce ambiguity. The chart at the back of each book gives the full *sandhi* system.

Fortunately it is not necessary to know these changes in order to start reading Sanskrit. For that, what is important is to know the form of the second word without *sandhi* (pre-*sandhi*), so that it can be recognized or looked up in a dictionary. Therefore we are printing Sanskrit with a system of punctuation that will indicate, unambiguously, the original form of the second word, i.e., the form without *sandhi*. Such *sandhi* mostly concerns the fusion of two vowels.

In Sanskrit, vowels may be short or long and are written differently accordingly. We follow the general convention that a vowel with no mark above it is short. Other books mark a long vowel either with a bar called a macron (*ā*) or with a circumflex (*â*). Our system uses the macron, except that for initial vowels in *sandhi* we use a circumflex to indicate that originally the vowel was short, or the shorter of two possibilities (*e* rather than *ai*, *o* rather than *au*).

When we print initial	before *sandhi* that vowel was
â,	*a*
î or *ê*,	*i*
û or *ô*,	*u*
âi,	*e*
âu,	*o*
ā,	*ā* (i.e., the same)
ī,	*ī* (i.e., the same)

ū,	*ū* (i.e., the same)
ē,	*ī*
ō,	*ū*
āi,	*ai*
āu,	*au*

', before *sandhi* there was a vowel *a*

FURTHER HELP WITH VOWEL SANDHI

When a final short vowel (*a*, *i* or *u*) has merged into a following vowel, we print ' at the end of the word, and when a final long vowel (*ā*, *ī* or *ū*) has merged into a following vowel we print " at the end of the word. The vast majority of these cases will concern a final *a* or *ā*.

Examples:

What before *sandhi* was *atra asti* is represented as *atr' âsti*

atra āste	*atr' āste*
kanyā asti	*kany" âsti*
kanyā āste	*kany" āste*
atra iti	*atr' êti*
kanyā iti	*kany" êti*
kanyā īpsitā	*kany" ēpsitā*

Finally, three other points concerning the initial letter of the second word:

(1) A word that before *sandhi* begins with *ṛ* (vowel), after *sandhi* begins with *r* followed by a consonant: *yatha" rtu* represents pre-*sandhi* *yathā ṛtu*.

(2) When before *sandhi* the previous word ends in *t* and the following word begins with *ś*, after *sandhi* the last letter of the previous word is *c* and the following word begins with *ch*: *syāc chāstravit* represents pre-*sandhi* *syāt śāstravit*.

(3) Where a word begins with *h* and the previous word ends with a double consonant, this is our simplified spelling to show the pre-*sandhi* form: *tad hasati* is commonly written as *tad dhasati*, but we write *tadd hasati* so that the original initial letter is obvious.

COMPOUNDS

We also punctuate the division of compounds (*samāsa*), simply by inserting a thin vertical line between words. There are words where the decision whether to regard them as compounds is arbitrary. Our principle has been to try to guide readers to the correct dictionary entries.

EXAMPLE

Where the Deva·nágari script reads:

कुम्भस्थली रक्षतु वो विकीर्णसिन्दूररेणुर्द्विरदाननस्य ।
प्रशान्तये विघ्नतमश्छटानां निष्ठ्यूतबालातपपल्लवेव ॥

Others would print:

kumbhasthalī rakṣatu vo vikīrṇasindūrareṇur dviradānanasya /
praśāntaye vighnatamaśchaṭānāṃ niṣṭhyūtabālātapapallaveva //

We print:

kumbha|sthalī rakṣatu vo vikīrṇa|sindūra|reṇur dvirad'|ānanasya
praśāntaye vighna|tamaś|chaṭānāṃ niṣṭhyūta|bāl'|ātapa|pallav" êva.

And in English:

"May Ganésha's domed forehead protect you! Streaked with vermilion dust, it seems to be emitting the spreading rays of the rising sun to pacify the teeming darkness of obstructions."

"Nava·sáhasanka and the Serpent Princess" I.3 by Padma·gupta

DRAMA

Classical Sanskrit literature is in fact itself bilingual, notably in drama. There women and characters of low rank speak one of several Prakrit dialects, an "unrefined" *(prākṛta)* vernacular as opposed to the "refined" *(saṃskṛta)* language. Editors commonly provide such speeches with a Sanskrit paraphrase, their "shadow" *(chāyā)*. We mark Prakrit speeches with ⌜opening and closing⌟ corner brackets, and supply the Sanskrit *chāyā* in endnotes. Some stage directions are original to the author but we follow the custom that sometimes editors supplement these; we print them in italics (and within brackets, in mid-text).

WORDPLAY

Classical Sanskrit literature can abound in puns *(śleṣa)*. Such paronomasia, or wordplay, is raised to a high art; rarely is it a *cliché*. Multiple meanings merge *(śliṣyanti)* into a single word or phrase. Most common are pairs of meanings, but as many as ten separate meanings are attested. To mark the parallel senses in the English, as well as the punning original in the Sanskrit, we use a *slanted* font (different from *italic*) and a triple colon *(⁝)* to separate the alternatives. E.g.

> yuktaṃ Kādambarīṃ śrutvā kavayo maunam āśritāḥ
> *Bāṇa/dhvanāv* an|adhyāyo bhavat' îti smṛtir yataḥ.
>
> It is right that poets should fall silent upon hearing the Kádambari, for the sacred law rules that recitation must be suspended when *the sound of an arrow ⁝ the poetry of Bana* is heard.
>
> Soméshvara·deva's "Moonlight of Glory" I.15

INTRODUCTION

Murári and His Work

Murári's 'Rama Beyond Price' (*Anargha/rāghava*) is reputed to be one of the most difficult literary texts in Sanskrit literature—and this is exactly why it was one of the most popular plays among pundits in India. Numerous commentaries have been written to facilitate its interpretation, and many of its stanzas are among the favorites in traditional verse anthologies. In spite of the great popularity of this play in traditional India, it has not been appreciated in the West. In most books on the history of Sanskrit literature, it is presented as too static to be a good drama and its language as too complicated to be good poetry. While it is true that much of the action, which reproduces the story of the 'Ramáyana' with a number of modifications, is performed behind the scenes, this convention is not unique to 'Rama Beyond Price,' or to Sanskrit drama. Moreover, Murári introduces a unique change into the plot of the Rama story, in the form of a complex political intrigue involving the minister of the monkeys, the minister of the demons and, indirectly, Vishva·mitra, the sage who is associated with King Dasha·ratha's court. Thus, Murári's Rama story is not merely about the hero who conquers the demon king; rather, it is a story of courtly discussions and intrigues culminating in the war. The hero, Rama, is in fact an innocent prince who is manipulated by various intriguers until he defeats the demon king and becomes a real hero.

Furthermore, Murári's sensibility to drama is also reflected in the fact that his language alludes constantly to dramatic terminology. These allusions form a kind of play within the play, while they also emphasize the theatrical nature of the court, which is the main scene of action.

Nevertheless, it is certainly true that 'Rama Beyond Price' is first and foremost a piece of poetry, and it is because of its poetic qualities that it has been a favorite in India. Murári's images use traditional conventions and conceits of Sanskrit poetry, but many of them are distinguished as particularly unusual and striking, and some of them—about the Vedic god Indra, for instance—are humorous. While most of the stanzas are readable without following the particularities of the plot, a few verses require some knowledge of the mythology and the main story of the 'Ramáyana.' Therefore, to facilitate the reading, the most common poetic conventions and mythological references have been collected and summarized on p. 28 ff. below.

This play is the only surviving work by Murári, but he may have written other pieces of poetry, for many stanzas attributed to him do not figure in 'Rama Beyond Price.' (These stanzas may, of course, be attributed to him because of his fame.) As is the case with most poets in Sanskrit, we know next to nothing about his life, and even his dates and his provenance are uncertain. It is commonly assumed that he came from Orissa, for he may refer to the procession of Puri in the prologue of the play, but it is questionable whether it is indeed the Puri festivities that are meant there. Moreover, even if he refers to the Puri procession, he may have come from a neighboring territory such as Andhra, where he has always been much revered. Judging from citations from his work and references to his person, he must have lived before the middle of the tenth century, and certainly after Bhava·bhuti, i.e., after the beginning of the eighth century. He gives his family (*gotra*) name in the prologue, but this information does not help us to situate him with more certainty in time and place.

Summary of the Plot

Act 1. The Discussion of the Sages

The prologue, a dialogue between the stage manager and his assistant, presents the play and its author, while emphasizing the fact that the story of Rama is the most noble subject matter of any literary composition. The act itself consists of the courtly conversation between King Dasha·ratha, Rama's father, and two sages, Vama·deva and Vishva·mitra. First, Dasha·ratha and Vama·deva appear onstage, and the sage reads out a message from the royal priest, Vasíshtha, to the king. In his message, Vasíshtha reminds the king of his royal obligation to fulfill the requests of those who approach him. Then Vishva·mitra, the second sage, arrives, led before the king by Vama·deva. They have a long polite conversation, after which Vishva·mitra makes his request. He asks Dasha·ratha to allow him to take Rama with him, so that he can protect the sacrifice that Vishva·mitra prepares, against the attack of demons. Dasha·ratha tries to argue that Rama is too young to perform such a difficult task, but Vishva·mitra is adamant, while he is also supported by Vama·deva, who reminds the king of Vasíshtha's advice. Finally, Rama and his brother, Lákshmana, are called in and are told to obey their preceptor. Vishva·mitra leaves with the two young brothers for his hermitage, and

Dasha·ratha, who is deeply affected by the separation from his son, goes to the harem to console Rama's mother, Queen Kaushályа.

Act 2. Childhood Exploits

The Sanskrit-Prakrit prelude with comic elements takes place at Vishva·mitra's hermitage, between two of the sage's disciples, Pashu·medhra ("He who has the Penis of a [Sacrificial] Animal") and Shunah·shepa ("He who has the Penis of a Dog"). Pashu·medhra tells Shunah·shepa how he was frightened by a stone changed into a woman, whom he took for a demoness. It turns out that this woman was the sage Gáutama's wife, who had been cursed to remain petrified until Rama's arrival in the hermitage, owing to her infidelity with the god Indra. Thus, the event announces the coming of Rama to the hermitage, whose task is to fight the demons. Shunah·shepa describes the demoness Tádaka to his friend while also explaining a political intrigue involving the demons and the monkey-king of Kishkíndha. It is Murári who introduced this political element into the plot of the epic, and it is present throughout the play.

Shunah·shepa explains that the monkey-king of Kishkíndha, Vali, formed an alliance with the demon king, Rávana, to be able to defend himself in case of a riot. Vali's minister, Jámbavan, disapproved of this alliance, and when his advice was not heeded he left the kingdom to meet Vali's younger brother, Sugríva, who aspired to the throne. Sugríva was then led to the fortress of Rishya·muka by the son of the wind, the monkey Hánuman, to be safe from his brother. At the same time, the demons arrived and set up a camp on the northern edge of the ocean, ready to help Vali in case of an insurrection. In the course of a battle, a number of demons reached the territory near Vishva·mitra's hermitage and were likely to cause trouble there.

The act starts with the appearance of Rama and his brother Lákshmana onstage, describing the beauty of the hermitage. While they are having a rest, Vishva·mitra arrives and points out the importance of the sacred place. During their conversation, they hear a cry for help, coming from the inhabitants of the hermitage, who are being attacked by the demoness Tádaka and her allies. Vishva·mitra tells Rama to aim at the demons with his arrow, but Rama at first hesitates to act against Tádaka, because she is a woman. Finally, he decides to obey and exits the stage. It is then announced from offstage that he has killed Tádaka and other demons. After he returns, all three enjoy the moonlit evening and night. Vishva·mitra then suggests that they go to Míthila, where his friend Jánaka rules, for there is another sacrifice being prepared there which is likely to be attacked by demons, and Rama could again help. Vishva·mitra also mentions that Jánaka would like to give his daughter, Sita, to the man who can string Shiva's bow, the Pináka, which is kept in the royal armory. Thus, all three leave for Míthila.

Act 3. The Breaking of Shiva's Bow

The Sanskrit-Prakrit prelude between the chamberlain and a lady from the harem informs us of the arrival of Rama, Lákshmana and Vishva·mitra in Míthila. The two characters discuss Rama's chances to be able to string Shiva's bow. It is also mentioned that Rávana has sent his priest, Sháushkala, to the court to ask for Sita's hand.

The act begins with the reception of the three newly arrived men by King Jánaka and his priest, Shatanánda. When Vishva·mitra asks the king to show them the bow, the arrival of Sháushkala, Rávana's priest, is announced. Jánaka receives him with due respect, in spite of his feelings toward the demon. Sháushkala also tries to hide his hostility toward the princes, who have killed many of his relatives. Sháushkala presents Rávana's request to marry Sita without undergoing the test of stringing Shiva's bow, for Rávana is a devotee of Shiva, and it would not be appropriate for him to try his strength on his deity's weapon. There follows a quarrel between Sháushkala and Shatánanda, while Rama and Lákshmana exit to see the bow in question. It is announced from behind the scenes by Lákshmana that Rama has broken the bow, meaning that he can marry Sita. Then, at Shatánanda's suggestion, three other girls are to be married to Rama's three brothers and arrangements are made for the marriages. The princes' father, Dasha·ratha, is sent for to come to Míthila, while the demon priest Sháushkala is outraged and predicts Sita's abduction by Rávana.

Act 4. Dasha·ratha Is Tricked

The political intrigue continues to develop, as we learn in the Sanskrit-Prakrit prelude from the conversation between Mályavan, the minister of demons, and Shurpa·nakha, Rávana's younger sister. The demoness tells Mályavan about the marriages in Míthila, and the minister reflects upon the growing enmity between Rama and Rávana. He is afraid that Rávana will do something politically too dangerous against Rama, risking his own kingdom for his vengeance. Mályavan waits so that with the help of Jámbavan's intrigues Rama will be taken far away, separated from his allies.

Bharata's mother, Kaikéyi, sends one of her maids, Mánthara, to convey her regards on the occasion of the marriages. While Mánthara falls asleep on her way, a huntress called Shrávana enters her body at Jámbavan's command, and leaves her own body for Hánuman to look after. Shrávana is also given the task of changing Kaikéyi's message and demanding the exile of Rama, Lákshmana and Sita, and the coronation of Bharata. Dasha·ratha will have to fulfill these requests, for earlier he promised Kaikéyi two boons. Thus, when Rama is in exile, thanks to Jámbavan's plot, it will be easier for Mályavan to organize Sita's abduction. Shurpa·nakha thinks that they need not wait until then, for Párashu·rama, the archenemy of all warriors, is preparing to fight with Rama, for Rama has broken the bow that belonged to Shiva, Parashu·rama's preceptor. Mályavan, however, does not believe that Párashu·rama should be able to defeat Rama, and suggests that they wait somewhat longer.

At the beginning of the act, Párashu·rama's arrival is announced from offstage. Both Párashu·rama and Rama enter, and there follows a long conversation between them, full of ironical remarks made by Rama while praising his enemy. They leave to fight behind the scenes, and Rama's victory over his enemy is soon announced. They reappear as friends, but Párashu·rama refuses Rama's invitation to come to his marriage and leaves for the forest to practice penance.

The two kings, Jánaka and Dasha·ratha, are happy to learn about Rama's triumph and plan to celebrate Rama's coronation before the marriages. Dasha·ratha is about to perform the rite when Lákshmana enters with Kaikéyi's message, transmitted by Mánthara: her requests to send Rama into exile and to consecrate Bharata as king. Dasha·ratha faints at this news, but Rama feels compelled to obey, in order to keep his father's promise. The act ends with Rama's leaving for the forest, together with Lákshmana and Sita.

Act 5. Sugríva's Consecration

The Sanskrit prelude relates many events not represented onstage, in a dialogue between Jámbavan and Shrávana. Shrávana tells about her return and relates Rama's victory over Párashu·rama, as well as the departure of Rama, Lákshmana and Sita. They cross the Ganges in the boat of Guha, who is the king of Nisháda hunters, and go to the Chitra·kuta mountain. Rama then meets his half brother, Bharata, from whom he learns about his father's death, but he refuses to return to the throne. Bharata leaves with Rama's sandals, which he is to install on the throne to signal that Rama is the real ruler of Ayódhya. Knowing that Rama mourns his father and is thus not to take up arms, two demons (Cruel and Corrupt) send a third one (Virádha) to attack Rama. But, as Jámbavan remarks, such rules about not taking up arms are not valid in case of imminent danger, and thus Rama is able to fight back and kill the demon. After performing the funerary rites of his father, Rama leaves for the hermitage of the sage Agástya. On the way, a crow (Dhara·dhara) attacks Sita, and Rama blinds one of its eyes with his arrow. Rama is received by the sages of the hermitage and stays in the Pancha·vati forest. The demoness Shurpa·nakha tries in vain to seduce him, and is eventually mutilated by Lákshmana. The two demons, Cruel and Corrupt, reply with an attack, but Rama kills all the demons. Jámbavan foresees that Rávana will certainly find a way to revenge this massacre and that he will abduct Sita. He then explains how this situation can be used by the dethroned monkey-king, Sugríva. Sugríva can make an alliance with Rama to help him liberate Sita, and in return Rama can support Sugríva in his aspirations, by defeating the ruling monkey-king, Vali. Jámbavan asks Shrávana to speak to Guha and get him to approach Rama and Lákshmana as a friend, to facilitate the alliance.

After Shrávana exits, Jámbavan meets Jatáyus, who is rushing to the Pancha·vati forest to warn Rama that Rávana and his uncle, Marícha, are roaming about there. Jatáyus flies farther and reports that Rama is lured away by Marícha disguised as a golden deer, and that Sita sends Lákshmana to help him. While the brothers are away, Rávana, disguised as a mendicant, enters the hermitage and abducts Sita in his chariot. Jatáyus follows them and exits from the scene.

This is the end of the prologue, after which Rama and Lákshmana enter. Lákshmana tries to console the dejected Rama. Then Guha cries for help behind the scenes. Lákshmana saves him by killing his attacker, the demon Kabándha. Guha tells Rama that he has been sent by Sugríva to seek alliance with Rama against Sugríva's brother, Vali, and to give Rama some of Sita's clothes, which fell from Rávana's chariot and were found by the monkeys. Rama decides to accept the alliance in order to get help to defeat Rávana.

Vali's voice is heard as he comes to meet Rama and Lákshmana. He is enraged to see that Lákshmana has kicked a heap of bones, belonging to a demon that Vali himself had killed. The warriors greet one another and there is a verbal combat between Rama and Vali, with stanzas of "insults-disguised-as-praises" (*nindā/stuti*). They both exit for the duel. Lákshmana and Guha report the fight, which ends with Rama's killing Vali with an arrow. They also relate then the consecration of Sugríva as the new monkey-king, that Vali's son, Ángada, shall nevertheless be Sugríva's successor, and that Hánuman, son of the Wind, and other monkeys are sent in search of Sita.

Act 6. Rávana's Defeat

In the Sanskrit prelude, the demon spy Sárana relates some news from Rama's camp to Rávana's counselor, Mályavan, and Shuka does the same from the battlefield. The news is the following: Ángada, Vali's son, is consecrated as the successor to the throne of Kishkíndha; the demon prince Vibhíshana leaves Lanka; Hánuman makes a visit to Lanka, where he is captured but frees himself and sets the city on fire; the monkeys have built a bridge over the ocean to Lanka; and Rama's army now camps at the very edge of the city, ready to attack it. Mályavan reflects on Rávana's situation becoming more and more difficult. Shuka reports that Narántaka has been killed by Ángada, and then the fights between Índrajit and Lákshmana and between Kumbha·karna and Rama are described from behind the scenes.

The three characters onstage react to the sad news of the deaths in their army. Then Rávana enters the battle, and the three characters exit to support him in the fight.

The act consists of the battle between Rávana and Rama behind the scenes, described by two semi-divine beings, *vi-dyā/dharas*. They watch the events from their flying chariot, and when Rávana is killed they sing in praise of him. They also relate the lamentations of Rávana's wife, the release of the deities captured by Rávana and the coronation of Prince Vibhíshana as king of Lanka.

Act 7. The Happiness of the Hero

Three stanzas recited offstage inform us that Sita's chastity was questioned, because she had spent some time in another man's house, but that she proved her innocence through a fire ordeal. The major part of the act describes the return of Rama to Ayódhya, accompanied by Sita, Lákshmana, Su-gríva and Vibhíshana. While they are flying over India in the celestial Púshpaka chariot, they describe the landscape, the cities, the moon, etc., and recall some episodes of Ra-ma's story. The act ends with the appearance of Vasíshtha, who performs Rama's coronation, and the royal family is reunited in Ayódhya. The last two verses close the drama with benedictions of poetic merit.

On the Sanskrit Text, the Translation and its Relation to the Commentaries

The text has been partially reedited here on the basis of available editions and edited ancient commentaries, but without attempting to provide a critical edition, which would be impossible to produce at the present state of research. Almost all the Sanskrit prose passages and all the Prakrit passages have been taken from the Pondicherry edition, but the verses have been reedited on the basis of the available editions and commentaries. For more details on the constitution of the text and the variants, see the website http://www.claysanskritlibrary.com. It is also on this site that the reader can find further explanations concerning some complex passages and allusions to grammatical, philosophical, aesthetic and other terms in the text, which make Murári's language sometimes so difficult both to understand and to translate.

Since 'Rama Beyond Price' was considered one of the most challenging pieces of poetry to interpret in India, a large number of commentaries have been written on it over the centuries. Twenty-six old commentaries have been identified thus far, of which only four have been edited; but only two out of these four can actually be considered available.

This translation has been prepared using these two available old commentaries, one by Ruchi·pati, given in the Bombay edition of the text, and one by Vishnu·bhatta, critically edited in the Pondicherry edition. When interpreting some particularly difficult stanzas, I also made use of an unedited Jain commentary by Jina·harsha·gani.

In a few instances, I have also cited a widely available modern commentary, Rāmacandra Miśra's *Prakāśa*, accompanied by a Hindi translation. There are many other modern commentaries that one could recommend for further study, such as Jīvānanda Vidyāsāgara's.

Although a great number of vernacular translations of 'Rama Beyond Price' exist, the only translation made into a Western language thus far is Karin Steiner's prose German translation of 1997, geared more to specialists than to a general audience. This German translation has also been consulted and occasionally cited. It is to be hoped that the present translation will correct the few mistranslations found there (see, e.g., 5.191) without adding further ones.

Sanskrit Drama

A few additional stage conventions of Sanskrit drama may be worth mentioning here.

The director or stage manager and his assistant, who appear in the Prologue to introduce the work, are also to play the main roles. The recurring instruction to "walk around" implies that the character should walk around the stage to indicate the changing of the scene, since no props are used for this purpose. Preludes, in which some important secondary characters can figure, also have the function to inform the audience about events that cannot be represented directly, usually because they involve a long lapse of time. Violence and killing are not to be represented on stage. That is why battles are usually either fought shortly behind the scenes and commented upon by the characters staying on stage or, if they are longer, reported by various characters.

Commonly Used Poetical Conventions in 'Rama Beyond Price'

On poetical conventions and the flora and fauna figuring in them, see:

WILHELM RAU "Poetical Conventions in Indian *Kāvya* Literature." In: *The Adyar Library Bulletin* 50 (1986): 191–197.

SALIM ALI and S. DILLON RIPLEY *Handbook of the Birds of India and Pakistan Together with Those of Bangladesh, Nepal, Bhutan and Sri Lanka,* Compact Ed. Delhi/Oxford/New York: Oxford University Press, 1983.

SURESH CHANDRA BANERJI *Flora and Fauna in Sanskrit Literature.* Calcutta: Naya Prokash, 1980.

R. SYED *Die Flora Altindiens in Literatur und Kunst.* 1990.

The following list of conventions and images commonly used in classical Sanskrit poetry and figuring in 'Rama Beyond Price' is not exhaustive. It enumerates the most frequently occurring conventions in the play to help the reader and to avoid repetitive explanations in the notes. In most cases the precise identification of the flora and fauna is not discussed, as that is beyond the scope of these explanatory notes.

BIRDS On *cakoras*, see THE MOON. On *cakra/vākas* (ruddy shelduck), see DARKNESS AND THE NIGHT. Peacocks dance in the rain or when the rain is to come. Swans or wild geese (*haṃsa*—a poetic rather than an identifiable bird) live in mountain caves.

DARKNESS AND THE NIGHT helps ladies who meet their lovers in secret at night. At night, medicinal herbs shine. *Cakra/vāka* couples (ruddy shelduck, *Tadorna ferruginea [Pallas]*) must separate during the night, owing to a curse.

ELEPHANTS carry pearls or jewels in their temples, which come out when they are in rut. They exude ichor when in rut, and the kind of ichor determines the quality of the elephant. Superior elephants exude particularly fragrant ichor, and therefore they are called "scent-elephants" (*gandha/gaja*). Eight elephants guard the eight directions of the world.

FAME is said to be white and to have a good scent.

FLOWERS Day lotuses blossom during the day, under the effect of the sun, and are said to sleep at night; night lotuses do the opposite, as they are thought to open under the effect of the moonlight. Eyes and faces, especially of beautiful women, are often pictured as lotuses. Feet of venerable or beautiful persons are also commonly said to be lotuses. *Saṃtānaka* is one of the five trees of Indra's paradise or its flowers, and the wives of gods are often said to wear garlands or head ornaments made of these flowers. The *priyaṅgu* creeper blossoms at the touch of a woman. *Kiṃśuka* flowers (*Butea monosperma*, SYED 208) are red and have a curved shape often compared to the shape of lion or tiger claws, or to the nail marks of a lover. Flowers of the *kadamba* tree (*Anthocephalus indicus*, SYED 149) blossom when thunderclouds arrive.

GOOSEBUMPS or, more correctly, the hair of the body standing on end, is a sign of excitement, usually of sexual arousal, both in men and women.

THE MOON AND MOONLIGHT The moon was produced from the milk-ocean when the gods and demons were churning it to obtain the nectar of immortality. Moonstones ooze away or exude drops of water under the effect of the moonlight. The night lotus blossoms because of the moonlight. The moon keeps separated lovers company. *Cakoras* (*Alectoris chukar chukar [JE Gray]*, a kind of partridge) feed on moonbeams. Moonbeams are cool and contain ambrosial nectar. The moon is identified with the ambrosial nectar of the gods. There is a hare or a deer in the moon, identified with its spot. Shiva wears the crescent moon on his head. A beautiful woman's face is often compared to the moon.

MOUNTAINS Mountains originally had wings, but Indra cut them off, except those of Mainága (son of Himálaya and Mena), because Mainága could hide himself in the sea, who was his friend. They are famous for having magic healing herbs growing on them (especially the Drona mountain), which glow at night. They can have precious stones in them which illuminate them at night. From the Málaya mountain comes a soothing breeze, smelling of sandalwood. The sun rises at the mythical Eastern Mountain and sets at the Western one. See also myths about the VINDHYA, HIMÁLAYA and MERU.

PRECIOUS STONES Pearls originate from drops of water filtered and thickened in oyster shells. See also under SNAKES and ELEPHANTS.

THE SEA contains a submarine fire. The sea is identified with the milk-ocean, which was churned by the gods and the demons to obtain the nectar of immortality. Before the ambrosial nectar, the churning also produced the Káustubha gem (which adorns Vishnu's chest), Dhanvántari (the physician of the gods), the *apsaras*es, Lakshmi (the Goddess of Fortune) and the moon. For the sea's hiding Mainága, see under MOUNTAINS.

SNAKES live in the dark underworld (*pātāla*) below the earth. They have a bright jewel on their heads and have no ears—they hear with their eyes. They are called "double-tongued" because of their split tongue. They feed on wind and inhabit the sandal tree. Gáruda, Vishnu's bird mount, is the greatest enemy of snakes. Female snakes conceive when thunderclouds arrive. Vásuki, the King of Snakes, has a thousand heads.

THE SUN makes its daily course on a chariot. Sunstones emit fire when exposed to it.

TREES For the sandal tree, see under SNAKES and MOUNTAINS. *Tamāla* trees (*Xanthochymus pictorius Roxb.*) are often mentioned in comparisons because of their particularly dark color.

WORLDS are usually said to be three, seven or fourteen in number. The three are heaven, earth and the space between them; the seven are these three and four additional ones above them; the fourteen comprise these seven and seven underworlds (none of which is hell).

Recurring Mythological References and Divine Attributes

In what follows, the most frequently occurring myths and divine attributes have been summarized, excepting the Rama story itself. Many of these myths are to be found in the text of the 'Ramáyana,' especially in its first and last books. Some of the versions of these myths are peculiar to 'Rama Beyond Price,' but such peculiarities have not been pointed out here. Most of the stories can easily be found in various epic and Puránic sources, and therefore I have refrained from giving references.

Agástya is a sage, the son of the gods Mitra and Váruna. At the sight of the nymph Úrvashi, the seed of these two gods fell into a jar at a sacrificial session, and Agástya was born. (Another part of their seed fell into water, from which the sage Vasíshtha was born.) Agástya once ate up and digested the demon called Vatápi. This demon had killed many a brahmin by taking the form of a sacrificial animal, which was served to the brahmins as a funerary meal by his brother. When the brahmins swallowed him, he cut up their bellies and came out. Agástya put an end to these killings by digesting the demon. He also once drank up the oceans because they had offended him and because he wanted to help Indra and the gods in the war against the Kaléya demons, who had hidden themselves in the waters. See also the story of Agástya and the Vindhya mountain, below.

BRAHMA is the creator of the world (a demiurge rather than the ultimate creator). He has four heads, which represent the four Vedas. He is seated on a lotus (grown from Vishnu's navel), from which he was born, and therefore he is often called "the lotus-born"; however, he is also called "self-born" (for, being the creator, he was not created). His vehicle is the swan or wild goose (*haṃsa*).

HIMÁLAYA is often considered to be the abode of the gods, particularly of Shiva. The Himálaya range personified is also father to Shiva's wife, Párvati, and the source of the earthly course of the Ganges.

INDRA is the king of the gods, the ruler of heaven. He has a thousand eyes and wields a bow in the form of the rainbow; he also brandishes a thunderbolt. He once seduced Ahálya, the wife of the sage Gáutama. The sage cursed Ahálya to become petrified until Rama came by to release her, and Indra to be unmanly. When the demon king Rávana attacked the city of the gods, the demon Megha·nada, using his magical power to become invisible, managed to capture Indra, who could not fight back because of Gáutama's curse. Megha·nada thus earned the title *Indra|jit*, "Conqueror of Indra." Megha·nada was later killed by Lákshmana. Indra lost his kingdom to Rávana, and regained it thanks to Rama's victory over the demon king. He was once helped by Dasha·ratha, Rama's father, in the fight against the *Asura* demons.

Kama, the God of Love was burned by Shiva's third eye (see under Shiva). The *makara* is his vehicle. The *makara* is a mythical animal of the sea, often translated as "crocodile" owing to the lack of any equivalent. It is also the sign of Capricorn in the zodiac, and is often drawn in musk, diluted *kuṅkuma* or sandalwood paste on women's skin as an ornament.

Meru is a mythical mountain made of gold and gems, situated at the center of the world, between the continents. The planets are said to revolve around Meru.

Rávana is the king of demons (*rākṣasas*), the ruler of Lanka, which originally belonged to Kubéra, the God of Treasures. He is the grandson of the sage Pulástya, and has ten heads and twenty arms. He once lifted up the Kailása mountain to show his force by shaking up Shiva in his abode, but Shiva stepped down, thus pulverizing Rávana's hands, which were squeezed under the mountain. Rávana cut off nine of his heads to honor Shiva with them as an offering, and was about to cut off his tenth head, when the god stopped him and offered him a boon. He chose to become the ruler of the world, not to be killed by a god or a man. In one verse, it is Brahma instead of Shiva who is mentioned in the same role. He was once imprisoned by the thousand-armed king, Árjuna Kartavírya, for attacking his territory and was once defeated by the monkey-king, Vali (Indra's son), who squeezed him under his armpit while doing his prayers at the sea.

Ságara is the solar king and had sixty thousand sons. He performed ninety-nine sacrifices, but, when he began the hundredth, Indra stole his sacrificial horse and went to the underworld (*pātāla*) with it. Ságara then sent his sons to seek out the horse, but they could not find it on earth, and so they started digging down to the underworld. By digging, they increased the boundaries of the ocean, which thus came to be called *Sāgara* ("made by the sons of Ságara"). When they met the sage Kápila, they accused him immediately of having stolen the horse, thus enraging the sage, who reduced them into ashes. It was only several thousands of years later that King Bhagi·ratha managed to bring the Ganges down to the underworld, and purified the ashes of his ancestors to convey their souls to heaven.

Shiva has the crescent moon on his head, wears ascetic's clothes, has the goddess Ganges in his hair and has a third eye on his forehead which can burn and destroy anything. He destroyed the God of Love with this third eye, who is thus often called "the bodiless." The God of Love had been sent to make him attracted to Párvati, who, in spite of this unsuccessful effort, later became Shiva's wife. Shiva has a form in which he is half woman, half man; the female side is often pictured as being identical to Párvati. He carries a skull in his hand as a begging bowl, and has to wander with it as a punishment for having cut off Brahma's fifth head. He has a snake instead of the brahminical sacred thread and a bull (Nandi) as his vehicle. His neck is black or dark blue (Skt. *nīla*), because when the gods and demons were trying to churn out the ambrosial nectar from the milk-ocean, the snake they used as a rope spat his venom into the ocean, and Shiva swallowed it to save the nectar. Párvati stopped the flow of the poison in Shiva's throat to save him, but his neck remained tainted. Shiva's dance marks the destruction of the world at the end of a cosmic period.

VINDHYA is a mountain, and was jealous of Mount Meru and wanted the sun to revolve around himself. When the sun refused, he started growing higher and higher to obstruct the sun's path. The gods were alarmed to see this, and asked the sage Agástya to solve the problem. Agástya asked the Vindhya to bend down so that he should be able to go to the South easily, and to stay that way until his return to the North. The Vindhya obeyed, but Agástya never returned from the South, and the Vindhya never became high.

VISHNU has a conch shell and a mace in his hands, and the Káustubha stone on his chest. His animal vehicle is the king of birds, Gáruda, the arch-enemy of snakes. Vishnu's wife is Shri/Lakshmi, the Goddess of Fortune. (Both the Káustubha and Shri were produced from the milk-ocean, when the gods were churning it to obtain the nectar of immortality.) One of Vishnu's avatars is the dwarf. The world was oppressed by a demon called Bali, and the gods sent Vishnu to remedy the situation. Vishnu took up the form of a dwarf to trick Bali, and asked for as much territory as he could cover in three steps. When Bali agreed, Vishnu returned to his universal form, and crossed all the three worlds with his three steps. Rama is considered to be an embodiment of Vishnu; sometimes Dasha·ratha's four sons are said to be Vishnu's four quarters.

Bibliography

EDITIONS, COMMENTARIES AND TRANSLATIONS OF THE ANARGHARĀGHAVA

(B) *Anargharāghavam with the commentary (ṭīkā) of Rucipati* (R), ed. DURGAPRASAD and WASUDEV LAXMAN SHASTRI PANSIKAR. (Kāvyamālā 5.) Bombay: Nirnaya Sāgar Press, 1908.

(C) *Anargharāghava*, ed. JIBANANDA VIDYASAGARA. Calcutta: Sucharu Press, 1875.

(J) *Anargharāghavam with the commentary of Jīvānanda Vidyāsāgara*, ed. by his sons ĀŚUBODHA VIDYĀBHŪṢAṆA and NITYABODHA VIDYĀRATNA. Calcutta: Vācaspatya, 1936.

(P) *The Commentary of Viṣṇubhaṭṭa on the Anargharāghava of Murāri*, vol. 1. *The Commentary of Viṣṇubhaṭṭa* (V), vol. 2. *The Anargharāghava of Murāri as Read by Viṣṇubhaṭṭa*, Notes, Appendices. Critical edition by HARINARAYANA BHAT, B.R. Pondicherry: Institut Français de Pondichéry, École Française d'Extrême-Orient (EFEO), 1998.

(T) Telugu character edition of the *Anargharāghava*, with the commentaries *Iṣṭārthakalpavallī* of LAKṢMĪDHARA, the *Hariharadīkṣitīya* of Harihara and the *Pañjikā* of Viṣṇubhaṭṭa, ed. Mysore: Cakravartyayaṅgār, 1905.

Working edition (in manuscript form) of LAKṢMĪDHARA's commentary (*Iṣṭārthakalpavallī*) on the *Anargharāghava*, prepared by H. N. BHAT at the EFEO in Pondicherry.

Anargharāghavam with Sanskrit commentary and Hindi translation (*Prakāśa*) by RĀMACANDRA MIŚRA. Varanasi: Chowkhamba Vidya Bhawan, 1960.

Jinaharṣagaṇi's Anargharāghavaṭīkā, Manuscript No. 655 / 1886–92. Poona: Bhandarkar Oriental Research Institute.

Steiner, K. 1997 *Anargharāghava: Das Schauspiel vom kostbaren Raghusspross. Einführung und Übersetzung. Drama und Theater in Südasien 1.* Wiesbaden: Harrassowitz Verlag.

OTHER SANSKRIT WORKS

Arthaśāstra of Kauṭilya, crit. ed., with a glossary by P. Kangle. 2nd edition. Bombay: University of Bombay, 1969.

Aṣṭādhyāyī of Pāṇini with English Translation by Sumitra M. Katre. Delhi: Motilal Banarsidass, 1989.

Āpastambadharmasūtra, ed. A. Chinnasvami Shastri, A. Ramanatha Shastri. Varanasi: Chaukhamba Sanskrit Series Office, 1932.

Uttararāmacarita of Bhavabhūti. *Uttararāmacarita (La dernière aventure de Rama) drame de Bhavabhuti traduit et annoté par Nadine Stchoupak*. Paris: Société d'Édition les Belles Lettres, 1968.

Ṛgveda: Ṛgvedasaṃhitā with the *Bhāṣya* of Sāyaṇācārya. ed. Narayanasarma Sonatakke and Chintaman Ganesh Kashikar. 5 vols. Poona: Vaidika Saṃśodhana Maṇḍala, 1931–51.

Kāvyādarśa of Daṇḍin with the commentary of S. K. Belvalkar and R. B. Raddi. Pariccheda 1, 2. Bombay: Bombay Sanskrit Series, 1920.

Daśarūpaka of Dhanaṃjaya. *Daśarūpam* with Dhanika's commentary. Ed. F. E. Hall. Calcutta: The Asiatic Society, 1989 (repr. of the ed. of 1865).

Nyāyamañjarī of Jayantabhaṭṭa, ed. K.S. Varadacharya. Mysore: University of Mysore, Oriental Research Institute Series, No. 116, 139, vols. 1, 2. 1969, 1983.

Pāṇini v. *Aṣṭādhyāyī*

Pratāparudrīya of Vidyānātha with the commentary *Ratnāpaṇa* of Kumārasvāmin, ed. V. Raghavan. Madras: Sanskrit Education Society, 1979.

"*Bṛhadāraṇyaka Upaniṣad*." In: *The Early Upaniṣads. Annotated Text and Translation*. P. Olivelle. Oxford: Oxford University Press, 1998.

Bhāgavatapurāṇa, ed. J. L. Shastri. Delhi: Motilal Banarsidass, 1983.

Manusmṛti with the commentary of Medhātithi. 2 vols. ed. Manasukharāy Mor, Calcutta 1967.

Mahāvīracarita of Bhavabhūti. Le Mahāvīracarita de Bhavabhūti accompagné du commentaire de Vīrarāghava. Nouvelle édition, traduction de la pièce et notes François Grimal. Pondicherry: Institut Français de Pondichéry, 1989.

Yājñavalkyasmṛti with the commentary *Mitākṣarā* of Vijñāneśvara and the *Vīramitrodaya* by Mitramiśra, ed. JAGANNATHA SHASTRI and KHISTE NARÁYANA SHASTRI. Varanasi: Chowkhamba Sanskrit Series Office, 1997.

Rāmāyaṇa of Vālmīki, crit. ed. in 7 vols. Baroda: Baroda Oriental Research Institute, 1960–75.

Rāmāyaṇa with Sanskrit Text and English Translation, 3 vols. Gorakhpur: Gita Press, 1995.

Vāyupurāṇa Vāyumahāpurāṇa. ed. VRAJAMOHANA CATURVEDA and NAG SHARAN SINGH. Delhi: Nag Publishers, 1983.

Sāhityadarpaṇa of Viśvanātha Kavirāja with two old commentaries. *Locana* by the author's son ANANTA DĀSA and *Vijñapriyā* by Bhaṭṭācārya Maheśvara Tarkālaṅkāra. Delhi: Bharatiya Book Corporation, 1988.

Subhāṣitaratnakoṣa, compiled by Vidyākara. Ed. D. D. KOSAMBI and V. V. GOKHALE. Cambridge Mass.: Harvard University Press, 1957.

SECONDARY LITERATURE

BROWNE, G. M. "Textual Notes on Vidyākara's *Subhāṣitaratnakoṣa.*" *Indo-Iranian Journal* 44 (2001): 21–24.

INGALLS, D. H. H. (tr.) *An Anthology of Sanskrit Court Poetry / Vidyākara's Subhāṣitaratnakoṣa.* Cambridge, Mass.: Harvard University Press, 1965.

JAMISON, S. "*Anargharāghava*: Das Schauspiel vom kostbaren Raghusspross. Einführung und Übersetzung. Drama und Theater in Südasien 1. Harrassowitz Verlag, Wiesbaden 1997. 314 pp." Review article in *Indo-Iranian Journal* 43 (2000): 173–177.

MAHALINGA SASTRI, Y. "Murári as a Poet." *Journal of Oriental Research, Madras* 19 (1950) pt. 3: 196–204.

STEINER, K. "Vālins Tod: Das *Anargharāghava* und seine Vorlagen I." *Indo-Iranian Journal* 42 (1999) : 235–247.

List of Characters

Characters marked with ⌜corner brackets⌟ speak Prakrit.

Stage Manager:	manager and director, may play the hero of the play, i.e. Rama
Actor:	the Stage Manager's assistant, may play the secondary role, here Lákshmana
Dasha·ratha:	king of Ayódhya, father to Rama, Lákshmana, Bharata and Shatrúghna
Vama·deva:	a priest, friend of Vishva·mitra; and messenger of Vasíshtha, who is the teacher of Dasha·ratha and of all the Raghu dynasty
Doorkeeper	
Warder	
Vishva·mitra:	a forest-dwelling ascetic, friend of Vama·deva; originally of the warrior caste, he became a brahmin through ascetism
Rama:	the hero of the play, Dasha·ratha's eldest son, considered to be an incarnation of Vishnu
Lákshmana:	Rama's brother and best friend
A bard	
Shunah·shepa:	A vedic student; a resident in Vishva·mitra's forest hermitage; his name means "Dog's penis"
⌜Pashu·medhra⌟:	a boy; another resident in Vishva·mitra's hermitage, a comic character; his name means "Animal penis"
Ascetics (offstage)	
Chamberlain:	chief officer of the royal household at Jánaka's court
⌜Kala·hánsika⌟:	a young woman from the Ladies Quarter at Jánaka's court

JÁNAKA:	king of Míthila, father of SITA, also called SIRA·DHVAJA "He whose Sign is the Plough"
SHATÁNANDA:	the chief royal priest of JÁNAKA
A MAN:	appearing from the rear stage
SHÁUSHKALA:	the royal priest of the demon king, RÁVANA
MÁLYAVAN:	the chief minister of the demon king, RÁVANA
SHURPA·NAKHA:	a demoness, RÁVANA's sister; her name means "she who has fingernails like winnowing baskets"
PEOPLE (OFFSTAGE)	
PÁRASHU·RAMA:	a brahmin warrior, son of JAMAD·AGNI (he is thus called JAMADÁGNYA in the Sanskrit text); the king ÁRJUNA KARTAVÍRYA once carried off JAMAD·AGNI's cow and was killed by PÁRASHU· RAMA; then the king's sons murdered JAMAD· AGNI while PÁRASHU·RAMA was away, upon which PÁRASHU·RAMA made the vow to exterminate all warriors; thus he is the arch enemy of kshatriyas; later he also came to be considered an incarnation of VISHNU
Jámbavan:	minister of the monkey king; he leaves VALI to serve the interest of VALI's brother, SUGRÍVA; an intriguer
SHRÁVANA:	a woman of the hunter caste, serving JÁMBAVAN
JATÁYUS:	a semi-divine vulture, a friend of DASHA·RATHA
GUHA:	king of the NISHÁDA hunters, allied with JÁMBAVAN
VALI:	the powerful king of the monkeys of Kishkíndha; during his absence from home to slay a demon, his younger brother,

	Sugríva, usurped his throne thinking him dead, but when Vali returned, Sugríva had to run away
Sárana:	a demon spy, serving Rávana
Shuka:	a demon serving Rávana
Ratna·chuda:	first Vidya·dhara; a semi-divine being; his name means "he whose diadem is made of gems"
Hemángada:	second Vidya·dhara; a semi-divine being; his name means "he whose armlet is made of gold"
Sugríva:	Vali's younger brother, exiled to Rishya·muka
⌜Sita⌟:	princess of Míthila, Jánaka's daughter, to become Rama's wife
Vibhíshana:	Rávana's brother, who quits Lanka and forms an alliance with the monkeys and Rama
Hánuman (offstage):	a powerful monkey, son of the Wind; he was cursed by Brahma to forget his heroic qualities

BENEDICTION

NIṢ|PRATYŪHAM upāsmahe bhagavataḥ
Kaumodakī|lakṣmaṇaḥ
koka|prīti|cakora|pāraṇa|paṭu|
jyotiṣmatī locane,
yābhyām ardha|vibodha|mugdha|madhura|
śrīr ardha|nidrāyito
nābhī|palvala|puṇḍarī|mukulaḥ
kamboḥ sa|patnī|kṛtaḥ.

api ca

viramati mahā|kalpe nābhī|
path'|âika|niketanas
tri|bhuvana|puraḥ|śilpī yasya
pratikṣaṇam Ātmabhūḥ
«kim adhikaraṇam? kīdṛk? kasya
vyavasthitir?» ity asāv
udaram aviśad draṣṭum, tasmai
jagan|nidhaye namaḥ.

To be free of all obstacles, we worship Vishnu's two eyes, the sun, which delights the sheldrake, and the moon, which feeds the *chakóra* with its beams—two luminaries, in whose light the lotus bud in the pond of His navel has become half-open while half-asleep, charming and sweet, a true rival of His conch shell.*

Moreover,

At the end of each cosmic aeon, Self-born Brahma, whose unique abode is the path formed by the Lord's umbilical cord, becomes the Creator of the three worlds. Every second, to see what to put where and how everything is arranged, Brahma enters the belly of He Who Is the Support of the Universe, Vishnu, to whom we pay our homage.

PRELUDE TO ACT I
PROLOGUE

1.5 SŪTRADHĀRAḤ: bho bho lavaṇ'|ôda|velā|tamāla|kandalasya tri|bhuvana|mauli|maṇḍana|mahā|nīla|maṇeḥ Kamalā|kuca|kalaśa|kelī|viracita|kastūrikā|pattr'|âṅkurasya bhagavataḥ Puruṣottamasya yātrāyām upasthānīyāḥ sabhā|sadaḥ! kutaś cid dvīp'|ântarād āgatena Kalahakandala|nāmnā kuśī|lavena raudra|bībhatsa|bhayānak'|âdbhuta|rasa|bhūyiṣṭhaṃ kam api prabandham abhinayatā nityaṃ kil' âyam udvejito lokaḥ. tat kasya cid abhimata|rasa|bhājaḥ prekṣaṇakasya prayog'|ânujñayā nāṭya|ved'|ôpādhyāya|Bahurūp'|ânte|vāsī madhya|deśīyaḥ Sucarita|nāmā Bharata|putro 'haṃ bhavadbhir anugṛhye. yataḥ:

prītir nāma sadasyānāṃ priyā raṅg'|ôpajīvinaḥ.
jitvā tad|apahartāram eṣa pratyāharāmi tām.

(ākāśe karṇaṃ dattvā) kiṃ brūtha, «vaideśiko bhavān, a|samagra|pātraḥ; katham īdṛśe karmaṇi pragalbhate?» iti! *(vihasya, sa|praśrayam añjalim baddhvā)* hanta bhoḥ, kim evam udīryate? bhavad|vidhānāṃ pariṣad|ārādhanī pravṛttir eva pātrāṇi samagrayiṣyati. yataḥ:

yānti nyāya|pravṛttasya tiryañco 'pi sahāyatām;
a|panthānaṃ tu gacchantaṃ s'|ôdaro 'pi vimuñcati.

At the end of the benedictory verses.

STAGE MANAGER: Venerable assembly, you have come here at the time of the festivities of the Lord Purushóttama, who is dark like the shoots of *tamála* trees in a coastal forest, or like the sapphire decorating the head of the ruler of the three worlds, or like the lines he draws playfully with musk on Lakshmi's round breasts. As you well know, an actor called the Source of Quarrel,* who comes from another continent somewhere, performs a play dominated by the sentiments of terror, disgust, fear and wonder, and thus always stirs up everyone here. Now I am pleased to serve you with a play of whichever sentiment you find appropriate. My name is Well-Behaving, I am an actor from the Central Province, a disciple of the great master of the theatrical art, Bahu·rupa.* I am greatly honored by you, for 1.5

> It is the delight of the spectator to which actors are devoted. I shall beat the person who takes this joy away, and shall bring it back to you.*

(listening) Are you asking yourselves how I dare embark on such a thing, being a stranger and not having all the actors? *(smiling and putting his hands together respectfully)* Alas, why are you speaking in this way? It will be my respectful duty toward people like you to gather the actors. For

> he who follows the path of virtue shall be helped even by the beasts, but even his brother shall abandon him who takes an evil course.*

(punar karṇaṃ dattvā) kiṃ brūtha, kiṃ brūtha, «tarhi prahit" êyam asmābhiḥ patrikā» iti?

1.10 *praviśya* NAṬAḤ *patrikāṃ dadāti.* SŪTRADHĀRO *gṛhītvā vācayati.*

«yatra samasta|puruṣ'|ârtha|rasa|niṣyandini—

cetaḥ|śuktikayā nipīya śataśaḥ
śāstr'|âmṛtāni kramād
vāntair akṣara|mūrtibhiḥ su|kavinā
muktā|phalair gumphitāḥ,
unmīlat|kamanīya|nāyaka|guṇa|
grām'|ôpasaṃvargaṇa|
prauḍh'|âlaṃ|kṛtayo luṭhanti su|dṛśāṃ
kaṇṭheṣu hāra|srajaḥ.

tasmai vīr'|âdbhut'|ārambha|gambhīr'|ôdātta|vastave
jagad|ānanda|kandāya saṃdarbhāya tvarāmahe.»

iti. *(vimṛśya sa|harṣa|smitam)* māriṣa! Rāmāyaṇam iti śṛṇoṣi tatra|bhavataḥ kavit"|âvatāra|prathama|tīrthasya valmīka|janmano mahā|muneḥ sarasvatī|niryāso, yaśaḥ|śarīram Ikṣvākūṇām.

(again listening) What are you saying? Are you saying that in that case you have sent me a written order?

An ACTOR *enters. He gives the* STAGE MANAGER *a letter. The* 1.10
STAGE MANAGER *takes it and reads aloud.*

"We look forward to a play in which the essence of all the four aims of men are brought out,

> whose excellent writer has filtered the nectar of hundreds of learned compositions through his mind, in due order, like the oyster shell filters water, and produced pearls in the form of words, which he then strung into necklaces. Such chains of words would have subtle poetic figures for decoration, a collection of well-known, desirable qualities for a string, and the hero for its central gem, to decorate the necks of the spectators instead of beautiful women.
>
> A composition in which the action is dominated by the sentiments of the heroic and the miraculous, whose subject matter is profound and noble, and which is a source of delight for the whole world—it is to such a play that we look forward."

(reflecting and smiling happily) My friend, you have surely heard about the 'Ramáyana,' the essence of poetry, written by the great Sage of the Anthill, the first master to bring down poetry from heaven. This work is the very embodiment of the Ikshváku dynasty's fame.

1.15 NAṬAḤ: atha kim?

SŪTRADHĀRAḤ: tad|pratibaddha|prabandh'|ânubandhinī pariṣad|ājñā.

NAṬAḤ: *(vihasya)* aho! sakala|kavi|s'|ârtha|sādhāraṇī khalv iyaṃ Vālmīkīyā subhāṣita|nīvī!

SŪTRADHĀRAḤ: māriṣa! kim ucyate!

api katham asau rakṣo|rājas
tatāpa jagat|trayīm?
api katham abhūd Ikṣvākūṇāṃ
kule Garuḍa|dhvajaḥ?
api katham ṛṣau divyā vācaḥ
svataḥ pracakāśire?
su|carita|parīpākaḥ sarva|
prabandha|kṛtām ayam.

1.20 tatr' âpi tāvan nirūpayāmi rūpakam abhirūpam īdṛśam.

muhūrtam iva sthitvā, smaraṇam abhinīya, s'|ôllāsam.

asti Maudgalya|gotra|sambhavasya mahā|kaver Bhaṭṭa|śrī|Vardhamāna|tanū|janmanas Tantumatī|nandanasya Murāreḥ kṛtir abhinavam Anargharāghavaṃ nāma nāṭakam. tat prayuñjānāḥ sāmājikān upāsmahe. *(vicintya sa|harṣam)* aho, ramaṇīyā khalv iyaṃ sāmagrī pariṣad|ārādhanasya!

yataḥ:

mad|vargyā rasa|pāṭha|gīti|gatiṣu
praty|ekam utkarṣiṇo,
Maudgalyasya kaver gabhīra|madhur'|

ACTOR: Yes, indeed. 1.15

STAGE MANAGER: Our audience's order refers to a play based on that work.

ACTOR: *(smiling)* The treasure of Valmíki's poetry* is the common property of the flock of all poets.

STAGE MANAGER: My friend, this is certainly so.

> How was it that the king of demons tormented the triple world? How was it that Gáruda-riding Vishnu was born in the family of the Ikshvákus? And how was it that the divine words manifested themselves spontaneously in the sage Valmíki? The poetic treatment of this is the ultimate reward of all poets.*

Well, then, from the dramas I shall select a delightful play 1.20
of this kind.

Stopping for a moment, he mimes remembering something, and then, with delight.

There is a new play entitled 'Rama Beyond Price,' written by the great poet Murári, son of Bhatta Vardhamána and Tántumati, born in the Maudgálya *gotra*. If we perform that play, we shall appropriately serve our audience. *(reflecting, with joy)* Hey, this is really excellent material to please our public.

For,

> My company is equally good at reciting, singing and acting according to the predominant sentiments. The poetic compositions* of the writer

ôdgārā girāṃ vyūtayaḥ.
dhīr'|ôdātta|guṇ'|ôttaro Raghu|patiḥ
kāvy'|ârtha|bījaṃ, munir
Vālmīkiḥ phalati sma yasya carita|
stotrāya divyāḥ giraḥ.

1.25 ayaṃ tu prācetasīyaṃ kathā|vastu bahubhir bahudhā praṇītam api, prayuñjāno n' âparādhyati śrotriya|putraḥ.

paśya:

yadi «kṣuṇṇaṃ pūrvair»
iti jahati Rāmasya caritaṃ,
guṇair etāvadbhir
jagati punar anyo jayati kaḥ?
svam ātmānaṃ tat|tad|
guṇa|garima|gambhīra|madhura|
sphurad|vāg|brahmāṇaḥ
katham upakariṣyanti kavayaḥ?

upakramamāṇaś ca sa kaviḥ svataḥ|prakāśita|śabda|brahmāṇam ācāryaṃ Prācetasaṃ girāṃ ca devatām ev' ôpaślokitavān:

«tam ṛṣiṃ manuṣya|loka|
praveśa|viśrāma|śākhinaṃ vācām
sura|lokād avatāra|
prāntara|kheda|chidaṃ vande.»

from the Maudgálya *gotra* abound in beautiful expressions of profound meaning. Rama is the best of the brave and noble-minded category of heroes and is the source of all poetic matter—it is to praise his deeds that the sage Valmíki obtained the divine words.

Although Valmíki's story has been recast by many in many ways, this son of a learned brahmin is by no means at fault to use it again. 1.25

Look,

If people say that this subject has been done to death by their predecessors and thus abandon the story of Rama, then who will be as virtuous as Rama in this world to excel like him? And writers whose poetic power is displayed in the beautiful and solemn words describing his important qualities*—how will they be able to perfect themselves?*

Now, to start with, that poet sang the praise of his master, Valmíki, in whom the power of words manifested itself spontaneously, and then he composed a hymn to the Goddess of Speech:

"I praise the sage who is the tree that provides a resting place for divine words when they enter this human world, who takes away their fatigue after their long descent from heaven."

1.30 «Dhātuś catur|mukhī|kaṇṭha|śṛṅgāṭaka|vihāriṇīm,
nitya|pragalbha|vācālām upatiṣṭhe Sarasvatīm.»

NAṬAḤ: *(sa|harṣam)* bhāva, tat prastūyatām. asya hi Maudgaly'|âyanānāṃ brahma'|rṣīṇām anvaya|mūrdhanyasya Murāri|nāma|dheyasya bāla|Vālmīker vāṅ|mayam amṛta|bindu|niṣyandi kandalayati kautukaṃ me.

SŪTRADHĀRAḤ: māriṣa! sthāne bhavataḥ kutūhalam. īdṛśam eva etat:

tat|tādṛg|ujjvala|Kakutstha|kula|praśasti|
saurabhya|nirbhara|gabhīra|mano|harāṇi
Vālmīki|vāg|amṛta|kūpa|nipāna|lakṣmīm
etāni bibhrati Murāri|kaver vacāṃsi.

NEPATHYE *dhruvā gīyate.*

1.35 ⌜diṇaara|kiraṇ'|ukkero piāaro ko vi jīva|loassa
kamala|maūl'|aṃka|pālī|gaa|mahuara|karisaṇa|viaḍḍho.⌟

SŪTRADHĀRAḤ: *(ākarṇya)* katham? upakrāntam eva nartakair, yad iyaṃ Daśarath'|ôtsaṅgād Rāma|bhadr'|ākarṣiṇo Viśvāmitrasya prāveśikī dhruvā. *(puro 'valokya sa|sambhramam)* aye! katham atra eva tatra|bhavataḥ kamala|yoni|janmano muner āyatanāt pratinivṛttena' rtv|ijā

"I worship the goddess who amuses herself at the crossroads of Brahma's four heads, in his throat, the goddess who is always bold in speech and talkative—Sarásvati." 1.30

ACTOR: *(with delight)* Sir, let's start. This young Valmíki called Murári, who is an eminent member of the Maudgálya family of wise brahmins, indeed produces poetry that creates, as it were, a shower of ambrosia drops—these lines have really aroused my curiosity.

STAGE MANAGER: My friend, your curiosity is indeed justified. His poetry is really of this kind.

Murári's words are rich in thought and beauty, having gained their preeminence* by praising the well-known dynasty of Kakútstha. They possess the abundance of a reservoir next to Valmíki's well of word-ambrosia.

The following song is heard from BEHIND THE SCENES.

There is someone who shines with the rays of the 1.35
sun and bestows happiness on the world of mortals. He skillfully attracts even a bee resting in the lap of a lotus flower.*

STAGE MANAGER: *(listening)* What? Have the actors already started? Because I hear the song announcing Vishva·mitra's entry, who is ready to take away Rama from Dasha·ratha's lap. *(looking ahead, agitated)* O, what's happening? Here is the sacrificial priest, Vama·deva. He has just returned from the hermitage of the venerable sage Vasíshtha, whose father is lotus-born Brahma himself.

Vāmadevena kim api tad|vācikam abhidhīyamāno ma-hā|rājo Daśarathas tiṣṭhati. tad ehi! na dvayos tṛtīyena bhavitavyam. āvām apy an|antara|karaṇāya sajjī|bhavā-vaḥ.

iti niṣkrāntau.

iti prastāvanā.

Vama·deva is conveying some message from Vasíshtha to Maharaja Dasha·ratha. So let's go— when two men are conversing, no third person is needed. And we are also going to prepare for our imminent tasks.*

Both exit.

End of the prologue.

ACT I
THE DISCUSSION OF THE SAGES

tataḥ praviśaty upaviṣṭo DAŚARATHO VĀMADEVAḤ *ca.*

I.40 DAŚARATHAḤ: aho, bahudhā śrutam api bhagavato Vasiṣṭhasy' ânuśāsanam, etan navaṃ navam iva pramodayati mām.

«Madhu|Kaiṭabha|dānav'|êndra|medaḥ|
plava|visr'|āmiṣam eva medin" îyam
adhivāsya, yadi svakair yaśobhiś
ciram enām upabhuñjate nar'|êndrāḥ.»

(sa|vimarśa|smitam) ṛṣe Vāmadeva,

tasy' ājñay" âiva paripā|layataḥ prajāṃ me
karṇ'|ôpakaṇṭha|palitaṃ|karaṇī jar" êyam
yad garbha|rūpam iva mām anuśāsti sarvam
ady' âpi, tan mayi gurur guru|pakṣa|pātaḥ.

VĀMADEVAḤ: kim ucyate! samāna|vṛtter api kasya cit, kva cid eva tārā|maitrī. tathā hi, sa bhagavān

I.45 sādhāraṇo Raghūṇāṃ gurur
bhavann api, viśeṣa|dṛṣṭis te.
n' āmodayati kim induḥ?
kumudaṃ punar asya sarvasvam.

DAŚARATHAḤ: Vāmadeva, mama hi guru|vacana|śravaṇa|tṛṣṇām aṅkuśī|karoti śrotra|vṛttir indriy'|ântar'|ânusāriṇo hṛdaya|gajasya. tan na kiṃ cid aparam avaśiṣyate.

DASHA·RATHA *enters seated, in* VAMA·DEVA*'s company.*

DASHA·RATHA: Although I have heard the venerable Vasíshtha's advice several times, each time it fills me with joy again and again. 1.40

> "This earth is a prey to be enjoyed, but one that still stinks with the overflowing fat of the two demon kings, Madhu and Káitabha. Kings can profit from this earth for a long time only if they perfume it with their own glory."

(reflecting with a smile) Venerable sage Vama·deva,

> I have protected my people according to his advice, and now old age has whitened my hair at the temples. But my master still instructs me in everything as if I were a small child—which shows how heavily he is biased in my favor.*

VAMA·DEVA: It is certainly true. Even though one acts in the same manner toward everybody, one may have some inexplicable attachment* toward a particular person. Just as the venerable Vasíshtha...

> Although he is the common teacher of all the Raghus, he looks at you differently. Is there anything that the moon would not fill with joy? Yet, the dearest friend of the moon is the white night-lotus.* 1.45

DASHA·RATHA: Vama·deva, my hearing has created a goad for my elephant of a heart, which would otherwise follow other organs of the senses: it is the desire to hear my teacher's word. So there is nothing else left to be said...

VĀMADEVAḤ: mahā|rāja! niḥśeṣam abhihitam. imāṃ tu sarva | saṃdeśa | saṃgraha | kārikāṃ kārikām atiprayatnena bhagavān bhavantam anusmārayati.

DAŚARATHAḤ: *(s'|ādaram)* avahito 'smi. kim ājñāpayati?

VĀMADEVAḤ:

1.50 hutam, iṣṭaṃ ca, taptaṃ ca, dharmaś c' âyaṃ kulasya te:
gṛhāt pratinivartante pūrṇa|kāmā yad arthinaḥ.

DAŚARATHAḤ: *(sa|harṣam)* suṣṭhu kṛtaṃ śirasy ācārya|vacanam.

kiṃ ca,

asmad|gotra|mahattaraḥ kratu|bhujām
ady' âyam ādyo Ravir
yajvāno vayam adya; sā bhagavatī
Bhūr adya rājanvatī;
adya svaṃ bahu|manyate sahacarair
asmābhir Ākhaṇḍalo,
yen' âitāvad Arundhatī|patir api
sven' ânugṛhṇāti naḥ.

VĀMADEVAḤ: rāja'|rṣe! sahaj'|ânubhāva|gambhīra|mahimāno yūyam ev' âitādṛśe yaśase. vayaṃ tu kevalam upadeṣṭāraḥ.

VAMA·DEVA: Maharaja, I have told you everything. But it is the following verse, which summarizes all messages, that the venerable Vasíshtha would like you to remember particularly.

DASHA·RATHA: *(with respect)* I am listening. What is his order?

VAMA·DEVA:

> Domestic and solemn rituals, ascetic observances and the social duties of your lineage are all achieved if you adhere to the following principle: those who come to make a request to you should leave your home with their desire satisfied. 1.50

DASHA·RATHA: *(happily)* I have taken my teacher's advice fully.*

Moreover,

> Today the Sun, noble ancestor of our family, is indeed the foremost of the sacrifice-consuming gods; today we perform sacrifices in the real sense of the word, and today the goddess Earth is really governed by a just ruler in our person; today Indra can think highly of himself as we accompany him—for Arúndhati's husband, Vasíshtha, himself has bestowed his infinite grace upon us.

VAMA·DEVA: Royal sage, it is you who possess solemn greatness through your innate dignity, for which you are so famous. We simply give advice to you.*

1.55 unnidrayati hi kumud'|ākaram
a|śaran|niśā|niśāta|nistuṣo 'pi tuṣāra|kiraṇaḥ;
sa punaḥ kim ucyate bhagavān,
dvitīyaḥ Parameṣṭhī, Vasiṣṭhaḥ?

api ca,

idaṃ vo yājyānām
uditam uditaṃ yat kulam abhūd,
yad iṣṭaṃ vā kurvann
a|kṛta Sagaraḥ pūrtam udadhim,
asau pūrveṣāṃ te
su|carita|patākā yad Amara|
sravantī— kṛtsno 'yaṃ
tri|bhuvana|guros tasya vibhavaḥ.

kiṃ ca,

Kauśika|svī|kṛtasy' âpi yad ājñ"|âtikramād abhūt
Triśaṅkor upabhogāya na dyaur api, na bhūr api.

1.60 *praviśya.*

PRATĪHĀRAḤ: jayatu, jayatu devaḥ! bhagavān Kauśiko dvāram adhyāste.

DAŚARATHAḤ: *(sa|saṃbhramam)* kiṃ Kauśikaḥ?

VĀMADEVAḤ: aham apy upasṛtya śrautena vidhinā puras|kṛtya praveśayāmi tapo|nidhim.

iti PRATĪHĀREṆA *saha niṣkrāntaḥ.*

For the cool-rayed moon awakens the white night-lotuses, even if it is misty and hazy, unlike on an autumn night. So what else can we say about the venerable Vasíshtha, who is a second Brahma?* 1.55

Moreover,

Your family of sacrificers had risen generation after generation; then, performing his sacrifice, Ságara filled the ocean with water; and the celestial Ganges has become a symbol of your ancestors' good action*—all this shows the might of the master of the three worlds Vasíshtha, who ultimately caused these events.*

Furthermore,

Tri·shanku did not obey Vasíshtha's order; then, even though he was accepted by Vishva·mitra, he obtained neither heavenly nor earthly enjoyments.*

The DOORKEEPER *enters.* 1.60

DOORKEEPER: Long live the king! Maharaja, the venerable Vishva·mitra is waiting at the door.

DASHA·RATHA: *(surprisedly)* Is it Vishva·mitra?

VAMA·DEVA: I shall go to receive this pious ascetic according to Vedic ritual and bring him here.

VAMA·DEVA *exits with the* DOORKEEPER.

1.65 DAŚARATHAḤ: *(sa|harṣam)*

> yaḥ kṣattra|dehaṃ paritakṣya ṭaṅkais
> tapo|mayair brāhmaṇam uccakāra,
> paro|rajobhiḥ sva|guṇair a|gādhaḥ,
> sa Gādhi|putro 'pi gṛhān upaiti.

tataḥ praviśati VĀMADEV' */ ôpadiśyamāna / vartmā* VIŚVĀMITRAḤ.

VIŚVĀMITRAḤ: sakhe Vāmadeva! kathaya, tvam adhun" âiva Vasiṣṭh'|āśramāt āgato 'si. kac cit kuśalī tāvad Arundhatī|nāmnā pati|vratā|mayena jyotiṣā saha|carita|dharmā sa tatra|bhavān Maitrā|varuṇiḥ?

VĀMADEVAḤ: viśeṣeṇa punar adya yājya|kulam upatiṣṭhamāne cirantana|priya|suhṛdi Kauśike.

1.70 VIŚVĀMITRAḤ: sakhe Vāmadeva! cireṇa «Daśaratho draṣṭavya» iti sarva|mano|rathānām upari vartāmahe.

VĀMADEVAḤ: *(sa|vinayam)* bhagavan Kuśika|nandana! dhanyaḥ khalv ayaṃ rājā sāvitro, yad enam evam anurudhyante bhavanto 'pi!

VIŚVĀMITRAḤ: sakhe! dhanya ev' âyam.

> naman|nṛpati|maṇḍalī|
> mukuṭa|candrikā|dur|dina|
> sphurac|caraṇa|pallava|
> pratipad'|ôkta|doḥ|sampadā
> anena sasṛjetarām
> turaga|medha|mukta|bhramat|
> turaṅga|khura|candraka|
> prakara|danturā medinī.

DASHA·RATHA: *(with delight)* 1.65

> The man who has destroyed his kshatriya body with the chisels of asceticism and created a new Brahmanic one,* he who is deeply pervaded by his own nonviolent, pure qualities, the son of Gadhi, is now coming to see us.*

VISHVA·MITRA *enters, with* VAMA·DEVA *showing him the way.*

VISHVA·MITRA: My friend Vama·deva, give me some news—you have just come from Vasíshtha's hermitage. I hope the venerable and righteous sage is well, together with his pious and devoted wife, radiant Arúndhati.*

VAMA·DEVA: He is especially happy today, for his dear old friend Vishva·mitra has come to see the family for whom he performs sacrifices.*

VISHVA·MITRA: My friend Vama·deva, for a long time my 1.70
foremost desire has been to see Dasha·ratha.

VAMA·DEVA: *(politely)* Venerable son of Kúshika, this king of the solar dynasty is indeed very fortunate that you show so much regard for him.

VISHVA·MITRA: My friend, he is indeed fortunate.

> His might has been fully demonstrated, as kings bending down their crowned heads before him threw light on his feet, which thus shone forth like flower shoots illuminated by the moonlight in the rain. He has made the earth uneven, marked by the crescent-shaped hooves of the wandering horse he unleashed at the rite of Ashva·medha.*

(puro 'valokya sa|harṣam)

1.75 cirād akṣṇor jāḍyaṃ
śamayati samast'|âsura|vadhū|
kac'|ākṛṣṭi|krīḍā|
prasabha|su|bhagam|bhāvuka|bhujaḥ,
tri|lokī|jaṅghāl'|ô-
jjvala|sahaja|tejā, Manu|kula|
prasūtiḥ, Sutrāmṇo
vijaya|saha|kṛtvā Daśarathaḥ.

sakhe Vāmadeva! iyam anena pīyūṣa|tuṣāra|śīkar'|āsāra|varṣiṇī su|jana|saṃvāda|kautuka|megha|rekhā paurastyen' êva marutā loka|nāthena sahasra|śikharī|kriyate.

VĀMADEVAḤ: bhagavan! adya khalu Dilīpa|kula|kuśala|kalpa|latā|nav'|âṅkura|granthibhir udgīryante kisalayāni, yad atra|bhavān api tri|bhuvana|sanātana|gurur evam asmai nar'|êndrāya spṛhayati!

iti parikrāmataḥ

DAŚARATHAḤ: *(sa|praśraya|sambhramam āsanād utthāy' ôpasṛtya ca)* bhagavan Kuśika|nandana! aikṣvākaḥ Paṅkti|ratho 'bhivādayate.

1.80 VIŚVĀMITRAḤ: svasti bhavate saha|parivārāya.

sarve yath''|ôcitam upaviśanti.

(looking ahead, with delight)

> His arms are particularly able,* for they pulled the hair of all the demon-wives, as if just playing roughly.* His inborn energy radiates quickly everywhere in the three worlds. Born in the family of Manu, he has won the battle against demons in the company of Indra. And it is he who heals the numbness of my eyes after a long time: Dasha·ratha. 1.75

My friend Vama·deva, just as the eastern wind multiplies the crests of the row of clouds that generously shower drops of ambrosia-like cool water, this sovereign multiplies the joy with which good subjects talk about him.

VAMA·DEVA: Venerable master, today the joys of Dilípa's* lineage, which are like the knotty new sprouts of the wish-fulfilling creeper, have been transformed into shoots, as it were, because even you, the eternal master of the three worlds, show so much affection for this king.

Then they both go around the stage.

DASHA·RATHA: *(rises from his seat respectfully and with excitement, and approaches* VISHVA·MITRA*)* Venerable son of Kúshika, Dasha·ratha of the Ikshváku dynasty salutes you.

VISHVA·MITRA: God bless you and everybody around you. 1.80

Then all are seated as is customary.

DAŚARATHAḤ: *(sa|praśrayam)* bhagavan Viśvāmitra!

kac cit kāntāra|bhājāṃ bhavati paribhavaḥ
ko 'pi śauvā|pado vā?
pratyūhena kratūnāṃ na khalu makha|bhujo
bhuñjate vā havīṃṣi?
kartuṃ vā kac cid antar|vasati vasumatī|
dakṣiṇaḥ sapta|tantur
yat samprāpto 'si? kiṃ vā Raghu|kula|tapasām
īdṛśo 'yaṃ vivartaḥ?

VIŚVĀMITRAḤ: *(vihasya)*

1.85 janayati tvayi, vīra, diśāṃ patīn
api gṛh'|âṅgaṇa|mātra|kuṭumbinaḥ
«ripur» iti śrutir eva na vāstavī,
pratibhay'|ônnatir astu kutas tu naḥ?

api ca,

datt'|Êndr'|â|bhaya|vibhram'|âdbhuta|bhujā|
saṃbhāra|gambhīrayā
tvad|vṛttyā śithilī|kṛtas tri|bhuvana|
trāṇāya Nārāyaṇaḥ,
antas|toṣa|tuṣāra|saurabha|maya|
śvās'|ânil'|āpūraṇa|
prāṇ'|ôttuṅga|bhujaṅga|talpam adhunā
bhadreṇa nidrāyate.

DASHA·RATHA: *(courteously)* Venerable Vishva·mitra,

> Has some wandering beast caused distress among the forest-dwelling ascetics? Or has someone disturbed the sacrifices and obstructed the gods to enjoy the offerings? Or is it that you are thinking of performing a sacrifice for which a piece of land would be compensation? Is one of these the reason for your coming here? Or is your visit the reward of the ascetic observances of the Raghu dynasty?

VISHVA·MITRA: *(smiling)*

> Mighty hero, you have transformed even the celes- 1.85
> tial guardians of the directions into householders who simply look after their home and courtyard. So any hearsay about the existence of enemies cannot be true—in which case, what could we be scared of?

Furthermore,

> In your heroic exploits, your miraculously strong arms assured Indra's safety while also embarrassing him, and released Vishnu-Naráyana from his duty to protect the three worlds. The sweet, cool breath of the deeply contented Vishnu is pouring nourishing life-force into the snake, which, thus swollen, serves as his bed: he is now happily sleeping on it.

DAŚARATHAḤ: *(sa/vailakṣya/smitam)* bhagavan Viśvāmitra! abhyamittrīṇasya tatra|bhavataḥ Sunāsīrasya nāsīra|pūrakeṇa padāti|param'|âṇunā mayā kadā cid uddhṛtaṃ dhanuḥ, tan|mūlo 'yam alīka|loka|pravādo bhagavantam āpyāyayati.

VIŚVĀMITRAḤ: *(s'/ôtprāśa/smitam)*

1.90 trailoky'|â|bhaya|lagnakena bhavatā
vīreṇa vismāritas
taj|jīmūta|muhūrta|maṇḍana|dhanuḥ|
pāṇḍityam Ākhaṇḍalaḥ.
kiṃ c' âjasra|makh'|ârpitena haviṣā
saṃphulla|māṃs'|ôllasat|
sarv'|âṅgīṇa|valī|vilupta|nayana|
vyūhaḥ, kathaṃ vartate?

VĀMADEVAḤ: mahā|rāja, bhū|Kāśyapa! yath" āha bhagavān Kauśikaḥ. svayam an|ekadhā su|dharmāyām adhyakṣī|kṛtam aham api kiṃ cid bravīmi.

tvayy ardh'|āsana|bhāji, kiṃnara|gaṇ'|ôd-
gītair bhavad|vikramair
antaḥ|saṃbhṛta|matsaro 'pi, bhagavān
ākāra|guptau kṛtī;
unmīlad|bhavadīya|dakṣiṇa|bhujā|
rom'|âñca|viddh'|ôccarad|
bāṣpair eva vilocanair abhinayaty
ānandam Ākhaṇḍalaḥ.

DAŚARATHAḤ: *(sa/smitam)* Vāmadeva! tvam api bhagavantaṃ Gādhi|nandanam ev' ânupraviṣṭo 'si.

etasmai samar'|âṅgaṇa|praṇayine

DASHA·RATHA: *(embarrassed, smiling)* Venerable Vishva·mitra, I indeed took up the bow once as a common foot soldier, when I was appointed to fight in the front line of the army of Lord Indra, who affronted his enemies himself. That is the source of these false rumors that please you.

VISHVA·MITRA: *(smiling jokingly)* My friend,

> With your heroic deeds, you have guaranteed the safety of the three worlds and made Indra forget how to use his (rain-)bow, which adorns the clouds every now and then for a moment. What is more, you have given him so many offerings in never-ceasing sacrifices that now his body has become plump all over and his folding flesh hides his thousand eyes—how can he go on living like this? 1.90

VAMA·DEVA: Maharaja, Father of the Earth, what Vishva·mitra said is true. I am also only saying what I have witnessed several times in the council of gods.

> While you shared half of your seat with him, he—although filled with jealousy, hearing the horse-headed celestial bards singing about your exploits—skillfully hid his feelings. With his thousand eyes becoming full of tears—for they were hurt by seeing the hair on your able arms* rising in thrill*—he feigned joy, the venerable Indra.

DASHA·RATHA: *(smiling)* Vama·deva, you also follow the example of our venerable Vishva·mitra.

> Who could stand up against this Indra, so fond of going to battle, whose famous colossal arms are il-

tiṣṭheta kaḥ prajvalad|
dambholi|dyuti|maṇḍal'|ôdbhaṭa|bhuja|
stambhāya Jambh'|âraye?
niryadbhir bahir eṣa roṣa|dahana|
jyotiḥ|sphuliṅgair iva
svai rajyadbhir ap' īkṣaṇaiḥ samatanod
āgneyam astraṃ dviṣām.

1.95 VIŚVĀMITRAḤ: *(sa|gauravaṃ* DAŚARATHA*|bāhum āmṛśan)* rāja'|rṣe Vasiṣṭha|śiṣya!

saṃvṛtto 'yaṃ yadi tava bhuja|
chāyayā samprat' Îndro
nirvighna|Śrīr, iyam abhinavā
kīdṛśī te praśastiḥ?
Ikṣvākūṇāṃ likhita|paṭhitā
svar|vadhū|gaṇḍa|pīṭha|
krīḍā|pattra|prakara|makarī|
pāśu|pālyaṃ hi vṛttiḥ.

DAŚARATHAḤ: bhagavan, sarv'|âdbhuta|nidhe! bhavantam ukti|pratyuktikay" âpy anugantuṃ ke vayam? evaṃ kila Triśaṅku|saṃkīrtan'|ôpākhyāna|pāra|dṛśvānaḥ paurāṇikāḥ kathayanti:

trās'|ôtkampa|tri|daśa|pariṣan|
mauli|māṇikya|mālā|
bāl'|āditya|prakara|kiraṇa|
smera|pād'|âravinde
prācīm etāṃ bhuvana|racanām
anyathā nirmimāṇe
kārpaṇy'|ôktīs tvayi racitavān
antarāyaṃ mah"|Êndraḥ.

luminated by the halo of his radiant thunderbolt? He created a weapon of fire against his foes, using his burning glances, which were like flashing sparks of his flaming rage.

VISHVA·MITRA: *(respectfully touching* DASHA·RATHA*'s arm)* 1.95
Royal sage, Vasíshtha's disciple,

Even if Indra's Fortune is unobstructed now, thanks to your protecting arms, this new eulogy of your deeds means nothing to you, for it has always been the well-known prescribed duty of the Ikshváku dynasty to look after the herd of female *mákaras** playfully drawn on the cheeks of goddesses.*

DASHA·RATHA: Venerable Vishva·mitra, source of all wonders! Who are we to follow you in your arguments? The bards who recite stories of yore and know fully the famous story of Tri·shanku say this:

The rows of rubies on the heads of the gods who were trembling with fear of you threw light on your lotus-feet as the gods bowed down*—just as the morning sun's rays illuminate the opening day-lotuses—when you were about to change this previous creation of the universe. But the great Indra, asking you to be compassionate, stopped you.*

(vihasya)

1.100 javād ārāddhuṃ tvām
upanamati varge divi|ṣadām
apavyasto mandair
ajani ratha|haṃsaiḥ Kamala|bhūḥ;
niyacchāmo jihvāṃ
na tava caritebhyaḥ, kim uta te
sudhā|sadhrīcīnām
atipatati vācām avasaraḥ.

(añjaliṃ baddhvā) bhagavan, prasīda tāvat! uttar'|ôttareṣāṃ mah"|ôtsavānāṃ kadā cid api na tṛpyanti puṃsāṃ hṛdayāni; yad iyaṃ tvad|upasthāna|sulabha|saṃbhāvan"|âtiprasaṅga|saṃgītaka|nartakī citta|vṛttir niyog'|ânugrahāya spṛhayati.

VIŚVĀMITRAḤ: *(vihasya)* Aindumateya! kim anyan niyojyam?

nirmukta|śeṣa|dhavalair, acal'|êndra|mantha|
saṃkṣubdha|dugdha|maya|sāgara|garbha|gauraiḥ,
rājann, idaṃ bahula|pakṣa|dalan|mṛg'|âṅka|
ched'|ôjjvalais tava yaśobhir aśobhi viśvam.

punar idānīm api,

1.105 yaśaḥ|stomān uccair
upacinu cakora|praṇayinī|
rasa|jñā|pāṇḍitya|
chidura|śaśi|dhāma|bhrama|karān;

(smiling)

> When all the gods were coming quickly to praise you, lotus-born Brahma, whose chariot was pulled by slowly flying swans, became worried to arrive so late.* I should not prevent my tongue from retelling your exploits, but the occasion to hear your ambrosia-like words should not be missed, either. 1.100

(putting his hands together) So venerable Vishva·mitra, be gracious to us. People's hearts are never satisfied with the great feast of mutual replies. My mind, a dancer who has appeared in a performance of great affection and respect,* which was eased by your presence, now desires to be favored by your command.

VISHVA·MITRA: *(smiling)* O son of Índumati, what else shall I say?

> White as the serpent king Shesha after leaving his slough, or as the depths of the milk-ocean, which was churned with the Lord of the Mountains as a churning stick, bright white as the radiant digit of the moon that breaks forth in the dark fortnight, such is your renown, o king, which has come to adorn this world.*

But now,

> You should acquire fame that resembles the white 1.105
> moonlight so much that it could confuse even the female *chakóra*'s refined tongue. And when your splendor has conquered the darkness, let the Sun,

api tvat|tejobhis
tamasi śamite rakṣatu diśām
asau yātrā|maitrīṃ
nabhasi nitarām Ambara|maṇiḥ.

kiṃ tu, katipaya|rātram āyudha|sadhrīcā Rāma|bhadreṇa saṃnihita|vaitānika|vratānām asmākam āśrama|padaṃ sanāthī|kariṣyate. api ca,

madhye|kṛtya ghanaṃ dhinoti jala|dhiḥ
svair ambubhir Medinīṃ,
hanti svaiḥ kiraṇais tamisram aruṇaṃ
kṛtv" ântarāle Raviḥ,
tvaṃ Rām'|ântaritaś ca pālaya nijair
eva pratāpaiḥ prajām;
īdṛk ko 'pi par'|ôpakāra|suhṛdām
eṣa svabhāvo hi vaḥ.

kiṃ ca,

dṛṣṭaḥ sākṣād *asura/vijayī*
nākināṃ cakra/vartī,
mātsyo nyāyaḥ kathayati yathā
Vāruṇī daṇḍa|nītiḥ,
pātāl'|êndrād *ahi/bhayamath' âsty*
eva nity'/ânuṣaktaṃ;
tan, naḥ puṇyair ajani bhavatā,
vīra, rājanvatī bhūḥ!

> that jewel of the sky, still remain good friends with the Directions while making his journey in the air.*

Now, for a few nights, let your well-armed Rama protect my hermitage, for I have made a vow to perform a sacrifice. Furthermore,

> The ocean satisfies the earth with its water through the clouds as intermediaries, the sun uses the dawn as a go-between to destroy the darkness with its rays. And you should protect your subjects with your own prowess, but through Rama. For such is the nature of friends who help others, such is your nature.

Moreover,

> We have seen that the *King of Celestials conquered the demons : King of Gods is a ruler conquering with demonic means.* Furthermore, the law of fish : And the law of the big fish devouring the small fish* tells us how the legal system of Váruna , *the Lord of the Waters : the God of Justice*, works. It is also inevitable *that one should always get scared of the snake who is : to be afraid of the treachery of allies when it comes to* the King of the Underworld. Therefore, our efforts have been rewarded in that the earth unlike the sky, the sea and the underworld has found a good king in your person, o hero!*

I.110 DAŚARATHAḤ: *(sa|viṣādaṃ sva|gatam)* katham idam asmākaṃ sa|kala|loka|śoka|śaṅk'|ûddharaṇa|śītalebhyaḥ Kauśika|pādebhyo Rāma|bhadra|pravāsa|vaimanasyam apy utpatsyate! dṛṣṭaṃ vā niḥśeṣ'|ānanda|niṣyandinīnām indu|kiraṇa|kandalīnāṃ kamalinī|nimīlanam aṅka|sthānam. *(vimṛśya)* kā gatiḥ?

kūrma|rāja|bhujag'|âdhipa|gotra|
 grāva|dik|karibhir eka|dhurīṇaḥ;
māṃ prasūya katham astu vigīto,
 hā, par'|ârtha|vimukho Raghu|vaṃśaḥ?

VIŚVĀMITRAḤ: *(sasmitam)* rāja'|rṣe! mama|kāro hi putreṣu rājñām upalālana|kleśāya kevalam, upabhogas tu prajānām. yath" âitad:

kaṣṭā vedha|vyathā, kaṣṭo nityam udvahana|klamaḥ
śravaṇānām; alaṅkāraḥ kapolasya tu kuṇḍalam.

DAŚARATHAḤ: bhagavan! param anugṛhītā vayam evam atra|bhavatā sambhāvyamānāḥ. kiṃ tu punar, «a|kṛt'|âstraḥ kṣīra|kaṇṭhaḥ ca vatso 'yam» iti pramugdho 'smi.

I.115 VIŚVĀMITRAḤ: *(vihasya)* sakhe! tatra|bhavantaṃ Maitrā|varuṇim ṛṣiṃ puro|dhāya carita|brahma|carya|vratasya dhanur|veda|saṃskārās tāvad asya Kṛśāśva|prasādād asmāsu āyatante.

DASHA·RATHA: *(sadly, aside)* How can it happen that the 1.110
venerable Vishva·mitra, who soothes the world by taking away the sharp pain of all its sufferings, causes so much sorrow for me with the idea of Rama's departure. Indeed, the moon's rays, which are white as the plantain tree, are a delight to everyone, yet they have the fault of closing up the day-lotuses. *(reflecting)* What can I do?

> Just like the tortoise-king, the ruler of snakes, the seven great mountains and the elephants who guard the eight quarters, our family, too, has the same burden;* but, alas, how can our Raghu dynasty be lauded after my birth, if we no longer care for others?

VISHVA·MITRA: *(smiling)* Royal sage, kings are attached to their sons only because they have painstakingly brought them up. But it is the subjects who can make use of the princes. Just as:

> It is the ears that feel the pain when they are pierced and it is the ears that get tired carrying their burden all the time; but it is the cheeks that are decorated by the earrings.

DASHA·RATHA: Venerable Vishva·mitra, I am greatly honored that you show so much regard for me. However, I do worry, because this small child of mine has not yet taken arms in his hands—he still drinks only milk.

VISHVA·MITRA: *(smiling)* My friend, under the guidance of 1.115
the venerable sage Vasíshtha, he has finished his studies of the Vedas, and thanks to my guru Krisháshva, I can be in charge of initiating him into the practice of archery.

DASARATHAḤ: *(sa|vinay'|ôparodham)* bhagavan! ucchvasitam api Raghu|rāja|bījānāṃ tvad|āyattam eva, kim punaḥ kārmuka|vidyā|sampradāyaḥ! śaṅke «sahasra|kiraṇa|kul'| âika|pakṣa|pāten' âiva sahasraṃ parivatsarān bhagavantaṃ Kṛśāśvam upāsīno divy'|âstra|mantr'|ôpaniṣadam adhyagīṣṭhā» iti.

VIŚVĀMITRAḤ: alaṃ ca te Rāma|bhadre 'pi «bālo 'yam» ity a|sambhāvanayā, dyāvā|pṛthivyos timira|tiras|kariṇīṃ taraṇir aṇutaro 'pi nija|tejasā tiras|karoti.

DAŚARATHAḤ: *(vihasya)* bhagavan, Kuśika|vaṃśa|keto! kasya punar tādṛśī talinā jihvā, yā tvām api bruvāṇam adhar'| ôttareṇa pratisaṃdhatte? *(apavārya)* Vāmadeva! evam atra|bhavān Kauśiko bravīti.

VĀMADEVAḤ: rāja'|rṣe! kim atra praṣṭavyā vayam?

1.120 Kauśiko 'rthī, bhavān dātā, rakṣaṇīyo mahā|kratuḥ;
rakṣitā Rāma|bhadraś ced, anumanyāmahe vayam.

api ca,

jagatī|bhāra|khinnānāṃ viśrāmo bhavatām ayam,
yad yathā|kāma|saṃpatti|prīt'|ârthi|mukha|darśanam.

DASHA·RATHA: *(politely, restraining his feelings)* Venerable sage, every breath of the Raghu princes depends upon you, and even more so the transmission of the science of archery. I think it is because you are biased in favor of this dynasty of the thousand-rayed Sun that you have learned the secret science of celestial mantra-weapons from Krisháshva for a thousand years.*

VISHVA·MITRA: Stop thinking that Rama is still a child, please. The sun, even when it is like a tiny atom, is capable of removing the veil of darkness that envelops the sky and the earth with its light.

DASHA·RATHA: *(smiling)* Venerable and eminent son of the family of Kúshika, who could have a tongue sharp enough to be able to reply to your arguments? *(aside)* Vama·deva, you have heard what the venerable Vishva·mitra says.

VAMA·DEVA: Royal sage, why are you asking me?

> Vishva·mitra asks for something, you are generous, 1.120
> and there is the great sacrifice to be protected. If
> Rama is to be the protector, I have no objection.

Moreover,

> It would be a great relief for you, who are tired of
> carrying the burden of the earth, to see the happy
> face of someone who has asked for something and
> obtained it to his liking.

kiṃ ca, viśeṣeṇa ca—

pūrayitum arthi|kāmān
Maitrā|varuṇena gotra|guruṇā te
saṃdiśatā saṃdiṣṭaḥ—
samādhi|dṛṣṭo 'yam ev' ârthaḥ.

I.125 DAŚARATHAḤ: Vāmadeva, evam etad!

dhyāna|maya|dṛṣṭi|pāta|
pramuṣita|kāl'|âdhva|viprakarṣeṣu
viṣayeṣu naiṣṭhikānāṃ
sarva|pathīnā matiḥ kramate.

(vimṛśya sva|gatam)

kriyāṇāṃ rakṣāyai
Daśaratham upasthāya vimukhe
munau Viśvāmitre
bhagavati gate samprati gṛhān
tapo|leśa|kleśād
upaśamita|vighna|pratibhaye
pravṛtte yaṣṭuṃ vā,
Raghu|kula|kath" âiv' âstam|ayate.

(muniṃ prati) bhagavan! loka|traya|guro! Gādhi|nandana!

I.130 tvaṃ ced dīkṣiṣyamāṇo me
Rāma|bhadraṃ pratīkṣase,
tan naḥ pati|vratā|vṛttam
iyaṃ carati Medinī.

(nepathy'|âbhimukham avalokya) kas, ko 'tra bhoḥ?

praviśya.

DAUVĀRIKAḤ: kim ājñāpayati devaḥ?

Furthermore, and in particular,

> The teacher of your family, Vasíshtha, has sent the message to tell you to fulfill the wishes of whoever asks you—he had surely foreseen these events through his meditative power.

DASHA·RATHA: Vama·deva, it must be so, I.125

> Objects that are far in space and removed in time are grasped by their yogic vision—the thought of ascetics thus reaches everywhere.

(reflecting, aside)

> The venerable sage Vishva·mitra has turned to Dasha·ratha to ask for the protection of his rites. If his request is refused and he now returns home to conquer the troubling impeders of his sacrifice himself by using some of his ascetic power, then the fame of the Raghu dynasty shall decline.*

(turning toward the ascetic) Master of the three worlds, son of Gadhi,

> If you really depend on my son, Rama, to perform I.130
> the sacrifice, then it means that this earth leads the life of a faithful wife of ours.*

(toward the rear stage) Who is that? Who is here?

The WARDER *enters.*

WARDER: What does Your Majesty command?

DAŚARATHAḤ: āhūyatāṃ Rāma|bhadraḥ!

VĀMADEVAḤ: Lakṣmaṇaś ca.

VIŚVĀMITRAḤ: *(sa/smitam)* ṛṣe! pṛthak|prayatn'|âpekṣī n' âyam arthaḥ: na khalu prakāśam antareṇa tuhina|bhānur ujjihīte!

DAUVĀRIKO *niṣkrāntaḥ*

tataḥ praviśato RĀMA|LAKṢMAṆAU.

RĀMAḤ: *(sa/harṣam)*

sur'|âdhīśa|krodhāj
  jagad aparathā kartum apare
purāṇa|brahmāṇo
  bhuvana|pitaraḥ sapta ca kṛtāḥ.
dhṛtās tuṣṭen' âmī
  bahir api ca vaiśvānara|pathāt
kathā paurāṇī yac
  caritam iti ha sma prathayati—

kathaṃ so 'pi bhagavān asmābhiḥ svayam upacariṣyate?

iti parikrāman puro 'valokya harṣ'/âtiśayaṃ nirūpayan

nūnaṃ vinaya|vinamrayos tāta|Vāmadevayos tṛtīyaḥ praśānta|pāvanīy'|ākṛtiḥ sa bhagavān Viśvāmitro bhaviṣyati.

LAKṢMAṆAḤ: *(s'/āścarya/smitam)* ārya,

ayam ayam īdṛśa|
  praśama|viśvasanīya|tanur
bhuvana|bhayaṃ|karīḥ
  katham adhatta ruṣo 'pi muniḥ?
sthitam idam eva vā
  mṛdu|mano|jña|tuṣāra|tamās

DASHA·RATHA: Call my dear Rama.

VAMA·DEVA: And Lákshmana.

VISHVA·MITRA: *(smiling)* Sage, he does not need to be called separately—the cool-rayed moon does not rise without its light.

The WARDER *exits.*

RAMA *and* LÁKSHMANA *enter.*

RAMA: *(with delight)*

> Enraged with the King of Gods, he created a new set of seven Brahmas, ancestors of the world, in order to perform a new and different creation. Then, propitiated by the gods, he agreed to keep them as a new constellation in the sky out of the way of the moon's path known by mankind.* He whose exploits of this kind have been transmitted in ancient stories...*

how shall I be able to serve him, the venerable Vishva·mitra?

He walks around the stage and looks forward, miming extreme delight.

Surely, the third person, calm and pure, in front of my father and Vama·deva, who politely bow down before him, must be the venerable Vishva·mitra.

LÁKSHMANA: *(surprised and smiling)* My brother,

> This very person, this ascetic who looks so calm and trustworthy, how could he be so angry that he made the world tremble? Or one should just think of the example of the medicinal herbs, which are tender, lovely and cool but suddenly become radiant in the dark.

tamasi sati jvalan-
ti sahas" âiva mah"|âuṣadhayaḥ.

RĀMAḤ: vatsa Lakṣmaṇa, evaṃ dur|avagāha|gambhīra|caritāś citrīyante mahāntaḥ. api ca,

vrata|vihati|karībhir apsarobhiḥ
saha jagad asya nigṛhṇato gṛṇanti
namad|amara|śiraḥ|kirīṭa|rocir|
mukulita|roṣa|tamāṃsi ceṣṭitāni.

VĀMADEVAḤ: *(dṛṣṭvā, sa|harṣaṃ)* katham? āgato Rāma|bhadraḥ? *(muniṃ prati)* bhagavan,

brahma|jyotir vivartasya caturdhā|deha|yoginaḥ
Ṛṣyaśṛṅga|caror aṃśaḥ prathamo 'yaṃ mahā|bhujaḥ.

1.150 VIŚVĀMITRAḤ: *(sa|harṣa|saṃbhramam avalokya)* Vāmadeva, kim ucyate! āraṇyakeṣu prakṛṣṭatamaṃ kim api brāhmaṇyam Ṛṣyaśṛṅgasya! na kevalam amunā vatsena brahma'|ṛṣir Vibhāṇḍaka eva putravatāṃ dhuram āropitaḥ, api tu rāja'|ṛṣir Daśaratho 'pi.

VĀMADEVAḤ: bhagavan, evam ev' âitat.

VIŚVĀMITRAḤ: (VĀMADEVAṂ *prati)*

ye Maitrāvaruṇiṃ purohitavataḥ
vaṃśe Manor jajñire
tās tā vainayikīḥ kriyā vidadhire
yeṣāṃ ca yuṣmā|dṛśaḥ,
teṣām añcalam eṣa te, Daśarathaḥ.

RAMA: Dear Lákshmana, great men surprise the world with their inscrutable and mysterious ways of acting. Furthermore,

> People evoke his exploits, such as when he was to punish the world as well as the nymphs who wanted to obstruct his observance, but the darkness of his wrath was reduced by the radiant crowns of the gods, who bent down before him.

VAMA·DEVA: *(seeing him, with delight)* What? Has Rama arrived? *(toward the ascetic)* Venerable sage,

> Of the offering made by Rishya·shringa,* in which he transformed his brahmanic radiance into four embodied beings, this strong-armed Rama was the first and foremost portion.

VISHVA·MITRA: *(looking at him with delight and excitement)* I.150
Vama·deva, indeed, among the forest-dwellers, it is Rishya·shringa's brahmanic power that is the most outstanding. Not only did he make the brahmin sage Vibhándaka the best of fathers by becoming his son, but he also made the royal sage Dasha·ratha an eminent father.*

VAMA·DEVA: Venerable sage, it was indeed so.

VISHVA·MITRA: *(to* VAMA·DEVA*)*

> Of the kings who were born in the dynasty of Manu and made Vasíshtha their family priest, and whom people like you have instructed in various ways, here is the king who was going to be the last one: your disciple, Dasha·ratha. But now the dynasty of Ikshvákus has been surely renewed, as

samprаty amī ye punar
jātās, te dhruvaṃ Ṛṣyaśṛṅga|tapasām
aiśvaryam Ikṣvākavaḥ.

RĀMA|LAKṢMAṆĀV *upasarpataḥ.*

I.155 VĀMADEVAḤ: vatsau! bhagavān eṣa niḥ|śeṣa|bhuvana|mahanīyo mahā|muniḥ Kauśikaḥ praṇamyatām!

RĀMA|LAKṢMAṆAU: *(upasṛtya)* bhagavan Viśvāmitra, sāvitrau Rāma|Lakṣmaṇāv abhivādayete.

VIŚVĀMITRAḤ: vatsau, āyuṣmantau bhūyāstām. *(iti bhujābhyām parigṛhya, sa/rom'/âñcaṃ* RĀMAṂ *ca nirvarṇya sa/bahu/mānam ātma/gatam)*

Vasiṣṭh'|ôktair mantrair
dadhati jagatām ābhyudayikīṃ
dhuraṃ samprаty ete
dinakara|kulīnāḥ kṣiti|bhujaḥ
gṛhe yeṣāṃ Rām'|ā-
dibhir api kalābhiś catasṛbhiḥ
svayaṃ devo Lakṣmī|
stana|kalaśa|vārī|gaja|patiḥ.

api ca,

I.160 tvaṃ tās tāḥ smṛtavān ṛco daśatayīs
tvat|prītaye yajvabhiḥ
Svāhā|kāram upāhitaṃ havir iha
tret"|âgnir ācāmati.
tvāṃ kṣīroda|jale|śayaṃ kratu|lihaḥ
pṛthvīm avātītarad
udvṛttā Daśa|kandhara|prabhṛtayo
nigrāhitāras tvayā.

these sons were born of Rishya·shringa's ascetic power.

RAMA *and* LÁKSHMANA *approach.*

VAMA·DEVA: Princes, please bow down to salute this great ascetic, worshipped by the whole world: the venerable Vishva·mitra. 1.155

RAMA AND LÁKSHMANA: *(approaching him)* Venerable Vishva·mitra, Rama and Lákshmana of the solar dynasty salute you.

VISHVA·MITRA: My dear sons, may you live long. *(He embraces them and then, thrilled, he observes* RAMA. *Aside, showing his appreciation.)*

These kings of the solar race shall now dutifully maintain the well-being of the worlds following Vasíshtha's advice, for Lord Vishnu himself has been incarnated in their house in four parts as Rama and his brothers, the lord who is like the king of elephants and is restrained only by the jar-like breasts of the Goddess of Good Fortune.

Moreover,

You have revealed the ten books of hymns of the 'Rig·veda,' and it is to please you that the three sacred fires here consume the offerings made with the recitation of "Svaha" and other ritual formulas.* You were sleeping in the milk-ocean, but the sacrifice-eating gods made you bring up the earth.* Now the haughty demons, ten-headed Rávana and the others, are also to be punished by you. 1.160

VĀMADEVAḤ: *(sa|smitam)* vatsau! ayam atra|bhavān bhavantau netum āgataḥ.

RĀMA|LAKṢMAṆAU: yad abhirucitaṃ bhavate tātāya ca.

DAŚARATHAS *tau sa|sneha|bahu|mānam ādāya «bhagavan Kauśika» ity ardh'|ôkte many'|ûtpīḍa|nigṛhyamāṇa|kaṇṭho* VĀMADEVASYA *mukham īkṣate.*

VĀMADEVAḤ: imau tau Rāma|Lakṣmaṇau. *(ity arpayati)*

1.165 VIŚVĀMITRAḤ *s'|ādaraṃ pratigṛhṇāti. nepathye śaṅkha|dhvaniḥ.* VĀMADEVO *nimittam anumodayamāno* DAŚARATHAM *ullāsayati. punar* NEPATHYE

VAITĀLIKAḤ: sukhāya mādhyaṃ|dinī saṃdhyā bhavatu devasya! saṃprati hi,

kirati mihire viṣvadrīcaḥ
karān ativāmanī
sthala|kamaṭhavad deha|chāyā
janasya viceṣṭate,
gaja|pati|mukh'|ôdgīrṇair āpyair
api trasa|reṇubhiḥ
śiśira|madhurām eṇāḥ kaccha|
sthalīm adhiśerate.

api c' êdānīm paṭīra|taru|koṭara|kuṭīram adhyāsīnāḥ,

pratyakṣara|sruta|sudhā|rasa|nirviṣābhir
āśīrbhir abhyadhika|bhūṣita|bhoga|bhājaḥ
gāyanti kañcuka|vinihnuta|roma|harṣa|
sved'|ōrmayas tava guṇān urag'|êndra|kanyāḥ.

VAMA·DEVA: *(smiling)* Princes, this venerable sage has come to take you away.

RAMA AND LÁKSHMANA: We do what pleases you and our father...

DASHA·RATHA *embraces them affectionately and with respect; he starts saying "Venerable* VISHVA·MITRA*" and then stops the sentence halfway as his voice is choked by sorrow and pain. Next he looks at* VAMA·DEVA*'s face.*

VAMA·DEVA: Here are Rama and Lákshmana.

He thus hands them over to VISHVA·MITRA. VISHVA·MITRA *takes them respectfully. Conch shells are blown behind the scenes.* VAMA·DEVA *is delighted to hear this auspicious sound and consoles* DASHA·RATHA. *Again from* BEHIND THE SCENES. 1.165

A BARD: May the midday hour be to the delight of His Majesty. For now,

> When the sun casts its rays in all directions, people's shadows become contracted, behaving like tortoises on dry land. And deers repose on the marsh, cool and pleasant, with dust-like water drops sprinkled from the trunks of tall elephants.

Furthermore, those who use the holes of sandal trees as huts...

> Their hoods are beautifully decorated with fangs that have lost their venom, because every letter of your praise produces ambrosia in them; their goosebumps and their drops of perspiration are

1.170 VIŚVĀMITRAḤ: sakhe Daśaratha, priyam api tathyam āha vaitālikaḥ.

mand'|ôddhūtaiḥ śirobhir maṇi|bhara|gurubhiḥ
 prauḍha|rom'|âñca|daṇḍa|
sphāyan|nirmoka|saṃdhi|prasarad|a|vigalat|
 saṃmada|sveda|pūrāḥ,
jihvā|yugm'|âbhipūrṇ'|ānana|viṣama|samud-
 gīrṇa|varṇ'|âbhirāmam
velā|śail'|âṅka|bhājo bhujaga|yuvatayas
 tvad|guṇān udgṛṇanti.

(sa|vinaya|vailakṣya|smitaṃ ca) rāja'|rṣe, pratyāsīdati dīkṣā|praveśa|kālaḥ. tad evaṃ|vidha|madhura|goṣṭhī|bhaṅga|niṣṭhurāṇāṃ prathame vayaṃ tāvad bhavitum icchāmaḥ.

DAŚARATHO RĀMA|LAKṢMAṆĀV *avalokya bāṣpa|bhara|taraṅgita|locano munim prati «bhagavan!» ity ardh'|ôkte vāk|stambhaṃ nāṭayati.*

VĀMADEVAḤ: *(sa|saṃbhramam)* bhagavan Kauśika, sādhaya! śivās te panthānaḥ, vatsayoś ca Rāma|Lakṣmaṇayoḥ.

1.175 *ity utthāya sarve yath"|ôcitam ācaranti.*

VIŚVĀMITRAḤ: evam āsyatām bhavadbhiḥ.

iti RĀJA|PUTRĀBHYĀM *anugamyamāno niṣkrāntaḥ.*

trapped under their skin while they sing about
your virtues, these daughters of the snake-king.

VISHVA·MITRA: My friend Dasha·ratha, the bard describes this faithfully and pleasantly. 1.170

They sway their heads slowly, weighed down by their head-jewels. Their skin is swelling with goose-bumps sticking out, which do not release their abundantly flowing sweat of pleasure from their pores. With their double tongues, their mouths* pronounce the sounds indistinctly, which is all the more delightful. Thus do serpent maidens sing about your virtues on the mountain slopes beside the sea.

(politely, with an embarrassed smile) Royal sage, the time to start the preliminaries of the sacrifice is near. Let me be the first to break up this pleasant gathering, harsh as this task may be.

DASHA·RATHA, *looking at* RAMA *and* LÁKSHMANA, *his eyes filled with flowing tears, starts saying "Venerable" to the ascetic and then mimes that he can no longer speak.*

VAMA·DEVA: *(with excitement)* Venerable Vishva·mitra, do proceed, and may your paths, as well as those of Rama and Lákshmana, be auspicious.

They all rise and observe the usual formalities. 1.175

VISHVA·MITRA: May you also remain prosperous.

Thus VISHVA·MITRA *exits, followed by the* TWO PRINCES.

DAŚARATHAḤ: *(dīrgham uṣṇaṃ ca niḥśvasya)* Vāmadeva, nūnam idānīm asmān iva tatra|bhavantaṃ Kauśikam apy a|kāraṇa|vatsalaṃ vatsalayati vatso me Rāma|bhadraḥ.

kac cid asmad|viyog'|ârti|duḥkhī duḥkhā|kariṣyati,
a|pūrva|viṣay'|āloka|sukhī vā sukhayiṣyati.

1.180 VĀMADEVAḤ: *(vihasya)* rāja'|rṣe, «vayaṃ Kauśiko v" êti» kva punar eṣa kakṣyā|vibhāgo Rāma|bhadra|mādhuryasya? paśya,

yad indor anveti
    vyasanam udayaṃ vā nidhir apām,
  upādhis tatr' âyaṃ
    jayati jani|kartuḥ prakṛtitā.
ayaṃ kaḥ saṃbandho
    yad anuharate tasya kumudaṃ?
  viśuddhāḥ śuddhānāṃ
    dhruvam an|abhisandhi|praṇayinaḥ.

DAŚARATHAḤ: *(vimṛśya)* evam etat.

ratn'|ākaro janayitā sahajaś ca vargaḥ
  kiṃ kathyatām amṛta|kaustubha|pārijātāḥ?
kiṃ tair a|cintyam? iha tat punar anyad eva
  tattv'|ântaraṃ kumuda|bandhur asau yad induḥ.

DASHA·RATHA: *(heaving a deep* sigh)* Vama·deva, now my dear Rama shall favor the venerable Vishva·mitra, who has an inexplicable attachment toward him, just as he favored me.

> Perhaps he shall suffer because of the separation from me and shall also make Vishva·mitra sad; or else he shall be delighted to see unknown things and thus also make Vishva·mitra happy.

VAMA·DEVA: *(smiling)* Royal sage, why should there be such 1.180
antagonistic rivalry for Rama's affection between you and Vishva·mitra. Look,

> That the sea follows the waxing and waning of the moon can be explained by the fact that the natural inclination of the father dominates.* But how does this relate to the case of the night-lotus, which imitates the moon's nature by opening up at night? Here the reason is surely that pure souls follow the pure, with inexplicable affection.*

DASHA·RATHA: *(reflecting)* Indeed, it must be so.

> The sea rich in pearls is the father of the Moon, whose brothers are the Káustubha gem, ambrosia and the coral tree of Indra's paradise—but what is there to say about them?* Yet there is something else, a relationship altogether different and unthinkable for all of these, which causes the moon to be called "the friend of the night-lotus."*

(puro 'valokya) katham̩, nayana|patham atikrāntaḥ sa|Rāma|Lakṣmaṇo bhagavān! tad vayam api vatsa|pravāsa|dur|manasaṃ devīṃ Kauśalyām upetya sāntvayāmaḥ.

1.185 *iti niṣkrāntāḥ sarve.*

(looking ahead) O, the venerable Vishva·mitra is already out of sight with Rama and Lákshmana. So I shall go and comfort Queen Kaushálya, who is also dejected to see that her son has gone away.

All exit. 1.185

PRELUDE TO ACT II
SANSKRIT-PRAKRIT PRELUDE

*tataḥ praviśati kuśān ādāya yajamāna/*ŚIṢYAḤ.

ŚIṢYAḤ: *(puro 'valokya)* aye, prabhāta|prāy"|âiva rajanī. tathā hi,

tamobhiḥ pīyante
gata|vayasi pīyūṣa|vapuṣi
jvaliṣyan|mārtaṇḍ'|ô-
pala|paṭala|dhūmair iva diśaḥ.
saro|jānāṃ karṣann
ali|mayam ayas|kānta|maṇivat
kṣaṇād antaḥ|śalyaṃ
tapati patir ady' âpi na rucām.

api ca,

2.5 jātāḥ pakva|palāṇḍu|pāṇḍu|madhura|
chāyā|kiras tārakāḥ;
prācīm aṅkurayanti kiṃ cana ruco
rājīva|jīvātavaḥ;
lūtā|tantu|vitāna|vartulam ito
bimbaṃ dadhac cumbati
prātaḥ|proṣita|rocir ambara|talād
ast'|âcalaṃ candramāḥ.

(sarvato 'valokya)

diṅ|maṇḍalī|mukuṭa|maṇḍana|padma|rāga|
ratn'|âṅkure kiraṇa|mālini garbhite 'pi
saukha|prasuptika|madhuvrata|cakravāla|
vācāla|paṅkaja|vanī|sarasāḥ sarasyaḥ.

api ca,

prācī|vibhrama|karṇikā|kamalinī|
saṃvartikāḥ samprati

A DISCIPLE *of the sacrificer* VISHVA·MITRA *enters, with sacred* kusha *grass in his hand.*

DISCIPLE: *(looking ahead)* It seems that the night is being taken over by the dawn. In fact,

As the moon made of ambrosia has lost its strength, darkness is covering the world, just as the veil-like smoke of the sun-stones prevails before they show their radiance. The Sun, Lord of All Light, does not yet burn to extract in an instant the bee from the lotus, as a magnet would a nail.

Moreover,

The stars scatter their pale and sweet light, resembling ripe onions; and the rays of dawn that ensure the lives of blue lotuses illuminate slightly the eastern direction. Now, as it dawns, the moon has lost its radiance and, with its large and round cobweb-like disk, it descends from the sky to kiss the Western Mountain. 2.5

(looking everywhere)

While that small shining ruby that decorates the crown of all directions, the sun, is still hidden with its garland of rays, lakes resound charmingly with swarms of bees who ask the lotuses if they have slept well.

Moreover,

Now, as if they were petals of a lotus earring worn playfully by the eastern direction, two or three rays

dve tisro ramaṇīyam ambara|maṇer
dyām uccarante rucaḥ.
stok'|ôcchvāsam ap' īdam utsukatayā
saṃbhūya kośād bahir
niṣkrāmad|bhramar'|âugha|saṃbhrama|bharād
ambhojam ujjṛmbhate.

2.10 api ca,

eka|dvi|prabhṛti|krameṇa gaṇanām
eṣām iv' âstaṃ|yatāṃ
kurvāṇā samakocayad daśa|śatāny
ambhoja|saṃvartikāḥ,
bhūyo 'pi kramaśaḥ prasārayati tāḥ
saṃpraty amūn udyataḥ
saṃkhyātuṃ sa|kutūhal" êva nalinī
bhānoḥ sahasraṃ karān.

kiṃ ca,

pratyāsanna|sur'|êndra|sindhura|śiraḥ|
sindūra|sāndr'|âruṇā
yat tejas|trasareṇavo viyad itaḥ
prācīnam ātanvate.
śaṅke saṃprati yāvad abhyudayate
tat tarku|ṭaṅk'|ônmṛjā|
rajyad|bimba|rajaś|chaṭā|valayito
devas tviṣām īśvaraḥ.

(puro 'valokya) katham idam uday'|âcala|mauli|māṇikyam arka|maṇḍalam ady' âpi na vihāya|sthalam alaṅ|karoti? tad asmad|guror vitāyamāna|yajñasya kula|pateḥ Kauśikasy' ādeśāt samid|āharaṇāya prasthito 'smi. tat tvaritataraṃ gacchāmi.

of the sun, that jewel of the sky, have gracefully risen to reach the sky. The day-lotus, although it was just going to take a little breath, has been overcome by the eagerness to release its burden, the swarming bees, from its calyx and is opening up fully.

Moreover, 2.10

As if counting the rays of the setting sun one by one, the lotus had closed up its thousand petals for the night. Now it is stretching them out again one by one, as if it wanted to count the thousand rays of the rising sun eagerly.

Furthermore,

Radiant dust particles, bright red like the vermilion decoration on the head of the elephant ridden by Indra nearby, start filling the space in the East. It seems now that they belong to the god who is enveloped in a circular mass of redness, shining as if it had just been polished perfectly with the chisel of the Creator:* the sun is rising.

(looking ahead) Why is it that the sun-disk, that jewel in the crown of the Eastern Mountain, is still not decorating the sky? Now, our master and guardian, Vishva·mitra, is preparing a sacrifice and has ordered me to gather some wood. I shall go without delay.

2.15 *iti parikrāmati.*

praviśya saṃbhrānto VAṬUḤ.

VAṬUḤ: ⌜ajja Suṇāseva! kiṃ vi acchariaṃ bhīsaṇaṃ ca vaṭṭaï.⌟

ŚUNAḤŚEPAḤ: *(sa|camat|kāraṃ parivṛtya)* sakhe Paśumeḍhra! kim āścaryaṃ bhīṣaṇaṃ ca vartate?

PAŚUMEḌHRAḤ: ⌜ajja «Rāmo tti ko vi khattia|kumāro āao» tti suṇia kouhalleṇa dhāvantassa sā tavo|vaṇa|ppanta|paḍiṭṭhiā patthara|puttiā sacca|māṇusī bhavia mama evva sammuhaṃ parāvaḍiā. taṃ pekkhia uttar'|āsaṅga|vakkalaṃ vi ujjhia palāio mhi.⌟

2.20 ŚUNAḤŚEPAḤ: *(vihasya.)* sakhe! sādhu kṛtam. diṣṭyā hi jīvataḥ punar āvṛttiḥ.

PAŚUMEḌHRAḤ: ⌜tā rakkhaü maṃ ajjo imāe duṭṭha|rakkhasīe muhāo.⌟

iti vepamānaḥ pādayoḥ patati.

ŚUNAḤŚEPAḤ: *(sa|smitam utthāpy' āliṅgya ca)* vayasya, śṛṇoṣy aucathyasya bhagavato Gautamasya maha"|rṣer Ahalyāṃ nāma dharma|dārān.

PAŚUMEḌHRAḤ: ⌜suṇomi, jā Jaṇaa|vaṃsa|purohiassa Saāṇandassa jaṇaṇī. tado tado.⌟

He goes around the stage. 2.15

A BOY *enters, confused.*

BOY: Mr Shunah·shepa, something miraculous and frightening has happened to me.

SHUNAH·SHEPA: *(turning around with surprise)* My friend Pashu·medhra, what sort of miraculous and frightening thing was it?

PASHU·MEDHRA: I heard today that a certain young kshatriya called Rama had come here. As I came running, eager to see him, the stone statue that had been erected at the edge of the hermitage suddenly approached me, in the form of a real woman. When I saw her, I was able to just barely escape, leaving behind even the bark garment that covered my shoulders.

SHUNAH·SHEPA: *(smiling)* Well done, my friend. Thank god 2.20
you have come back alive.

PASHU·MEDHRA: So please protect me from the mouth of that terrible demoness, my noble friend.

Trembling, he falls at SHUNAH·SHEPA*'s feet.*

SHUNAH·SHEPA: *(smiles, lifts him up and embraces him)* My friend, you must have heard about Ahályа, the lawful wife of the great sage, the venerable Gáutama.

PASHU·MEDHRA: Yes, I have. She is mother to Shatánanda, who is the official priest appointed to the house of Jánaka. So what happened?

2.25 ŚUNAḤŚEPAḤ: s" êyam purā Puruhūta|khaṇḍita|caritrā tasya dīrgha|tapaso muner manyunā nijam etad indriya|daurbalyam evaṃ vivartamānam anubhavantī, saṃpraty asya Raghu|rāja|putrasya tejasā tasmād andha|kārāt niramucyata. tad alam āvegena!

PAŚUMEḌHRAḤ: *(unmīlya cakṣuṣī sarvato 'valokya)* ⌜aho! ajjassa pasāeṇa jīva|loe paḍiṭṭhio mhi. taha vi, saṅkā|jaro ajja vi maṃ ṇa pariccaaï. tā, muhuttaṃ vīsamīaü.⌟

ŚUNAḤŚEPAḤ: sakhe, bhayam iti kim etad brāhmaṇasya? tat paryavasthāpay' ātmānam.

ity upaviśataḥ.

PAŚUMEḌHRAḤ: *(ciraṃ viśramya sa|vismayam)* ⌜kahaṃ visaa|maa|taṇhā|jhalaṃ|jhalīe bhaavado Hariṇā vi hariṇaā viḍambīadi?⌟

2.30 ŚUNAḤŚEPAḤ: *(vihasya)* sādhu bravīti bhavān. alpīyān khalv ayaṃ lokaḥ! katham aihika|sukh'|âdhyavasāy'|āsvāda|lubdhair amūr bhūyasyo rātrayaḥ parāhaṇyante. kiṃ tu mano|hāribhir āhāryair viṣayair āhūyamānasya locana|dvayasy' âpi ko 'pi jano vivekam aṅkuśayituṃ n' ēṣṭe. kiṃ punaḥ, Sahasra|nayanasya tādṛśa|vibhave Marutām patyuḥ. cakṣuḥ|prītim udbhavantīm anūdbhavanti c' âparāṇi Kusuma|cāpa|cāpalāni.

SHUNAH·SHEPA: Some time ago, she was made unfaithful to 2.25
her husband by Indra, and her husband, that ascetic of great power, became so enraged that he transformed her body into this petrified form. But, thanks to the radiant power of Prince Rama, she has been liberated from this darkness of her senses. Hence you need not be so scared of her.

PASHU·MEDHRA: *(opens his eyes and looks around)* O, thanks to your kindness, I have come back to the world of living beings. Yet I still cannot get rid of my feverish alarm. So, Mr. Shunah·shepa, let us rest here for a while.

SHUNAH·SHEPA: My friend, why would a brahmin be afraid? Pull yourself together.

They sit down.

PASHU·MEDHRA: *(resting for a while, then with surprise)* How come even the venerable Indra, dazzled by the mirage-like senses, can be transformed into a beast?

SHUNAH·SHEPA: *(smiling)* You speak the truth. This world 2.30
of the senses is of little importance. So one wonders why people deprive themselves of that much more important stay in heaven, being eager to taste worldly pleasures. Yet one does not learn to control the judgment of one's two eyes, which are attracted to pleasant things as their objects. And how much less can Indra, Lord of the Winds, do so, given that he has a thousand eyes to overpower him. Now, when visual pleasure is aroused, other senses also get carried away by the God of Love.

PAŚUMEḌHRAḤ: *(vihasya)* ⌈maṇṇe, edāe muṇi|ghariṇīe puṇṇa|paripāo Rāma|bhaddassa pavāse kāraṇam.⌋

ŚUNAḤŚEPAḤ: idaṃ tāvat prathamam.

PAŚUMEḌHRAḤ: *(s'|âbhyarthanam.)* ⌈ajja, duīaṃ vi suṇiuṃ imiṇā de vaaṇeṇa pajjūsuo mhi.⌋

ŚUNAḤŚEPAḤ: sakhe, tvayi kim a|kathanīyaṃ nāma? asti Kiṣkindhāyām Puraṃdarasya nandano Vālī nāma plavaṅga|rājaḥ. taṃ ca rajanī|cara|cakra|varttinā Daśakandhareṇa pravṛddha|maitrīkam avalokya tu vānar'|âcchabhalla|golāṅgūla|prabhṛtīnām ācāryaḥ sarv'|âmātyānām anumato Jāmbavān avādīt.

2.35 PAŚUMEḌHRAḤ: *(vihasya, sa|kautukam)* ⌈tado tado.⌋

ŚUNAḤŚEPAḤ: tataś ca, «rājan! māyāvinī khalv iyaṃ rākṣasa|jātiḥ. viśeṣataś ca Mahendr'|âvaskanda|kandalita|vikramaḥ pitṛ|vairī tav' âyaṃ Rāvaṇaḥ. api ca, tvadīya|dor|mūla|pīḍana|galita|pauruṣo na viśva|vijay" îti svayam āśaṅkanīyaḥ. n' âpi sāmant'|ântara|jighṛkṣāyām antarāla|vartini samudre laghu|samutthaḥ. tad anena virāddha|maṇḍalena *sur'|âsura|jayinā* rākṣasa|rājena maittram an|arth'|ânubandhi. kiṃ ca, sarvath" êyam an|upakāriṇī Pulasty'|âpatye prītir iti bhagavān ih' ôdāharaṇaṃ Hariṇ'|âṅka|śekharaḥ. tathā hi,

PASHU·MEDHRA: *(smiling)* I think that the reason Rama has come here is that the meritorious acts of the ascetic's wife have borne their fruit.

SHUNAH·SHEPA: That is surely one of the reasons.

PASHU·MEDHRA: *(begging)* I am also eager to hear the other reason from you, sir.

SHUNAH·SHEPA: My friend, is there anything I would not tell you? There lives a monkey-king called Vali, son of Indra, in Kishkíndha. He began to be on friendly terms with the king of demons, ten-headed Rávana, and this was observed by Jámbavan, the preceptor of monkeys, bears, apes and the like. So Jámbavan, with the approval of all the ministers, spoke up.

PASHU·MEDHRA: *(smiling, with curiosity)* What did he say? 2.35

SHUNAH·SHEPA: Then he said:* "Your Majesty, the race of demons is full of magic tricks. And this is especially true of the demon whose prowess has been renewed by attacking the great Indra, and who is thus also your father's enemy: Rávana. Moreover, the reason he has not conquered the whole world yet is that you have deprived him of his manliness by squeezing him under your armpit—therefore he is all the more suspicious. And, with the sea lying between us, he cannot come here quickly to help if you want to attack a neighboring king.* Therefore, it makes no sense to be allied *with this conqueror of gods and demons : with this conqueror of the gods, who conquered them with unfair means,** with this rákshasa ruler whose kingdom is hostile. Furthermore, the venerable Shiva, who wears the moon in his hair, is himself

ukṣā ratho, bhūṣaṇam asthi|mālā,
bhasm'|âṅga|rāgo, gaja|carma vāsaḥ,
ek'|ālaya|sthe 'pi dhan'|âdhināthe
sakhyau daś" êyaṃ Tri|pur'|ântakasya»

PAŚUMEḌHRAḤ: ⌜aṃho! thera|bhallūassa mant'|ôvaṇṇāso parihāsa|kusala" â. tado tado.⌟

ŚUNAḤŚEPAḤ: tataś ca, tad|vacanaṃ «jarā|pralapitam» ity upahasati har'|īśvare, upāṃśu tad|anumatyā mah"|âmātyasya kesariṇaḥ putro Hanūmān kumāraṃ Sugrīvam ādāya Ṛṣyamūkaṃ nāma parvata|durgam anupraviṣṭaḥ.

2.40 PAŚUMEḌHRAḤ: *(s'|ākūtam)* ⌜ajja! jo so māruī «tellokka|mallo» tti suṇīadi⌟

ŚUNAḤŚEPAḤ: atha kim.

PAŚUMEḌHRAḤ: *(sa|vicikitsam)* ⌜ajja! jaha taha vā hou, sāmī sāmī evva. taṃ pariccaïa ṇa sariso tārisassa mahā|bhāassa paḍiūla|pariggaho.⌟

the example to illustrate that when one takes delight in Pulástya's sons* it leads to no good in any case. To explain,

> He has a bull instead of a chariot, his jewelry consists of a garland of bones, he uses ashes instead of fragrant unguents and his clothes are a piece of elephant hide. Although he lives where the Lord of the Riches does,* who is his friend, this is Shiva's plight."

PASHU·MEDHRA: Hey, that old bear knows how to give advice, and he even has a sense of humor. And then what happened?

SHUNAH·SHEPA: When the monkey-king laughed at these words, saying it was the babbling of an old man, then, with Jámbavan's secret consent, Hánuman, son of the chief minister Késarin, took Prince Sugríva with him and they left for that inaccessible mountain called Rishya·muka.

PASHU·MEDHRA: *(with enthusiasm)* Sir, that son of the Wind, Hánuman, is known as the best wrestler in the three worlds. 2.40

SHUNAH·SHEPA: Indeed.

PASHU·MEDHRA: *(with hesitation)* Sir, be that as it may, a lord always remains a lord. It is not appropriate for a noble-minded person such as Hánuman to leave his master and take the side of the enemy.

ŚUNAḤŚEPAḤ: *(vihasya)* sakhe! pur" âiva kil' âyam Āñjaneyaḥ bhagavataḥ Sahasra|kiraṇād vyākaraṇam adhīyānas tad|ātmajanmano vānara|yoneḥ Sugrīvasya sāhāyakam abhiprāya|jño guru|dakṣiṇī|cakāra.

PAŚUMEḌHRAḤ: *(s'|ānandam)* ⌜huṃ. tā uiaṃ evva jaṃ guru|putto sa|bbamhacārī vā aṇuvaṭṭīaï. tado tado.⌟

2.45 ŚUNAḤŚEPAḤ: tataś ca, ahi|bhay'|ôpajāpa|jarjaraṃ suhṛd|balam ity upaśrutya, rākṣasa|rājaḥ Khara|Dūṣaṇa|Triśirobhir mah"|âmātyair adhiṣṭhitam ātma|bal'|âika|deśaṃ sindhor udīci kūle Vāli|pratigrahāya prāhiṇot.

PAŚUMEḌHRAḤ: ⌜kahaṃ a|parihīṇa|mitta|dhammo vi so rakkhaso!⌟

ŚUNAḤŚEPAḤ: sakhe, kim ucyate. Rāvaṇaḥ khalv asau.

priyā|kartuṃ kasmai
  cana nija|śiraḥ|kartana|rasa|
prahṛṣyad|romā yaḥ,
  sa param iha Laṅkā|parivṛḍhaḥ.
vilakṣa|vyāpāraṃ
  kim api dadṛśur yasya daśamaṃ
śiras, te mūrdhānaḥ
  kṣaṇa|hṛta|punar|janma|su|bhagāḥ.

PAŚUMEḌHRAḤ: *(sa|kautukam)* ⌜tado tado.⌟

2.50 ŚUNAḤŚEPAḤ: tataḥ Suketu|sutā nāga|sahasra|bala|dhāriṇī Tāḍakā nāma rākṣasī tasmād anīkād āgatya manuṣya|maṇḍala|vihāra|kautukād imām asmadīyāṃ bhūmim adhivasati.

SHUNAH·SHEPA: *(smiling)* My friend, formerly, when Hánuman learned the science of grammar from the thousand-rayed Sun, he then, knowing his master's intention, became friends with his guru's son, the monkey-born Sugríva. Thus, through this friendship, Hánuman paid off his debt to his preceptor.

PASHU·MEDHRA: *(happily)* Right. It is indeed proper for him to follow his fellow student, who is also the son of his preceptor. And then?

SHUNAH·SHEPA: Hearing that treason and treachery divides 2.45
his ally's house, the king of demons sent over a part of his own forces to the northern seashore, an army that was led by his chief ministers, Cruel, Corrupt and Three-Headed, in order to support Vali.

PASHU·MEDHRA: What a true friend he is, this demon.

SHUNAH·SHEPA: My friend, this is just natural. We talk about Rávana here.

> He was thrilled by the idea* of cutting off his own heads in order to delight someone—such is the greatest lord of Lanka. Moreover, those nine heads, which had the fortune to be able to grow out again in a second, looked at the tenth head as the idle one.

PASHU·MEDHRA: *(with interest)* And then?

SHUNAH·SHEPA: Then Sukétu's daughter, a demoness called 2.50
Tádaka, who is strong like a thousand elephants, left that army of demons because she wanted to divert herself among humans. Now she lives in our territory.

PAŚUMEḌHRAḤ: ⌜«ṇāa|sahāsa|balā itthi tti» a|suṇia|puvvaṃ eaṃ! tado tado.⌟

ŚUNAḤŚEPAḤ: tataś ca, śrautasya vidheḥ pratyūham asyāḥ śaṅkamānaḥ kula|patir imau Rāma|Lakṣmaṇāv ānītavān.

PAŚUMEḌHRAḤ: ⌜jāṇe Rāma|bhaddo tti rakkhasāṇaṃ uvariaṃ avaïṇṇo khu eso.⌟

ŚUNAḤŚEPAḤ: sakhe! evam ev' âitat. «Rāma|bhadra» iti ko 'pi catur|akṣaro rākṣasa|śikṣā|siddha|mantraḥ. viśeṣeṇa punar idānīṃ Kauśikena bhagavatā brahma|jyotiṣas tādṛśaṃ vivartaṃ divy'|âstra|mantra|pārāyaṇam āścaryam adhyāpitaḥ.

2.55 PAŚUMEḌHRAḤ: ⌜maṇṇe manta|maīhiṃ attha|devaāhiṃ samaṃ bal'|âïbalāo sattīo vi Rāme saṃkamissanti tti.⌟

ŚUNAḤŚEPAḤ: atha kim. tad api saṃvṛttam eva.

PAŚUMEḌHRAḤ: ⌜ajja! ṇaṃ bhaṇāmi: jaï ṇiā jevva sattīo, ṇiā jevva attha|vijjāo, tā kiṃ ti attaṇo viggh'|ôvasame Rāhavassa gāraaṃ appei tatta|bhavaṃ Kosio?⌟ *(vihasya)* ⌜aha vā pāhuṇia|hattheṇa sappa|māraṇaṃ kkhu edaṃ?⌟

ŚUNAḤŚEPAḤ: sakhe, an|abhijño 'si. svayaṃ prayogād ante|vāsibhiḥ prayogo mahimānam ācāryāṇām upacinoti. paśya,

PASHU·MEDHRA: I have never heard of a woman who is as strong as a thousand elephants! And then?

SHUNAH·SHEPA: Then our master, fearing that she could obstruct his Vedic sacrifice, brought Rama and Lákshmana here.

PASHU·MEDHRA: I understand that a certain Rama has come over here to control the demons.

SHUNAH·SHEPA: Yes, my friend. The name of Rama is a magical formula of four letters, to be recited as protection against demons. Especially because now the venerable Vishva·mitra has taught him all the celestial mantric weapons, which are the wonderful transformations of brahmanic power.

PASHU·MEDHRA: I assume that, together with the divine 2.55
mantric weapons, the power and superpower *mantras* will also be transmitted to him.

SHUNAH·SHEPA: Of course, they have already been taught to him.

PASHU·MEDHRA: Sir, I would then say that if it is about the venerable Vishva·mitra's own *mantras* and his own divine weapons, why does he want to make Rama famous for conquering the impeding demons? *(smiling)* Or is it the well-known case of letting your guest kill the serpent in your house?

SHUNAH·SHEPA: My friend, you do not understand this. If one's students excel, it increases the teacher's fame more than if he himself excels. Look,

sthāneṣu śiṣya|nivahair viniyujyamānā
vidyā gurum hi guṇavat|taram ātanoti.
ādāya śuktiṣu balāhaka|viprakīrṇai
ratn'|ākaro bhavati vāribhir ambu|rāśiḥ.

2.60 PAŚUMEḌHRAḤ: ⌜ajja! sohaṇaṃ mantesi. aṇṇaṃ kiṃ vi pucchidu|kāmo mhi.⌟

ŚUNAḤŚEPAḤ: tat kim?

PAŚUMEḌHRAḤ: ⌜savvahā ṇiūḍhaṃ vi vāṇarāṇaṃ cha|gguṇṇaṃ ayyeṇa kahaṃ paḍivaṇṇaṃ?⌟

ŚUNAḤŚEPAḤ: sakhe, sarvam etad Ayodhyā|yātrāyāṃ samādhi|mayena cakṣuṣā sākṣāt|kṛta|tri|bhuvana|vṛttāntasya tāta|Viśvāmitrasya mukhād aśrauṣam. *(sarvato 'valokya)* aho prābhātikī tri|bhuvana|lakṣmīḥ! tathā hi,

pratyagra|jvalitaiḥ pataṅga|maṇibhir
nīrājitā bhānavaḥ
sāvitrāḥ kuruvinda|kandala|rucaḥ
prācīm alaṃ|kurvate.
prauḍha|dhvānta|karālitasya vapuṣaś
chāyā|chalena kṣaṇād
a|prakṣālita|nirmalaṃ jagad, aho,
nirmokam unmuñcati.

2.65 api ca,

pītvā bhṛśaṃ kamala|kuḍmala|śukti|koṣā
doṣātanīṃ timira|vṛṣṭim atha sphuṭantaḥ.
niryan|madhuvrata|kadamba|miṣād vamanti
bibhranti kāraṇa|guṇān iva mauktikāni.

> If a teacher appoints his students to an appropriate task, it is his qualities that their knowledge will prove. It is because the sea makes the water that fills the clouds go through the mother-of-pearl that it is called the "source of gems."

PASHU·MEDHRA: You speak eloquently, sir. I should also like to know something else. 2.60

SHUNAH·SHEPA: What is it?

PASHU·MEDHRA: How have you learned about these stratagems* of the monkeys, if they have kept them so secret?

SHUNAH·SHEPA: My friend, I have heard about all this while traveling to Ayódhya, from the mouth of the venerable Vishva·mitra, for he can see everything that happens in the three worlds through his yogic eye. *(looking in every direction)* Look how the world is wonderful at dawn:

> The sunbeams illuminated by the freshly inflamed sun-stones look like ruby-sprouts that adorn the eastern direction. The world, whose body was terrifying with its thick darkness, leaves its slough of shadows in a second, and—look!—it becomes spotless without any washing.

Moreover, 2.65

> The lotus buds have quickly drunk the outpouring darkness of the night—like oyster shells would drink water—but they are fully open now. They release the departing swarm of bees, just as oysters would produce pearls of the same color as that of the water.*

api ca,

vikasita|saṃkucita|punar|
 vikasvareṣv ambujeṣu dur|lakṣyāḥ;
kalikāḥ kathayati nūtana|
 vikāsinīr madhulihām arghaḥ.

(ūrdhvam avalokya, ādityaṃ ca nirvarṇya)

2.70 kaṭubhir api kaṭhora|cakravāk'|ôt-
 kara|viraha|jvara|śānti|śīta|vīryaiḥ
timira|hatam ayaṃ mahobhir añjañ
 jayati jagan|nayan'|âugham Uṣṇa|bhānuḥ.

tad anujānīhi māṃ samid|āharaṇāya.

PAŚUMEḌHRAḤ: ⌜ahaṃ vi khattia|kumārāṇaṃ daṃsaṇe ukkhaṃṭhio mhi. tā kahehi, tā kahiṃ pekkhāmi?⌟

ŚUNAḤŚEPAḤ: *(vihasya)* nanv etāv eva yajña|vāṭam uttareṇa vihāra|bhūmiṣu krīḍataḥ. tad upetya niḥ|śaṅkam avalokaya.

iti niṣkrāntau.

2.75 *iti miśra/viṣkambhakaḥ*

Furthermore,

> The new buds are difficult to distinguish among the lotuses that already opened, closed and are about to open up again. It is only the adoration of the bees that betrays which are the freshly opening buds.

(looking up, gazing at the sun)

> May he be victorious, whose rays—pungent as 2.70
> they may be—are able to appease and cool down the sharp and burning pain of the shelduck when they are separated from each other, he who takes away the blindness of the world's eyes by anointing them with its splendor: the sun.

So let me go and fetch some wood.

PASHU·MEDHRA: And I am very curious to see these two princes. Tell me, where could I find them?

SHUNAH·SHEPA: *(smiling)* They are now playing on the pasture, north of the sacrificial grounds. You can go and see them there without problem.

Both exit.

End of the Sanskrit-Prakrit prelude. 2.75

ACT II
CHILDHOOD EXPLOITS

tataḥ praviśato RĀMA|LAKṢMAṆAU.

RĀMAḤ: vicitram idam āyatanaṃ siddh'|āśrama|padaṃ nāma bhagavato Gādhi|nandanasya!

tat|tādṛk|tṛṇa|pūlak'|ôpanayana|
kleśāc cira|dveṣibhir
medhyā vatsatarī vihasya baṭubhiḥ
s'|ôlluṇṭham ālabhyate.
apy eṣa pratanū|bhavaty atithibhiḥ
s'|ôcchvāsa|nāsā|puṭair
āpīto madhu|parka|pāka|surabhiḥ
prāg|vaṃśa|janm'|ânilaḥ.

LAKṢMAṆAḤ: ārya! atr' âiva kila,

2.80 devaḥ kaustubha|kiñjalka|nīl'|ôtpalam asau Hariḥ
svayaṃ kim api tat tepe tapaḥ kapaṭa|Vāmanaḥ.

ittham etan mahā|tīrtham adhyāsīnā dvi|jātayaḥ
a|kuto|bhaya|saṃcārāḥ ṣaṭ|karmāṇi prayuñjate.

(anyato dṛṣṭvā.) ārya,

paśy' âite paśu|bandha|vedi|valayair
audumbarī|danturair
nitya|vyañjita|gṛhya|tantra|vidhayo
ramyā gṛha|sth'|āśramāḥ.
yatr' âmī gṛha|medhinaḥ pracalita|
svā|rājya|siṃh'|āsanā
vaitāneṣu kṛpīṭa|yoniṣu puro-
ḍāśaṃ vaṣaṭ|kurvate.

Then RAMA *and* LÁKSHMANA *enter.*

RAMA: Look, how wonderful this place is, the sacred hermitage of the venerable Vishva·mitra.

> The disciples became the enemies of the sacrificial calf long ago, for they had to take pains to gather those thick bunches of grass to feed it—now they are killing it, smiling ironically. Meanwhile, the guests inhale with widened nostrils the steam coming from the sacrificial hall, a steam that smells sweet with the welcome offerings prepared to receive them—they seem to be slowly drinking it up.

LÁKSHMANA: My brother, and here,

> God Vishnu, who is like a blue lotus (his Káustubha gem being its blossom), himself practiced hard asceticism to become the trickster dwarf.* 2.80
>
> Thus, brahmins live and work in this highly sacred place without fear, performing their six pious acts.*

(looking elsewhere) My brother,

> Look, here are some *udúmbara* wood sticks on the round altars of the animal sacrifice, making them uneven. All of this shows that in this wonderful hermitage of householders the domestic sacrificial duties are regularly observed.* Here these householders make the throne of the heavenly kingdom shake* by their constant offering of rice in the sacrificial fires.

RĀMAḤ: *(sa|harṣa|smitam)* vatsa! ehi, ito 'pi tāvat kṛt'|ârtha-yāvaś cakṣuṣī. prasanna|pāvano 'yam ṛṣīṇāṃ samavāyaḥ. idam amīṣām,

2.85 pūrayitv" êva sarv'|âṅgam atiriktāḥ śirā|tatīḥ
jaṭā|rūpeṇa bibhrāṇaiḥ śirobhir gahanaṃ sadaḥ.

kiṃ ca,

tapaḥ|kṛśatarair aṅgaiḥ sraṣṭum ākāritair iva,
sāyaṃ prātar amī puṇyam agni|hotram upāsate.

iti parikrāmataḥ

LAKṢMAṆAḤ: *(sa|hāsam.)* ārya, ramaṇīyam ito vartate:

2.90 bāleya|taṇḍula|vilopa|kadarthitābhir
etābhir agni|śaraṇeṣu sa|dharmiṇībhiḥ
uttrāsa|hetum api daṇḍam udasyamānam
āghrātum icchati mṛge, munayo hasanti.

RĀMAḤ: *(parikrāman sa|kautuk'|ânurāgam.)* vatsa! ito 'pi tāvat.

ārdra|prasūtir iyam aṅgaṇa|yajña|vedi|
nediṣṭham eva hariṇī tṛṇute tṛṇaṃ ca
vatsīya|tāpasa|kumāra|kar'|ôpanīta|

RAMA: *(smiling with delight)* My friend, and here we can make our eyes fully contented. The sight of this group of sages is soothing and purifying.

> Here is their assembly: an impenetrable forest of matted locks of hair carried on their heads, locks that appear as if they were a mass of veins coming out of their bodies, after going through all their limbs. 2.85

Furthermore,

> Their limbs are very much emaciated by the practice of asceticism, as if they were the lines of a sketch. They perform their holy fire rituals every morning and evening.

They both walk around the stage.

LÁKSHMANA: *(smiling)* My brother, look, there is something delightful here.

> Annoyed by the disappearance of the sacrificial rice grains, the wives of these sages took up some sticks in the sacrificial halls to chase away the deer, which then started sniffing at the sticks although they were meant to frighten them—all this to the great delight of the sages themselves. 2.90

RAMA: *(walking around the stage, with curiosity and affection)* My little brother, come over here.

> This doe near the sacrificial altar in the courtyard has just borne her fawn and is now grazing there, while looking at her fawn, who is happy to be fed

nīvāra|nirvṛtam apatyam avekṣate ca.

itaś ca,

viṣvak tapo|dhana|kumāra|samarpyamāṇa|
śyāmāka|taṇḍula|bhṛtāṃ ca pipīlikānām
śreṇībhir āśrama|pathāḥ prathamāna|citra|
pattr'|āvalī|valayino mudam udvahanti.

2.95 LAKṢMAṆAḤ: aho, paśūnām api prasava|vātsalyam! aho, śiśūnām api sat|karma|tāc|chīlyam!

RĀMAḤ: *(anyato 'valokya)*

muni|viniyoga|vilūna|pra-
rūḍha|mṛdu|śādvalāni barhīṃṣi,
go|karṇa|tarṇako 'yaṃ
tarṇoty upakaṇṭha|kaccheṣu.

iti parikrāmataḥ

LAKṢMAṆAḤ: *(anyato 'valokya)* ārya,

2.100 iyam ebhir ālavālaiḥ
pade pade granthilāsu kulyāsu
tīvra|rayā jala|veṇī
pravahati viśramya viśramya.

RĀMAḤ: vatsa, sādhu dṛṣṭam.

ālavāla|valayeṣu bhū|ruhāṃ
māṃsala|stimitam antar'|ântarā
keralī|cikura|bhaṅgi|bhaṅguraṃ
sāraṇīṣu punar ambu dṛśyate.

with rice grains from the hands of the affectionate sons of the ascetics.

And here,

As the ants collect the millet and rice grains scattered by the young sons of the ascetics in all directions, they form rows, which make the paths of the hermitage delightful: they adorn the ground with circles that look like long and variagated lines of musk drawing.*

LÁKSHMANA: You see how much animals love their offspring 2.95
and how even young children are aware of what a good act is.

RAMA: *(looking elsewhere)*

The *kusha* grass that had been cut on the sages' orders has regrown and become tender and green—this fawn is grazing it on the riverbank nearby.

They both walk around the stage.

LÁKSHMANA: *(looking elsewhere)* My brother,

This quick stream of water, flowing in the winding 2.100
channels of trenches around the trees here and there, runs down, stopping for a while every now and then.

RAMA: My little brother, you have observed this very well.

The water remains abundant and steady flowing in the trenches dug around the trees, but in the channels it becomes unevenly winding again, like the curly hair of Keralan women.

tad ehi! bhagavatīṃ kauśikīm ālokayantau muhūrtam ātmānam punīvahe. *(parikramy' âvalokya ca.)* kva cit sāṃkrāmiko 'pi viśeṣo naisargikam atiśete. tathā hi,

jaḍa|svaccha|svādu|
prakṛtir upahūt'|êndriya|gaṇo
guṇo yady apy āsām
ayam ayuta|siddho vijayate,
tath" âpy utkarṣāya
sphurati saritām āśrama|sadām
idānīṃ vānīra|
druma|kusuma|janmā parimalaḥ.

2.105 LAKṢMAṆAḤ: ārya, purastād anu|Kauśikī|tīram avalokaya!

tair medhā|janana|vrata|praṇayibhir
vyūhair baṭūnām iyaṃ
siktā nitya|vasanta|vibhramavatī
ramyā palāś'|āvalī.
etasyāṃ hariṇ'|âri|pāṇi|ja|sṛṇi|
śreṇi|śriyaḥ korakā
gopāyanti tapo|vanaṃ vana|kari|
krīḍā|kar'|ākarṣaṇāt.

NEPATHYE: Rāma|bhadra, kiyac ciram avalokanena kṛt'|ârthī|kriyante tapo|vana|bhūmayaḥ. saṃprati hi—

So come, let us purify ourselves by seeing the holy river of Káushiki.* *(after walking around the stage, looking)* Sometimes acquired qualities may override natural ones:

> Rivers are always cool, pure and sweet by nature, and they also attract the senses—this is their inseparable and inherent nature. However, what makes the rivers of the hermitage superior is that now they possess the fragrance of the flowers blossoming on the reeds that grow on their banks.

LÁKSHMANA: My brother, look, near the bank of the river Káushiki in front of us, 2.105

> In order to fulfill their vow of producing mental and physical strength, the brahmin boys have watered this row of charming *kínshuka* trees, which are always delightful, as if they enjoyed a never-ending spring season. Their buds, which are beautiful, like the row of the hook-like claws of a lion, protect, as it were, the hermitage from the wild elephants, who would otherwise playfully pull everything out with their trunks.

BEHIND THE SCENES: Dear Rama, if you look at the hermitage for a while, it will have attained everything it could desire. For now,

pariṇamayati jyotir|vṛttyā
yajūṃṣi rucāṃ patiḥ
kim api śaminaḥ Sāvitr'|ākhyam
rahasyam upāsate.
gurur ayam anuṣṭhāsyan mādhyan|
dinīṃ savana|kriyām
iha makha|vidhau nedīyāṃsaṃ
bhavantam apekṣate.

RĀMAḤ: *(a|śrutim abhinīya s'|ânurāgam)*

2.110 vārāṃs trīn abhiṣuṇvate, vidadhate
vanyaiḥ śarīra|sthitīr,
aiṇeyyāṃ tvaci saṃviśanti, vasate
c' âpi tvacaṃ tāravīm,
tat paśyanti ca dhāma n' âbhipatato
yat cārmaṇe cakṣuṣī;
dhanyānāṃ virajas|tamā bhagavatī
cary" êyam āhlādate.

NEPATHYE *punas tad eva paṭhyate—«pariṇamayat' ity» ādi.*

RĀMAḤ: *(śrutvā sa|saṃbhramam ūrdhvam avalokya)* katham, gagana|madhyam adhyārūḍho bhagavān Nidāgha|dīdhitiḥ! tad ehi. yajña|vāṭam adhiṣṭhāya bhagavataḥ krameṇa kṛt'|āhnikasya Kauśikasya pratyanantarī|bhavāvaḥ.

iti parikrāmataḥ

LAKṢMAṆAḤ: *(sarvato dṛṣṭvā)* ārya, paśya,

2.115 uddāma|Dyumaṇi|dyuti|vyatikara|
prakrīḍad|ark'|ôpala|
jvālā|jāla|jaṭāla|jāṅgala|taṭī|
niṣ|kūja|koyaṣṭayaḥ

The sun makes the sacrificial formulas efficient with its light, while the ascetics recite the powerful Sávitri *mantra*. Our master is here, just about to perform the midday libation, and would like you to be near now, in the sacrificial rite.

RAMA: *(miming that he has not heard it, then affectionately)*

These sages take a ritual bath three times a day, they maintain their bodies with fruits and roots found in the forest, they sit on black antelope skin and wear garments made of bark, they see the power that worldly eyes cannot behold; thus this pure,* holy observance of the blessed ascetics makes us rejoice.* 2.110

The same verse, "The sun makes the sacrificial formulas...," is recited BEHIND THE SCENES, *as before.*

RAMA: *(hears it and looks above in confusion)* The sun has already reached the top of the sky! Come, the venerable Vishva·mitra has already performed his daily ritual duties in order at the sacrificial area, so let us approach him.

They both walk around the stage.

LÁKSHMANA: *(looking everywhere)* My brother, look,

The lapwings no longer sing on the arid land, which blazes everywhere with flaming sun-stones playing with the powerful sunlight that falls on them. Bathing in the heat of the earth,* the sun-beams are cruelly blinding our eyes; there is not a 2.115

bhaum'|ôṣma|plavamāna|sūra|kiraṇa|
krūra|prakāśā dṛśor
āyuṣ|karma samāpayanti, dhig, amūr
madhy'|âhna|śūnyā diśaḥ.

antikatamā c' êyaṃ yajña|vāṭa|bhūmiḥ. tad etan nyagrodha|chāyā|maṇḍalam adhyāsīnā ṛtv|ijaḥ pratyavekṣāvahe. galita|yauvane punar ahani bhagavantaṃ drakṣyāvaḥ.

RĀMAḤ: evam astu.

iti parikramya nāṭyena upaviśataḥ

LAKṢMAṆAḤ: *(pārśvato dṛṣṭvā)*

2.120 madhye|vyoma krīḍayitvā mayūkhān
bhānor bimbe lambamāne krameṇa
svairaṃ svairaṃ mūlataḥ pādapānāṃ,
paśya, chāyāḥ kaś cid ākarṣat' îva.

RĀMAḤ: *(samantād avalokya)* vatsa, madhyan|dinam atikrāntam iti, kim etad dinam apy atikrāntam eva. tathā hi,

gagana|śikhām Uday'|âdrer
adhirūḍhāḥ kaṣṭam arka|ratha|harayaḥ
Asta|mahīdharam adhunā jhaṭ-
iti sukhen' âvarohanti.

LAKṢMAṆAḤ: ārya, nūnam adya parāpatiṣyanti rakṣāṃsi. yad ayam adhvara|vedikā|saṃnidhānaṃ Śunaḥśepa|mukhād bhagavān upādhyāyaḥ praśāsti.

RĀMAḤ: *(sa|roṣ'|âhaṃkāram)* vatsa, yady evaṃ syāt,

living being anywhere around under the midday sun—what a terrible time of the day.

The sacrificial area is very close now. Let us sit in the shade of the fig tree and watch the officiating priests. Then, later in the day, we shall see the venerable Vishva·mitra, too.

RAMA: Let us do so.

They both walk around the stage and mime sitting down.

LÁKSHMANA: *(looking toward one side of the stage)*

Look, while the sun-disk is gradually going down making its rays play in the air, it looks as if somebody was gently pulling the shades of trees from their roots. 2.120

RAMA: *(looking everywhere)* My brother, midday has passed and now the day itself has also ended:

The horses of the Sun's chariot, having mounted on the top of the sky from the Eastern Mountain with difficulty, have now descended to the Western Mountain easily, in a second.

LÁKSHMANA: My brother, now the demons are going to infest the grounds: that is why our venerable master has commanded you through Shunah·shepa to be near the sacrificial altar.

RAMA: *(with anger and pride)* My little brother, if it is so, then

2.125 kalp'|ânta|karkaśa|Kṛtānta|bhayaṃ|karaṃ me
niṣpraghnataḥ kratu|vighāta|kṛtām amīṣām
nīrākṣasāṃ vasumatīm api kartum adya
puṇy'|âha|maṅgalam idaṃ dhanur ādadhātu.

LAKṢMAṆAḤ: *(vihasya)* katham, rajanī|cara|vināś'|ôtkaṇṭhā|visaṃsthulam ārya|hṛdayam a|dīrgha|darśinaṃ Kauśikam api saṃbhāvayati!

a|vidyā|bīja|vidhvaṃsād ayam ārṣeṇa cakṣuṣā
kālau bhūta|bhaviṣyantau vartamānam avīviśat.

RĀMAḤ: kim ucyate. tatra|bhavān Viśvāmitraḥ,

prajñāta|Brahma|tattvo 'pi, svargīyair eṣa khelati
gṛha|stha|samay'|ācāra|prakrāntaiḥ sapta|tantubhiḥ.

2.130 api ca,

ārdrī|kṛto vinaya|namra|mah"|Êndra|mauli|
mandāra|dāma|makaranda|rasair iv' âyam
prakrānta|kuṇḍalita|nūtana|bhūta|sargas
traiśaṅkavaṃ caritam adbhutam ātatāna.

I am going to kill those impeders of sacrifices with this bow of mine, which is as frightening as the terrible God of Death at the end of the world. Before it makes the whole world free of demons, may it ritually declare this day to be a most auspicious one.* 2.125

LÁKSHMANA: *(smiling)* You see, your heart is agitated, for it longs to exterminate the demons—indeed, it regards even Vishva·mitra as shortsighted!

Destroying the cause of ignorance, Vishva·mitra made the past and the future fuse into the present with his yogic eye.

RAMA: Yes, indeed, the venerable Vishva·mitra is as you describe him.

Although he knows the true nature of *Brahman*, he amuses himself with sacrifices undertaken according to the rules laid down for householders, in order to obtain heaven.*

Moreover, 2.130

It is as if he had been bathed in the sap coming from the flower garland* of Indra's headdress when the god bowed down politely in front of him. Vishva·mitra had made and then withdrawn a new creation of the world, and filled the life of King Tri·shanku with miracles.*

LAKṢMAṆAḤ: *(puro 'valokya sa|harṣam)*

svābhir adhvara|caryābhiḥ śrautam arthaṃ kṛt'|ârthayan,
aye, kula|patiḥ so 'yam ita ev' âbhivartate.

tataḥ praviśati dīkṣita|veṣo VIŚVĀMITRAḤ.

2.135 RĀMAḤ: *(nirvarṇya sa|bahu|mānam)* vatsa Lakṣmaṇa, paśya,

karmaṇaḥ śrūyamāṇasya vyañjanair adhik'|ôjjvalām
tapas|tejo|mayīṃ lakṣmīm adya puṣṇāti no guruḥ.

VIŚVĀMITRAḤ: *(parikrāman sa|harṣam)* hanta, kṛta|kṛtya|prāyam ātmānaṃ paśyāmaḥ. yataḥ,

nirvṛtto bahu tāvad adhvara|bhujām
ātarpaṇo 'yaṃ vidhir,
dāyādena samaṃ Suketu|duhitā
c' âdy' âiva ghāniṣyate.
pāṇau|kṛtya punar Vṛṣadhvaja|dhanur|
dhvaṃs'|âika|śulkāṃ vadhūm,
Aikṣvāke sura|kārya|dikṣu calati
svāsthyaṃ vidhātāsmahe.

RĀMA|LAKṢMAṆĀV *utthāya upasarpataḥ*

2.140 VIŚVĀMITRAḤ: (RĀMAM *aticiraṃ nirvarṇya sa|sneha|kautukam)*

eṣa vaihārikaṃ veṣam ādadhāno dhanur|dharaḥ
tattvam āntaram asmākam amṛtair iva limpati.

UBHAU: *(upasṛtya)* Rāma|Lakṣmaṇau Dāśarathī abhivādayete.

LÁKSHMANA: *(looking ahead, with delight)*

Here is the one who fulfills his Vedic duties with
his sacrifices—our master is coming this way now.

VISHVA·MITRA *enters, dressed as a Vedic initiate.*

RAMA: *(seeing him, with respect)* My little brother Lákshmana, look, 2.135

With the signs indicating that he is performing a Vedic ritual, our preceptor now further increases his radiance of ascetic power.

VISHVA·MITRA: *(walks around the stage, with delight)* O, I cannot ask for more, for

This rite to propitiate the sacrifice-consuming gods has almost ended, and the demoness Tádaka, Sukétu's daughter, together with her son, shall be slain today. Then Rama will marry the girl whose hand he will gain by breaking Shiva's bow, and when he has left for the South to do what the gods want him to, then I shall be fully satisfied.

RAMA *and* LÁKSHMANA *stand up and approach him.*

VISHVA·MITRA: *(looking at* RAMA *for a while, then with affection and curiosity)* 2.140

In clothes meant for playing but with the bow in his hand, he fills my heart with ambrosia.

BOTH OF THEM: *(approaching him)* Rama and Lákshmana, Dasha·ratha's sons, salute you.

VIŚVĀMITRAḤ: *(āliṅgya)* vatsau, kim anyad āśāsmahe?

> yuvābhyām abhinirvṛtta|yoga|kṣemasya Vajriṇaḥ
> aiśvarya|prakriyā|mātra|kṛt'|ârthāḥ santu hetayaḥ.

2.145 *ubhau tūṣṇīm adho|mukhau staḥ.*

VIŚVĀMITRAḤ: *(vihasya)* vatsau, samantād upaśīlito 'yaṃ saṃniveśaḥ. kac cid asmadīyās tapo|vana|vihāra|bhūmayo ramayanti vām, upasnehayati vā gārhasthyam ṛṣīṇām?

UBHAU: *(sapraśrayam)* bhagavan,

> ramyam etad, a|ramyaṃ vā, kaḥ paricchettum arhati?
> kiṃ tu dvay'|âtigaṃ cittam adya nau paśyator abhūt.

iti yath"|ôcitam upaviśataḥ

2.150 VIŚVĀMITRAḤ: *(s'|ākūta|smitam.)* vatsau,

> iha vaneṣu sa kaitava|Vāmano
> munir atapta tapāṃsi purātanaḥ.
> tam iva vām avalokya tapasvino
> nayanam adya cirād udamīmilan.

ubhau muhūrtam unmanī|bhavataḥ.

VIŚVĀMITRAḤ: *(sva|gatam)* aye, kim apy utsāha|vardhanāya prāg|bhavīyam antaḥ|karaṇam anusmāritam anayoḥ. tad etāvad ev' âstu. anyataḥ kṣipāmi. *(pratyag avalokya prakāśam)* katham, Udaya|giri|kāśmīra|kuṅkuma|kedārasya

VISHVA·MITRA: *(embracing them)* My sons, how could I bless you,

> You have ensured well-being for Indra, who brandishes the thunderbolt.* Now may his weapons be satisfied simply to show his sovereignty.

Both remain silent and look down. 2.145

VISHVA·MITRA: *(smiling)* My sons, you have seen every corner of this place. I hope the grounds of our hermitage are to your delight and that the households of the sages are pleasing.

BOTH: *(politely)* Master,

> Who would be entitled to say if this hermitage is delightful or not? However, we can confirm that today, by seeing it, our minds have become purified.

They take a seat, as appropriate.

VISHVA·MITRA: *(smiling, with emotion)* My dear sons, 2.150

> It was in this hermitage that a sage of old, Vishnu, practiced asceticism to become the trickster dwarf.* Seeing you two as if seeing him, the ascetics today were really able to use their eyes after a long time.

Both are excited for a moment.

VISHVA·MITRA: *(aside)* Well, to boost their courage, I have made their minds remember their acts in a previous life. This much of it should be enough, now I shall draw their attention to something else. *(looking to the west,*

prabhāta|saṃdhyā|latāyāḥ prathama|stabako Gabhasti|mālī hast"|ânuhastikayā kutūhalinībhir dig|aṅganābhir vāruṇīṃ diśaṃ yāvad upanītaḥ.

ayam api khara|yoṣit|karṇa|kāṣāyam īṣad|
visṛmara|timir'|ōrṇā|jarjar'|ôpāntam arciḥ;
mada|kala|kalaviṅkī|kāku|nāndī|karebhyaḥ
kṣitiruha|śikharebhyo bhānumān uccinoti.

2.155 api ca,

mantra|saṃskāra|saṃpannās tanvad audanvatīr apaḥ
etat trayī|mayaṃ jyotir Ādity'|ākhyaṃ nimajjati.

RĀMAḤ: *(sarvato nirūpya)* vatsa, Lakṣmaṇa,

tāpanair eva tejobhiḥ pluṣṭa|nirvāṇa|mecakāḥ
diśo jātāḥ, pratīcī tu samudācarati kramāt.

kiṃ ca,

2.160 kāṃ cid bibhrati bhūtim āśrama|bhuvo
vaitāna|vaiśvānara|
jvāl"|ôpaplavamāna|dhūma|valabhī|
vibhrānta|dig|bhittayaḥ.

saying aloud) When the dawn appears on the Eastern Mountain like a creeper in a field of Kashmiri saffron, the matchless bunch of flowers it produces is the sun, which the directions—desirous women as they are—hand from one to another until it reaches the West. Look, it has already reached there!

> The light of the sun is split up by the darkness that slowly crawls in—it looks like the red ears of a she-ass with dark wool-like threads at the edges. The treetops echo the high-pitched melodious song of the excited hen sparrows, which sounds like the benedictory verse of a play, while the sun is withdrawing its light from there.

Moreover, 2.155

> To make the water of the ocean purified by mantras, this light, which contains the three Vedas and is called the sun, is sinking into it.

RAMA: *(looking everywhere)* My little brother Lákshmana,

> After being scorched by the heat of the sun, the directions became extinguished and black—except for the West, which is now about to follow their example in due course.

Furthermore,

> This hermitage is so majestic—its roof, which is no longer distinguishable from its surrounding walls, is formed by the expanding smoke coming from the flames of sacrificial fires. And we can hear the brahmin boys manifesting their rivalry pleasantly 2.160

śrūyante baṭavas tṛtīya|savana|
svādhyāya|dīrghān api
spardhā|bandha|mano|haraṃ prati muhuḥ
svān drāghayantaḥ svarān.

VIŚVĀMITRAḤ: vatsa, Rāghava,

unmuktābhir divasam adhunā
sarvatas tābhir eva
sva|chāyābhir niculitam iva
prekṣyate viśvam etat.
paryanteṣu jvalati jala|dhau
Ratna|sānau ca madhye
citr'|âṅg" îyaṃ ramayati tamaḥ|
stoma|līlā dharitrī.

LAKṢMAṆAḤ: *(sa|nirvedam)*

tejo|mayaṃ tamo|mayam
anyatarasyāṃ tad eva dik|cakram;
kim api vicitrā Dhātuḥ
sṛṣṭir iyam bhuvana|koṣasya.

2.165 *(sarvato 'valokya)*

cūḍā|ratnaiḥ sphuradbhir viṣa|dhara|vivarāṇy
ujjvalāny ujjvalāni
prekṣyante; cakravākī|manasi niviśate
sūrya|kāntāt kṛśānuḥ;
kiṃ c' âmī śalyayantas timiram ubhayato
nirbhar'|âhas|tamisrā|
saṃghaṭṭ'|ôdbhūta|sandhy"|ânala|kiraṇa|kaṇa|
spardhino bhānti dīpāḥ.

RĀMAḤ: *(vilokya)*

viśvaṃ cākṣuṣam astam asti hi, tamaḥ|

by making the high-pitched syllables even more high-pitched again and again during the Vedic recitation at the third Soma-pressing.

VISHVA·MITRA: My dear Rama,

The shadows of the universe, which were scattered during the day, seem to be fully covering the world now.* While the ocean is in flames at the horizon and Mount Meru shines bright in the center with its jeweled peak, the all-supporting earth delights us with the colors of her body as she is playing with the thick darkness.

LÁKSHMANA: *(humbly)*

Whether it is in flames or covered with darkness, it is the same wide world—it is Brahma who produced this multicolored variety when he created this sphere.

(looking everywhere) 2.165

The holes of poisonous snakes are blazing with their bright head-jewels here and there; from the sun-stones, the fire enters the hearts of the shelduck;* and the stars that pierce the darkness look like tiny sparkles of the radiant sunset, whose fire was produced by the violent friction of the day and the night on both sides.*

RAMA: *(watching)*

The visible world has disappeared, only darkness

kaivalyam aupādhika|
prācy|ādi|vyavahāra|bīja|virahād
diṅ|mātram eva sthitam.
gṛhyante bhaya|hetavaḥ paṭubhir apy
akṣ'|ântarair, bhāti ca
dhvānte n' âpaghanena vastu, vacasā,
jñāta|svareṇ' âmukaḥ.

kiṃ ca,

2.170 āḥ, sarvataḥ sphuratu kairavam; āḥ, pibantu
jyotsnāṃ kaṣāya|madhurām adhunā cakorāḥ;
yāto yad eṣa caram'|âcala|cūḍā|cumbī
paṅke|ruha|prakara|jāgaraṇa|pradīpaḥ.

ghanatara|timira|ghuṇ"|ôtkara|
jagdhānām iva patanti kāṣṭhānām
chidrair amībhir uḍubhiḥ
kiraṇa|vyājena cūrṇāni.

NEPATHYE *kalakalaḥ. sarve sa|saṃbhramam ākarṇayanti. punas tatr' âiva:*

nirmajjac|cakṣur|antar|bhramad|atikapila|
krūra|tārā, nar'|âsthi|
granthiṃ dant'|ântarāla|grathitam a|viratam
jihvayā ghaṭṭayantī,
dhvānte 'pi vyātta|vaktra|jvalad|anala|śikhā|
jarjare vyakta|karmā
nirmāntī, gṛdhra|raudrīṃ divam upari pari-
krīḍate Tāḍak" êyam.

reigns, and because the source that helps us to orient ourselves* has gone, the directions are left undetermined. Our non-visual perception becomes oversensitive, seeing sources of fear in every corner. In the darkness, objects are not recognized by their form but through their sound, and people are identified by their familiar voices.

Moreover,

The white night-lotuses shall open up everywhere 2.170
and the *chakóra*s shall now drink the sweet and fragrant moonlight, for the luminary that wakes up the day-lotuses has gone to kiss the head of the Western Mountain.*

The carpentry of the sky is devoured by the woodworms of the thick darkness; and from the wormholes—the stars—falls sawdust in the guise of starlight.*

Noise of confusion from behind the scenes. All of them listen with concern. Then, from BEHIND THE SCENES *again.*

She is hollow-eyed and her deep-red and frightening eyeballs are rolling inside; she is constantly licking human sinews stuck between her teeth; one can see what she is doing even in the dark, which she splits up with the flames blazing in her open mouth; she is now making the sky terrifying like a vulture, she is playing right above us—here is Tádaka.

tret"|âgni|kuṇḍa|pūraṃ ca varṣanto rudhira|chaṭāḥ
himsrāḥ Subāhu|Mārīca|miśrā naḥ parivṛṇvate.

2.175 VIŚVĀMITRAḤ: *(s'|ākūtam)* kathaṃ, Tāḍakā?! vatsa Rāma| bhadra,

vidhānam ānuśravikaṃ gṛheṣu naḥ
pratiṣkirantī kim iyaṃ pratīkṣyate?
Subāhu|mukhyaiḥ samam ātatāyibhir
gṛhāṇa cāpaṃ, nigṛhāṇa Tāḍakām!

RĀMAḤ: *(sa|ghṛṇ'|âtirekam)* bhagavan, striyam imām...

NEPATHYE: a|brahmaṇyam, a|brahmaṇyam! bho, tāta Viśvāmitra, rākṣasaiḥ kiyac ciraṃ paribhūyāmahe! prahīyatām adhijya|dhanvā Dāśarathiḥ!

RĀMAḤ: *(vihasya nepathy'|âbhimukham avalokya)* bāla'|rṣe, Śunaḥśepa! muhūrtaṃ dhīro bhava!

2.180 alaṃ kliśitvā gurum; alpako 'yaṃ
vidhis, tvad|ājñ" âiva garīyasī naḥ.
na Kauśikasya tvayi dharma|putre
putre Madhucchandasi vā viśeṣaḥ.

VIŚVĀMITRAḤ: *(vihasya)* vatsa, kṛtam uttar'|ôttareṇa. nanv ayaṃ nedīyān āśram'|ôpaghātaḥ.

LAKṢMAṆAḤ: *(sa|vyatham iva sva|gatam)*

mīmāṃsate kim āryo 'yaṃ Kauśike 'py anuśāsati?
vācam eṣām ṛṣīṇāṃ hi śāstram ev' ânuvartate.

> The demons headed by Subáhu and Marícha are showering streams of blood to fill up our three sacred fire pits, and now they are surrounding us.

VISHVA·MITRA: *(with surprise)* Tádaka? How come? My dear 2.175
Rama,

> Why are you waiting for her to obstruct the Vedic sacrifice in our home? Take up your bow and kill Tádaka, together with the other murderers headed by Subáhu!

RAMA: *(filled with compassion)* My master, but to kill this woman...

FROM BEHIND THE SCENES: Help! How terrible! O venerable Vishva·mitra, we are going to be defeated by the demons. Send Rama here with his well-strung bow!

RAMA: *(smiling, looking at the rear of the stage)* Young sage, Shunah·shepa! Hold on for a second,

> Our master should not suffer any longer; this is a 2.180
> small task and I respect your order. Vishva·mitra treats you, his spiritual son, like Madhu·cchandas, his real son.

VISHVA·MITRA: *(smiling)* My son, enough of this conversation, or else this hermitage will be soon destroyed.

LÁKSHMANA: *(with anxiety, aside)*

> Why is my elder brother hesitating even when Vishva·mitra commands him? For it is the words of such sages that make the law.*

RĀMAḤ: *(sva|gatam)*

2.185 gurv|ādeśād eva nirmīyamāṇo
n' â|dharmāya strī|vadho 'pi sthito 'yam.
adya sthitvā śvo gamiṣyadbhir alpair
lajj" âsmābhir mīlit'|âkṣair jit" âiva.

kiṃ tu,

dīrghaṃ prajābhir atikautukinībhir ābhir
asminn a|kīrti|paṭahe mama tāḍyamāne
jyotir|mayena vapuṣā jagad|anta|sākṣī
lajjiṣyate kula|gurur, bhagavān Vasiṣṭhaḥ.

NEPATHYE:

alam iṣṭvā makhān, mūrkhāḥ,
khaḍga|dhār" êyam asti naḥ,
a|davīyān ayam panthāḥ
svar|lokam upatiṣṭhate.

2.190 RĀMAḤ: *(śrutvā sa|roṣaṃ sa|saṃbhramam utthāya sa|vinayam añjaliṃ baddhvā)* bhagavan, jagat|traya|guro Gādhi|nandana,

Daśaratha|gṛhe saṃbhūtaṃ mām
avāpya dhanur|dharaṃ
«dinakara|kul'|āskandī ko 'yaṃ
kalaṅka|nav'|âṅkuraḥ?»
iti hi vanitām enāṃ hantuṃ
mano vicikitsate.
yad adhikaraṇaṃ dharma|stheyaṃ,
tav' âiva vacāṃsi naḥ.

RAMA: *(aside)*

It is to obey the word of my master that I should kill this woman, which thus will not be against the law. Here I am today, but, as an insignificant mortal, I will have left the world by tomorrow—by closing my eyes for this moment, I can conquer this shame.* 2.185

Yet,

People full of gossip will keep going around as drum-beating heralds to proclaim this shameful act of mine. And then he who can witness the end of the world with his radiant body, the preceptor of my dynasty, the venerable Vasíshtha, will be very much ashamed of me.

FROM BEHIND THE SCENES:

Stop offering your sacrifices, idiots. Here is the blade of a sword, which is the shortest way that leads you to heaven.

RAMA: *(hears this, gets up angrily and is confused, then politely folds his hands together)* Venerable Vishva·mitra, Lord of the Three Worlds, 2.190

There will be a new stain on the solar dynasty* because of me, born in the house of Dasha·ratha, if I take up this bow—this is why my heart hesitates to kill this woman. But your word can be the only source to determine my duty.

(iti praṇipatya) bho mā bhaiṣṭa, mā bhaiṣṭa, tapo|dhanāḥ!

rajanicara|camūr amūr apāsyann
ayam aham āgata eva, Rāmacandraḥ.
Kuśika|suta|kuś'|âgra|toya|bindor
idam anukalpam aveta kārmukaṃ me.

iti dhanur āropayan niṣkrāntaḥ.

2.195 LAKṢMAṆAḤ: *(s'|āśaṅkaṃ sva|gatam)* diṣṭyā kṣātreṇa dharmeṇa kaumāram a|śūnyam āryasya tāvad āsīt. *(nepathy'|âbhimukham avalokya, harṣaṃ nāṭayan, prakāśam)* bhagavan Kauśika! purastād ārye dhṛta|dhanuṣi

vāyavy'|âstra|vyatikara|nirā-
lambanas tāḍakeyaḥ
prāpto jīvan|maraṇam asubhir
viprayuktaḥ Subāhuḥ.
kṛtt'|ônmuktā bhuvi ca karuṇ'|āś-
carya|bībhatsa|hāsa|
trāsa|krodh'|ôttaralam ṛṣibhir
dṛśyate Tāḍak" êyam.

VIŚVĀMITRAḤ: *(vilokya)* vatsa Lakṣmaṇa! vismayena pramodena ca paravanto vayaṃ na vācām īśmahe. vaktavyaṃ vā kim asti? na khalv iyam adyatanī vaḥ pratiṣṭhā.

(falling on his knees) O ascetics, do not be afraid.

> I have come to chase away that army of night-walking demons, here I am, Rama. Think of the drop of holy water on the tip of the sacred *kusha* grass held by Vishva·mitra—such is the strength of my bow.

Stringing his bow, RAMA *exits.*

LÁKSHMANA: *(worried, aside)* Thank god he has followed the law of warriors and thus made his childhood fruitful. *(looking toward the rear of the stage, showing his joy, aloud)* Venerable Vishva·mitra, look ahead. While Lord Rama takes up his bow, 2.195

> Hit by an arrow of the Wind,* Subáhu, Tádaka's son, lost support and reached death while still moving,* being deprived of his life-force. And here she is, torn asunder and left on the ground in front of the sages, who are trembling with compassion, wonder, disgust, laughter, fear and anger while looking at her—this is Tádaka.

VISHVA·MITRA: *(looking)* My son, Lákshmana. Overwhelmed with wonder and joy, I cannot speak. And what could one say in any case? Such great acts are not new among you,

dik|kūlaṃkaṣa|kīrti|dhauta|viyato
nirvyāja|vīr'|ôddhatās
te yūyaṃ Raghavaḥ prasiddha|mahaso,
yaiḥ so 'pi dev'|âdhipaḥ
bibhrāṇair asur'|âdhirāja|vijaya|
krīḍā|nidānaṃ dhanuḥ
Paulomī|kuca|pattra|bhaṅga|racanā|
cāturyam adhyāpitaḥ.

LAKṢMAṆAḤ: bhagavan, paśya,

2.200 adya naiśā|carīṃ senām enām unmūlayad ayam,
ādhānaṃ vīra|dharmasya nirmāya tvām upasthitaḥ.

praviśya.

RĀMAḤ: *(sa|vailakṣyam)*

Pūṣā Vasiṣṭhaḥ Kuśik'|ātmajo 'yaṃ
trayas ta ete guravo Raghūṇām.
mahā|muner asya girā kṛto 'pi,
straiṇo vadho māṃ na sukhā|karoti.

(āśramam avalokya)

2.205 pratyāsanna|Tuṣāra|dīdhiti|kara|
kliśyat|tamo|vallarī|
balyābhir makha|dhūma|vallibhir amī
saṃmīlita|vyañjanāḥ
śvaḥ|saṃcīvarayiṣyamāṇa|baṭuka|
vyādhauta|śuṣyat|tvaco
nidrāṇ'|âtithayas tapodhana|gṛhāḥ
kurvanti naḥ kautukam.

The sky is whitened by your fame that spreads in all directions, you are distinguished as genuine heroes, and your power is well known, descendants of Raghu. Since you* took up the bow, with which you easily slew the demon king in power, all that was left for the king of the gods was to learn the tricks of how to make drawings on the breasts of his wife.

LÁKSHMANA: Look, my master,

Rama has annihilated this army of demons, and thus set an example of how to fulfill the duties of a warrior. Here he is now at your service. 2.200

RAMA *enters.*

RAMA: *(embarrassed)*

The Sun, Vasíshtha and Vishva·mitra—these are the three preceptors of the Raghu dynasty. Even if I killed a woman only to obey this great sage, Vishva·mitra, it does not make me happy.

(looking toward the hermitage)

The outlines of the buildings are obscured by the streaks of smoke coming from the sacrifices, streaks that strengthen the effect of the patches of darkness dispersed only by the rays of the rising moon. The bark garments that the brahmin students have washed and are to wear tomorrow are drying while the guests are sleeping there—such are the houses of the ascetics, which delight me so much. 2.205

(puro 'valokya)

sphurati purato mādyan|mādyac|
cakora|vilocana|
prakara|kiraṇa|śreṇī|datta|
sva|hasta|ghanaṃ mahaḥ;
hṛdaya, laghu mā bhūḥ, preyo|dar-
śana|pratibhūr ayaṃ
kuvalaya|dṛśām indur netre
sudhābhir anakti naḥ.

unmīlanti mṛṇāla|komala|ruco
rājīva|saṃvartikā|
saṃvarta|vrata|vṛttayaḥ katipaye
Pīyūṣa|bhānoḥ karāḥ.
apy agrair dhavalī|bhavatsu giriṣu
kṣubdho 'yam unmajjatā
viśven' êva tamo|mayo nidhir apām
ahnāya phenāyate.

(sa|nirvedam)

2.210 indur yady Uday'|âdri|mūrdhni na bhaved
ady' âpi, tan mā sma bhūn;
nāsīre 'pi tamaḥ|samuccayam amūr
unmūlayanti tviṣaḥ.
apy akṣṇor mudam udgiranti, kumudair
āmodayante diśaḥ,
saṃpraty ūrdhvam asau tu lāñchanam abhi-
vyaṅktum prakāśiṣyate.

(sa|harṣam)

kāśmīreṇa dihānam ambara|talaṃ,

(looking ahead)

The moonlight shines forth, becoming thicker with the support of the rays of light coming from the eyes of the *chakóra* birds, who get more and more intoxicated.* O hearts, do not despair, for here is the moon, which guarantees that the lotus-eyed women will see their beloved; it anoints our eyes with ambrosia.

A few rays of the moon are spreading out, as tender as lotus filaments, fulfilling their vow to close the new petals of the blue day-lotus. As the moonbeams whiten the mountain peaks, the ocean full of darkness seems to be stirred up by the appearance of the world and looks as if it suddenly started bubbling.*

(disheartened)

If the moon does not appear today on top of the Eastern Mountain, then let it not come up—even then, its rays shall destroy the thick darkness in front of it.* They gratify the eyes, they perfume the directions with lotuses; so that now, if the moon itself appears, the only thing it will be able to do is to show its sign: its spot. 2.210

(with joy)

It smears the surface of the sky with saffron, it rivals the faces of women with beautiful eyebrows and

vāma|bhruvām ānana|
dvai|rājyaṃ vidadhānam, indu|dṛṣadāṃ
bhindānam ambhaḥ|śirāḥ,
pratyudyat|Purūhūta|pattana|vadhū|
datt'|ârghya|darbh'|âṅkura|
kṣīb'|ôtsaṅga|kuraṅgam aindavam idaṃ
bimbaṃ samujjṛmbhate.

etāś ca,

Paulomī|kuca|kumbha|kuṅkuma|rajaḥ|
svājanya|janm'|ôddhatāḥ
śīt'|âṃśor dyutayaḥ Puraṃdara|purī|
sīmnām upaskurvate.
etābhir lihatībhir andha|tamasāny
udgrathnatībhir diśaḥ
kṣoṇīm āstṛṇatībhir antaratamaṃ
vyom' êdam ojāyate.

2.215 api ca,

n' âiv' âyaṃ bhagavān udañcati śaśī
gavyūti|mātrīm api
dyām ady' âpi; tamas tu kairava|kula|
śrī|cāṭu|kārāḥ karāḥ
mathnanti sthala|sīmni, śaila|gahan'|ôt-
saṅgeṣu saṃrundhate,
jīva|grāham iva kva cit kva cid api
chāyāsu gṛhṇanti ca.

(jyotsn"|âtiśayaṃ nirūpya)

kiṃ nu dhvānta|payodhir eva kataka|
kṣodair iv' êndoḥ karair
atyaccho 'yam, adhaś ca paṅka|malinaḥ

breaks up the channels in which the moonstone flows;* it has a deer* inside, which was greeted by the nymphs in Indra's heaven, and then got drunk with the guest-offering of tender *darbha* grass mixed with honey—here it is, the moon-disk rising.

And these

Rays of the cool-lighted moon are proud to be born related to the saffron powder on the round breasts of Indra's wife;* they adorn the borders of Indra's heavenly realm. They lick up the blind darkness, throw light in each direction, cover the earth, and make the intermediary space shine bright.

Moreover, 2.215

His Lordship the Moon is still not coming up to reach the sky, even though the sky is only a few miles away from him; yet his rays, which flatter the lotus-beauties, destroy some darkness in the horizon, block it in the slopes of forested mountains and imprison it here and there in the shades.*

(looking at the bright moonlight)

Is it that the moonbeams have purified this sea of darkness, leaving the shades below, just as powdered *kátaka* nuts purify water from mud?* Or is it

chāy"|âpadeśād abhūt?
kiṃ vā tat|kara|kartarībhir abhito
nistakṣaṇād ujjvalaṃ
vyom' âiv' êdam itas tataḥ ca patitāś
chāyā|chalena tvacaḥ?

parikramya pārśvato 'valokya

2.220 dala|vitati|bhṛtāṃ tale tarūṇām
iha tila|taṇḍulitaṃ Mṛg'|âṅka|rociḥ
mada|capala|cakora|cañcu|koṭī|
kavalana|tuccham iv' ântar" ântar" âbhūt.

(vibhāvya ca)

tri|bhuvana|tamo|luṇṭākīnām,
aho, mihira|tviṣām
abhividhir asau koka|śreṇī|
manaḥsv avaśiṣyate.
kṣudham api tamaḥ sākṣād antaḥ
praviśya vinighnataḥ
Śaśadhara|karān a|cchinn'|âgrāṃś
caranti cakorakāḥ.

api c' êdānīm,

tathā paurastyāyāṃ
diśi kumuda|kedāra|kalikā|
kapāṭa|ghnīm induḥ
kiraṇa|laharīm ullalayati.
samantād unmīlad|
bahala|jala|bindu|stabakino
yathā puñjāyante
pratiguḍakam eṇ'|âṅka|maṇayaḥ.

that the sky has become white because the moon has cut it with its rays everywhere, as a carpenter cuts wood with his adze, and the pieces of the sky's bark have fallen here and there in the form of patches of shade?

He walks around the stage and gazes at one side.

Here, under the large leaves of trees, the moonlight is dispersed and looks like rice grains in the midst of sesamum seeds; it seems to be pecked at here and there by the curved beaks of *chakóra*s trembling with desire. 2.220

(reflecting)

The sunbeams destroy the darkness of the three worlds, but alas, now they remain here only to pervade the hearts of the shelduck.* And the moonbeams with their pointed tips, which visibly destroy both darkness and the hunger of the *chakóra*s when they enter them, are being grazed by these birds.

And now,

In the eastern direction, the moon spreads out a flood of its rays, capable of breaking up the closed buds in the lotus fields. It plays with its beams in such a way that they gather the moonstones into round heaps everywhere, each of which becomes like many water drops clustered together.*

2.225 *parikrāmann ūrdhvam avalokya*

taruṇa|tamāla|komala|
malīmasam etad ayaṃ
kalayati candramāḥ kila
kalaṅka iti bruvate,
tad an|ṛtam eva; nirdaya|
Vidhuṃtuda|danta|pada|
vraṇa|vivar'|ôpadarśitam
idaṃ hi vibhāti nabhaḥ.

kiṃ ca,

rucibhir abhitaṣ ṭaṅk'|ôtkīrṇair
iva trasa|reṇubhir
yad uḍubhir api chedaiḥ sthūlair
iva bhriyate nabhaḥ.
prakṛti|malino bhāsvad|bimb'|ôn-
mṛjā|kṛta|karmaṇas
tad ayam api hi tvaṣṭuḥ kunde
bhaviṣyati candramāḥ.

LAKṢMAṆAḤ: *(sarvato dṛṣṭvā)*

2.230 bhūyastarāṇi yad amūni tamasvinīṣu,
jyotsnīṣu ca praviralāni tataḥ pratīmaḥ:
saṃdhy"|ânalena bhṛśam ambara|mūṣikāyām
āvartitair uḍubhir eva kṛto 'yam induḥ.

(vihasya) hanta, yathā|dharmam ev' âitat.

yat pīyūṣa|mayūkha|mālini tamaḥ|
stom'|âvalīḍh'|āyuṣāṃ
netrāṇām apamṛtyu|hāriṇi puraḥ
sūry'|ōḍha ev' âtithau

He goes around the stage and then looks up. 2.225

The moon bears this thing, dark and tender like a young *tamála* tree, which people call a "spot." But this is not true; it seems rather like a piece of the sky made visible by the cruel demon, Rahu,* whose teeth have bitten a gaping wound in the moon at that place.

Moreover,

The space is filled with rays of moonlight, as if with dust particles produced by a chisel, and with the stars, which are like larger chunks. The next thing in the turner's lathe of the Creator, the carpenter of our world, who has already polished the sun-disk round, must be the naturally spotted moon.

LÁKSHMANA: *(looking everywhere)*

Since the stars are many on dark nights, but few when the moon shines bright, we fancy that by the fire of sunset, in the crucible of the sky, the stars suddenly melt together to produce the moon. 2.230

(smiling) It indeed behaves according to the law.

When, after sunset, the moon with its rays of ambrosia arrives as a guest to lengthen the lifetime of our eyesight, which would otherwise be taken away by the thick darkness, the lotuses turn away from it. That is why, in return, the moon seems

ambhojāni parāñci; tan nijam agham
dattv" êva tebhyas, tato
gaur'|âṅgī|vadan'|ôpamā|su|kṛtam ā-
datte patir yajvanām.

VIŚVĀMITRAḤ: *(sarvato 'valokya sa/smitam)* ahaha! nāma|dheya|mātra|mādhuryād a|param'|ârtha|dṛśvāno vipralabhyante viṣayiṇaḥ. tathā hi,

smerā diśaḥ, kumudam udbhiduraṃ, pibanti
jyotsnā|karambham udaraṃ|bharayaś cakorāḥ.
āḥ, kīdṛg Atri|muni|locana|dūṣikāyām
«pīyūṣa|dīdhitir» iti prathito 'nurāgaḥ?

2.235 (RĀMAṂ *ca dṛṣṭvā sa/harṣa/smitam)* katham, ayaṃ kaumār'|âṅka|vijaya|pratyāgato 'pi Tāḍakā|nigraheṇa hṛṇīyamāṇaḥ sahasā n' ôpatiṣṭhate vatsaḥ. (LAKṢMAṆAM *prati.)* vatsa Saumitre, asmākam anena vṛttāntena pradoṣa|lakṣmīr iyam anūdyate. paśya,

niśā|carāṇāṃ tamasāṃ nihantā
puro 'yam udgacchati Rāma|candraḥ.
ath' ôllasadbhir nayanair munīnām
ayaṃ kumudvān ajani pradeśaḥ.

to give its spot to them and takes away their form, which resembles the fair face of a beautiful woman. This master of sacrificers exchanges his sin for their virtue.*

VISHVA·MITRA: *(looking everywhere, smiling)* Alas, mortals who do not see the ultimate truth are cheated by things that are agreeable only in their name:

The directions manifest themselves, the lotuses open up without any help, and the gluttonous *chakóras* are drinking the moonlight as if it was curded barley. Ah, then why does everyone show so much affection for the moon, a drop of rheum in the eye of the sage Atri,* to call it "the one whose rays are made of ambrosia"?

(seeing RAMA, *smiling with delight)* This boy has come back 2.235
from his first victory over the enemy, which was only a sham fight for him,* yet he is embarrassed to have defeated Tádaka and suddenly refrains from approaching me. *(to* LÁKSHMANA*)* My son, Lákshmana, these events re-create the beauty of the nightfall for us. Look,

The killer of the demons comes here in front of us, Rama, as the moon, destroyer of darkness.* Thus, this place has become full of night-lotuses, as the lotus-eyes of the sages have opened up to see him.

RĀMAḤ: *(vibhāvya)*

madayati yad utpanno dugdh'|â-
mbu|dher ayam ambu|dhīn;
nayati nayanād Atrer jāto
mudaṃ nayanāni ca;
tad akhila|sura|śreṇī|sādhā-
raṇa|praṇayā Śacī|
sahacara|caru|sthālī Somaḥ
samañjasam īhate.

(sa|lajjam upasṛtya) bhagavan Kuśika|nandana! abhivādaye.

2.240 VIŚVĀMITRAḤ: *(sa|sneha|bahu|mānam āliṅgya)* vatsa Raghu|nandana! ittham eva,

prakṛṣṭa|kartr|abhiprāya|kriyā|phalavato vidhīn
prayuñjānās tvayā, vīra, paripālyāmahai vayam.

RĀMAḤ: śirasā pratigṛhītam ācārya|vacanam.

VIŚVĀMITRAḤ: *(samara|dhūli|dhūsaritaṃ* RĀMASYA *kapolam unmārjayan)* vatsa! yat satyam, amunā naktaṃcara|vyatikareṇa priya|suhṛdā Sīradhvajena vitanyamāne vaitānike karmaṇi kampitam eva me hṛdayam.

RĀMAḤ: *(sa|gauravam.)* bhagavan! ka eṣa Sīradhvajo nāma, yam adya te tri|bhuvana|durlabho 'yaṃ priya|suhṛc|chabda|prayogaḥ kam api mahimānam āropayati?

2.245 VIŚVĀMITRAḤ: vatsa, śṛṇoṣi Videheṣu Mithilāṃ nāma nagarīm.

RAMA: *(reflecting)*

> Since it was produced from the milk-ocean, it delights the seas; and, as it was born from the eye of Atri, it pleases the eyes; it is also Indra's sacrificial pot that contains the offerings, and it is thus equally favored by all the gods—in this way, the moon tries to satisfy everyone equally.

(approaching timidly) My master, Vishva·mitra, I salute you.

VISHVA·MITRA: *(embracing him with love and respect)* My 2.240
son, Rama, in this way,

> May you protect us, brave hero, while we perform our sacrificial duties, which produce results for the benefit of those who accomplish them perfectly.

RAMA: I obey my master's command.

VISHVA·MITRA: *(wiping* RAMA*'s cheeks, which have become stained with dust in the battle)* My son, it is true that, fearing the disaster that the demons could have caused in the sacrifice of my dear friend Sira·dhvaja, my heart was indeed trembling.

RAMA: *(with respect)* My master, who is this person called Sira·dhvaja, onto whom you bestow so much respect that you use the word "dear friend," an appellation that no one could hope for in the three worlds.

VISHVA·MITRA: My son, you must have heard about the city 2.245
called Míthila in the country of Vidéha.

RĀMAḤ: yatr' êdam āścarya|dvayaṃ janāḥ kathayanti—sa-kala|rāja|dur|ākarṣam aindu|śekharaṃ dhanur, lāṅgala|mukh'|ôllikhita|viśvaṃbharā|prasūtir a|garbha|saṃbhavā ca mānuṣī.

VIŚVĀMITRAḤ: *(vihasya)* atha kim.

RĀMAḤ: *(sa|kautukam)* tataḥ kiṃ tasyām?

VIŚVĀMITRAḤ:

2.250 asau Sīradhvajo rājā, yo devād Dyumaṇer api
adhyaiṣṭa Yājñavalkyasya mukhena Brahma|saṃhitām.

tasya saṃnyasta|śastrasya purāṇa|rāja'|rṣer Janaka|vaṃśa|jan-mano dīkṣā|vilopa|śaṅkā paryākulayati mām. tad etam, āyuṣmantau, vidhi|śeṣam asmadīyaṃ samāpya, sahas" âiva Mithilām upatiṣṭhāmahe.

RĀMAḤ: *(sa|harṣam apavārya)* vatsa Lakṣmaṇa, mam' âpi taruṇa|rohiṇī|ramaṇa|cūḍā|maṇi|praṇayini bāṇ'|āsane ciraṃ kautukam asti.

LAKṢMAṆAḤ: *(sahāsam)* āryāyām a|yoni|jāyāṃ kanyāyāṃ ca.

RĀMAḤ: *(sa|roṣa|smitam.)* katham, anyad eva kim api praha-sanaṃ sūtrayati bhavān! *(muniṃ prati)* bhagavann Ikṣ-vāku|kula|guro! yad abhirucitam bhavate.

2.255 *iti parikramya niṣkrāntāḥ sarve.*

RAMA: About which people tell two miraculous things: one is Shiva's bow, which not a single king manages to string, the other is the lady who was born not from a womb but from the earth, in the furrow of a plowshare.

VISHVA·MITRA: *(smiling)* Exactly.

RAMA: *(with curiosity)* What about that place?

VISHVA·MITRA:

> There lives King Sira·dhvaja, having learned the 2.250
> sacred texts from Yajnaválkya's mouth, who had
> been taught by the sun god himself.

This old royal sage, who has studied the learned treatises, was born in the house of Jánaka. It is because I was afraid to make an omission in his Vedic initiatory rite that I was so concerned. So let us finish our ritual duties and leave for Míthila quickly, my friends.

RAMA: *(with delight, aside)* My dear Lákshmana, I have been curious for a long time to see that bow so dear to Lord Shiva, who wears the crescent moon as a beautiful head-jewel.

LÁKSHMANA: *(laughing at him)* As well as to see the noble girl who was not born from a womb.

RAMA: *(angry but smiling)* So you are making fun of me again. *(to the sage)* My master, preceptor of the Ikshvákus, whatever you wish us to do...

They all go around the stage and exit. 2.255

PRELUDE TO ACT III
SANSKRIT-PRAKRIT PRELUDE

tataḥ praviśati KAÑCUKĪ.

KAÑCUKĪ: *(jarā|vaiklavya|visaṃsthulāni kati cit padāni gatvā, ātmānaṃ prati sa|khed'|ôpālambham.)*

gātrair girā ca vikalaś, caṭum īśvarāṇāṃ
kurvann, ayaṃ prahasanasya naṭaḥ kṛto 'smi.
tan māṃ punaḥ palita|varṇaka|bhājam enaṃ
nāṭyena kena naṭayiṣyati dīrgham āyuḥ?

(puro vibhāvya.) aye, Sītā|pād'|ôpajīvinī Kalahaṃsikā.

3.5 *praviśya* KALAHAṂSIKĀ.

KALAHAṂSIKĀ: ⌜ayya! paṇamāmi!⌟

KAÑCUKĪ: vatse, kalyāṇinī bhūyāḥ.

KALAHAṂSIKĀ: ⌜ayya, cireṇa kudo tumhe?⌟

KAÑCUKĪ: *(vimṛśya)* tat kiṃ na kathyate? vatse, viditam ev' âitad bhavatyā: tat|tādṛg adbhutaṃ dāraka|dvayam ādāya bhagavān Kauśiko yajamānaṃ Sīradhvajam upasthita iti.

3.10 KALAHAṂSIKĀ: ⌜aha iṃ. ayya, pahavaṃ ṇāma|heaṃ a tāṇaṃ suṇiduṃ atthi me koduhallam.⌟

KAÑCUKĪ: vatse, kathayāmi.

trayas|triṃśat|koṭi|
tri|daśa|maya|mūrter bhagavataḥ
Sahasr'|âṃśor vaṃśe
jayati jagad|īśo Daśarathaḥ.

The CHAMBERLAIN *enters.*

CHAMBERLAIN: *(afflicted by old age, makes a few stumbling steps, then, exhausted, scolds himself)*

> Praising my masters without having the voice or the limbs to do so, I have been made a comic actor. With my gray hair for greasepaint, in what play will I still be made to act, directed by this long life of mine?

(looking ahead) Here is Kala·hánsika, who serves her ladyship, Sita.

KALA·HÁNSIKA *enters.* 3.5

KALA·HÁNSIKA: Sir, I salute you.

CHAMBERLAIN: Young lady, may you be blessed.

KALA·HÁNSIKA: Sir, where have you been for such a long time?

CHAMBERLAIN: *(reflecting)* Why would I not tell you? Young lady, you know very well that the venerable Vishva·mitra, accompanied by two extraordinary young men, has come to see Maharaja Jánaka, who commanded a sacrifice.

KALA·HÁNSIKA: Yes, I know, sir, and I am curious to know 3.10
their names and from which family they are.

CHAMBERLAIN: Young lady, here is their story.

> In the lineage of the thousand-rayed Sun, whose body is made of the thirty-three highest gods, there is a victorious king, ruler of the world, named Dasha·ratha. When his rough weapons provoked the

yad astrair a|snigdhair
asura|yuvati|śvāsa|pavana|
prakope siddhe na
spṛśati śata|koṭiṃ Śata|makhaḥ.

imau tasya viśāṃ|patyur ātmajau Rāma|Lakṣmaṇau,
yayor Bharata|Śatrughnau anujau dvandva|cāriṇau.

KALAHAṂSIKĀ: ⌜jaha amhāṇaṃ ghare bhaṭṭi|dāriā Sīdā, Ummilā, Maṇḍavī, Suaïttī a.⌟ *(vicintya harṣaṃ nirūpayantī.)* ⌜kahaṃ, mahā|ula|ppasūā khu ede kumārā.⌟ *(muhūrtam iva sthitvā, dīrgham uṣṇaṃ ca niḥśvasya.)* ⌜kudo amhāṇaṃ īrisaṃ bhāa|heaṃ.⌟

3.15 KAÑCUKĪ: bhavati, mā viṣīda. sarvam bhadraṃ bhaviṣyati deva|brāhmaṇa|prasādāt.

KALAHAṂSIKĀ: ⌜tado tado.⌟

KAÑCUKĪ: tataś ca vṛddh'|ântaḥ|purāṇām abhyarthanayā tau vikartana|kula|kumārau dṛṣṭvā, nivartamānaḥ purodhasā Gautamen' āhūya rāja|putrīṇāṃ saubhāgya|devat"|ārādhanāya saṃvihito 'smi.

KALAHAṂSIKĀ: *(sa|harṣam.)* ⌜ayya! savva|jaṇa|maṇīsid'|âṇuūlaṃ via tatta|hodo Sadāṇandassa vaaṇam.⌟

KAÑCUKĪ: vatse, evam ev' âitat. na khalv a|gambhīram Āṅgiraso bravīti.

3.20 KALAHAṂSIKĀ: ⌜tā kiṃ maṇṇeha? Saṃkara|sar'|âsaṇ'|ārovaṇa|vvavasāeṇa rā'|êsiṇo Jaṇaassa païṇṇā|sāhasaṃ ṇivvahadi Rāhavo?⌟

storming sighs of the demon-wives,* Indra did not even need to touch his thunderbolt.*

Those two young men are this king's sons: Rama and Lákshmana. They have two younger brothers who are inseparable: Bharata and Shatrúghna.

KALA·HÁNSIKA: Just as in our house, where we have the Princess Sita with Úrmila, and Mándavi with Shruta·kirti. *(reflecting, then showing delight)* These princes also come from a great family... *(She stops for a moment, then heaves a long, deep sigh.)* How could we be so fortunate?

CHAMBERLAIN: Young lady, do not despair, with the help of 3.15
the gods and brahmins everything will be all right.

KALA·HÁNSIKA: So then what happened?

CHAMBERLAIN: Then I was sent by the elder members of the ladies' quarters to go and see these two princes of the solar dynasty, and on my return I was called upon by the royal priest, Shatánanda, who appointed me to perform the worship of the fortune-bringing deities for the benefit of the princesses.

KALA·HÁNSIKA: *(with delight)* Sir, Shatánanda's words seem to express what is everybody's desire.

CHAMBERLAIN: Young lady, it is indeed so. This sage born in the family of Ángiras never says anything superficial.

KALA·HÁNSIKA: Do you think that Rama will meet the dif- 3.20
ficult requirement* set forth by the royal sage, Jánaka, and be able to bend Shiva's bow?

KAÑCUKĪ: vatse, asmān api tarko 'yaṃ taralī|karoti. tathā hi,

pūrṇe 'pi karmaṇi, hateṣv api rākṣaseṣu,
vijñāya Maithila|sutām api vīrya|śulkām,
bālaṃ pituḥ priyatamaṃ Raghu|rāja|putram
etāvatīṃ bhuvam ṛṣiḥ katham āninaya?

KALAHAṂSIKĀ: *(smaraṇam abhinīya, sa|viṣādam)* ⌜ayya! paütti|visesa|lāheṇa dum|maṇāamāṇaṃ attāṇaṃ paṃcāliā|keli|vvāvāreṇa viṇoaantīṃ bhaṭṭi|dāriaṃ pekkhia, paḍivattuṃ āadāe ayyassa daṃsaṇeṇa mae visumaridaṃ. imiṇā uṇa de rakkhasa|ṇāma|ggahaṇeṇa saṃsumarāvida mhi.⌟

KAÑCUKĪ: *(sa|viṣādam)* vatse, kīdṛśī sā pravṛttir, yā tava bhartṛ|dārikām api dur|manāyayati?

3.25 KALAHAṂSIKĀ: ⌜jaha kila Sīdā|devīṃ patthiduṃ Dasa|ggīva|purohido paraādo tti.⌟

KAÑCUKĪ: *(tatr' âvajñāṃ nāṭayan, sa|harṣam)* katham, etāvad api kāryaṃ vatsā Jānakī jānāti, yad anen' ôdantena dur|manī|bhūyate? nūnam idānīm asyāḥ kṛt'|âvataraṇa|maṅgalāny aṅgāni yauvanasya panthānam īkṣante.

CHAMBERLAIN: Young lady, this is exactly what has been on my mind:

> The sacrifice has been successfully performed, the demons got killed, and Vishva·mitra also knows that the hand of the Princess of Míthila can be obtained by a heroic act—so for what other reason could that sage have brought this young boy, the Raghu prince, his father's dearest son, to such a distant land?*

KALA·HÁNSIKA: *(acting as though she remembers something, then with concern)* Sir, the princess had heard some news, which made her very unhappy, and I saw her trying to chase away her grief by playing with a doll. Then I came here to learn the cause of her grief, but I forgot about it all when I saw Your Honor. Now that you mention the demons, it makes me think of this story again.

CHAMBERLAIN: *(with concern)* Young lady, what is this news that makes even your princess so sad?

KALA·HÁNSIKA: It is that the royal priest of ten-headed Rá- 3.25
vana has arrived to ask for Princess Sita's hand.

CHAMBERLAIN: *(showing his contempt, then with delight)* How come the young Sita has learned about this event, and how can this news even make her sad? Surely, her body, which has received all the auspicious blessings, is looking forward to the path of young age.*

KALAHAMSIKĀ: *(vihasya)* ⌜ayya! evvaṃ ṇ' êdam. ayyo tti sa-ḍhilī|kaa|lajjā saṃpadi evva aṇuhūdaṃ kiṃ ti ṇivedemi.⌟ *(saṃskṛtam āśritya)*

an|ākūtair eva
priya|sahacarīṇāṃ śiśutayā
vacobhiḥ pāñcālī|
mithunam adhunā saṃgamayitum
upādatte no vā,
viramati na vā; kevalam iyam
kapolau kalyāṇī
pulaka|mukulair danturayati.

KAÑCUKĪ: *(sa/harṣam.)* diṣṭyā cirasya jīvadbhir asmābhir yauvanavatī vatsā Vaidehī draṣṭavyā. *(sa/smitam.)* tatas tataḥ.

3.30 KALAHAMSIKĀ: ⌜tado a, tāhiṃ ujjuāhiṃ ṇibbandhijjamāṇā lajjiduṃ vi lajjedi.⌟

KAÑCUKĪ: *(vihasya, sa/kautukam)* vatse, saṃkīrṇe vayasi khalv iyaṃ vartate. atra hi,

mano 'pi śaṅkamānābhir bālābhir upajīvyate
a|ṣaḍ|akṣīṇa|ṣāḍ|guṇya|mantrī Makara|ketanaḥ.

KALAHAMSIKĀ: *(sa/lajjam)* ⌜ayya! sohaṇaṃ mantesi. savvassa vy aṇuhava|saṃvāiṇī de vāā.⌟

KAÑCUKĪ: vatse,

3.35 tadātva|pronmīlan|
mradima|ramaṇīyāt kaṭhinatāṃ
nicitya pratyaṅgād
iva taruṇa|bhāvena ghaṭitau,
stanau saṃbibhrāṇāḥ

KALA·HÁNSIKA: *(smiling)* Sir, it is indeed so. You are a noble person, so I do not feel so shy and shall tell you another thing that happened. *(She resorts to Sanskrit to say what follows.)*

> According to the account of her dear friends, who are too young to have any particular intention, today this lovely girl refused to make her pair of dolls sleep together, nor did she stop playing with them; she just stayed there with the small buds of goosebumps spreading over her cheeks.

CHAMBERLAIN: *(with delight)* Fortunately, since I have lived long, I can see Princess Sita in her full-blown youth. *(smiling)* And then?

KALA·HÁNSIKA: As these simple-minded friends of hers kept 3.30
teasing her, she became too shy even to be ashamed.

CHAMBERLAIN: *(smiling, with interest)* Young lady, she is now in between two stages of life. In this condition,

> young girls, who are suspectful even of their own hearts, employ the *Mákara*-bannered God of Love as their confidential defense minister.

KALA·HÁNSIKA: *(shyly)* Sir, you are perfectly right. What you say is confirmed by everyone's experience.

CHAMBERLAIN: Young lady,

> Their youth seems to have withdrawn all hardness 3.35
> from their bodies, which start to become tender and lovely at this age, while all the firmness is being put into their breasts; they are withdrawn for a moment, but then become bold, as desire is

kṣaṇa|vinaya|vaiyātya|masṛṇa|
smar'|ônmeṣāḥ keṣām
upari na rasānāṃ yuvatayaḥ.

KALAHAMSIKĀ: *(vihasya)* ⌜hodu! ṇa kiṃ vi tumhehiṃ sudaṃ!⌟

KAÑCUKĪ: vatse, na tāvad ayam artho 'dy' âpi rāja|gocarī|bhavati. yadi ca syāt, kim etāvatā?

KALAHAMSIKĀ: ⌜had'|āso Rāvaṇo devīṃ pariṇedi!⌟

KAÑCUKĪ: *(vihasya.)*

3.40 haste|kariṣyati jagat|traya|jitvaro 'pi
kas tādṛśo duhitaraṃ Janak'|ēśvarasya?
prāṇ'|âdhikaṃ vipula|hastavatām ap' îdam
traiyambakaṃ kim api kārmukam antar|āyaḥ.

n' âpi Daśa|kandhar'|ânurodhena svayaṃ pratijñātam anyathā kariṣyati mahā|kṣatriyo Videha|rājaḥ. tan na kiṃ cid etat.

KALAHAMSIKĀ: *(niḥśvasya)* ⌜evvaṃ hodu! ayya! saṃpadi kahiṃ te Rāma|Lakkhaṇau?⌟

KAÑCUKĪ: nanv etāv eva devat"|āgāra|vedikāyām,

munīn Kauśika|Vaideha|
Gautamān abhirādhyataḥ,
ḍhaukitau jñāna|karmabhyām
mokṣa|svargāv iva svayam.

slowly awakening in them; they are the sweetest of
all, aren't they?—such are young women.*

KALA·HÁNSIKA: *(smiling)* All right. So you have not heard anything?

CHAMBERLAIN: Young lady, this matter has not reached the king's ears yet. And, if he has heard it, then what?

KALA·HÁNSIKA: Then that damned Rávana will marry the princess!

CHAMBERLAIN: *(smiling)*

Even if he is the conqueror of the three worlds, who 3.40
is he to marry King Jánaka's daughter? For there is
Shiva's bow, more powerful than the hands of the
strongest men, which stands there as an obstacle.

And the great warrior, the King of Vidéha, will not break his promise to satisfy ten-headed Rávana. So there is nothing to be afraid of.

KALA·HÁNSIKA: *(sighing)* Let us hope it will be so. Sir, where are Rama and Lákshmana now?

CHAMBERLAIN: Now, at the raised seat in the temple,

They are propitiating the three sages: Vishva·mitra, Jánaka and Shatánanda. Rama and Lákshmana embody what one obtains through knowledge and ritual: final release and heaven.

3.45 tad ehi. mahac ciram āgatayor āvayoḥ. kany"|ântaḥ|puram eva gacchāvaḥ.

iti niṣkrāntau.

iti miśra|viṣkambhakaḥ.

So come, we have been chatting for a long time. Let us go to the young ladies' quarters. 3.45

Both exit.

End of the Sanskrit-Prakrit prelude.

ACT III
THE BREAKING OF SHIVA'S BOW

tataḥ praviśati JANAKO, VIŚVĀMITRAḤ, ŚATĀNANDO, RĀMA|LAKṢMAṆAU *ca.*

JANAKAḤ: *(sa|harṣam)* bhagavan Viśvāmitra,

3.50 lumpann a|dṛṣṭa|jāmātṛ|saṃpadāṃ śucam adya naḥ;
tvad|āgamana|janm" âyam ānandaḥ su|dināyate.

api ca,

adya pradakṣiṇa|śikh"|ā|valayaḥ Kṛśānur
aśnāti me jana|padeṣu vaṣaṭ|kṛtāni.
tvat|tejasi sphurati śāntika|pauṣṭikeṣu,
svāṃ ca srucaṃ śithilam Āṅgiraso bibharti.

VIŚVĀMITRAḤ: sakhe, Sīradhvaja! cirasya śāntaḥ puṣṭaś ca tav' âyaṃ jana|padaḥ,

yatra tvaṃ brahma|mīmāṃsā|tattva|jño daṇḍa|dhārakaḥ,
purodhāś c' âiva yasy' âsāv Aṅgiraḥ prapitā|mahaḥ.

3.55 *(smitaṃ kṛtvā.)* jāmātur a|darśana|janm" âyaṃ śokaḥ punar asmākam upaśamayitum avaśiṣyate. kiṃ ca, śoka|harṣau nāma loka|yātr" êyam bhavataḥ. tathā hi,

yajūṃṣi taittirīyāṇi mūrtāni vamati sma yaḥ,
sa yogī Yājñavalkyas tvāṃ ved'|ântān adhyajīgapat.

JÁNAKA, VISHVA·MITRA, SHATÁNANDA, RAMA, *and* LÁKSHMANA *enter.*

JÁNAKA: *(with delight)* Venerable Vishva·mitra,

> Grief could have overcome us today, because we 3.50
> have not been lucky enough to find an appropriate son-in-law—but this grief is now gone, as the joy to see you arrive makes our day cloudless.

Moreover,

> Today, the flames go around clockwise* while the fire consumes the offerings made to it in our kingdom. Your power radiates everywhere as the ritual acts to promote welfare and prosperity are performed, and the sage Shatánanda can keep his sacrificial ladle unused.*

VISHVA·MITRA: My friend, Jánaka, your kingdom has been peaceful and prosperous for a long time. . .

> Here, where you, a true philosopher, an expert of brahmanical knowledge, are the ruler, for whom the grandson of Ángiras, Shatánanda, performs the priestly duties.

(smiling) Now, what remains for us to do is to chase away the 3.55
grief you feel because you cannot find a son-in-law. In any case, what are these worldly experiences, happiness or grief, for you? For,

> He who revealed the form of sacrificial formulas according to the Tittiriya tradition of Vedic texts, the yogi Yajnaválkya himself, taught you Vedic philosophy.

LAKṢMAṆAḤ: *(jan'|ântikam.)* ārya, ayaṃ sa rājā Vaidehaḥ, pavitram a|parimey'|āścaryam yasy' âpadānam upādhyāyād anuśrūyate.

RĀMAḤ: *(sa|pramod'|ânurāgam.)* vatsa, sa ev' âyaṃ Śatapatha|kath"|âdhikārī puruṣaḥ, praṇāyyāy'|ânte|vāsine yasmai bhagavān vājasaneyo Yājñavalkyaḥ śuklāni yajūṃṣi provāca.

VIŚVĀMITRAḤ: *(muhūrtaṃ nirvarṇya)*

3.60 nijāya tasmai gurave yatīnāṃ
jaitrāya viśrāṇita|go|sahasram,
taṃ go|sahasr'|âdhipateḥ praśiṣyam
upāsmahe Maithilam ātitheyam.

JANAKAḤ: *(sa|praśrayam)* bhagavan, yat kiṃ cid anyad abhidadhāsi, tatra prabhaviṣṇur bhavān eva. tatra|bhavatas tu Sahasra|mayūkh'|ânte|vāsino yog'|īśvarād bhagavato Yājñavalkyād adhyayanam iti mahīyas" îyam asmākaṃ yaśaḥ|patākā.

VIŚVĀMITRAḤ: *(vihasya)* bho mahā|yogin!

kiṃ Yājñavalkyo, Janakaḥ kim evaṃ?
na vaḥ sva|rūpaṃ kavayo 'pi vidyuḥ.
pravāha|nityān adhikṛtya yuṣmān
sahasra|śākhāḥ śrutayaḥ prathante.

LÁKSHMANA: *(aside to* RAMA*)* My brother, this is that king, Jánaka, about whose virtuous and incomparably miraculous deeds we heard from our master.

RAMA: *(happily, with affection)* My little brother, he is the man who has figures in the Shata·patha Bráhmana, who studied the Vedas without attachment to this world, and to whom Yajnaválkya, founder of the tradition of the white Yajur·veda, revealed the sacrificial formulas.

VISHVA·MITRA: *(looking at* JÁNAKA *for a moment)*

> He has given a thousand cows to his preceptor, who won against the other ascetics;* he is the disciple of the thousand-rayed Sun's disciple—we honor him, the King of Míthila, who always receives his guests in the right manner. 3.60

JÁNAKA: *(politely)* No matter what you say, venerable Vishva·mitra, you shall outwit me in this conversation. But the real reason for my becoming famous is that I had the honor of studying under the guidance of the best of yogis, the venerable disciple of the thousand-rayed Sun.

VISHVA·MITRA: *(smiling)* O great yogi,

> What kind of person is Yajnaválkya? What sort of man is Jánaka? Even the seers are unable to explain your true nature to us. Thanks to your uninterrupted chain of preceptors and disciples, the holy scriptures have been revealed in their thousands of branches.

ŚATĀNANDAḤ: bhagavan, evam īdṛśāḥ khalv amī tri|bhuvana|mahanīya|mahimāno manīṣiṇaḥ.

3.65 JANAKAḤ: *(sa|vailakṣya|smitam)* bhagavan,

nirmāya kārmaṇam ṛcām agha|marṣaṇīnām
 unmārjanīr jagad|aghāni tav' âdya vācaḥ
śrotuṃ cira|praṇayi|kautukam asti ceto.
 duḥkhā|karoti punar eṣa mam' ârtha|vādaḥ.

tad virama. *(iti śirasy añjaliṃ ghaṭayati.)*

VIŚVĀMITRAḤ: *(sa|smitam, asy' âñjalim udghāṭayan)* sakhe Sīradhvaja! saṃhriyatām añjaliḥ. amī tūṣṇīṃ|bhūtāḥ smaḥ. Kātyāyanī|kāmuka|kārmuk'|āropaṇa|pravīṇena duhituḥ patyā sampraty a|paryuṣita|pratijño bhūyāḥ!

LAKṢMAṆAḤ: *(apavārya)* ārya, paras|param eteṣāṃ pauruṣ'|ôtkarṣa|praśaṃsā|ramaṇīyaḥ pāvano 'yam ṛṣīṇāṃ samavāyaḥ.

3.70 RĀMAḤ: vatsa, yad āttha.

smaranti lok'|ârtham amī kila śrutīr
 iti pratiṣṭhām adhigantum īśmahe.
paraṃ yad eṣāṃ punar asti vaibhavaṃ,
 tad eta eva vyatividrate yadi.

JANAKAḤ: *(sa|harṣam)* param anugṛhīto 'smi.

SHATÁNANDA: Venerable Vishva·mitra, such are indeed those sages, whose fame has spread in the three worlds.

JÁNAKA: *(smiling in embarrassment)* Venerable Vishva·mitra, 3.65

> My heart has for a long time been eager to hear your words, which perform the magic of the purificatory Rigvedic chants and destroy the sins of the world. But these affirmations praising me make me uneasy.

So please stop. *(He puts his folded hands on his head.)*

VISHVA·MITRA: *(smiling, making* JÁNAKA'*s arms descend)* My friend, Jánaka, do not beg me with folded hands. I am not going to say anything. May your promise be fulfilled and your daughter's future husband be able to take up the bow of Párvati's husband.

LÁKSHMANA: *(aside)* My brother, they praise each other's manly qualities, which makes their meeting pleasant; their conversation has a purificatory effect.

RAMA: My little brother, as you say, 3.70

> They transmit Vedic knowledge for the sake of this world—this is what we are able to understand about their greatness. But only they can possibly understand each other's real power.

JÁNAKA: *(with delight)* I am very much honored.

samasyā vā sāmnāṃ,
bahir|a|bahir|aṃhaḥ|parimṛjām
ṛcāṃ vā saṃvādaḥ,
kim api yajuṣāṃ vā paripaṇaḥ,
tvad|āśīr|vādo 'yaṃ
bahu|viṣaya|sākṣāt|kṛta|phalo
varaṃ me vatsāyāḥ
kathayati puro|varttinam iva.

VIŚVĀMITRAḤ: *(s'|ākūta|smitam)* sakhe Sīradhvaja. evam etat.

3.75 davīyasyo dūrād
a|patham iha c' âmutra ca śucām
tri|vedī|vākyānām
an|aticira|bhagnā iva khilāḥ.
śruti|grāhyaṃ jyotiḥ
kim api bahir|antar|mala|muṣo
mṛjāyā majjānaḥ
kva nu vipariyanti dvi|ja|giraḥ?

ŚATĀNANDAḤ: *(sva|gatam)* nūnaṃ Rāma|bhadram eva jāmātaram abhisaṃdhāya bhagavān ayaṃ punaḥ punar vakr'|ôktibhiḥ Sīradhvajam parimohayate. bhavatu! aham asya prarocan"|ârtham a|saṃvidāna iva pṛcchāmi. *(prakāśaṃ, muniṃ prati)* kasy' êdaṃ Śakunta|rāja|ketor iva Kaustubha|Śrīvatsau dāraka|ratna|dvayam?

VIŚVĀMITRAḤ: *(vihasya, sva|gatam)* sādhu, vatsa Śatānanda! yad etat kṛtaṃ tīrthaṃ vivakṣitasya vastunaḥ sukh'|âvatārāya. *(prakāśam)* vatsa Gautama, Kakutstha|kula|kumārāv etau.

Like the synthesis of Samavedic songs, like the truthfulness of Rigvedic chants, which purify external and internal sins, like the stock of Yajurvedic formulas, such are your words of blessing, which have come true on many different occasions. They now talk about my daughter's bridegroom as if he were present here.

VISHVA·MITRA: *(smiling purposefully)* My friend, Jánaka, it is true.

Very distant and far beyond any grief of this or the next world, they are like untouched lands—made of Vedic words—which have just been plowed. They are made of light that one can perceive only by hearing, they purify internal as well as external impurities, being as they are the core of purity itself—such are the words of brahmins. In what could they prove to be wrong? 3.75

SHATÁNANDA: *(aside)* Surely, this venerable sage thinks already of Rama as the king's would-be son-in-law, and confuses Jánaka with repeated allusions. All right, to please him, I shall inquire as if I were ignorant. *(aloud, to the sage)* Venerable Vishva·mitra, to whom do these two dear boys belong, who are like the Káustubha gem and Shri·vatsa mark on Gáruda-bannered Vishnu?*

VISHVA·MITRA: *(smiling, aside)* Well done, my friend, Shatánanda. You have given a cue so that I can easily introduce the subject I wanted to talk about. *(aloud)* My friend, Shatánanda, these are two princes of the Kakútstha dynasty.

ŚATĀNANDAḤ: *(sa|pratyabhijñam iva)*

putr'|ârthe jagad|eka|jāṅghika|yay'|ûd-
dāma|bhramat|kīrtinā,
cātur|hotra|vitīrṇa|viśva|vasudhā|
cakreṇa cakre makhaḥ
rājñā Paṅkti|rathena, yatra sakala|
svar|vāsi|sarv'|âtithau
sa sven' âiva phala|pradaḥ phalam api
sven' âiva Nārāyaṇaḥ.

3.80 tat kim etāv eva tau Dāśarathī, yau kila Rāma|Lakṣmaṇāv iti Tāḍakā|mathana|maṅgal'|ôdghāta|vitīrṇa|divy'|âs-tra|mantra|pārāyaṇena bhagavat" âiva vinītau vaitānasya karmaṇaś chidrā|pidhāna|dakṣiṇayā bhagavantam upā-sāṃbabhūvatur?

VIŚVĀMITRAḤ: atha kim.

JANAKAS *tau sa|sneha|bahu|mānam paśyati.*

ŚATĀNANDAḤ: tad anayoḥ kataro Rāmaḥ, kataro Lakṣma-ṇaḥ?

VIŚVĀMITRAḤ: *(RĀMAṂ nirdiśan)* vatsa, Āṅgirasa,

3.85 ye catvāro dinakara|kula|
kṣattra|saṃtāna|mallī|
māl"|âmlāna|stabaka|sa|dṛśā
jajñire rāja|putrāḥ.
Rāmas teṣām a|carama|bhavas,
Tāḍakā|kāla|rātri|
pratyūṣo 'yaṃ su|carita|kathā|
kandalī|mūla|kandaḥ.

SHATÁNANDA: *(as if he were recognizing them)*

> King Dasha·ratha, whose fame had reached everywhere in the form of his swift sacrificial horse, unique in this world, the king who had rewarded his four officiating priests with the gift of the whole earth, performed a sacrifice to have sons.* The guests invited were all the inhabitants of heaven; and he who makes all sacrifices fruitful, Vishnu-Naráyana, himself came to be the result obtained through the sacrifice.*

So are these Dasha·ratha's two sons, Rama and Lákshmana, 3.80
whom you yourself taught and to whom you transmitted the science of the divine mantra-weapons to strike down and kill Tádaka successfully? Are they the ones who honored you with the gift of destroying all obstacles to your sacrifice?

VISHVA·MITRA: Yes, indeed.

JÁNAKA *looks at them with affection and respect.*

SHATÁNANDA: So which of them is Rama and which is Lákshmana?

VISHVA·MITRA: *(pointing at* RAMA*)* My dear friend, Shatánanda,

> Four princes were born, four unfading flower clus- 3.85
> ters in the jasmine garland of the line of warriors in the solar dynasty. Here is Rama, the eldest of them, the dawn that ended the night of Tádaka's threat, the root of what is a plantain tree of good acts.

(LAKṢMAṆAM *nirdiśya)* ayaṃ c' âparo Lakṣmaṇaḥ.

ŚATĀNANDAḤ: bhagavan, diṣṭyā Vasiṣṭha|prasūtaṃ kṣattram ṛddhyati.

JANAKAḤ: *(vihasya)* sādhu bhagavan, asmā|dṛśīṣu praviśya krīḍasi.

krodh'|âgnau Puruhūta|huṃ|kṛti|parā-
bhūta|Triśaṅku|trapā|
saṃpāta|jvalite jagat|traya|mayīṃ
tvayy āhutiṃ juhvati,
saṃbhrānt'|ôpanatasya nāṭita|jarā|
vaiklavya|śīrṇ'|âkṣarāḥ
pratyūhāya babhūvur Ambuja|bhuvo
devasya cāṭ'|ûktayaḥ.

3.90 tam api nāma bhagavantaṃ yajamānam anye gopāyitāraḥ.

ŚATĀNANDAḤ: rāja'|rṣe, evam etat. kiṃ punar na dīkṣiṣyamāṇāḥ krudhyant' îti rakṣitāraṃ kṣatriyam upādadate.

JANAKAḤ: *(sa|harṣaṃ* RĀMA|LAKṢMAṆAU *nirvarṇya, jan'|ântikam)* bhagavan Śatānanda,

bhavati na tathā Bhānoḥ śiṣye
gurau vasato mama
svayam api munau Viśvāmitre
gṛhān adhitiṣṭhati,
Daśaratha|sutāv etau dṛṣṭvā
yath" ôcchvasitaṃ manaḥ
śithilayati me pratyag|jyotiḥ|
prabodha|sukh'|āsikām.

(pointing at LÁKSHMANA*)* And the other one is Lákshmana.

SHATÁNANDA: Venerable Vishva·mitra, thank god, warriors begotten by Vasíshtha prosper.

JÁNAKA: *(smiling)* Well done, venerable Vishva·mitra. Adapting yourself to people like me, you just play with us.

> When you were making a sacrifice of the three worlds into the fire of your wrath kindled by the deep shame of Tri·shanku, who had been humiliated by the roaring Indra,* then lotus-born Brahma, being confused by this destruction of his creation,* bowed down to you and uttered some flattering hymns of garbled words—as if he had been hindered by his feigned old age—to interrupt you.

Still, may others protect and help you with your sacrifices! 3.90

SHATÁNANDA: Royal sage, may it be so. As initiates of a sacrifice should not be angered, they need to employ a warrior to protect them.

JÁNAKA: *(looking at* RAMA *and* LÁKSHMANA *with delight, aside to* SHATÁNANDA*)* Venerable Shatánanda,

> My heart had never been so delighted by the presence of my preceptor, the Sun's disciple, when I lived in his house, nor by the arrival of the sage Vishva·mitra in our home, as it is now by seeing these two sons of Dasha·ratha. My mind forgets even the joy of knowing the Supreme Self.

ŚATĀNANDAḤ: rāja'|rṣe Vaideha, īdṛśam ev' âitat. mam' âpi rāja|putrāv etau sākṣāt|kurvato vatse Sīt"|Ōrmile na hṛdayād avarohataḥ.

3.95 JANAKAḤ: (VIŚVĀMITRAM *prati)* bhagavan,

idaṃ vayo, mūrtir iyaṃ mano|jñā,
vīr'|âdbhuto 'yaṃ carita|prarohaḥ.
imau kumārau, bata, paśyato me
kṛt'|ârtham antar|naṭat' îva cetaḥ.

VIŚVĀMITRAḤ: *(s'|ôtprāsa|hāsam)* sakhe Sīradhvaja, hṛdayam ev' āmantrayasva: kim|arthaṃ kṛt'|ârtham as' îti.

JANAKAḤ: *(sa|khedam)*

yad|gotrasya prathama|puruṣas
tejasām īśvaro 'yam,
yeṣāṃ dharma|pravacana|gurur
brahma|vādī Vasiṣṭhaḥ,
ye vartante tava ca hṛdaye
su|ṣṭhu saṃbandha|yogyās
te rājāno; mama punar asau
dāruṇaḥ śulka|setuḥ.

3.100 RĀMA|LAKṢMAṆAU: *(jan'|ântikam)* katham, asmadīyāḥ kathāḥ prastūyante!

VIŚVĀMITRAḤ: *(sa|smitam)* rāja'|rṣe, yadi śulka|saṃsth" âiva kevalam antar|āyas, tan na kiṃ cid etat.

JANAKAḤ: *(sa|khedaṃ vimṛśann, apavārya)* bhagavan Āṅgirasa,

yad vidann api Videha|nandinī|
pāṇi|pīḍana|vidher mah"|ârghatām
evam āha munir eṣa Kauśikaḥ,

SHATÁNANDA: Royal sage, Jánaka, it is indeed so. When I see these two princes, they remind my heart of our dear little Sita and Úrmila.

JÁNAKA: *(to* VISHVA·MITRA*)* Venerable Vishva·mitra, 3.95

> Look at their youthfulness, their handsome appearance, their eminent deeds, heroic and admirable. When I behold these two princes, my heart, having all its desires fulfilled, almost dances with joy.

VISHVA·MITRA: *(smiling ironically)* My friend, Jánaka, then ask your heart why it has obtained all its desires.

JÁNAKA: *(with distress)*

> These kings whose paternal ancestor is the Lord of the Luminaries, to whom Vasíshtha, the preceptor of the Vedas, taught the words of law and religion—these kings who are so dear to your heart would make very good husbands. But I have a promise to fulfill strictly, concerning the bride-price.

RAMA AND LÁKSHMANA: *(whispering to each other)* Look, they are talking about our affairs. 3.100

VISHVA·MITRA: *(smiling)* Royal sage, if the only obstacle is that promise concerning the bride-price, it is not even worth mentioning.

JÁNAKA: *(reflecting, with pain, aside)* Venerable Shatánanda,

> What this sage Vishva·mitra has just said—though he knows what a great price is required in order to obtain Sita's hand—confuses my mind very much.

tena muhyati cirāya me manaḥ
tad eva sthāṇavīyaṃ vā dhanuḥ syād idam īdṛśam,
etad|āropaṇaṃ nāma paṇo vā mama jarjaraḥ.

3.105 ŚATĀNANDAḤ: śāntaṃ pāpaṃ, śāntaṃ pāpam.

dur|laṅgham Īśvara|śar'|âsanam, a|pramocya|
śulka|grahas tvam asi; sarvam idaṃ tath" âiva.
kiṃ tv asya Rāghava|śiśoḥ sahaj'|ânubhāva|
gambhīra|bhīṣaṇam ati|sphuṭam eva vṛttam.

JANAKAḤ: *(muniṃ prati)* bhagavan Kauśika, ciram api vikalpayan na bhavad|girām abhidheyam ady' âpi niścinomi.

VIŚVĀMITRAḤ: *(vihasya)* tad upadarśaya kārmukam aindu|śekharam. Rāma|bhadra eva vyākarotu.

RĀMAḤ: *(sa|harṣaṃ, sva|gatam)* katham alīka|vikalpair ātmānaṃ vinodayāmi? nanv ayaṃ mam' âiva kautukaṃ pūrayitum aiśvaraṃ dhanur abhyarthayate bhagavān. *(*JANAKAṂ *ca dṛṣṭvā, sa|vimarśam)* ahaha,

3.110 «bālena saṃbhāvyam idaṃ ca karma
bravīti ca pratyayito maha"|rṣiḥ.»
iti dhruvaṃ mantrayate nṛpo 'yaṃ.
datte kim atr' ôttaram? ākulo 'smi.

JANAKAḤ: *(muhūrtam iva sthitvā, dīrgham uṣṇaṃ ca niḥśvasya)* bhagavan, kva tādṛśaṃ bhāga|dheyam asmākam, yena bhagavatā Viśvāmitreṇa nāthavanto vayaṃ Maithilīm etasmai Raghu|kula|kumārāya pratipādya cirāya carit'|ârthā bhavāmaḥ?

RĀMO *lajjate.*

> Either this bow of Shiva is to be strung by Rama,
> as said, or my promise about it will be broken.

SHATÁNANDA: God forbid! 3.105

> Shiva's bow is hard to string, and your promise about the bride-price should not be broken—this is the state of the matter. However, Rama's conduct has clearly proved that his innate power is frightening and limitless.*

JÁNAKA: *(toward the sage)* Venerable Vishva·mitra, I have been thinking about what you said for a long time, but I still do not quite understand what you meant.

VISHVA·MITRA: *(smiling)* Then show us Shiva's bow, and Rama himself shall interpret my words for you.

RAMA: *(with delight, aside)* Why, am I deluding myself with false hopes? But the sage must be asking for Shiva's bow in order to satisfy my curiosity! *(looking at* JÁNAKA, *reflecting)* Alas,

> The king surely says to himself: "This great sage is quite confident that even a child can perform the task." So how will he react to this request? —This is what worries me. 3.110

JÁNAKA: *(waiting for a moment, then, with a deep sigh)* Venerable Vishva·mitra, how could I be so lucky to be able to give Sita to this Raghu prince and fulfill my greatest wish after a long time, thanks to your gracious help?*

RAMA *is bashful.*

JANAKAḤ:

yat|kodaṇḍa|samarpita|tri|bhuvana|
chidrā|pidhāna|vratam
jātaṃ rohitam eva kevalam apa-
jyā|bandham aindraṃ dhanuḥ,
te 'pi prekṣya purā śar'|âsanam idaṃ
maurvī|kiṇa|śyāmikā|
kastūrī|surabhī|kṛtān abibharur
vyarthaṃ bhujān bhū|bhujaḥ.

3.115 VIŚVĀMITRAḤ: sakhe Sīradhvaja, kathaṃ mahā|puṇya|rāśim ātmānam avamanyase?

tvad|bhāga|dheyam api tādṛśam, utsavānām
etādṛśāṃ vayam api prasamīkṣitāraḥ.
santy eva viśva|bhuvan'|â|bhaya|dāna|śauṇḍāḥ
kṣoṇī|bhujaḥ, param amī tu na Rāma|bhadraḥ.

LAKṢMAṆAḤ: *(sva|gatam)* katham, etad upādhyāyen' âiv' âbhihitam, yad asmi vaktu|kāmaḥ.

JANAKAḤ: bhagavan! satyam, a|cintyo hi maṇi|mantr'|âuṣadh'|ādīnām iva Raghu|rāja|ḍimbhānām anubhāvaḥ. param etad bravīmi:

Gir'|īśen' ārāddhaṃ
tri|jagad|avajaitraṃ, diviṣadām
upādāya jyotiḥ
Sarasi|ruha|janmā yad asṛjat,
Hṛṣīk'|ēśo yasminn
iṣur ajani, maurvī Phaṇi|patiḥ,
puras tisro lakṣyaṃ,
dhanur iti kim apy adbhutam idam.

JÁNAKA:

> Indra's bow has bestowed the task of protecting the three worlds onto the bows of some powerful kings, and has become a straight rainbow, without its bowstring attached.* Yet even these kings, when they saw Shiva's bow—although their arms seemed almost scented by the musk that their calluses resembled after stringing so many bows—were completely helpless.*

VISHVA·MITRA: My friend, Jánaka! Why do you lament your 3.115
fate when you have so much luck.

> You are very fortunate and we are here to witness that wedding feast. There are indeed eminent kings capable of bestowing safety upon the world, but Rama simply does not belong to the same category.

LÁKSHMANA: *(aside)* Why, my master has just said exactly what I was about to remark.

JÁNAKA: Venerable Vishva·mitra, it is true that just as the power of precious stones, mantras, medicinal herbs and the like is unimaginable, so is it with the power of the Raghu princes. But I must also tell you something.

> It was requested by Shiva, Lord of the Mountains, and it was fashioned by Brahma, out of the radiance of the gods put together, to conquer the three worlds. Vishnu has become its arrow, the Lord of the Serpents its string and the three demon-cities its target—this is the story of this miraculous bow.

3.120 ŚATĀNANDAḤ: āḥ kim anayā Pināka|praśasti|prapañcikayā? tad etat Kauśikam eva pramāṇayanto bahu|manyāmahe. api ca, kim a|śakyaṃ Rāma|bhadrasya?

utpādayan kam api kauṇapa|koṭi|homam,
tejo|hutāśana|samindhana|sāmidhenīm
yas Tāḍakām akṛta bāla|sakhaiḥ pṛṣatkair,
īṣaj|jayaḥ sphuṭam anena Daś'|ānano 'pi.

nepathy'|ârdha|praviṣṭaḥ PURUṢAḤ.

PURUṢAḤ: deva, Daś'|ānana|purohitaḥ Śauṣkalo nāma ma-hā|rājaṃ didṛkṣate.

ŚATĀNANDAḤ: *(s'|ôdvegam.)* āḥ! āgacchatu.

3.125 PURUṢO *niṣkrāntaḥ.*

RĀMAḤ: *(sa|vyayaṃ, jan'|ântikam)* vatsa Lakṣmaṇa, katham antarito 'yam anena dur|ātmanā rākṣasena Kām'|āri|kār-muka|paricaryā|mah"|ôtsavaḥ?

LAKṢMAṆAḤ: na kevalam ayam... *(ity ardh'|ôktau hasati.)*

RĀMAḤ *sa|praṇaya|roṣa|smitaṃ tam apāṅgena paśyati.*

praviśya.

3.130 ŚAUṢKALAḤ: *(pratyekam avalokya, ātma|gatam)* katham, atr' âiva Janaka|Śatānandābhyāṃ puras|kṛto viśveṣām as-mākam a|mitro Viśvāmitraḥ. *(vicintya)* tiṣṭhatu. hatako 'yam. *(hastaṃ dakṣiṇena dṛṣṭvā)* aye, kāv etau kṣatriya| brahma|cāriṇau?

SHATÁNANDA: What is the point in praising Shiva's bow in such an elaborate way? I take Vishva·mitra's words as true, and respect him. Moreover, what could be impossible for Rama? 3.120

> He is preparing for a miraculous sacrifice of thousands of demons, for which, with the help of his childhood friends, his arrows, he has already used Tádaka as mantric fuel to kindle the fire of his power—he shall surely conquer even ten-headed Rávana easily.

From behind the scenes, a MAN *comes halfway onto the stage.*

MAN: Your Majesty, the sacrificial priest of ten-headed Rávana, Sháushkala, desires to see you.

SHATÁNANDA: *(with agitation)* Ah, let him enter.

The MAN *exits.* 3.125

RAMA: *(with alarm, aside to* LÁKSHMANA*)* My dear Lákshmana, how come this ill-willed demon is hindering the great festive adoration of Shiva's bow?

LÁKSHMANA: My brother, and not only this... *(He laughs in the middle of the sentence.)*

RAMA *casts a side glance in his direction, smiling with affection, but also with irritation.*

Then SHÁUSHKALA *enters.*

SHÁUSHKALA: *(looking at each of them, then aside)* Here is our archenemy, received by Jánaka and Shatánanda—Vishva·mitra.* *(reflecting)* Let this wretched one be here. *(looking to his right)* O, who are these two warriors doing their Vedic studentship? 3.130

puṇya|lakṣmīkayoḥ so 'yam anayor pratibhāsate
mauñjy|ādi|vyañjanaḥ śānto vīr'|ôpakaraṇo rasaḥ.

nisarg'|ôdagram idaṃ ca dāraka|dvayam.

pārśve trayāṇām eteṣām
ṛk|sāma|yajuṣām iva,
rūpābhyāṃ vidhi|mantrābhyām
atharv" êva pradīpyate.

(vimṛśya) nūnaṃ sa eṣa Lakṣmaṇa|dvitīyo Rāma|hatakaḥ, Kauśikam ṛṣim anuplavamāno Mithilām upasthitaḥ. *(sa|krodha|śokam)* hā, vatse Suketu|kula|nandini Tāḍake! katham īdṛśān manuṣya|ḍimbhāt tādṛśo daiva|dur|vipākas te saṃvṛttaḥ. kaṣṭam, Anaraṇya|vaṃśa|janmanaḥ kṣatriya|vaṭor an|ātma|veditā.

3.135 Sund'|âsur'|êndra|suta|śoṇita|śīdhu|pāna|
dur|matta|mārgaṇa|nir|argala|vīra|garvaḥ
drohaṃ cakāra Daśa|kaṇṭha|kuṭumbake 'pi;
so 'yaṃ baṭuḥ Kuśika|nandana|yajña|bandhuḥ.

bhavatu. draṣṭavyam asya bhuja|śauṇḍīryam. *(upasṛtya, prakāśam)* api sukhino yūyaṃ Janaka|miśrāḥ?

JANAKAḤ: sv|āgataṃ Paulastya|purohitasya. ita āsyatām.

ŚAUṢKALAS *tathā karoti.*

> They possess both purity and royal fortune, and it is not only the heroic sentiment they suggest but, with their sacred threads and other holy attributes, also the sentiment of tranquility.

These two princes are powerful by nature.

> They are distinguished next to the three sages by their appearance, just as the Atharvaveda is distinguished by its rites and mantras compared with the Rig-, Sama- and Yajur-vedas.*

(reflecting) Ah, this is that wretched Rama, who, together with Lákshmana, has followed Vishva·mitra all the way to Míthila. *(with anger and grief)* Ah, my dear Tádaka, Sukétu's beloved daughter! How could it happen that a human child like this brought such great misfortune upon you! Alas, this young warrior born in the family of Anaránya* overestimates himself.

> His heroic pride remained unchallenged as his arrow got intoxicated by drinking the blood* of the demon king's, Sunda's, son. Thus, he offended the whole race of ten-headed Rávana. This is he, that child who helped Vishva·mitra to complete his sacrifice. 3.135

All right, let us see how powerful his arms are. *(approaching them, aloud)* Are you well, venerable Jánaka?

JÁNAKA: We welcome Rávana's royal priest. Pray be seated.

SHÁUSHKALA *does so.*

JANAKAḤ: api kuśalaṃ te rājño Rāvaṇasya? atha vā,

3.140 vipadāṃ pratikartāro yasy' ôpāyair atharvabhiḥ
tvādṛśāḥ santi, kiṃ tasya kalyāṇam anuyujyate?

ŚAUṢKALAḤ: *(vihasya)* śrotriya Sīradhvaja, pratyakariṣyām' âiva vayaṃ, yadi sva|bhuja|daṇḍa|maṇḍalī|mattavāraṇī|valayit'|ôraḥ|prāsāda|su|sthita|catur|daśa|bhuvana|lakṣmī|mah"|ântaḥ|pure Laṅkā|patau kim api pratikāryam abhaviṣyat. paśya,

yac|ceṣṭāḥ samanīka|sīmani pari-
trastaḥ parāñcann api
pratyakṣī|kurute Sahasra|nayanaḥ
pṛṣṭh'|ôdbhavair akṣibhiḥ,
cakre vartma ca nāga|loka|jayinīṃ
yātrām iva prastuvan
yaḥ Kailāsam udasya, kīdṛśam upā-
dānaṃ tu tasy' āpadām?

LAKṢMAṆAḤ: *(s'|âmarṣaṃ, jan'|ântikam)* ārya, katham asau sahasra|bhuj'|Ârjuna|Vālibhyām avalīḍha|śaurya|sāro dur|ātmā Rāvaṇaḥ prastūyate?

RĀMAḤ: vatsa, mā m" âivam. mahānto hi tādṛśāḥ. kiṃ ca.

JÁNAKA: Is your king, Rávana, in good health? Or, I should say,

> Why should we inquire about the well-being of someone for whom people like you shall remedy any bad incident with Atharvavedic mantras? 3.140

SHÁUSHKALA: *(smiling)* Learned Jánaka, we would indeed act if there was anything to remedy for the benefit of the King of Lanka. But he keeps the Goddess of the Fortune of the Fourteen Worlds in well-being in the large harem of his heart inside the palace of his bosom, which is surrounded by the fence of his many colossal arms. You see,

> At the climax of the battle, his heroism was witnessed by the eyes on the back of the thousand-eyed Indra, although he was about to escape, trembling with fear. And, as if making an expedition to conquer the underworld of serpents, Rávana created a downward path by raising Mount Kailása. What could cause him distress?

LÁKSHMANA: *(in anger, aside to* RAMA*)* My brother, why is ill-willed Rávana, whose heroic pride has been shattered to pieces* by the thousand-armed Árjuna Kartavírya as well as by Vali, being praised?

RAMA: My dear Lákshmana, do not say such a thing, for heroes like him do have grandeur.

3.145 syātāṃ nāma Kap'|îndra|Hehaya|patī
tasy' âvagāḍh'|ântara|
sthemānau, Daśa|kaṃdharasya mahatī
skandha|pratiṣṭhā punaḥ.
sadyaḥ pāṭita|kaṇṭha|kīkasa|kaṇ'|ā-
kīrṇāṃ yad|aṃsa|sthalīṃ
sven' êbh'|âjina|pallavena muditaḥ
prāsphoṭayad Dhūr|jaṭiḥ.

api ca,

Maghonas tad ghoraṃ
kuliśam alasī|kṛtya samare,
bhunakti svā|rājyaṃ
tri|bhuvana|bhaṭo 'yaṃ Daśa|mukhaḥ;
Śriyo nānā|sthāna|
bhramaṇa|ramaṇīyāṃ capalatām
avacchidya, svasminn
api bhuja|vane vāsayati yaḥ.

ŚATĀNANDAḤ: *(*ŚAUṢKALAM *prati)* brahman, satyam ayam īdṛśo rākṣasa|rājaḥ.

ŚAUṢKALAḤ: rāja'|rṣe Janaka,

3.150 saṃtuṣṭe tisṛṇāṃ purām api ripau
kaṇḍūla|dor|maṇḍala|
krīḍā|kṛtta|punaḥ|prarūḍha|śiraso
vīrasya lipsor varam,
yācñā|dainya|parāñci yasya kalahā-
yante mithas «tvaṃ vṛṇu!
tvaṃ vṛṇv!» ity abhito mukhāni sa Daśa-
grīvaḥ kathaṃ kathyatām?

It is true that the monkey-king, Vali, and Árjuna Kartavírya have deeper inner power and stamina than him, but ten-headed Rávana has some special force in his shoulders. For when he cut his own heads off, and his shoulders were covered with the particles of his bones, then Shiva, being contented, dusted those particles off immediately, with the edge of his own elephant-skin attire. 3.145

Moreover,

He has paralyzed Indra's frightening thunderbolt in a battle and is now enjoying the kingdom of heaven, that conqueror of the three worlds, ten-headed Rávana. And he also disciplined the Goddess of Good Fortune, who, charmingly fickle, had been wandering in various places—she is now kept in the forest of Rávana's arms.

SHATÁNANDA: *(to* SHÁUSHKALA*)* Brahmin, the demon king is indeed as you describe him.

SHÁUSHKALA: Royal sage, Jánaka,

When Shiva, although he was the Enemy of the Three Demon Cities, was propitiated by Rávana, who, hoping for a boon, playfully cut off his own heads with his arms, eager to offer them, his heads grew out again. But then, ashamed at the idea of begging, they turned away and started quarreling with each other on all sides, saying, "You should choose a boon, you should choose." Now, how would it be possible to describe such a hero? 3.150

so 'pi,

kanyām a|yoni|janmānaṃ varītuṃ prajighāya mām
purodhasā Gautamena guptasya bhavato gṛhān.

VIŚVĀMITRAḤ: sakhe Sīradhvaja, paśya paśya! Pināka|darśan'|ôllāsikā|visaṃsthula|citta|vṛttir iva vatso Rāma|bhadraḥ.

JANAKAḤ: *(vihasya)*

3.155 kim etad eva bhagavann abhidhīye punastarām?
Ikṣvākavo Videhāś ca paravantas tvayā vayam.

ŚAUṢKALAḤ: bho Sīradhvaja, kim idam asmākam ākāśa|vacanam? uta duṣ|pariccheda ev' âyam artho, yad uttaram api na pratipadyase?

dātavy" êyam avaśyam eva duhitā
kasmai cid; enām asau
dor|līlā|masṛṇī|kṛta|tri|bhuvano
Laṅkā|patir yācate.
tat kiṃ mūḍhavad īkṣase? nanu kathā|
goṣṭhīṣu śaṃsanti nas
tvad|vṛttāni paro|rajāṃsi munayaḥ
prācyā Marīcy|ādayaḥ.

ŚATĀNANDAḤ: brahman, cirāya dattam eva uttaram asmābhiḥ.

ŚAUṢKALAḤ: hanta, rāja|putrī|samarpaṇād anyat kīdṛśaṃ tat?

And he, Rávana himself,

> Has sent me to ask for the girl who was not born from a womb, Sita, for him to marry; so here I am to see you in your home, where you are well protected by your sacrificial priest, Shatánanda.

VISHVA·MITRA: My friend, Jánaka, look. It seems that our dear Rama's mind cannot concentrate on anything else; it is so eager to see Shiva's bow, the Pináka.

JÁNAKA: *(smiling)*

> Venerable Vishva·mitra, I do not need to be reminded of the same thing again and again. The Ikshvákus and we, the Videhas, both obey your commands. 3.155

SHÁUSHKALA: Jánaka, am I talking to the air, then? Or is the matter I have raised so difficult to decide that you cannot give an answer? Look,

> Your daughter must be given to someone, and the King of Lanka, whose arms easily forced the three worlds to obey him, is asking for her hand. So why are you staring like an idiot? In our conversations, the old sages like Maríchi always praise your virtuous deeds...

SHATÁNANDA: Brahmin, we gave you our reply long ago.

SHÁUSHKALA: Ah, what else is it if not the giving of the princess?

3.160 ŚATĀNANDAḤ: śṛṇu.

śāṃbhavaṃ cāpam āropya yo 'smān ānandayiṣyati,
pūrṇa|pātram iyaṃ tasmai Maithilī kalpayiṣyate.

ŚAUṢKALAḤ: śāntaṃ pāpaṃ, śāntaṃ pāpam. ahaha, yuṣmākam apy amūny akṣarāṇi.

ten' âṅgulī|śata|nighṛṣṭa|Kubera|śaila|
kaṇṭh'|ôkta|doḥ|kuliśa|kandala|vikrameṇa
māheśvareṇa mahatā Daśa|kandhareṇa
karm' êdam īdṛśam an|āryam api kriyeta?

ŚATĀNANDAḤ: *(vihasya)* brahman,

3.165 ayaṃ mahā|kṣatriya|gotra|janmā
dṛḍha|pratijño Janak'|âdhirājaḥ.
na cāpam āropayitā Daś'|āsyas.
tvam eva jānāsi yad uttaraṃ naḥ.

ŚAUṢKALAḤ: *(s'|âmarṣam)*

māheśvaro Daśa|grīvaḥ, kṣudrāś c' ânye mahī|bhujaḥ.
Pināk'|āropaṇaṃ śulkam. hā, Sīte, kiṃ bhaviṣyasi?

ŚATĀNANDAḤ: *(sa|roṣa|vyatham)* brahman, evam anena dhanuṣā kim api vinay'|ādhikārikam adhyāpyate, yad adya paraṃ māheśvaras te Rāvaṇo 'pi saṃvṛttaḥ.

SHATÁNANDA: Listen, 3.160

He who shall delight us by stringing Shiva's bow
shall receive Sita as a champion receives his cup.*

SHÁUSHKALA: God forbid, you talk about the same conditions for us!

Even Mount Kailása eulogized the courage of the thunderbolt-like arms of great Rávana in the fight, although his hundred fingers had uprooted it. But our ten-headed hero is a devotee of Shiva, so how could he perform such a base act as to string his master's bow?

SHATÁNANDA: *(smiling)* Brahmin,

King Jánaka was born in a family of great warriors 3.165
and he cannot break his promise. Ten-headed Rávana will not string that bow, so you know exactly our reply to you.

SHÁUSHKALA: *(angrily)*

Ten-headed Rávana is a devotee of Shiva, the other kings are despicable, and the bride-price is the stringing of Shiva's bow—poor Sita, what will become of you?

SHATÁNANDA: *(with anger and agitation)* Brahmin, thus this bow seems to have taught you a good lesson on how to behave, for from now on even your Rávana is a devotee of Shiva.

Śambhor ādhāram acalam utkṣeptuṃ bhuja|kautukī
māheśvaro dhanuḥ kraṣṭum, aho, te Daśa|kandharaḥ.

3.170 ŚAUṢKALA/*varjam anye smayante.*

ŚATĀNANDAḤ: *(sa|roṣ'|âvahittham)* Rāma|bhadra,

tad etad āropaya cāpam Īśa|
prakoṣṭha|bhasma|pratirūṣita|jyam.
śaury'|ôṣma|bhājāṃ bhajatāṃ mukhāni
sva|bāhu|maurvī|kiṇa|kālik" âiva.

ŚAUṢKALAḤ: *(sa|krodham)* are, re Śatānanda, kim udbhrānto 'si, yad evam asmad|agre mahā|rājam Paulastyam adhikṣipasi? kathaṃ, te māṇikya|parihāṇena gairika|parigrahaḥ, yad evaṃ Daśa|grīvam avamanyamānasya te manuṣya|pote 'nurāgaḥ? yadi vā, bhavantaṃ Gautamam apahāya duli|cakṣuṣi Sahasr'|âkṣe bhavato mātur Ahalyāyāḥ.

ŚATĀNANDAḤ: *(sa|roṣa|hāsam)* kim āttha, re, kim āttha asmad|agra iti?

3.175 VIŚVĀMITRAḤ: *(sa|praṇaya|roṣam iva)* vatsa Gautama, virama śuṣka|kalahāt. atithir ayam asmākam upādhyāyo Daśa|kandharasya. *(vyathamānau* RĀMA|LAKṢMAṆAU *ca dṛṣṭvā, vihasya)* vatsa Rāma|bhadra, dhanur|grah'|ôpasarpaṇam abhyanujānāti te Janak'|ânvaya|purodhāḥ.

His arms were happy to uproot the mountain that is Shiva's home, but today, when it comes to stringing the bow, he has become a devotee of Shiva, that ten-headed Rávana of yours.

All are smiling except SHÁUSHKALA. 3.170

SHATÁNANDA: *(concealing his anger)* My dear Rama,

Bend this bow, whose string has been smeared with the ashes fallen from Shiva's forearm, and may the faces of those kings who burn with heroic pride get charred with envy to become like the calluses on their arms, blackened by their bowstrings.*

SHÁUSHKALA: *(with anger)* Hey, Shatánanda, have you gone mad, the way you are insulting King Rávana in front of us? Why, you reject ruby to accept red chalk when you despise ten-headed Rávana and are attached to a human child. Well, of course, your mother, Ahálya, too, left the venerable sage Gáutama to love Indra, who is dotted with his thousand eyes like a female tortoise with plates...

SHATÁNANDA: *(smiling with anger)* What are you saying? What are you saying right before us?

VISHVA·MITRA: *(as if angry out of affection)* My dear Shatánanda, do not quarrel pointlessly. This preceptor of ten-headed Rávana is our guest. *(seeing that* RAMA *and* LÁKSHMANA *are quite agitated, then smiling)* My Rama, Jánaka's family priest commands you to go and string the bow. 3.175

RĀMAḤ: yad ādiśanti guravaḥ.

iti sa|vinaya|lajjā|kautukaṃ parikramya LAKṢMAṆENA *saha niṣkrāntaḥ.*

ŚAUṢKALAḤ: rāja'|rṣe Sīradhvaja, dhanyo 'si. purā khalu param'|ēśvara|paricary"|âpadāne nikṛtteṣu navasu mūrdhasu,

varaṃ tādṛk karm'|âd-
bhuta|sadṛśam a|prekṣya kim api
prarohad|vailakṣyaṃ
Pura|vijayino yena dadṛśe,
tad unmārṣṭuṃ yena
tri|bhuvanam api prārthitam idaṃ,
tad eva tvayy arthī
bhavati daśamaṃ Rāvaṇa|mukham.

3.180 ŚATĀNANDAḤ: *(utthāya, nepathy'|âvalokitakena sa|harṣ'|âdbhutam.)* paśyantu bhavantaḥ!

yasminn eka|dhanuṣmato bhagavataḥ
khaṭvāṅga|pāṇer asāv
ākṛṣṭo guṇatāṃ gato 'py ahi|patiḥ
karṇ'|âvataṃsāyate,
unmuktaś ca pur" êva bhūṣaṇa|padaṃ
yāti prakoṣṭh'|ântare. . .

JANAKA *autsukyaṃ nāṭayati.*

ŚATĀNANDAḤ:

Kākutsthena tad eva Bhārgava|guroḥ
kodaṇḍam ākṛṣyate.

RAMA: As my master commands.

Thus he goes around the stage, showing politeness, bashfulness and eagerness, then exits with LÁKSHMANA.

SHÁUSHKALA: Royal sage, Jánaka, you are very fortunate. Long ago, after Rávana had cut his nine heads to worship Shiva in a noble way,

> There remained one, which saw that Shiva felt increasingly ashamed for not finding a reward to match this miraculous act; then it asked for the three worlds only to relieve the Demon-Killer's embarrassment. It is this tenth head of Rávana which is making a request to you now.

SHATÁNANDA: *(stands up, looks toward the rear stage and then, with delight and surprise)* Please look over there, 3.180

> In the bow of that unrivaled archer, the skull-staff-carrying Shiva, the Snake King, although playing the role of the bowstring, used to adorn the Lord's ear when it was pulled by Him as far as His ears. Then, when the arrow was released, it used to become an ornament of the god's forearm again. That very bow... *

JÁNAKA *shows his restlessness.*

SHATÁNANDA:

> That very bow of the Lord who taught archery to Párashu·rama is now strung by Rama.

3.185 *nepathye kalakalaḥ. sarve s'|ātaṅkaṃ paśyanti. punar* NEPATHYE

rundhann aṣṭa Videhḥ śrutīr, mukharayann
aṣṭau diśaḥ, kroḍayan
mūrtīr aṣṭa Mah"|ēśvarasya, dalayann
aṣṭau kula|kṣmābhṛtaḥ,
tāny akṣṇā badhirāṇi pannaga|kulāny
aṣṭau ca saṃpādayann,
unmīlaty ayam ārya|dor|bala|dalat|
kodaṇḍa|kolāhalaḥ.

JANAKAḤ: *(sa|harṣa|viṣād'|âdbhutam)* katham, bhagnam api!

ŚATĀNANDAḤ:

Vaidehī|kara|bandha|maṅgala|yajuḥ|
s'|ûktaṃ dvi|jānāṃ mukhe,
nārīṇāṃ ca kapola|kandala|tale
śreyān ulūlu|dhvaniḥ.
peṣṭuṃ ca dviṣatām upaśruti|śataṃ
madhye|nabho jṛmbhate
Rāma|kṣuṇṇa|Mah"|ôkṣa|lāñchana|dhanur|
dambholi|janmā ravaḥ.

3.190 ŚAUṢKALAḤ: *(sa|viṣād'|âdbhutam, ātma|gatam)* aho, kṣatriya|sphuliṅgasya dur|ātmanaḥ sarva|karmīṇam ūṣmāyitam.

JANAKAḤ: *(sa|harṣaṃ pādayor nipatya)* bhagavan Kuśika|nandana,

iyam ātma|guṇen' âiva krītā Rāmeṇa Maithilī.
sva|gṛha|vyavahārāya Lakṣmaṇāy' Ōrmil" âstu naḥ.

Tumult behind the scenes. All are looking worried. Then, again from BEHIND THE SCENES. 3.185

Deafening Brahma's eight ears,* making the eight directions resound, pervading the eight forms of Shiva,* shattering to pieces the eight great mountains of the world, making the eight snake-kings deaf by blinding them,* the bow produces an overwhelming noise as it is being broken by the strong arms of my noble brother.

JÁNAKA: *(delighted, then sad but impressed)* How can it be even broken?

SHATÁNANDA:

In the mouths of our priests, the mantra-hymns resound on the auspicious occasion of Sita's wedding, and women are making the pleasant sound *ululu* in the hollow of their cheeks.* To destroy the enemies, a roaring comes forth, echoed in the sky to reach hundreds of ears—the sound of the bull-riding Shiva's thunderbolt-like bow, as it has just been broken by Rama.*

SHÁUSHKALA: *(unhappy and surprised, aside)* Ah, this ill-willed sparkle of a warrior has generated enough energy to perform any task. 3.190

JÁNAKA: *(delighted, falling on his knees)* Venerable Vishva·mitra,

Rama has bought Sita with his own merit; now let us give Úrmila to Lákshmana, to fulfill our duty as a father.*

VIŚVĀMITRAḤ: *(sa|smitam)* sakhe Sīradhvaja, yad abhirucitam bhavate.

ŚATĀNANDAḤ: (JANAKASYA *karṇe evam ev' êti kathayitvā)* bhagavan Kauśika, mam' âpi Candra|śekhara|śar'|âsan'|āropaṇa|prathama|priya|vādino 'dya pāritoṣikaṃ dhārayasi.

3.195 VIŚVĀMITRAḤ: *(vihasya)* vatsa, dīyate. kim abhipraiṣi?

ŚATĀNANDAḤ: Kuśadhvaja|duhitṛbhyāṃ Māṇḍavī|Śrutakīrtibhyām Bharata|Śatrughnāv abhyarthaye.

VIŚVĀMITRAḤ: evam astu. (ŚATĀNANDAṂ *haste gṛhītvā, sa|smitam)* vatsa, sarvam asmābhir vidhātavyam. āgamayasva tāvad Daśaratham.

JANAKAḤ: tarhi prahīyatām bhagavān Āṅgirasaḥ priya|suhṛdam Uttara|kosal'|ēśvaram ānetum.

VIŚVĀMITRAḤ: evam astu.

3.200 ŚATĀNANDAḤ: *(utthāya)* bhagavan, kim anyad asti vācikam?

VIŚVĀMITRAḤ: vatsa, nisṛṣṭ'|ârtho 'si. gamyatām.

ŚATĀNANDO *niṣkrāntaḥ.*

VIŚVĀMITRAḤ: *(harṣaṃ nāṭayan, ātma|gatam)*

dor|līlā|dalit'|Êndu|śekhara|dhanur|
    vyākhyāta|vikrāntinā
  Kākutsthena kṛto Videha|nṛpatis
    tīrṇa|pratijñā|bharaḥ.
paśyāmaś ca suhṛd|gṛhān nava|nav'|ôn-

VISHVA·MITRA: *(smiling)* My friend Jánaka, whatever pleases you. . .

SHATÁNANDA: *(after saying something into* JÁNAKA*'s ear)* Venerable Vishva·mitra, I was the first to announce the good news that Shiva's bow had been strung, so you owe me a gift.

VISHVA·MITRA: *(smiling)* It shall be given, what is your wish? 3.195

SHATÁNANDA: I would like Bharata and Shatrúghna to marry Kusha·dhvaja's daughters, Mándavi and Shruta·kirti.

VISHVA·MITRA: Let it be so. *(taking* SHATÁNANDA*'s hand, smiling)* My friend, we should make all the arrangements. Please do bring Dasha·ratha here.

JÁNAKA: Then let us send Shatánanda for our dear friend, Dasha·ratha, King of Úttara·kósala.

VISHVA·MITRA: Let it be so.

SHATÁNANDA: *(stands up)* Venerable sage, is there any other 3.200
message to take?

VISHVA·MITRA: My friend, this is all you need to do, you may go now.

SHATÁNANDA *exits.*

VISHVA·MITRA: *(showing his delight, aside)*

> Shiva's bow, broken so easily by Rama's arms, has amply showed the valor of this descendant of Kakútstha, who thus also enabled Jánaka, the King of Vidéha, to keep his promise. Now let us see our friends' houses as they are being prepared for the wedding feast.* Today, our blessings bear their

mīlad|vivāh'|ôtsavān
Aikṣvākeṣu ca Maithileṣu ca phalanty
asmākam ady' āśiṣaḥ.

3.205 ŚAUṢKALAḤ: *(vailakṣya|roṣābhyāṃ smayamānaḥ)* bho Sīradhvaja, puruṣa|prakarṣ'|ādhāne hi vidyā|vṛddha|saṃyogād bahir|aṅgāni vayāṃsi, yad anayā prahīṇa|labdha|kanyayā yauna|saṃbandh'|ôpasthitaṃ Pulastya|kulam upekṣamāṇo varṣīyān api komala|prajño 'si. *(munim prati.)* ṛṣe Kauśika, n' âdy' âpi kiṃ cid atikrāmati. tav' âpi Laṅkā|patau Tāḍakā|vadh'|âparādham apamārṣṭum ayam eva śreyān avasaraḥ.

KAUŚIKAS *tatr' âvajñāṃ nāṭayati.*

JANAKAḤ: bhagavan, ehi. svayam upetya Rāma|bhadra|vadana|candra|candrikā|pravāhe nirvāpayāmi tāvad alīka|dhanur|dhara|sahasra|prārthyamāna|Maithilī|kadarthitam ātmānam. na hi mihira|marīci|paricaya|pacelimasya hima|kara|bimba|saṃpātād aparo 'pi kaś cid a|gadaṅ|kāraḥ kairav'|ākarasya.

ity utthāya parikrāmataḥ.

ŚAUṢKALAḤ: *(sa|khedam ākāśe)* hā tapasvini Sīte, hat" âsi. Paulastya|prārthit" âpi vicāryase.

3.210 tri|bhuvana|vijaya|śriyaḥ sa|patnīṃ
janayatu ko bhavatīm an|ātma|tantrām?
sva|janam api na te nirūpayāmaḥ;
kim api vidārya bhuvaṃ vinirgat" âsi.

fruit for the benefit of everyone in the house of Ikshváku and in Míthila.

SHÁUSHKALA: *(smiling, ashamed and angry)* Jánaka, when it comes to judging whether someone is superior, age counts less than accumulated knowledge. You looked down upon Rávana when he wanted to marry the girl who had been found abandoned in the furrow—though you are an elderly person, you have little intelligence. *(toward the sage)* Vishva·mitra, it is still not too late now; you still have an excellent opportunity before the King of Lanka to atone for your sin of having killed Tádaka. 3.205

VISHVA·MITRA *shows his comtempt.*

JÁNAKA: Venerable sage, please come. I am about to go myself to delight my heart, which has been pained by the innumerable false archers who had asked for Sita, in the cooling light of the moon-like face of our dear Rama. For nothing heals the white night-lotuses scorched by the touch of sunbeams better than the contact with the moon.

Thus they stand up and go around the stage.

SHÁUSHKALA: *(with pain, in the air)* O poor Sita, how miserable you are! Although Rávana himself has asked you to marry him, your fate still remains undecided.

Who shall make you, a person dependent on others, a rival of the Goddess of Fortune of the Three Worlds? We cannot even know who your relatives are, you have come to this world by miraculously splitting up the surface of the earth. 3.210

(sa|roṣaṃ JANAKAṂ *prati)*

paurāṇībhir an|eka|vikrama|kathā|
gāthābhir arthāpitās
te vīrasya jayanti rākṣasa|pater
doḥ|stambha|dambholayaḥ,
yān utprekṣya viśoṣayan mada|mayaṃ
maireyam Airāvaṇaḥ
bhūṣā|sragbhir abhūd amartya|madhupa|
śreṇīṣu sādhāraṇaḥ.

teṣu satsu,

vṛthā saj|jana|saṃbandha|sat|kāreṇ' âsi vañcitaḥ
Paulastya|hasta|vartinyā Sītayā tu bhaviṣyate.

3.215 *(s'|ākṣepaṃ nepathy'|âbhimukham avalokya)*

samantād uttālaiḥ
sura|sahacarī|cāmara|marut|
taraṅgair unmīlad|
bhuja|parigha|saurabhya|śucinā
svayaṃ Paulastyena
tri|bhuvana|bhujā cetasi kṛtām,
are Rāma, tvaṃ mā
Janaka|nṛpa|putrīm upayathā.

(sa|vimarśam ātma|gatam) aho, gambhīram idam upasthitaṃ vastu. tan mantriṇaṃ Mālyavantam eva puras|kṛtya Laṅk"|ēśvarasya nivedayāmi.

iti niṣkrāntāḥ sarve.

(angrily, to JÁNAKA*)*

The thunderbolt-like strong arms of the king of demons have been sung by bards in various tales about his heroic deeds—and they shall remain victorious! Seeing these arms, Indra's elephant witnessed its sweet ichor dry up.* Then, with only the flower decorations left on it, it became a common creature for the heavenly bees.*

Since Rávana's arms have this power,

It does not matter that you have been tricked out of the honorable alliance with a good person. You shall see that Sita will end up in Rávana's hands.

(looking toward the rear of the stage, with accusation) 3.215

The white fame* of Rávana's club-like arms are spread by the upward gusts of wind as the goddesses fan him everywhere with yak tails; this lord of the three worlds himself wants King Jánaka's daughter, so, Rama, you shall not marry her!

(reflecting, aside) This matter has become very serious. So first I shall talk to our minister, Mályavan, and then I must go and inform the King of Lanka.

All exit.

PRELUDE TO ACT IV
SANSKRIT-PRAKRIT PRELUDE

tataḥ praviśati MĀLYAVĀN.

MĀLYAVĀN: *(jṛmbhamāṇaś cakṣuṣī parimṛjya)* aye, vibhāta|prāy" âiva rajanī. tathā hi,

stok'|ônnidra|Nidāgha|dīdhiti|mahas|
tandrālu|candr'|ātapās
tyāyante kakubho rathāṅga|gṛhiṇī|
gārhasthya|garhā|bhidaḥ.
ady' âpi sva|kulāya|śākhi|śirasi
sthitvā ruvanto muhus
tūṣṇīṃ pratyabhijānate bali|bhujaḥ
bhītāḥ sva|yūthya|svarān.

api ca,

4.5 prācīṃ vāsaka|sajjikām upagate
bhānau diśāṃ vallabhe,
paśy' âitā rucayaḥ pataṅga|dṛṣadām
āgneya|nāḍiṃ|dhamāḥ
lokasya kṣaṇadā|niraṅkuśa|rasau
saṃbhoga|nidr"|āgamau
koka|stoma|kumudvatī|vipinayor
nikṣepam ātanvate.

(sarvato nirūpya) hanta! samantād āmodamāna|paura|saṃbhogamayī khalv iyaṃ Daśa|grīvasya bhuj'|ârgala|paripālitā rājadhānī.

itaḥ paurastyāyāṃ
kakubhi vivṛṇoti krama|dalat|
tamisrā|marmāṇam
kiraṇa|kalikām Ambara|maṇiḥ.
ito niṣkrāmantī

MÁLYAVAN *enters.*

MÁLYAVAN: *(yawning and rubbing his eyes)* O, the night has almost turned into dawn:

While the moonbeams are exhausted by the heat of the sun, which is slowly waking up, the directions are becoming visible to put an end to the shelduck's cursing of domestic life.* And now the crows, staying in their nests on treetops, start crowing—but each time they get scared and keep silent again; thus do they recognize the voices of their own flock.

Furthermore,

When the sun, the beloved of all directions, comes to meet the East, who has been impatiently expecting him, then look, these rays, which kindle the fire in the veins of the sun-stones, transfer the joys and the sleep that people relished at night without disturbance onto the shelduck and the white night-lotuses.* 4.5

(looking in all directions) O, this capital protected by Rávana's strong arms is enjoyed by its happy citizens everywhere.

Here, in the eastern direction, the sun, jewel of the sky, unfolds its as yet tender rays, which slowly pierce the heart of the night. Here a maiden comes out to rub off the marks of the *mákara* design, originally drawn with musk on her own body but now imprinted on the chest of him who has just taught her pleasures.

nava|rati|guroḥ proñchati vadhūḥ
sva|kastūrī|pattr'|âṅ-
kura|makarikā|mudritam uraḥ.

api ca,

ayaṃ mṛdu mṛṇālinī|
vana|vilāsa|vaihāsikas
tviṣāṃ vitapate patiḥ;
sa|padi dṛśyamānā nijāḥ
stanau pulakayanti ca
utpala|dṛśāṃ priy'|ôraḥ|sthale
viparyayita|vṛttayo
ghusṛṇa|paṅka|pattr'|âṅkurāḥ.

4.10 itaś ca,

priya|vasater apayāntyo,
mithaḥ karambita|kar'|âmbu|janmānaḥ,
karaja|vraṇa|virala|stana|
pulakam amūḥ kim api vivadante.

(anyataś ca dṛṣṭvā) ito ramyataraṃ vartate:

prabhāte pṛcchantīr
anu|rahasa|vṛttaṃ sahacarīr,
nav'|ōḍhā na vrīḍā|
mukulita|mukh" îyaṃ sukhayati.
likhantīnāṃ pattr'|âṅ-
kuram a|niśam asyās tu kucayoś—
camat|kāro!—gūḍhaṃ
karaja|padam āsāṃ kathayati.

Moreover,

> Here is the Sun, the lord of lights, shining forth gently, becoming the clown to amuse the day-lotuses. And now the lotus-eyed women can see the designs they had drawn on their bodies in diluted kunkuma as printed the other way around on the chests of their lovers, a sight that makes the hair on their breasts stand on end.

And here, 4.10

> These women, coming back from the houses of their lovers, holding one another's lotus-like hands, are quarreling about something that has caused goosebumps on their breasts in between the nail marks. . . *

(looking elsewhere) And here is also something very delightful,

> At dawn, when her friends ask her about the secret happenings of the night, the newlywed bride, closing her mouth out of bashfulness, does not delight them with her reply. But when they draw the designs on her breasts without interruption, then—look what happens!—it is the nail marks there that tell her hidden secret to them.

(muhūrtam anudhyāya) aho! yataḥ prabhṛti Vaidehī|varaṇāya prahitena purodhasā kathyamānaṃ Kakutstha|kula|kumārasya tādṛśaṃ mānuṣyak'|âtiśayam aśṛṇavam, tataḥ prabhṛti kaṣṭāṃ daśām anubhavāmi. tathā hi,

4.15 tat tādṛśaṃ katham ud|eti manuṣya|loke
tejo 'dbhutaṃ? nirabhisaṃdhi na tāvad etat!
tāny eva c' âsya caritāni Daś'|ānanasya;
dhik, cintayā rajanir akṣiṣu naḥ prabhāti.

api ca,

śrutvā duḥ|śravam adbhutaṃ ca Mithilā|
vṛttāntam, antaḥ|patac|
cint"|âpahnava|sāvahittha|vadanas
tad|dig|vikīrṇa|smitaḥ,
helā|kṛṣṭa|sur'|âvarodha|ramaṇī|
sīmanta|saṃtānaka|
srag|vās'|ôjjvala|pāṇir apy avati māṃ
vatso na Laṅk"|ēśvaraḥ.

(vimṛśya, ākāśe.) ahaha, dāruṇ" êyam asmākaṃ cira|jīvitā.

prīte Vidhātari purā paribhūya martyān,
vavre 'nyato yad a|bhayaṃ sa bhavān ahaṃyuḥ.
tan marmaṇi spṛśati mām ati|mātram adya;
hā vatsa, śāntam, atha vā Daśa|kaṃdharo 'si.

(reflecting for a moment) Alas, ever since the priest who had been sent to ask for Sita's hand related to me that story of the prince of the Kakútstha dynasty, a story that surpasses anything that one could imagine of a human being, I have been suffering very much:

How can one have a miraculous power like this in the world of humans? It was surely not created without any reason... And the reason must be Rávana's misbehavior. It is this terrible anxiety which keeps my eyes wide open all night. 4.15

Moreover,

Having heard the bad news about the miracles that happened in the city of Míthila, he did not show his feeling on his ten faces, concealing the anxiety that fell upon his heart—he just smiled in that direction. Although his hands have become fragrant as he playfully pulled the hair of the maidens from the celestial harem, who were wearing tiaras of coral flowers, he still does not please me, my dear King of Lanka.*

(reflecting, then in the air) Alas, this long life of mine is very harsh.

Long ago, when he propitiated the Creator, then despising humans, our haughty lord chose the boon to be invincible to all except humans. Now—alas my young lord!—it is this story which disturbs my heart so much. But God forbid such thoughts, you are ten-headed Rávana.

4.20 *(sa|vimarśam.)* aho Maithilasya nṛpater a|kārya|jñatā.

Viśvāmitra|vaśī|kṛte hṛdi, vayaṃ
mā bhūma sambandhinas;
te dṛṣṭā na kathaṃ purāṇa|munayo
mānyāḥ Pulasty'|ādayaḥ?
jāmāt" âpi mah"|êndra|mauli|valabhī|
paryaṅka|ratn'|âṅkura|
jyotsnā|puṣṭa|nakh'|êndu|dīdhitir ayaṃ
n' âpekṣito Rāvaṇaḥ.

(puro 'valokya.) kathaṃ Mithilā|vṛttāntam upalabdhuṃ prahitā cirayati me vatsā Śūrpaṇakhā?

praviśya ŚŪRPAṆAKHĀ.

ŚŪRPAṆAKHĀ: *(sa|harṣam)* ⌜aṃho, somma|sundara|viāha|ṇevaccha|lacchī|vitthāria|kanti|ppa|bbhārāiṃ Rahu|ula|kumārāṇaṃ muha|puṇḍarīāiṃ pekkhantī, juucchieṇa vi māā|māṇusī|bhāveṇa, kaa|tthā mhi. aṃho, sā tārisī guṇāṇaṃ païiī, jaṃ vivakkha|hattha|paḍiā vi suhāvei.⌟

4.25 MĀLYAVĀN: *(dṛṣṭvā sa|sneham.)* katham, vatsā Śūrpaṇakhā! vatse, ayam aham. ito bhavatī.

(thoughtfully) Well, the King of Míthila did not know his duty. 4.20

His heart was under Vishva·mitra's control, so let us concede that he could not want us to be his relations. But how could he ignore the respected old sages, Pulástya and the others?* And he whose crescent-shaped toenails became more radiant as they were illuminated by the light of the pointed jewels in Indra's crown, which formed a royal resting couch for him,* he was not even considered to be a future son-in-law.

(looking ahead) Now, why is my dear Shurpa·nakha, whom I have sent to obtain some news from Míthila, delaying coming?

SHURPA·NAKHA *enters.*

SHURPA·NAKHA: *(happily)* When I saw the lotus-like faces of the Raghu princes, with their foreheads becoming more radiant with the richness of their soft and beautiful costumes worn for the wedding, then, although I had to put up the appearance of a human female—something rather disgusting for me—I was fully satisfied. Such is the nature of good qualities: they delight everybody, even if they happen to belong to one's enemy.

MÁLYAVAN: *(seeing her, with affection)* This is my dear Shurpa·nakha! Here I am—come over here, my child. 4.25

ŚŪRPAṆAKHĀ: ⌜kahaṃ, ettha evva aṭṭālaa|sihara|vaṭṭi|paggīve mādā|maho. amho, dū|siliṭṭhaā duṭṭha|kammāṇaṃ, jaṃ dāṇiṃ paāara|kiliṇṇa|loaṇo paḍikkhaṇa|jimbhiā|pasāria|muha|kuhara|diṭṭha|hiaa|ṭṭhia|kaṭhiṇa|kajja|bhāro aṇṇo via ko vi dīsaï. aha vā sāmaṇṇassa vi garīaṃso khu manti|bhāvo, viseseṇa uṇa sāhasa|ras'|ekka|vvavasāa|caṇḍa|cariassa amha sāmiṇo Rāvaṇassa. jāṇāmi maṃ evva paḍivālaanto ciṭṭhaï tti. jāva ṇaṃ uvasappāmi.⌟ *(sa/viṣādam upasṛtya)* ⌜ayya, vandāmi!⌟

MĀLYAVĀN: vatse, kalyāṇinī bhūyāḥ! ita āsyatām. api Bharata|Śatrughnābhyāṃ sah' âiva Vaideham upasthito Daśarathaḥ?

ŚŪRPAṆAKHĀ: *(upaviśya.)* ⌜ayya, Dasarahe āade kumārāṇaṃ godāṇa|maṃgale a saṃvutte, mae paviṭṭhaṃ Mihilā|ṇaaraṃ.⌟

MĀLYAVĀN: *(niḥśvasya.)* ati|prakāśo 'yam artho, yathā nirvṛtta|kara|grahaṇā Jānakī.

4.30 ŚŪRPAṆAKHĀ: ⌜aha iṃ.⌟

MĀLYAVĀN: *(vimṛśya.)* aho dur|ātmanaḥ kṣatriya|brāhmaṇasya Kuśika|vaṃśa|janmano dur|nāṭakam.

SHURPA·NAKHA: O, my grandfather* is up there, on the very top of a pointed tower. Alas, all his difficult duties have accumulated in an unfortunate way! His eyes are now exhausted because he is always awake, and, because he keeps opening his mouth when yawning every second, one can see the heavy burden he carries in his heart—he does not look like himself at all. Or, rather, one could say that it is a difficult task to be a minister even for an ordinary ruler, how much more so for our lord Rávana, whose only occupation is to do something reckless, terrifying everybody with what he does. I know my grandfather is waiting for me, so I shall approach him. *(approaching him)* Sir, I salute you.

MÁLYAVAN: My child, may you be prosperous. Pray be seated. Has Dasha·ratha gone to Míthila together with Bharata and Shatrúghna?

SHURPA·NAKHA: *(sits down)* Sir, it was when Dasha·ratha had already arrived and the ritual of tonsure* had been performed for the princes that I entered the city of Míthila.

MÁLYAVAN: *(sighing)* Then it is clear that Sita's marriage has been performed.

SHURPA·NAKHA: Of course. 4.30

MÁLYAVAN: *(reflecting)* This is the wicked arrangement of that ill-willed warrior-brahmin,* son of Kúshika, Vishva·mitra.

yajñ'|ôpaplava|śāntaye pariṇato
rājā sutaṃ yācitas;
taṃ c' ānīya vinīya c' āyudha|vidhau
te jaghnire rākṣasāḥ.
traiyakṣaṃ vidalayya kārmukam, atha
svī|kārya Sītām, ito
no vidmaḥ kuhanā|viṭena baṭunā
kiṃ tena kāriṣyate.

ŚŪRPAṆAKHĀ: ⌜ayya! evvaṃ ṇedaṃ. so tu mae bamhaṇo Vasiṭṭha|mah|esiṇo vi pura|phurando diṭṭho.⌟

MĀLYAVĀN: *(vihasya.)* vatse, tapobhir asya brāhmaṇ'|ādeśo 'pi sthānivad|bhāvena kṣatra|kāryaṃ na jahāti. kiṃ ca, svabhāva|madhuro 'pi Kākutstha|baṭur autpattikena brāhmeṇa brāhmaṇyena ca janmanā tri|jātakān muner adhīyann avarīṇa|śīlaḥ pariṇaṃsyate.

4.35 a|vinaya|bhuvām a|jñānānāṃ
śamāya bhavann api
prakṛti|kuṭilād vidy"|âbhyāsaḥ
khalatva|vivṛddhaye.
phaṇi|bhaya|bhṛtām ast' ûccheda|
kṣamas tamasām asau
viṣa|dhara|phaṇā|ratn'|āloko
bhayaṃ tu bhṛśāyate.

The old king was asked to give his son to him, in order to eliminate the impeders of his sacrifice; having taken the son, Vishva·mitra taught the science of arms to him and thus many a demon got killed. Then he made that child break the bow of the three-eyed Shiva and marry Sita. So now we do not know what that chap, that hypocrytical rogue, will make him do.

SHURPA·NAKHA: Sir, it is indeed so. I have seen that brahmin, Vishva·mitra, myself, when he rose up even against the great sage, Vasíshtha.

MÁLYAVAN: *(smiling)* My child, although he has become the equivalent of a brahmin through asceticism, he cannot give up acting like a warrior, because he still retains his original nature. Moreover, in addition to his natural birth and second birth as an initiate into Vedic studies, he had a third one when he got transformed into a brahmin: a thrice-born indeed.* Now, although this young Rama is sweet by nature, he did his studies with this thrice-born, and thus he is likely to have become corrupted.

Although the aim of learning is to destroy igno- 4.35
rance—ignorance being also at the root of bad conduct—if the teaching comes from someone whose nature is crooked it shall only increase wickedness. Although the light of a jewel may be able to destroy darkness together with the fear of snakes one experiences in the dark, it increases fear if it comes from the hood of a cobra.

bhavatu. kim atikrānt'|ôpavarṇanena? katham idānīṃ svayaṃ grahītum uttiṣṭhamāno rākṣasa|patiḥ pratikartavyaḥ syāt?

ŚŪRPAṆAKHĀ: ⌜ayya, ṇa khu bala|moḍiṃ pariharia ko vi aṇṇo uvāo takkīadi.⌟

MĀLYAVĀN: vatse, mā m" âivam. mahān doṣo hi tādṛśena dharma|vijayinā vīra|prakāṇḍena parigṛhītāyā Vaidehyāḥ prasahy' âpahāraḥ. paśya,

doḥ|stambha|dvaya|darpa|ḍambaram iti
  spaṣṭaṃ na vispandate
Vaidehī|kara|bandha|sūcanam iti
  prastauti na vrīḍayā.
ity ālocya kṛta|smitair munibhir ā-
  diṣṭena yena kṣaṇād
āttaṃ vanditam āñcitaṃ ca sahasā
  bhagnaṃ ca tādṛg dhanuḥ.

4.40 katham asmadīyaṃ niśā|cara|nātham ātatāyinam anujānīmaḥ?

ŚŪRPAṆAKHĀ: *(niḥśvasya.)* ⌜jaha ṇirūviaṃ mādā|maheṇa. aho, kālassa māha|ppaṃ, jaṃ dāṇiṃ ti|huaṇa|jaa|lacchī|līlā|vandī|āre mahā|rāe Rāvaṇe vi evvaṃ mantīaï.⌟

MĀLYAVĀN: kiṃ ca, vatse,

All right, enough of this description of the past. Now, how could we help the king of demons, who is intent upon taking Sita with him?

SHURPA·NAKHA: Sir, apart from using force against Rama, no other means can be devised.

MÁLYAVAN: My child, do not talk like this. It would be a great mistake to take away Sita by force, for she has been married to an outstanding hero, who won her with honest means. Look,

> He did not make a move in an unambiguous way, because he thought it would have been taken as boasting and showing off his colossal arms. He did not want to start it, because he was embarrassed that it would be understood as a sign that he wanted to marry Sita. Seeing this, the smiling sages commanded him to act, and thus he immediately took up that bow, worshipped it, and strung it, breaking it suddenly.

So how could we approve of our demon Lord's kidnapping 4.40
his wife?

SHURPA·NAKHA: *(with a sigh)* You are absolutely right, grandfather. How powerful time is, that now even our Maharaja Rávana, who easily imprisoned the Goddess of Good Fortune and Victory Over the Three Worlds, is spoken of in these terms.

MÁLYAVAN: And what is more, my child,

munir api gurur divy'|âstrāṇāṃ
babhūva; div'|âukasām
Ajagava|dhanur|bhaṅge tāvān,
aho, sa mah"|ôtsavaḥ.
Raghu|pati|guṇa|krītīm etām
avehi jagat|trayīṃ;
vipariṇamate daurjanyaṃ tu
prabhutva|padena naḥ.

ŚŪRPAṆAKHĀ: ⌜ko saṃdeho. tassiṃ vivāha|mah"|ûsave savvaṃ mae paccakkhī|kaaṃ.⌟

4.45 MĀLYAVĀN: tad evam eka|loṣṭa|vadhaḥ syāt. tathā hi, Mithilāṃ praviśya balād ākṛṣyamāṇe kalatre kathaṃ titikṣate Raghu|rāja|putraḥ? taṃ c' ôttiṣṭhamānaṃ paura|jāna|padāḥ prakṛtayo 'py anūttiṣṭheran, kim punar, aṅga|saṃbandhino bāndhavāḥ. yath" ôktam: «āraṇyo 'gnir iva duḥ|saha|duḥkh'|âmarṣajaṃ tejo vikramayati puruṣam, maṇḍalasya c' ânugrāhyo bhavat' îti.»

ŚŪRPAṆAKHĀ: *(dīrgham uṣṇaṃ ca niḥśvasya)* ⌜ayya, kiṃ dāṇiṃ juttaṃ?⌟

MĀLYAVĀN: śṛṇu vatse, kārya|jñ" âsi. asti van'|âukasāṃ mantrī Jāmbavān nāma. sa Mataṅg'|āśrama|vāstavyām upasṛtya Śramaṇāṃ nāma siddha|śabarīm abhyarthitavān, yathā: «asya Vālino vairāgyeṇa kṣīṇā lubdh'|âpacāritāḥ prakṛtayaḥ Kiṣkindhāyāṃ kumāraṃ Sugrīvam abhiṣekṣyamāṇāḥ sāmavāyikam aikṣvākaṃ Rāma|bhadram apekṣante.»

The sage Vishva·mitra himself taught him the divine weapons, and what a great feast the gods had when he broke Shiva's bow! So know this triple world to be won over by Rama with his qualities. And if we talk about our supremacy, it will be misinterpreted as wickedness.

SHURPA·NAKHA: This is the case, no doubt. I have witnessed all this myself at that great wedding feast.

MÁLYAVAN: And there would be a pure massacre of our army.* In other words, if we go to Míthila and take his wife by force, then could this Raghu prince tolerate that? And if he rises against us, then all his subjects from cities and the countryside will follow him, and even more would his relations and allies! As it is said: "if a king is ill-treated then the heat of anger and unbearable pain will make him fight bravely and he will be unstoppable like a forest fire; then he will be also supported by the circle of his neighboring kingdoms."* 4.45

SHURPA·NAKHA: *(heaving a deep sigh)* Sir, what would be the best to do, then?

MÁLYAVAN: Listen, my child, you understand the state of affairs. Now, there is a minister of the jungle beasts, who is called Jámbavan. He visited Shrámana, a woman from a mountain tribe, who has perfected herself in the obtainment of supernatural powers and now lives in sage Matánga's hermitage, and he addressed the following request to her: "the subjects of the kingdom of Kishkíndha are miserable because of the indifference of their king Vali, and they have become needy and humiliated. They

ŚŪRPAṆAKHĀ: ⌜kadhaṃ khattia|podo Vāli|ṇiggahe vi sahāo samikkhīaï? tado tado.⌟

MĀLYAVĀN: tataś ca, « ‹Ayodhyātaḥ Kaikeyyā Bharata|vārt"|āharaṇāya preṣitā Mantharā nāma vṛddha|dāsī kaṭhora-tara|taraṇi|kiraṇa|tāpa|vajra|jvāl"|âvalīḍha|jīvitā Mithilā|prāntare tiṣṭhat' îti› nidāgha|kiraṇ'|ânte|vāsī sa|tīrthyam ṛṣiṃ Yājñavalkyam upasthāya, saṃpraty eva nimeṣa|mātrān nivṛtto Hanūmān kathayati. atas tvam apy asmad|anurodhena Hanumad|avekṣita|sva|śarīrā para|pura|praveśa|vidyayā Mantharā|śarīram adhitiṣṭhantī Mithilām upetya pratyayitā saṃvidhānakam idaṃ Daśaratha|go|care kariṣyasi. itthaṃ|bhāvinā guru|nideśa|caryā|prasaṅgena paṅka|pāṣāṇa|taru|viṣama|kaṇṭaka|vyāla|bahulāṃ Daṇḍak'|âraṇyānīm anupraviṣṭaḥ sarvathā vaideśiko rāja|putraḥ kārya|gauravān niyatam eṣa Vāli|vadha|pūrvakeṇa pratīkāra|saṃdhinā Sugrīvam upagṛhṇīyād.» iti.

intend to consecrate Prince Sugríva as a king, and expect Rama of the Ikshváku dynasty to help them."

SHURPA·NAKHA: How could that warrior child be expected to help to defeat Vali? And then?

MÁLYAVAN: Then Jámbavan continued with the following words addressed to Shrámana: "Hánuman, who has just returned from Míthila in a second, after paying homage to the sage Yajnaválkya—since they had the same preceptor: the fiery-rayed Sun—says the following: 'from Ayódhya, Kaikéyi sent an old servant maid called Mánthara to learn the tidings of Bharata, but her life was taken by the piercing and flaming hot rays of the harsh sun, and she is now in an abandoned road leading to Míthila.' Therefore, following my instructions, and since you know how to enter someone else's body, you should take up residence in Mánthara's corpse, while Hánuman will look after your own body. Then go to Míthila, and when you have obtained everybody's trust there, convey our version of the story to Dasha·ratha. After this, Prince Rama will be obliged to act according to his elder's instructions as they were given to him, and will go to the Dándaka jungle, impassable with its marshes, rocks and trees, infested with hostile beings and beasts of prey. He will be a stranger there, and, because the task he has to perform will be important, he shall surely kill Vali to enter into an alliance of mutual help with Sugríva."

4.50 ŚŪRPAṆAKHĀ: *(sa|kautukam.)* ⌈ayya, kiṃ uṇa taṃ saṃvihāṇaaṃ?⌋

MĀLYAVĀN: *(karṇe)* evam iva. *(iti kathayati.)*

ŚŪRPAṆAKHĀ: *(hasantī)* ⌈aho, buḍḍha|ricchassa kuḍilaā kajja|kusalaā a!⌋

MĀLYAVĀN: tataś ca, «s" âpi śabara|yoginī Sugrīva|guṇ'|ânurāgeṇa sarvaṃ tath" êty urasī|kṛtya, tad" âiva Videh'|âbhimukhī prasthit" êti» me Jana|sthāna|nivāsibhir niśā|carair āgatya niveditam. tad amunā ca Jāmbavat|prayogeṇa phalavatā Virādha|prabhṛtibhir adhiṣṭhiteṣu Vindhya|giri|gahvareṣu viharataḥ su|karaṃ kalatr'|âpaharaṇam. asmadīyās tu māyāḥ sur'|âsura|prathama|lekhā|yodhasya Vibudha|pati|vitīrṇa|māyā|parihāra|mahā|mantra|dhāriṇo Daśarathasya samīpe na prabhavanti.

ŚŪRPAṆAKHĀ: *(sa|vicikitsam.)* ⌈ayya! uvaṇadassa evvaṃ karīadi?⌋

4.55 MĀLYAVĀN: *(vihasya)* sādhu, vatse. vṛddha|saṃvādinī te dṛṣṭiḥ. yad āhur: «yo hy upanatasya putra|dārān abhimanyate, tasy' ôdvignaṃ maṇḍalam a|bhāvāy' ôttiṣṭhate.»iti. kim punar, asmāsu n' âiṣa nisarga|tejasvī saṃśraya|vṛttim ātiṣṭhate.

SHURPA·NAKHA: *(with curiosity)* Sir, but what is Jámbavan's "version of the story"? 4.50

MÁLYAVAN: *(into her ears)* Like this... *(Thus he tells her.)*

SHURPA·NAKHA: *(laughing)* Look, how cunning and resourceful that old bear is!

MÁLYAVAN: And demons living in Jana·sthana in the Dándaka jungle have come and informed me that the woman from the tribe of mountaineers who had turned into an ascetic was so moved by Sugríva's qualities that she agreed to everything and left for Míthila immediately. Then, following Jámbavan's promising scheme, it will be easy to take away Rama's wife, while her husband is wandering about in the thick forests of the Vindhya mountain, inhabited by Virádha and other demons. Yet our tricks cannot deceive Dasha·ratha, for after he had fought in the first line in the battle of gods against demons, Lord Indra gave him a powerful *mantra* to use against any witchcraft.

SHURPA·NAKHA: *(with interest)* Sir, so is this what we would do once Rama comes to our forest and depends on our grace?

MÁLYAVAN: *(smiling)* Well observed, my child. Your insight is that of an elderly person. For it is also said: "he who covets the wives and children of a king who has become dependent will provoke the aggrieved country he has conquered to revolt with the intention to destroy him."* But this Rama, who is powerful by nature, will never really depend on us for shelter. 4.55

ŚŪRPAṆAKHĀ: ⌜aṇṇaṃ bhaṇāmi. avi evvaṃ karissaï Rāma|bhaddo?⌟

MĀLYAVĀN: kaḥ saṃśayaḥ? lok'|ôttaraṃ kim api rūpam unmīlayanto jagati rājy'|ôpabhogebhyo jugupsante mah"|ânubhāvāḥ.

ŚŪRPAṆAKHĀ: ⌜kiṃ ca, aṇṇaṃ vi aṇ|atth'|antaraṃ tattha havissadi tti takkemi.⌟

MĀLYAVĀN: *(sa|harṣam.)* kīdṛśaṃ tat?

4.60 ŚŪRPAṆAKHĀ: ⌜mae Jaṇaa|ṇaarādo ṇikkantāe suaṃ, jaha khuḍia|Sirikaṇṭha|sar'|âsaṇassa Dāsarahiṇo macchareṇa saala|khattia|ka'|ando Parasurāmo parāao tti.⌟

MĀLYAVĀN: sarvam upapadyate.

bhuj'|ârgalita|Narmadā|
makara|cakra|daṃṣṭr'|âṅkura|
vraṇa|prakara|karkaśaṃ
kim api bibhrad ugraṃ vapuḥ
sa, yena paraśau huto
nṛpatir Arjunaḥ kautukād,
asau katham upekṣate
guru|dhanur|vyalīkaṃ muniḥ?

param anen' âpi sakala|mūrdh'|âbhiṣikta|kaṇṭha|rudhir'|âvaseka|paṅkila|kuṭhāreṇa dur|abhibhavo Dāśarathiḥ.

SHURPA·NAKHA: I'll tell you something else. Will Rama do as foreseen?

MÁLYAVAN: No doubt. Great souls appear to have an extraordinary nature that is beyond our world; they are disgusted by mundane royal pleasures.

SHURPA·NAKHA: What's more, I think there may be another thing, not altogether useless for our cause, that will happen.

MÁLYAVAN: *(with delight)* What, exactly?

SHURPA·NAKHA: When I left the city of King Jánaka, I heard 4.60
that Párashu·rama, the exterminator of all kshatriyas, became jealous of Rama, who had broken Shiva's bow; and Párashu·rama has returned to the city.

MÁLYAVAN: Everything fits!

> With his battle-axe, just because he felt like it, he made a fire sacrifice from King Árjuna Kartavírya, whose terrifyingly strong body had been roughened with wounds afflicted by the sharp fangs of *mákaras* in the Nármada River, whose flow he had stopped with his arms.* Now, how could this sage ignore the shameful act that happened to his preceptor's bow?*

But even Párashu·rama, who has a battle-axe stained with the blood sprinkled on it from the throats of all the warriors whose heads had once been consecrated as kings, will not be able to conquer Rama easily.

ŚŪRPAṆAKHĀ: *(s'|âsūyam.)* ⌜duddha|muhe vi edassiṃ khattia|baḍue evvaṃ saṃbhāvedi mādā|maho!⌟

4.65 MĀLYAVĀN: vatse, n' âitāvaj jānāsi.

sarva|rājaka|dur|dharṣaṃ sarva|deva|mayaṃ dhanuḥ
bhañjatā Rāma|bhadreṇa vijigye bhuvana|trayam.

idānīṃ tu,

rājanya|rudhir'|âmbhodhi|kṛta|tri|ṣavaṇo muniḥ,
prāptaḥ Paraśurāmo 'yaṃ na vidmaḥ kiṃ kariṣyati.

tad ehi. rāja|kulam eva gacchāvaḥ.

4.70 *iti niṣkrāntau.*

iti miśra|viṣkambhakaḥ

SHURPA·NAKHA: *(with indignation)* Although this warrior child has still milk smeared on his face, my grandfather thinks rather highly of him!

MÁLYAVAN: My child, you have not understood this. 4.65

> By breaking the bow made of all the gods, a bow that all the kings tried to string in vain, Rama has won the three worlds for himself.

And now,

> He whose three daily rituals are performed with the sea of blood flowing from the bodies of warriors, the sage Párashu·rama, has arrived here—and we do not know what he shall do.

So come, let us go to the royal palace.

Both exit. 4.70

End of the prelude in Sanskrit and Prakrit.

ACT IV
DASHA·RATHA IS TRICKED

NEPATHYE: bho, bho! Janak'|âgni|hotra|paricārakāḥ, pādyaṃ pādyam. arghyam arghyam.

ā janma brahma|cārī,
pṛthula|bhuja|śilā|stambha|vibhrājamāna|
jyā|ghāta|śreṇi|saṃjñ"|ân-
tarita|vasumatī|cakra|jaitra|praśastiḥ,
vakṣaḥ|pīṭhe ghan'|âstra|
vraṇa|kiṇa|kaṭhine saṃkṣṇuvānaḥ pṛṣatkān,
prāpto rājanya|goṣṭhī|
vana|gaja|mṛgayā|kautukī Jāmadagnyaḥ.

api ca,

4.75 eṣa straiṇa|kapola|kuṅkuma|lipi|
stey'|âtibhīrau bhuje
bibhrāṇaś catur|anta|rāja|vijayi
jyā|nāda|raudraṃ dhanuḥ,
tūṇāv eva punastarāṃ draḍhayati
svād antarasmāt paṭād
ākṛṣṭaiḥ kuśa|cīra|tantubhir abhi-
kruddho munir Bhārgavaḥ.

tataḥ praviśati śara|cāpa|hastaḥ kruddh'|ôddhato JĀMADAGNYAḤ.

JĀMADAGNYAḤ: *(sa|khedam.)* yathā|mṛṣṭa|bhojinā Kṛtāntena pratyavasitās tādṛśāḥ sāṃyugīnāḥ. vartamāne tu,

BEHIND THE SCENES: Hey, attendants of Jánaka's fire sacrifice, get water to wash his feet, bring the offerings.

> Since his birth, he has been practicing chastity. Instead of stone-engraved panegyrics lauding him as the conqueror of the world on columns, marks carved by the string of his bow sing his praise, marks that adorn his thick, colossal arms.* His chest* is so rough with the scarred wounds caused by harsh weapons that he can sharpen his arrows on it. Here he comes, Párashu·rama, son of Jamad·agni, eager to hunt down warriors as if they were wild elephants.

Moreover,

> In his hands, which would be much too afraid to efface* the saffron dye on the cheeks of women, he carries a bow, terrifying with its resounding string, a bow that has conquered all the kings of the world. Now he is again fixing his two quivers with threads of his *kusha* grass rags, drawn out of his upper garment—he looks enraged, this sage of the Bhrigu clan. 4.75

PÁRASHU·RAMA, *proud and enraged, enters with a bow and arrows in his hands.*

PÁRASHU·RAMA: *(with fatigue)* The warriors seem to have been consumed by the God of Death, who eats whatever is savory for him. And now,

śastrā|śastri|kath" âiva kā? nava|bhavad|
gīrvāṇa|pāṇiṃ|dhamāḥ
panthāno divi saṃkucanti; Vasudhā
vandhyā, na sūte bhaṭān;
Lakṣmīr apy aravinda|saudha|valabhī|
nirvyūha|paryaṅkikā|
viśrāntair alibhir na kuñjara|ghaṭā|
gaṇḍ'|ôdgatair modate.

(sa|vimarś'|āścaryam)

4.80 Śaṃbhau yad guṇa|vallarīm upanayaty
ākṛṣya karṇ'|ântikaṃ,
bhraśyanti tri|pur'|âvarodha|su|dṛśāṃ
karṇ'|ôtpala|śreṇayaḥ,
svaṃ c' āsphālayati prakoṣṭhakam imām
unmucya, tāsām, aho,
bhidyante valayāni; Dāśarathinā
tad bhagnam aiśaṃ dhanuḥ.

sa|roṣa|vikaṭam parikrāmayan

bho, bho Videhāḥ! kva Rāmo Dāśarathiḥ?

yasmin Arjuna|doḥ|sahasra|nalaka|
prodgacchad|asra|cchaṭā|
jihvāle juhavāṃ|babhūvima ruṣā
rājanya|sattām api,
adya prāk|kavala|grahasya vighasī|
bhūteṣv api kṣatriya|
kṣudreṣu kṣudhitaś cireṇa paraśus;
ten' âyam anviṣyate.

Can we hear any stories of warfare at all? The paths that lead to heaven are getting congested with recent candidates to the divine ranks, who hustle and jostle. The earth has become barren and no longer gives birth to soldiers. Even the Goddess of Fortune cannot enjoy the presence of bees that come from the temples of battle elephants in rut, only of bees that rest on lotuses as on ivory couches in the bedroom of a palace.*

(reflecting, with astonishment)

When Shiva prepared to use his bow and drew its creeper-like string up to his ears, the lotuses that deck the ears of beauties in the harem of the Three Demon Cities dropped down. When he released the string and made it twang against his forearm, then—look!—the bangles of these demonesses got shattered.* And Rama broke this very bow of the Lord. 4.80

With anger and pride, he walks around the stage.

Hey, inhabitants of Vidéha, where is Rama, son of Dasha·ratha?

In my wrath, I once offered the whole race of warriors as sacrifice into its flames formed by the streams of blood coming from Árjuna Kartavírya's one thousand broken* arms. This battle-axe of mine, which, after a long fast, has become hungry even for warrior-morsels left over from its previous feast, is now looking for Rama.

tataḥ praviśati sa|dhairya|saṃbhramo DĀŚARATHIḤ.

4.85 DĀŚARATHIḤ:

sākaṃ Śakti|dhareṇa tatra|bhavato
devād Bhavānī|pater
yaḥ samyañcam avāpa cāpa|nigamaṃ
samyañci sāmāni ca,
śūrāṇāṃ ca tapasvināṃ ca paramāṃ
kāṣṭhām adhiṣṭhāsnubhis
tejobhir bhagavān asau Bhṛgu|patir
diṣṭy" âdya darśiṣyate.

JĀMADAGNYAḤ: *(sa|khed'|ôpālambham, ātmānaṃ prati)*

«bhasm'|âṅkur' êti» khuralī|kalahe Kumāram
apy ākṣipan paruṣa|roṣa|ras'|ândha|cetāḥ,
dṛṣṭo 'smi yaḥ kṛta|mitho|hasitaṃ Śivābhyām,
tac|cāpa|bhaṅgam api, hā, masṛṇaḥ śṛṇomi.

(vimṛśya ca) aho, mām araṇya|vāsinam upaśrutya dur|ātmanā Raghu|kula|kuṭumbakena dūram ucchvasitam. *(kiṃ cid uccaiḥ)*

4.90 re Kākutsthāḥ! kathaṃ vaḥ śruti|viṣayam ayaṃ
n' āgamad Bhārgavīyo
duḥ|sāmant'|âpacāra|pracita|pitṛ|vadh'|â-
marṣa|nistāra|bandhuḥ,
vārān āsanna|viṃśān viśasita|viṣama|
kṣatra|jāti|prarohaḥ
krodhād utkṛtta|garbh'|āmiṣa|rudhira|vasā|

RAMA, *courageous and excited, enters.*

RAMA: 4.85

In the company of spear-holding Skanda, he learned the real art of archery as well as all the Samavedic verses from Bhaváni's husband, Lord Shiva himself. He whose power has reached the highest degree that heroes or ascetics can hope to attain, the venerable chief of the Bhrigu clan, Párashu·rama, shall show himself today—how lucky I am!

PÁRASHU·RAMA: *(troubled and reproachful, aside)*

My mind being blinded by the harsh feeling of wrath, I insulted even Skanda when quarreling about archery, calling him the son of a false ascetic.* Then, seeing this, Shiva and his wife laughed at me. And now that I hear that my master's bow has been broken, should I stay calm?

(reflecting) Since the son of the Raghu dynasty, that ill-willed Rama, thinks I am a forest-dwelling ascetic, he has gone much too far... *(somewhat aloud)*

Hey, sons of the Kákutsthas dynasty, have you not heard about Párashu·rama's friend, who helped him to avenge his father's murder, committed due to an offense of a wicked warrior?* That friend killed the vile descendants of warriors twenty-one times, and then, enraged, sliced up even the warrior fetuses in their mothers' wombs—thus has he 4.90

visra|gandhiḥ kuṭhāraḥ?

RĀMAḤ: *(dṛṣṭvā, sa|harṣa|bahu|mānam)*

jetāraṃ Daśa|kandharasya rabhasād
doḥ|śreṇi|niḥśreṇikā|
tuly'|ārūḍha|samasta|loka|vijaya|
Śrī|pūryamāṇ'|ôrasam
yaḥ saṃkhye nijaghāna Hehaya|patiṃ,
śatror mukhaṃ dṛṣṭavān
yaḥ pṛṣṭhaṃ dadato 'pi Ṣaṇmukha|jaye,
so 'yaṃ kṛtī Bhārgavaḥ.

(kṣaṇaṃ ca nirvarṇya, sa|smitam) aho, saṃkīryamāṇ'|ân|eka|ras'|ânubhāva|gambhīra|madhuro 'yam asy' ābhogaḥ.

jaṭāṃ dhatte mūrdhā,
paraśu|dhanuṣī bāhu|śikharam,
prakoṣṭho raudr'|âkṣaṃ
valayam, iṣu|daṇḍān api karaḥ,
prarūḍha|prauḍh'|âstra|
vraṇa|vikaṭa|raudr'|âdbhutam idaṃ
praśāntām aiṇeyīṃ
tvacam api ca vakṣaḥ kalayati.

4.95 *(ity upasarpati.)*

JĀMADAGNYAḤ: *(vilokya)* katham, asau śrūyamāṇa|guṇ'|ânurūpa|kalpit'|ākāra|saṃvādī Dāśarathiḥ. sādhu, re, rājanya|pota, sādhu!

become stinking with their flesh, blood and marrow. This friend of Párashu·rama is his battle-axe.

RAMA: *(seeing him, with delight and respect)*

Out of wrath, he has killed him on whose thousand arms the Goddess of Victory Over the Whole World used to climb up happily as if on a thousand ladders, all at once, to reach his heart; yes, he has killed the conqueror of ten-headed Rávana, the ruler of the Háihayas, Árjuna Kartavírya, in a battle. And he saw the face of the fleeing enemy when he won a fight against the six-headed Skanda*—here he comes, powerful Párashu·rama.

(looking at him for a moment, then with a smile) His appearance is powerful but pleasant, as it makes one experience a combination of various impressions.

His head has matted locks of hair, he carries a battle-axe and a bow on his shoulder, a rosary of *rudráksha* beads on his forearm and arrows stuck in his hand instead of a cane. His chest is frightening, terrible and extraordinary, with the wounds inflicted upon it by powerful weapons—yet he wears an antelope skin over it, suggesting peaceful asceticism.

(approaching him) 4.95

PÁRASHU·RAMA: *(looking at him)* What? This is Rama coming, whose appearance seems to suit his qualities that I have heard about. All right, young warrior, well done.

sa|vidham upasaran sa|mūla|kāṣaṃ
kaṣita|nṛp'|ânvayam adya māṃ dhinoṣi,
harim iva kari|kumbha|kūṭa|koṭi|
prakaṭa|kaṭhora|nakh'|âṅkuraṃ kuraṅgaḥ.

RĀMAḤ: *(sa|smitam)* bhagavan Bhārgava! guru|garbha|rūpayor etāvad ev' ântaram. kiṃ ca,

ādeṣṭā bhagavān Bhṛgur jananayor
autpattika|brāhmayor;
devo Dhūrjaṭir astra|karmaṇi gurur;
vīryaṃ tu dūre girām.
sapta|dvīpavatīṃ dadad bhuvam abhi-
praiṣi dvi|jān Kaśyapa|
prāyān, a|pratim'|ânubhāva, bhavate
kasmai cid asmai namaḥ.

4.100 JĀMADAGNYAḤ: are, kṣatriya|ḍimbha! tav' ânena sattva|saujanya|pauruṣ'|ôtkarṣeṇa kim apy antar|āpyāyito 'smi. kiṃ tu,

nārācaiḥ Kṛtavīrya|nandana|vadhū|
bāṣpa|priyaṃ|bhāvukair
utpādya kṣataj'|ôdam arṇavam atha
nyuptaṃ pitṛbhyaḥ payaḥ.
saṃpraty asya samasta|bāhuja|bhujaḥ
krodhasya nirvāsyataḥ
kṣuṇdāno dhanur aindu|śekharam, aho,
jāto bhavān indhanam.

It delights me to see you approach me today, after I exterminated all the kings and their dynasties; just as an approaching deer delights a lion whose sharp and pointed claws are known by thousands of highly situated elephant temples.

RAMA: *(smiling)* Venerable Párashu·rama of the Bhrigu clan, elders and youngsters are indeed divided by the difference you have mentioned.*

Your natural and brahmanic births have both been ensured by the venerable Bhrigu;* and Shiva, the god with matted locks, taught you the use of weapons—words cannot describe your heroic qualities. You treated all brahmins like Káshyapa* when you gave them the world with its seven continents. You whose power is incomparable, here I am to salute you, who are beyond praise.

PÁRASHU·RAMA: Hey, warrior child, I am quite moved by 4.100
your excessive goodness, truthfulness and manliness.* Yet,

My arrows, inviting tears in the eyes of Árjuna Kartavírya's wives, created a sea of blood, which then served as a water offering for my ancestors. Now my wrath, whose fire consumed all the warriors and was about to be extinguished, is being kindled again by you, who, alas!, have broken moon-bearing Shiva's bow.

RĀMAḤ: *(smitvā)* bhagavan,

bāla|svabhāva|sulabhena kutūhalena
kṛṣṭaṃ dhanur bhagavato Vṛṣabha|dhvajasya.
tatr' ānuṣaṅgikam a|maṅgalam īdṛśaṃ tu
saṃvṛttam; atra na mayā gaṇitas tvam āsīḥ.

JĀGADAGNYAḤ: *(sa|roṣam.)* āḥ, kṣatriya|ḍimbha! katham Pramatha|nātha|pratham'|ânte|vāsinaṃ Paraśurāmam api bhavān n' âjīgaṇat?

4.105 Mahā|seno yasya,
pramada, Yama|daṃṣṭrā|sahacaraiḥ
śarair mukto jīvan
dvir iva śara|janmā samabhavat,
imāṃ ca kṣatrāṇāṃ
bhuja|vana|mahā|durga|viṣamām
ayaṃ vīro vārān
ajayad upaviṃśān Vasumatīm.

RĀMAḤ: śāntaṃ, śāntam. prasīda bhagavan. a|vimṛśya|kāritayā na gaṇito 'si, na punar avalepāt.

strīṣu pravīra|jananī jananī tav' âiva,
devī svayaṃ bhagavatī Girij" âpi yasyai
tvad|dor|vaśī|kṛta|Viśākha|mukh'|âvaloka|
vrīḍā|vidīrṇa|hṛdayā spṛhayāṃ|babhūva.

RAMA: *(smiling)* Sir,

I tried to string the honorable Shiva's bow, just out of curiosity, which is a common and natural thing in children. Then, as a result, that inauspicious event happened*—but I did not think about your reaction at the moment.

PÁRASHU·RAMA: *(angrily)* How could you disregard Párashu·rama, the foremost disciple of the Lord of Goblins, you foolish kshatriya?

O careless child, Skanda was spared by Párashu·ra- 4.105
ma's arrows, which resembled the fangs of the God of Death, and thus he obtained a second shara-birth while still alive.* It is me, heroic Párashu·rama, who conquered the earth twenty-one times, although it was inaccessible and very hard to penetrate, being covered, as it was, with a jungle of warriors' arms.

RAMA: Do not get agitated, please; do not be so angry. It is out of forgetfulness that I did not think of you, and not out of vanity.

Your mother was the only woman to give birth to an excellent hero. Even Párvati herself envied her, while the goddess's heart was torn apart with shame to see her Skanda's face after he was defeated by your strong arms.*

JĀMADAGNYAḤ: *(vihasya)*

anubhava|punar|uktāṃ muñca naḥ stotra|caryām!
upanamaya tad etat Kauśik'|ôpajñam astram!
kṣipati na khalu kālaṃ vīra|goṣṭhī|vinoda|
priya|paraśur ayaṃ me bāhur udyacchamānaḥ.

4.110 RĀMAḤ: *(sva/gatam)* aye, bhagavantaṃ Viśvāmitram api spṛśati. bhavatv evaṃ tāvat! *(sa/dhairya/smitam prakāśam)*

bhū|mātraṃ kiyad etad arṇava|mayaṃ
tat sādhitaṃ hāryate
yad vīreṇa bhavā|dṛśena vadati
triḥ|sapta|kṛtvo jayam.
ḍimbho 'yaṃ, nava|bāhur, īdṛśam idaṃ
ghoraṃ ca vīra|vratam;
tat krodhād virama! prasīda bhagavan!
jāty" âiva pūjyo 'si naḥ.

JĀMADAGNYAḤ: *(sa/krodhaṃ sva/gatam)* aho, dur|ātmano rājanya|potasya mahā|vīra|prahatāyāḥ paddhater a|skhalitam ukti|pratyukti|vaidagdhyam. *(prakāśam)* āḥ, pāpa, jāty" âiva kevalam ahaṃ pūjanīyaḥ Paraśurāmaḥ? katham ady' âpi nirāyudho 'si?

vinaya|niculitair bhavad|vacobhiḥ
kim api navaṃ vivṛṇadbhir aṅkam antaḥ,
ayam ajani karaḥ Kṛtānta|daṃṣṭrā|
krakaca|kaṭhora|kuṭhāra|dur|nirīkṣyaḥ.

PÁRASHU·RAMA: *(smiling)*

> Stop praising me politely—you are only repeating what is well known. Now take up that weapon of yours that Vishva·mitra invented. My arm cannot wait as it raises its battle-axe, which is so fond of entertaining the assembly of heroes.*

RAMA: *(aside)* Ah, he drags even Vishva·mitra into this story. 4.110
Let it be, then. *(aloud, smiling bravely)*

> Even this earth with its oceans is nothing to you. As a hero, you conquered it and then let it go to others, so that it now sings about your twenty-one victories. Here I am, a child, with weak arms—and the heroic duty to perform is very frightening. So suppress your anger and be appeased, my lord. I honor you for your very birth.*

PÁRASHU·RAMA: *(angrily, aside)* This ill-willed kshatriya child is perfect in debate; his words follow the tracks beaten by great heroes without fail. *(aloud)* Ah, shame on you, you honor Párashu·rama only because of his brahmanic birth?! How come you are still unarmed?

> Hearing your speech, which tries to conceal yet another wickedness in your heart with politeness but at the same time cannot help revealing it, my hand is becoming terrifying to behold, as it carries this cruel battle-axe, sharp as the saw-like fangs of the God of Death.

(uccaiḥ) aho, nu khalu bhoḥ!

4.115 trailokya|trāṇa|śauṇḍaḥ
Sarasi|ja|vasater yaḥ prasūto bhujābhyāṃ,
sa kṣatraṃ nāma varṇaḥ
kuliśa|kaṭhinayor yasya doṣṇor vilīnaḥ
jvālā|jihvāla|kāl'|â-
nala|kavala|bhaya|bhrānta|dev'|âsurāṇi
vyātanvāno jaganti
jvalati munir ayaṃ Pārvatī|dharma|putraḥ.

NEPATHYE: bhagavan Bhārgava, Bhārgava,

a|pravṛtti|viṣayaṃ vitanvataḥ
kṣatra|śabdam iyam eva medinī
dakṣiṇā tava babhūva yajvano.
muñca saṃprati tu śuṣkam āyudham!

JĀMADAGNYAḤ: aye, praśānta|gambhīra|svaraḥ ka eṣaḥ? Janakena bhavitavyam. *(tad|abhimukham avalokya)* rāja'|rṣe Sīradhvaja, bhagavataḥ Sūrya|śiṣyāt purāṇa|vājasaneyino Yājñavalkyād adhīta|brahma|siddhānto gṛhīta|vākya ev' âsi. kiṃ tu, n' âyam avasaraḥ śiṣṭ'|ânurodhasya.

(loudly) Hey, you,

> That caste called the warrior caste, created from the arms of the lotus-born Brahma* and so proud of their task to protect the three worlds, was annihilated by the hard, thunderbolt-like arms of the sage who, burning with his rage now, makes the gods and the demons of this world flee, for they are scared of being devoured by the tongue-like flames of the apocalyptic fire of his wrath. Here I am, this sage, adopted son of the goddess Párvati. 4.115

BEHIND THE SCENES: Venerable Párashu·rama,

> You have made the word "warrior" useless,* and you have received the due donation for your sacrifice of warriors: the earth itself. So now put down your weapon, which is no longer of use to you.

PÁRASHU·RAMA: Who is it, with such a deep and calm voice? It must be Jánaka. *(looking in his direction)* Royal sage, Jánaka, you have studied the doctrine of the Vedas from the old Yajnaválkya, who founded the White Yajur·veda and himself was a disciple of the sun god himself. Therefore, your word is always respected. However, this is not an occasion when one acts according to the advice of the learned.

avanim adhika|viṃśān abhyavaskandya vārān,
avabhṛtha|bhṛtakebhyaḥ sampradāya dvi|jebhyaḥ,
viramati ramaṇīyād dvandva|yuddhāt kathaṃ me
nikhila|nṛpati|hatyā|dṛṣṭa|sāraḥ kuṭhāraḥ?

4.120 *punar* NEPATHYE

Bhṛgu|tilaka! namas te! muñca vaimatyam etat!
kuru karuṇam idānīṃ mānasaṃ, māna|śauṇḍa!
vahati bata kim astraṃ putra|bhāṇḍe 'pi Rāme
tri|jagad|a|bhaya|dāna|sthūla|lakṣo bhujas te?

JĀMADAGNYAḤ: *(RĀMAṂ prati)* aye, dhīra|karkaśa|svaraḥ ka eṣaḥ?

RĀMAḤ: *(sa/praśrayam)* bhagavan, ayaṃ tāto Raghu|patiḥ.

JĀMADAGNYAḤ: *(sa/vyatham)* dhik, sarvataḥ kṣatra|kaṇṭak'|ôdbhedaḥ! *(nepathy'/âbhimukham)* bho, bho rājan Daśaratha! asman|nāma|dheya|mātra|mitreṇa sūnunā mān'|ârho 'si. kiṃ punar, an|abhijña ev' âsi vīra|vyavahārasya.

4.125 Puramathana|dhanur|vimardan'|ôtthaṃ
pradahad ahar|divam asti tīvram arciḥ;
Raghu|Janaka|kuṭumba|bāṣpa|pūraiḥ
param iha śāntim uśanti śastra|bhājaḥ.

It has conquered the world twenty-one times and handed it over to brahmins who acted as officiating priests at the end of this ritual offering and purified everything. Now, how could it refrain from an enjoyable duel, this battle-axe of mine, which has demonstrated its force when it killed all the kings of the world?

Again, FROM BEHIND THE SCENES 4.120

Jewel of the Bhrigu clan! We pay homage to you. Give up your hostility and make your heart compassionate now, respectable one. Your arm is most generous when it drives away the distress of the three worlds. Alas, why does it brandish a weapon against Rama, who could be your son?

PÁRASHU·RAMA: *(to* RAMA*)* Who is this man with a profound but harsh voice?

RAMA: *(politely)* Sir, this is my father, the king of the Raghu dynasty.

PÁRASHU·RAMA: *(with distress)* Fie, everywhere these generations of damned warriors. *(toward the rear of the stage)* Hey, King Dasha·ratha, this son of yours is my friend only because his name is the same as mine, and therefore I duly respect you, too. But you do not understand the way in which heroes act.

This violent flame of anger, caused by the destruction of Shiva's bow, keeps burning me all the time. 4.125
And armed men like myself obtain final tranquility in this world only if the flowing tears of the

punar NEPATHYE

ā Jāmadagnya! kim evam atiprasaktaḥ saṃnyasta|śastrān api balād dhanur grāhayasi?

JĀMADAGNYAḤ: *(sa/roṣam)* are Videha|prasava|pāṃsana,

«ayam adhipatir bhāsām ek'|ân-
taro bhavato gurus,
tvam asi tapasā yad varṣīyān»
iti sma titikṣyase.
katham asi dhanur|nāma|grāhī?
tad eṣa samāpyase:
mama hi sakala|kṣatr'|ālambha|
krator amṛtaṃ bhavān.

4.130 NEPATHYE: Bhārgava, Bhārgava! Cyavan'|ādi|vṛddha|vākya|gaurava|nigṛhīta|saṃprahāra|kriyā|samabhihārasya bhavataḥ parame brahmaṇi vartamānasya punar upaplavante buddhayaḥ. tad virama! kiyac ciram iyam aparam iva bhavantaṃ nāṭayiṣyaty āyudha|piśācikā?

JĀMADAGNYAḤ: *(vihasya)* aho, yājya|kula|snehaḥ Śatānandam ākulayati. bhavatu, sāntvayāmi tāvad enam. *(tad/abhimukham)* Āṅgirasa,

families of Raghu and Jánaka extinguish their fire of wrath.*

Again, FROM BEHIND THE SCENES

Ah, Párashu·rama, why are you so determined to fight as to force even those who had put down their arrows to take their bows up again?

PÁRASHU·RAMA: *(angrily)* O you wretched man from Vidéha,

The Sun, Lord of All Light, is indirectly your teacher, and you have practiced asceticism harder than I—therefore I should forgive you. But how dare you talk of taking up a bow? It is for this that you shall die. You are the leftover I will now use to complete my sacrifice in which I have already killed all the other warriors.

FROM BEHIND THE SCENES: Párashu·rama, listening to the 4.130
word of your respected elders such as Chyávana, you restrained yourself in the practice of armed fight and turned to religious thought*—yet your mind is still not calm. Refrain from this fight. For how long will this demon of war make you dance to his tune, just as he did before?

PÁRASHU·RAMA: *(smiling)* His affection for the family that employs him for sacrifices makes Shatánanda concerned. All right, I shall appease him. *(in* SHATÁNANDA*'s direction)* Shatánanda, son of Ángiras,

nṛpas te pālyo 'yaṃ
    mama paśu|puroḍāśa|rasikaḥ;
  pṛthivyām a|vyāj'|ôd-
    bhaṭa|bhuja|bhṛtaḥ santi Raghavaḥ.
amīṣām utsiktaṃ
    kim api kulam utkṛtya lavaśo,
  vidhātā tat sarvaṃ
    yad abhirucitaṃ te Bhṛgu|patiḥ.

NEPATHYE: āḥ pāpa, kṣatriyā|putra, kṣatriya|bhrūṇa|hatyā| mahā|pātakin! nisarga|niṣprāṇaṃ hi praharaṇam Ikṣvākūṇāṃ brāhmaṇeṣu; tair yādṛśas tādṛśo vā soḍhavyo 'si. katham evam atikrāmann asmākam api brahma|varcasān na bibheṣi?

JĀMADAGNYAḤ: *(sa|roṣa|hāsam)* are, brahma|bandho, bāndhakineya, Gautama|gotra|pāṃsana!

4.135 kuryuḥ śastra|kathām amī yadi Manor
    vaṃśe manuṣy'|âṅkurāḥ,
  syāc ced brahma|gaṇo 'yam ākṛti|gaṇas
    tatr' êṣyate ced bhavān,
saṃrājāṃ samidhāṃ ca sādhakatamaṃ
    dhatte chidā|kāraṇaṃ,
  dhiṅ, maurvī|kuśa|karṣaṇ'|ôlbaṇa|kiṇa|
    granthir mam' âyaṃ karaḥ.

Your king takes pleasure in duly offering animals and other oblations, he shall therefore be under my protection; but members of the Raghu dynasty have naturally strong arms to fight with on the surface of this earth.* I will just cut into pieces those of them who are much too haughty, and then will do whatever pleases you.

FROM BEHIND THE SCENES: Shame on you, son of a warrior woman, you who committed the sin of killing warrior fetuses. The weapons of the Ikshváku dynasty are naturally without force if used against brahmins. Whatever you do to them, they will forgive you. But why, transgressing all rules, are you still not afraid of our brahmanic power?

PÁRASHU·RAMA: *(laughing angrily)* O, wretched brahmin, son of a bitch, shame of the Gáutama family,

If these young men born in the family of Manu can babble about taking up their arms and if brahmins are brahmins only because they look similar* (and if you also count yourself among them), then, alas, why does this hand of mine, rough with many scars caused by pulling the sharp string of my bow, carry the battle-axe, which is the best instrument to cut up kings as well as firewood for sacrifices?* 4.135

NEPATHYE: Bhārgava, Bhārgava!

tvaṃ vedavān asi Vasiṣṭha|guroḥ sa|nābhiḥ,
Svāyaṃbhuvaḥ sa bhagavān prabhavo gurus te;
ten' âtimātra|masṛṇaṃ hṛdayaṃ madīyam
ady' âpi na truṭati. śāmyatu te ku|dṛṣṭiḥ!

JĀMADAGNYAḤ: *(s'|ôccair|hāsam)* kim āttha, re, Daśaratha? «n' âdy' âpi hṛdayaṃ truṭat' îti?» kathaṃ vā truṭyatu, yāvad eṣa na vyāpriyate paraśuḥ?

NEPATHYE: ā Jāmadagnya, gurūn apy adhikṣipasi.

4.140 puro|janmā n' âdya
prabhṛti mama Rāmaḥ, svayam ahaṃ,
na putraḥ pautro vā
Raghu|kula|bhuvāṃ ca kṣiti|bhujām;
a|dhīraṃ dhīraṃ vā
kalayatu jano mām ayam ayaṃ,
mayā baddho duṣṭa|
dvija|damana|dīkṣā|parikaraḥ.

JĀMADAGNYAḤ: *(s'|âvajñaṃ* RĀMAṂ *prati)* are, kim ayaṃ Lakṣmaṇo bhavantam puro|janmānaṃ na vyapadiśati?

RĀMAḤ: *(sa|vailakṣya|smitam)* prasīda bhagavan! sa ev' âyaṃ yauvanād arvācīne niraparādha|madhure vayasi vartamāno, yāni kāni cid akṣarāṇi pralapati.

JĀMADAGNYAḤ: *(sa|smitam)* katham etāvaty api mām a|mṛṣyamāṇam āśaṅkase? tvad|anuvartī khalv ayaṃ tvām eva astam|ayamānam anv|astam|ayiṣyate. nirvāntaṃ hi savitāraṃ taraṇi|maṇir apy anu|nirvāti. *(nepathyam prati)*

FROM BEHIND THE SCENES: Párashu·rama,

> You have Vedic learning and you come from the same family as our preceptor, Vasíshtha. Your venerable father is a descendant of the Self-born Brahma.* That is why my too sensitive heart is still not broken in spite of your hurting words.* Now, let your hostile glances* be appeased.

PÁRASHU·RAMA: *(laughing loudly)* What did you say, Dasha·ratha? That your heart is still not broken? Why should it break when my battle-axe still has not been used?

FROM BEHIND THE SCENES: O Párashu·rama, you insult even our elders,

> From now on, Rama is not my elder brother; I am myself, not the son or grandson of kings born in the Raghu dynasty.* And no matter whether people of this world find me cowardly or brave, I have got everything ready for my initiation into the taming of wicked brahmins. 4.140

PÁRASHU·RAMA: *(with contempt, toward* RAMA*)* Why does Lákshmana refuse to call you his elder brother?

RAMA: *(embarrassed, smiling)* Forgive him, sir. He is still in that tender and innocent age before puberty, he just babbles.

PÁRASHU·RAMA: *(smiling)* How come even in this matter you are not sure of my indulgence? Lákshmana, this true follower of yours, will go after you when you depart from this world. When the sun is down, the sun-stones do not shine, either. *(toward the rear of the stage)* Well

sādhu re, Lakṣmaṇa, sādhu! kaniṣṭhataro 'pi varaṃ bhavān, na punar ayaṃ vṛthā|jyeṣṭho Rāmas te.

prāg uccaiḥ|śirasaṃ kṣurapra|nakharaiḥ
 Krauñc'|âdri|dantāvalaṃ
bhittvā haṃsa|mayāni mauktika|phalāny
 ākīrya paryāpitām
saiṃhīṃ vṛttim adhiṣṭhite 'pi hi mayi,
 kṣātreṇa kalpena te
diṣṭyā kautukam ābhigāmikam asi
 tvaṃ ko 'pi vīr'|âṅkuraḥ.

4.145 NEPATHYE: Bhārgava, Bhārgava! dur|vijñānam idam arvāk phala|niṣpatter ābhigāmikaṃ sāṃgrāmikaṃ vā.

RĀMAḤ: *(sa|roṣam, nepathy'|âbhimukham)* ā vatsa, ko 'yam adyatanas te dur|vinaya|praroho, yo gurūn api kṣetrī|karoti?

NEPATHYE: ārya, tūṣṇīm asmi. kṣamasva Jāmadagnya, niyantrito 'ham āryeṇa.

JĀMADAGNYAḤ: *(vihasya)* are Rāma, kathaṃ vācam eva sūnṛtām asmad|abhiyoga|praśamanīṃ samarthayase? kavaca|haro 'si; śastrair eva pratikriyantāṃ śastrāṇi. kiṃ ca re,

rājanyebhyo janma vaivasvatebhyo;
 cakre cāp'|ācāryakaṃ Kauśikaś ca;
kṣātrīṃ caryām evam unmuñcatas te
 gotr'|ākṣepī vajra|lepaḥ kalaṅkaḥ.

done, Lákshmana, well done. Although you are younger, you are better than Rama, this good-for-nothing elder brother of yours.

> Once I split the high Krauncha mountain* with my sharp-tipped arrows and made the swans born in its caves disperse—just as a lion would tear apart a tall elephant using his claws and scatter the pearls produced in the elephant's temples. Yet, as your attitude is worthy of a warrior, luckily you have aroused my curiosity to approach you, you tiny hero.

FROM BEHIND THE SCENES: Párashu·rama, before we see the result of your interest in us it is difficult to know if you are curious to approach us or to fight against us. 4.145

RAMA: *(angrily, toward the rear of the stage)* My little brother, why are you behaving so incredibly badly today that you attack even your elders?

FROM BEHIND THE SCENES: My brother, I shall keep quiet. Please forgive me, Párashu·rama, my brother has restrained me.

PÁRASHU·RAMA: *(smiling)* Hey, Rama, how is it that you can still say soothing words to make me refrain from fighting? You are old enough to wear an armor; you should reply with weapons to weapons. Moreover,

> You were born in the solar dynasty and Vishva·mitra taught you the science of archery. If you do not behave as a warrior should, you will be a disgrace to your family, an ineffaceable stain on their name.

4.150 RĀMAḤ: *(sa|garva|smitam)* bhagavan, satyam etat.

jātaḥ so 'haṃ dinakara|kula|
kṣatriya|śrotriyebhyo,
Viśvāmitrād api bhagavato
dṛṣṭa|divy'|âstra|pāraḥ;
asmin vaṃśe kathayatu jano
dur|yaśo vā yaśo vā,
vipre śastra|grahaṇa|guruṇaḥ
sāhasikyād bibhemi.

JĀMADAGNYAḤ: *(sa|krodham)* āḥ, pāpa dur|mukha! Vasiṣṭha iva, Viśvāmitra iva svasti|vācaniko brāhmaṇas te Paraśurāmaḥ. *(sa|vyatham)* dhik, kaṣṭam! evam uccāvaca|vācaḥ kṣatriyāḥ śrūyante! *(krodh'|âtiśayaṃ nāṭayan)* ayam ayaṃ bhoḥ,

saha Daśaratham ady' ôt|kṛtya putraiś caturbhir
Janaka|kula|kabandha|skandha|nirgatvarībhiḥ.
nava|rudhira|latābhiḥ kḷpta|līlā|patākāṃ
raṇa|bhuvam atiraudrīṃ Rudra|śiṣyaḥ karomi.

RĀMAḤ: *(sa|roṣam)* ā Jāmadagnya! k" êyaṃ vāg|vibhīṣikā? dūram atikrāmati prasaṅge, kadā cid Ikṣvākavo 'pi dur|manāyante.

4.155 JĀMADGNYAḤ: *(sa|bhrukuṭī|bhaṅgam)* tataḥ kim?

RAMA: *(smiling proudly)* My lord, it is true. 4.150

I was born in the family of learned warriors of the solar dynasty, and I have demonstrated that I have really learned the science of weapons from the venerable Vishva·mitra. No matter if people call this dynasty famous or infamous, what I am afraid of is the gravely violent act of taking up arms against a brahmin.

PÁRASHU·RAMA: *(angrily)* You wretched creature showering abuses, you take Párashu·rama for someone like Vasíshtha or Vishva·mitra, whose job is to distribute benedictions. *(with pain)* What a shame that warriors can be heard to say such things. *(showing extreme wrath)* Now, here I am,

I shall cut Dasha·ratha and his four sons into pieces, and, to make a festive pole, I shall use the fresh streams of blood coming from the headless bodies that once belonged to members of Jánaka's family, instead of using creepers. Thus shall I make the battlefield frightful, being as I am the disciple of the Terrifying Shiva.

RAMA: *(angrily)* Párashu·rama, what is this scarecrow type of speech that is meant to frighten us? When such arguments go much too far, even members of the Ikshváku dynasty can sometimes become vexed...

PÁRASHU·RAMA: *(frowning)* And then? 4.155

RĀMAḤ: *(s'|âvaṣṭambham.)* tataś ca,

tais triḥ|saptabhir eva rāja|vijayair
yat te bhuja|stambhayoḥ
kṛtvā toraṇa|mālikāṃ, punar amuṃ
dvā|viṃśam āripsate;
drakṣyāmi tvayi vartamānam adhunā
tac cāpa|vidy"|âdbhutaṃ;
Śambhos tasya hi kevalena dhanuṣā
kṛṣṭena tuṣṭir na me.

JĀMADAGNYAḤ: *(sa|saṃrambham)* kim āttha, re, kim āttha? *(«drakṣyāmi tvayi vartamānam» iti triḥ paṭhitvā, sa|vyatham)* aho, sarvataḥ samidhyamāna|dāruṇasya roṣa|jāta|vedaso Videha|Dilīpayoḥ kulaṃ nāma kati bhaviṣyanty āhutayaḥ? *(uccaiḥ)* bho bhoḥ, sapta|dvīpa|kula|parvata|vartino rājānaḥ, cetayadhvam!

yena svāṃ vinihatya mātaram api,
kṣatr'|âsra|madhv|āsava|
svād'|âbhijña|paraśvadhena vidadhe
niḥkṣatriyā medinī,
yad|bāṇa|vraṇa|vartmanā śikhariṇaḥ
Krauñcasya haṃsa|cchalād
ady' âpy asthi|kaṇāḥ patanti, sa punaḥ
kruddho munir Bhārgavaḥ.

RAMA: *(firmly)* Then,

> Just as a gateway is decorated by a garland of flowers, your colossal arms have been adorned by your twenty-one victories over kings, thanks to your wonderful mastery of the science of archery, which now longs for a twenty-second victory, and which I would like to see myself now. For I have not been satisfied simply by stringing Shiva's bow.

PÁRASHU·RAMA: *(with confusion)* What did you say? *(he repeats three times "your wonderful mastery of the science of archery," etc., then, with pain)* In the cruel fire of my anger, which is being kindled in every possible way now,* how many sacrifices can Dilípa's and Vidéha's families provide? *(loudly)* Kings of the seven continents and the seven mountains, beware, beware!

> With his battle-axe—which, after he killed even his own mother with it,* learned the taste of the flowing blood of warriors as if it were sweet wine—he made this earth free of kshatriyas. From the wounds where he pierced Mount Krauncha with his arrows, the fragmented bones of the hillside are still falling out in the form of swans.* It is this sage of the Bhrigu clan, Párashu·rama, who is enraged again.

4.160 RĀMAḤ: *(sa|hāsam)*

nṛpān a|pratyakṣān
kim apavadase? nanv ayam ahaṃ
śiśu|krīḍā|bhagna|
Tripurahara|dhanvā tava puraḥ.
ahaṃkāra|krūr'|Âr-
juna|bhuja|vana|vraścana|kalā|
nisṛṣṭ'|ârtho bāhuḥ,
kathaya, kataras te? praharatu!

JĀMADAGNYAḤ: āḥ pāpa, vikartana|kula|kalaṅka! punastarāṃ tad eva Pārvatī|dayita|kodaṇḍa|dalanam udbhāvayasi. ahaha, kṣatriyo 'pi Bhārgavasya Kārtavīrya|vijayinaṃ bhuja|daṇḍam anviṣyati. aho, garīyān kālo, yad a|śruta|caram api śrāvayati, a|dṛṣṭa|caram api darśayati! api ca, re re rājanya|kīṭa,

jānāsy eva, yathā pitur paribhavan
hom'|ârjunīm Arjuno
mat|kodaṇḍam an|eka|rājaka|vadha|
svādhyāyam adhyāpipat.
ten' âiv' âsti bhavatsu yady api mama
krodho 'yam autsargikas,
tat saṃpraty upasarjanaṃ; guru|dhanur|
bhaṅgād ayaṃ hetumān.

RĀMAḤ: Jāmadagnya, paṭac|carī|bhūtā khalv iyaṃ purātanī kīrti|patākā. nanv idānīm eva draṣṭavyam. *(nepathy'|âbhimukham)* vatsa, Lakṣmaṇa! dhanur, dhanuḥ!

RAMA: *(laughing at him)* 4.160

> Why are you abusing kings who are not present? Here I am, standing before you, I who have broken Shiva's bow out of childish play. Now tell me which of your arms was appointed to show your skill in cutting off the thousand arms of the proud and cruel Árjuna Kartavírya; tell me which is the arm that will strike!

PÁRASHU·RAMA: Wretched stain of the solar dynasty, you are evoking again that you have broken the bow of Párvati's beloved husband. And although you are also a warrior, you are seeking Párashu·rama's arm that defeated Árjuna Kartavírya. What difficult times these are, which make one hear what has never had to be heard, and show things one has never had to behold. Now, listen, you worm of a kshatriya,

> You know well that Árjuna Kartavírya, by taking away my father's sacrificial cow, made my bow learn the lesson of how to kill innumerable kings. It is because of him that I am irritated by your kind in general. But that is not the case now. For I am enraged because you broke my preceptor's bow.

RAMA: Párashu·rama, these old stories about your fame are like ragged clothes... But I would like to see your heroism now. *(Toward the rear of the stage.)* My brother, Lákshmana, give me my bow...

4.165 JĀMADAGNYAḤ: are, an|ātma|jña kṣatriya|vaṭo!

tac cāpam Īśa|bhuja|pīḍana|pīta|sāraṃ
prāg apy abhajyata, bhavāṃs tu nimitta|mātram.
rājanyaka|pradhana|sādhanam asmadīyam
ākarṣa kārmukam idaṃ Garuḍa|dhvajasya!

ākṛṣṭena punar amun" âiva dhanuṣā kil' âsmān abhiyokṣyase. kṣatra|vadha|sattre dīkṣitānāṃ cirasya hotā paraśur asmākam asty eva.

iti RĀMASYA *haste dhanur arpayati.*

RĀMAḤ: *(gṛhītvā)* Bhārgava! samantād utkhātinī bhūmir iyam. tad ehi, vimarda|kṣama|pradeśam avatarāvaḥ.

4.170 JĀMADAGNYAḤ: *(sa|roṣaṃ, vikaṭaṃ parikrāman)* bho bhoḥ, kṣātreṇa brāhmeṇa ca tejasā vikatthamānāḥ!

bhavatu śaraṇa|do vā sarva|śastr'|âbhisāraḥ,
pratividadhatu v" âsminn āśiṣo vaijayikyaḥ,
a|Daśaratham a|Rāmaṃ nir|Videh'|êndram urvī|
valayam iha vidhatte roṣaṇo Raiṇukeyaḥ.

PÁRASHU·RAMA: You miserable fool of a kshatriya, you really do not know your limits, 4.165

> That bow had already lost its force, for it had been exhausted of being strung by Shiva's arms, and broke by itself even before that day—you were a mere instrument in that process. Now string this bow of mine, with which I killed all the kshatriyas, and which comes from the Garuda-bannered Vishnu himself.

Then, when you have strung this bow, you can fight against me with it. For I will still have this sacrificial priest of old, who acted for me when I was initiated in the sacrifice of warriors: my battle-axe.

Thus he places his bow in RAMA*'s hands.*

RAMA: *(takes it)* Párashu·rama, this ground is uneven everywhere, so come, let us go to a place that will bear our fight.

PÁRASHU·RAMA: *(angrily and fiercely, he walks around the stage)* You who are boasting with your heroic as well as brahmanic force,* here, 4.170

> All the weapons may come together to protect them, and people may sing benedictions to assure their victory, but no matter what, now the earth shall be made free of Dasha·ratha, Rama and the King of Vidéha by the enraged Párashu·rama, son of Rénuka.

iti niṣkrāntau.

NEPATHYE: bho bhoḥ, paura|jāna|padāḥ! pravartyatāṃ māṅgalikam ātodyam. prasajyatām ayaṃ Vaidehī|vivāh'|ôtsavo Jāmadagnya|vijay'|ôtsavena!

«kanyā kā cid ih' âpi karmaṇi paṇaḥ
syād» ity asūyā|valat|
Sīt"|âpāṅga|mayūkha|māṃsala|mukha|
jyotsn"|âvaliptīṃ divam
kurvāṇena Ragh'|ûdvahena cakṛṣe
nārāyaṇīyaṃ dhanuḥ,
saṃdhāy' âtha śaraś ca Bhārgava|gati|
cchedād amoghī|kṛtaḥ.

4.175 *tataḥ praviśato* RĀMA|JĀMADAGNYAU.

RĀMAḤ: bhagavan Bhārgava!

parair āhūtānāṃ
vihitam api śastraṃ, bhavatu naḥ
prakṛtyā viprebhyaḥ
punar a|kṛta|śastrā Raghu|bhuvaḥ.
cirād aṇḍīreṇa
tvayi tad api Rāmeṇa guṇitaṃ;
tapo|vidyā|vīra|
vrata|maya! mayi kṣāmyatu bhavān.

JĀMADAGNYAḤ: *(vihasya)* kim aparāddham asmāsu vatsena?

yad|artham asmābhir iha prakopitas
tad adya dṛṣṭvā tava dhāma vaiṣṇavam,
viśīrṇa|sarv'|āmayam asmad|āntaraṃ
cirasya kaṃ cil laghimānam aśnute.

Both exit.

FROM BEHIND THE SCENES: Citizens of towns and all the provinces, play the festive music to celebrate this auspicious event: now, after Sita's wedding, we can also celebrate the victory over Párashu·rama.

> Rama caused the sky to be lightly covered with the moonlight of Sita's beautiful* face, which was radiating with sidelong glances as she turned her head, thinking with jealousy that another girl could become the award in this competition.* Rama strung Vishnu-Narayana's bow and he made the arrow he fixed on it fulfill its function unfailingly by destroying Párashu·rama's way to heaven.*

Then RAMA *and* PÁRASHU·RAMA *reenter.* 4.175

RAMA: Venerable Párashu·rama,

> Although I have taken up my arms against an enemy who challenged me, members of the Raghu dynasty are not of the kind to fight against brahmins. For a long time, this haughty Rama obeyed this rule with respect to you, o sage rich in ascetic power, knowledge and heroism, you who keep your vows, please forgive me.

PÁRASHU·RAMA: *(smiling)* What is the fault you are supposed to have committed against me?

> I provoked you to see your power, which I understood today to belong to Vishnu himself. So now my heart is freed of all affliction; after a long time it has attained some relief.*

4.180 RĀMAḤ: ita ito bhavān.

JĀMADAGNYAḤ: *(cubukam unnamayya, sa|smitam)* vatsa, a|praśastaḥ khalv āraṇyakānāṃ jana|padeṣu cira|pracāraḥ. tat kva punar asmān neṣyasi?

RĀMAḤ: bhagavan, bhagavato Yājñavalkyasya āvasathe kṛt'|ātitheya|saṃvidhānau tāta|Janakau bhavantam anupālayataḥ.

JĀMADAGNYAḤ: vatsa, a|parihāryam eva hy ātithyaṃ rājanya|śrotriyāṇām. kiṃ tu punar evaṃ|vidha|vaikhānas'|ôcit'|ācāra|skhalita|vilakṣo na śaknomi dharm'|ācāryaṃ Yājñavalkyam upety' âvalokayitum. ācāras tu dūrād eva kṛto 'pi kṛtaḥ syāt. *(kiṃ cid uccaiḥ, nepathy'|âbhimukham)*

yasya smṛtiṃ pratīkṣante catur|varge manīṣiṇaḥ,
namo bhagavate tasmai Yājñavalkyāya yogine.

4.185 NEPATHYE:

gāyatrī tri|padā devī pāpmānam apahantu te.
punantu pāvamānyas tvām ṛdhnotu brahma te param.

JĀMADAGNYAḤ: bhagavan, apatrapamāṇo na bhavantaṃ draṣṭum utsahe. tad anumanyasva mām araṇya|gamanāya.

RAMA: Come over here, my lord. 4.180

PÁRASHU·RAMA: *(lifting up* RAMA*'s chin, smiling)* My child, it is not commendable for forest-dwelling ascetics to move around in villages for such a long time. So where are you leading me?

RAMA: My lord, in the venerable Yajnaválkya's home, my father and Jánaka have made the necessary preparations to receive their noble guest and are waiting for you.

PÁRASHU·RAMA: My son, a reception prepared by eminent warriors is not to be refused, but I am rather ashamed of not having behaved as an ascetic should, and cannot go there to face my spiritual teacher, Yajnaválkya. However, one can perform duties of politeness even from a distance. *(somewhat aloud, turning toward the rear of the stage)*

> He whose sacred teaching about the four aims of men is followed by all the sages, homage to him, the venerable yogi, Yajnaválkya.

FROM BEHIND THE SCENES: 4.185

> May the three lines of the Gayátri *mantra* destroy your sins; may the purificatory mantras cleanse you and may your spiritual knowledge increase.

PÁRASHU·RAMA: My lord, I am much too ashamed to see you. Please give me your approval so that I can go to the forest.

NEPATHYE:

śivās te panthāno;
 vraja nija|gṛhebhyas nija|gṛhān;
kim anyat? sarveṣāṃ,
 guṇa|maya, śiro|mālyam asi naḥ;
tri|lokī|nirmāṇa|
 sthiti|nidhana|bandhor Madhu|bhido
bhavān mūrtiḥ ṣaṣṭhī
 Bhṛgu|kulam adhiṣṭhāya ramate.

4.190 JĀMADAGNYAḤ: vatsa, Rāma|bhadra.

RĀMAḤ: ājñāpaya!

JĀMADAGNYAḤ: nivartasva. nūnam idānīṃ kṛta | kautuk' | āgāra|maṅgal'|ôpacāraḥ śvaśura|lokas tvām pratīkṣate.

iti parikramya niṣkrāntaḥ.

RĀMAḤ: *(s'|ôdvegam)* katham, gato bhagavān? tad aham api tāta|samīpam eva gacchāmi. *(iti parikrāman puro 'valokya)* kathaṃ, tātaś ca Janakaś c' êta ev' âbhivartete. *(ity upasarpati.)*

4.195 *tataḥ praviśato* JANAKA|DAŚARATHAU *rājānau, anyonyam pariṣvajya.*

JANAKAḤ:

su|caritam idam aitihāsikānāṃ
 na hṛdi viraṃsyati, yat tav' âiṣa vatsaḥ
Bhṛgu|suta|paraś'|ûdarād virājat
 sahaja|vijitvaram ācakarṣa tejaḥ.

FROM BEHIND THE SCENES:

> May your paths be favorable. Go home from what is also your home now. What else shall I say to you, the most virtuous of all? You are like a crown for us. As a member of the Bhrigu clan, you can rejoice to be the sixth incarnation of Lord Vishnu, who governs the creation, maintenance and destruction of this triple world.

PÁRASHU·RAMA: My son, dear Rama. . . 4.190

RAMA: I listen to your order.

PÁRASHU·RAMA: Please go home. The household of your father-in-law has prepared a festive reception to please you in your new home; they are surely waiting for you now.

He goes around the stage and exits.

RAMA: *(alarmedly)* What, you have already left? Then I shall also go to see my father. *(He goes around the stage, then looks ahead.)* Look, my father and Jánaka are coming this way. *(He approaches them.)*

The two kings, JÁNAKA *and* DASHA·RATHA, *enter holding each other.* 4.195

JÁNAKA:

> Bards will never cease to remember this good deed of your son: he took the kshatriya-conquering inborn radiance out of Párashu·rama's battle-axe.

DAŚARATHAḤ: *(puro 'valokya sa|harṣam)* katham, āgata eva vatso Rāma|bhadraḥ.

JANAKAḤ: sakhe, mahā|rāja Daśaratha, paśya paśya!

4.200 cirāt kṣātraṃ tejas
tri|jagad|upajīvyaṃ janayitā,
vidhātā sarveṣām
upari Savitāraṃ kula|bhṛtām,
vinetā varṇānāṃ
Bhṛgu|pati|bhujā|darpa|nikaṣo,
mahā|vīraḥ, śrīmān
ayam amṛtam akṣṇor vikirati.

DAŚARATHAḤ: *(nirvarṇya sa|sneham)* sakhe Sīradhvaja, Raghu|rāja|dharm'|âdhikāra|sarva|dhurīṇaḥ śiśur api vatso 'yam. tad asmin jarasā dur|vahaṃ varṇ'|āśrama|bhāram āropya, kv' âpi tapo|vane Dilīpa|kul'|ôcitena vidhinā śeṣam āyur upabubhukṣāmahe.

JANAKAḤ: sakhe Daśaratha, sādhu te hṛdayam īdṛśam. kramād evam anuṣṭhātavyam.

RĀMAḤ: *(upasṛty' âbhivādayate.)*

JANAKAḤ: ehy ehi, vatsa Rāma|bhadra. *(iti sa|harṣam āliṅgati.)*

4.205 DAŚARATHAḤ: *(sa|harṣaṃ* RĀMAM *āliṅgya)* sakhe Janaka, Rāma|bhadram abhiṣektuṃ Jāmadagnya|vijaya|prītir eva śreyān avasaraḥ. kāla|kṣepe punaḥ ko hetuḥ?

DASHA·RATHA: *(looking ahead, with delight)* Look, my dear Rama has arrived.

JÁNAKA: My friend, Maharaja Dasha·ratha, look,

> After a long time, he is the first to make the glory of kshatriyas shine forth to be enjoyed in the three worlds. He is the one to have established the Sun as the foremost ancestor of all. As the leader of all castes, he has tested the pride of Párashu·rama's arms. Here he is, this eminent great hero, filling our eyes with ambrosia. 4.200

DASHA·RATHA: *(observing him, with affection)* My friend, Jánaka, although this son of mine is still a child, he has already taken up the burden of lawfully governing the Raghu dynasty. Now I shall also confer all my social duties onto him, which I find difficult to fulfill at this old age. Then I shall go to a hermitage, just as our ancestors used to do, to spend the rest of my life there.

JÁNAKA: My friend, Dasha·ratha, your intention is appropriate. You should do so in due course.

RAMA: *(Approaches and greets them.)*

JÁNAKA: Come over here, my dear child, Rama. *(He embraces him with delight.)*

DASHA·RATHA: *(embracing* RAMA *with joy)* My friend, Jánaka, our happiness to see Rama conquer Párashu·rama provides a good occasion to perform his consecration. In fact, why should we postpone it? 4.205

praviśya.

LAKṢMAṆAḤ: iyam āryāyā Manthar'|ôpanītā madhyam'|âmbāyāḥ patrikā.

RĀJĀNĀV *anyonyaṃ sa|vitarkam paśyataḥ.*

RĀMAḤ: *(sa|harṣam)* vatsa Lakṣmaṇa, api sa|parivārāyāḥ kuśalam ambāyāḥ kathayaty āryā Mantharā?

4.210 LAKṢMAṆAḤ: ārya, atha kim.

RĀMAḤ: *(sa|harṣam)* nūnam asmat|pravāsa|daurmanasyam ambāṃ pīḍayati.

JANAKAḤ: *(*LAKṢMAṆA*|hastāt patrikāṃ gṛhītvā vācayati.)*

svasti mahā|rājāya Daśarathāya. Kaikeyī vijñāpayati, yathā:

tan me vara|dvayam urī|kṛta|pūrvam eva
  yāce: bibhartu Bharatas tava rājya|lakṣmīm.
varṣāṇi tiṣṭhatu catur|daśa Daṇḍakāyām
  Saumitri|Maithilasutā|sahitaś ca Rāmaḥ.

4.215 *iti* RĀJĀNAU *mūrcchataḥ.*

RĀMAḤ: *(śirasi pattrikāṃ nidhāya)* vatsa Lakṣmaṇa, asmad|ārādhana|sah'|âdhyāyinīṃ prajāvatīm ādāya purastād gaccha.

LAKṢMAṆO *niṣkrāntaḥ.*

LÁKSHMANA *enters.*

LÁKSHMANA: Here is a letter from Queen Kaikéyi,* brought by Mánthara.

The TWO KINGS *look at each other thoughtfully.*

RAMA: *(happily)* My dear brother, Lákshmana, has Mánthara brought good news of the queen and her family?

LÁKSHMANA: My brother, I am sure she has. 4.210

RAMA: *(happily)* Surely, it is because we are away from her that she may be grieved.

JÁNAKA: *(takes the letter from* LÁKSHMANA*'s hand and reads it out)*

Hail to Maharaja Dasha·ratha. Kaikéyi is making the following request.

> I beg you to grant these two requests you promised me long ago to fulfill without knowing what they were. The first is that Bharata should inherit your kingdom, and the second is that Rama should go and stay in the Dándaka forest for fourteen years, together with Lákshmana and Sita.

The TWO KINGS *faint.* 4.215

RAMA: *(touching his head with the letter)** My little brother, Lákshmana, take your sister-in-law, who will help you to cheer me up,* and go ahead.

LÁKSHMANA *exits.*

RĀMAḤ: tātau, samāśvasitaṃ samāśvasitam! *(iti paṭ'|ântena vījayati.)*

JANAKAḤ: *(samāśvasya, ākāśe lakṣyaṃ baddhvā)*

4.220 pāṇir gṛhīto Raghu|puṃgavena;
devaḥ purāṇaḥ śvaśuro Vivasvān;
pitā svayaṃ Kekaya|cakra|vartī;
karm' êdam etādṛśam, āḥ, kim etat?

iti mūrcchati.

RĀMAS *tath" âiva paṭ'|ântena vījayati.*

DAŚARATHAḤ: *(āśvasya)*

ko 'py eṣa vāṅ|manasayor ativṛtta|vartmā,
bhāvo hutāśana|mayaś ca tamo|mayaś ca;
bhoktṛtva|mātram iha me punar īdṛśaṃ māṃ,
hā vatsa, Rāma, katham utsahase vihātum?

4.225 *(vimṛśya)* hā, vatse Jānaki, niśā|carāṇām ātitheyī|bhavituṃ Daśaratha|gṛhaṃ praviṣṭ" âsi.

iti mūrcchati.

RĀMAḤ: tātau, samāśvasitaṃ samāśvasitam!

JANAKAḤ: *(āśvasya, ākāśe lakṣyam baddhvā)* sādhu, sakhi Kaikeyī, sādhu, yad asyā viśvaṃbharā|duhitur me vatsāyāḥ patyur anuvṛttir eva prasādī|kṛtā. *(vimṛśya, sa|vyatham)*

RAMA: My elders, please take heart. *(He fans them with the edge of his garment.)*

JÁNAKA: *(recovering, he looks at something in the air)*

> She was married to the foremost of Raghus, Dasha·ratha; the ancestor of her father-in-law is the sun god; her father is the King of Kékaya himself. Alas! How could Kaikéyi do such a terrible thing? 4.220

He faints again.

RAMA *fans him with the edge of his garment again.*

DASHA·RATHA: *(recovering)*

> Here I am in this indescribable state, full of fire and darkness, which is beyond the range of what words can explain or the mind can understand. Now that I have no choice but to bear what is meted out to me,* how could you leave me in this state, my dear Rama?

(reflecting) My dear daughter, Sita, you have entered the house of Dasha·ratha only to be received by demons. 4.225

He faints.

RAMA: My elders, please take heart.

JÁNAKA: *(recovering, looking at something in the air)* Well done, our friend, Kaikéyi. You have been generous enough to let my daughter, the child of the earth, follow her husband. *(reflecting, with pain)*

dhanuṣmantau vatsau,
Daśa|mukha|bhujair ūṣmalatamāḥ
pradeśās te; vatsā
śiśur, a|śiva|vṛttāḥ vana|bhuvaḥ;
priyai rājā muktair
asubhir apamārṣṭi svam ayaśaś;
caritra|vyatyāsaḥ,
sakhi, katham ayaṃ Kekaya|kule?

4.230 kaṣṭaṃ ca! vayam api katham anena jana|padeṣu bahulī|bhaviṣyatā Bharata|yauva|rājya|lakṣmī|karṇa|pūra|tamāla|pallavena Kaikeyī|duryaśasā mūrdhānam unnamayya lokasya mukhaṃ drakṣyāmaḥ?

RĀMAḤ: *(utthāya)* tāta Janaka, yathā sva|sthaṃ tātaṃ śṛṇomi, tathā yatasva.

iti niṣkrāntaḥ.

DAŚARATHAḤ: *(āśvasy' ôtthāya ca.)* vatsa Rāma|bhadra, paripālaya mām.

iti JANAKENA *dhāryamāṇo niṣkrāntaḥ.*

The two princes are good archers, but those places are extremely dangerous because of the presence of ten-headed Rávana. Princess Sita is an innocent child and the forest grounds are very pernicious. Now King Dasha·ratha shall give up his precious life and thus remove the stain on his fame. My friend, Kaikéyi, why is this change to hostile behavior in the family of Kékayas?

Alas, the bad reputation of Kaikéyi will be like a dark *tamála* shoot* to adorn the ears of the Goddess of Fortune under the rule of Bharata as heir apparent; and now that it will widely spread everywhere in the country, I will not be able to appear in public holding up my head to face people's gazes. 4.230

RAMA: *(rising)* Venerable Jánaka, please make all effort so that I hear about the well-being of my father.

RAMA *exits.*

DASHA·RATHA: *(recovers and rises)* My dear son, Rama, protect me.*

Held by JÁNAKA, DASHA·RATHA *exits.*

PRELUDE TO ACT V
SANSKRIT PRELUDE

tataḥ praviśataḥ ŚRAVAṆĀ|JĀMBAVANTAU.

JĀMBAVĀN: tatas tataḥ.

ŚRAVAṆĀ: tato Mithilāyā niṣkramya, Mantharā|kalevaraṃ vikīrya, Māruti|pratyavekṣitaṃ sva|śarīram adhiṣṭhāya, Gaṅgāyāṃ Śṛṅgaverapuraṃ nāma puram āgatya bhūt" âsmi.

JĀMBAVĀN: tatas tataḥ.

5.5 ŚRAVAṆĀ: tataś c' ânupadam eva tasmin, «imau Rāma|Lakṣmaṇau, iyaṃ Sīt" êti» sarvataḥ śabdo mahān abhūt.

JĀMBAVĀN: *(sa|harṣam)* tatas tataḥ.

ŚRAVAṆĀ: tataś ca, «kāv etau Rāma|Lakṣmaṇau?» iti karṇa|dhār'|âdhipatinā Guhen' âham anuyuktā niveditavatī:

putrīyatā Daśarathena muni|prasādāt
prāptāḥ purāṇa|puruṣasya kalāś catasraḥ.
tāsām ayaṃ guṇa|mayaḥ prathamaḥ kumāro,
dhīr'|ôddhataḥ punar asāv aparaḥ tṛtīyaḥ.

JĀMBAVĀN: Śravaṇe, sādh' ûktam. tatas tataḥ.

5.10 ŚRAVAṆĀ: tataś ca, udak'|ânta|nivartit'|ānuyātrika|bandhu|vargaḥ sa|saṃbhram'|ôpagatena Guhen' ôpanītāṃ nāvam adhiruhya,

tīrtvā Bhūteśa|mauli|srajam Amara|dhunīm
ātman" âsau tṛtīyas,
tasmai Saumitri|maitrī|mayam upakṛtavān
ātaraṃ nāvikāya.

Enter JÁMBAVAN *and* SHRÁVANA.

JÁMBAVAN: And then?

SHRÁVANA: Then I left the city of Míthila and discarded Mánthara's body, to take up my own, which had been looked after by Hánuman. Thus, I went to the town called Shringa·vera·pura, on the bank of the Ganges.

JÁMBAVAN: And then?

SHRÁVANA: Then, as I arrived there, some noisy tumult took 5.5
place and people kept saying that Rama, Lákshmana and Sita had come there.

JÁMBAVAN: *(with delight)* And then?

SHRÁVANA: Then the king of those navigators,* Guha, asked me who these Rama and Lákshmana were and I replied:

> Thanks to a sage's grace, Dasha·ratha, who desired to have sons, obtained four quarters of Vishnu, the primeval man, as four sons. Here is the first and best quarter, Prince Rama; and the other one is the third, the heroic Lákshmana.

JÁMBAVAN: Shrávana, exactly as you said. And then?

SHRÁVANA: Then Rama asked his relatives who were trav- 5.10
eling with him to stop at the bank of the river. They took Guha's boat, which Guha himself had brought there quickly.

> Accompanied by Sita and Lákshmana, Rama crossed the Ganges, the river of gods, which decorates Shiva's head; and in return for this service he gave the ferryman his friendship, which is as strong as his bond with Lákshmana. Then Rama's path

vyāma|grāhya|stanībhiḥ śabara|yuvatibhiḥ
kautuk'|ôdañcad|akṣaṃ
kṛcchrād anvīyamānaḥ kṣaṇam acalam atho
Citrakūṭam pratasthe.

JĀMBAVĀN: hanta, mahat karuṇam!

ŚRAVAṆĀ: ārya, karuṇa|bhayād eva tasminn iṅgudī|taru|mūla|deśe kumārayor jaṭā|grathaṇa|vṛttāntam antar|hitavaty asmi.

JĀMBAVĀN: Śravaṇe, sarvam etat kalyāṇ'|ôdarkaṃ bhaviṣyati. tatas tataḥ.

5.15 ŚRAVAṆĀ: ahaṃ tu Niṣāda|pati|prītaye tatr' âiv' âtiṣṭham. atīte ca gaṇa|rātre, sa|prakṛti|jāna|padaḥ pitṛ|svarg'|ārohaṇa|vārt"|âbhidhāyī Dāśarathir dvitīyo Rāma|bhadram Ayodhyām ānetuṃ ten' âiva pathā Citrakūṭam upāgataḥ.

JĀMBAVĀN: *(sa|śaṅkam)* tatas tataḥ.

ŚRAVAṆĀ: tataś ca, tasmin: «ārya, lokeṣu Kekayānām an|alpa|kīrti|stambham ākalpaṃ nikhanatā ken' âpi vidhinā chalitas tātaḥ. pratigṛhāṇa Raghūṇāṃ dhuram!» iti punaḥ punar anubandhī Rāmeṇa śarīra|spṛṣṭikayā pratyādiṣṭaḥ, kṛta|jaṭā|parigraho Bharataḥ Śarabhaṅga|muni|preṣitāṃ Rāmasya pādukāṃ bhadr'|āsanam adhiropya, prajānām ābhyudayikam avekṣamāṇaḥ, tad" âiva Nandigrāmaṃ gatavān.

was not easy to follow for the upward-looking curious eyes of the young Shabara women, whose large breasts could hardly be embraced by anyone*—for he left immediately for the Chitra·kuta mountain.

JÁMBAVAN: What an ordeal!

SHRÁVANA: Sir, it is because I was afraid of arousing pity for them that I did not tell you first that the two princes had made matted locks for themselves under the *íngudi* tree.

JÁMBAVAN: Shrávana, all this will have a happy ending. And then what happened?

SHRÁVANA: To please the King of Nishádas, Guha, I stayed 5.15
at the same place. And, after a number of nights, Dasha·ratha's second son, Bharata, arrived with his ministers and subjects, with the news that their father had gone to heaven; and then he also left for the Chitra·kuta mountain, following the same path, in order to take Rama back to Ayódhya.

JÁMBAVAN: *(with anxiety)* And then what happened?

SHRÁVANA: When they met, Bharata kept saying that by means of some plot that undermined forever the long-standing fame of the Kékayas,* their father was cheated and that Rama should now accept being the Raghu king; but Rama replied only with a warning gesture.* Then Bharata also transformed himself into an ascetic with matted locks and put Rama's sandals, which had been sent through the sage Shara·bhanga, on the throne.*

JĀMBAVĀN: *(sa|harṣam)* hanta, phalitam asmad|vyavasāya| Śravaṇā|pariśrāmābhyām. tatas tataḥ.

ŚRAVAṆĀ: tataś ca, «āśaucam āsthitasya kṣatriyasya pratiṣiddham astra|grahaṇam» iti chidr'|ânveṣibhir jana|sthāna|vāstavyaiḥ Khara|Dūṣaṇa|prabhṛtibhis tatra Virādho nāma rākṣasas tīkṣṇaḥ prahitaḥ.

5.20 JĀMBAVĀN: *(vihasya)* dhiṅ mūrkhāḥ! ātipātike hi kārye rājñāṃ sadyo viśuddhiḥ. tatas tataḥ.

ŚRAVAṆĀ: tataś ca, Virādha|vadha|kṣaṇ'|ākṣipta|hṛdaye duḥ|saha|śoka|dīrgh'|âhnīm aurdhva|daihikīm pituḥ kriyām ativāhya, bhagavatā catuḥ|samudra|muṣṭiṃ|dhayena Vindhy'|âcala|cāpal'|ārambha|visrambha|ghātinā Vātāpi|dānava|dīrgha|nidrā|maṅgala|kalaśena kalaśa|yoninā sa|nāthām araṇya|vīthīṃ pratiṣṭhamāne Dāśarathau, pathi Dhārādharo nāma vāyasaḥ sahas" aiva Vaidehīm upādravat.

JĀMBAVĀN: *(sva|gatam)* idaṃ tāvad apaśakunaṃ nāma. *(prakāśam)* tatas tataḥ?

ŚRAVAṆĀ: tataś ca,

rakṣo|'bhicāra|caru|bhāṇḍam iva stanaṃ yo
devyā Videha|duhitur vidadāra kākaḥ,
aiṣīkam astram adhikṛtya tadā tam akṣṇā
kāṇī|cakāra caramo Raghu|rāja|putraḥ

Seeking the prosperity of the subjects, Bharata left for Nandi·grama.

JÁMBAVAN: *(happily)* Our efforts and Shrávana's diligence have borne their fruit.* And then?

SHRÁVANA: Since a warrior who has become impure due to his contact with the dead is not allowed to take up his arms, Cruel, Corrupt and other demons living in Jana·sthana, eager to find a vulnerable point of Rama to attack, sent there a surly demon called Virádha.

JÁMBAVAN: *(smiling)* Those idiots! If a king has an urgent 5.20
task to perform, he is immediately purified anyway. And then?

SHRÁVANA: Then Rama, with his heart set on killing Virádha, first performed the funerary rites for his father for some long days spent in deep sadness and left for the forest ruled by jar-born Agástya: the sage who once drank up the four oceans, who confidently put an end to the foolish efforts of the Vindhya mountains and who served as the water pot to protect the eternal sleep of the demon Vatápi.* But, on their way to that forest, a crow called Dhara·dhara suddenly attacked Sita.

JÁMBAVAN: *(aside)* But this is a bad omen. *(aloud)* And then?

SHRÁVANA: Well, then,

> As if Princess Sita's breast contained an offering
> to perform black magic for demons,* the crow at-
> tacked it, but was made blind in one eye by the ar-
> row sent from the bow of the eldest* Raghu prince,
> Rama.

5.25 JĀMBAVĀN: tatas tataḥ?

ŚRAVAṆĀ: tataś ca,

> krameṇ' âiva Sutīkṣṇ'|ādīn upasthāya mahā|munīn,
> Agastya|śāsanād āste Pañcavaṭyāṃ Ragh'|ûdvahaḥ.

JĀMBAVĀN: *(sa|harṣam)* tarhi hasta|stha ev' âsmākam. kiyad antaram Ṛṣyamūka|Janasthānayoḥ?

ŚRAVAṆĀ: ārya, na khalv ady' âpi śrotavyaṃ śṛṇoṣi.

5.30 JĀMBAVĀN: avahito 'smi.

ŚRAVAṆĀ: tatra ca, kāmukī Rāma|bhadram anupraviśya «rasaṃ dāsyām' iti» saṃkalpita|pati|droha|pātakinī Śūrpaṇakhā Lakṣmaṇa|roṣa|hutabhuji karṇa|nās'|âuṣṭhamayībhis tisṛbhir āhutibhiḥ prāyaś|cittayāṃ|cakre.

JĀMBAVĀN: *(s'|āśaṅkam)* ahaha, mahān an|artha|kandaḥ saṃvṛttaḥ. atha bhaginyās tādṛśaṃ viḍambanam avalokya, Khar'|ādibhiḥ kiṃ pratipannam?

ŚRAVAṆĀ: *(vihasya)* ārya, kiṃ pratipannam? yad Rāma|bhadre dhṛta|dhanuṣi pratipadyate.

JÁMBAVAN: And then? 5.25

SHRÁVANA: Then,

> the Raghu prince paid homage to the sages, Sutíkshna and the others in due course, and stayed in the Pancha·vati hermitage, following Agástya's advice.

JÁMBAVAN: *(with delight)* So he is in our hands. What is the distance between the Rishya·muka mountain and Jana·sthana?

SHRÁVANA: My lord, you have not yet heard everything you needed to.

JÁMBAVAN: I am listening. 5.30

SHRÁVANA: In that forest, the demoness Shurpa·nakha, who was desirous of Rama, followed him to give him some "drinks."* She thus committed the crime of acting against her imaginary husband,* and was punished by making a triple offering, as it were, of her ears, nose and lips, which were consumed by Lákshmana's fire of anger.*

JÁMBAVAN: *(with alarm)* Ah, this will be the source of some great disaster. When Cruel and the other demons saw what a terrible thing happened to their sister, what did they do?

SHRÁVANA: *(smiling)* My lord, what could they do? They did what one can do against Rama, who carries his bow.

JĀMBAVĀN: *(sa|hāsam)* tat kiṃ te 'pi Vāli|sāhāyak'|ôpasthāyino Virādha|yātrā|prahatam adhvānam anuprapannāḥ?

5.35 ŚRAVAṆĀ: atha kim.

JĀMBAVĀN: Śravaṇe, prarūḍham idānīṃ Rāma|Rāvaṇayor vairam.

ŚRAVAṆĀ: *(hasantī)* ārya, manye Khara|Dūṣaṇa|prabhṛtīnām abhibhav'|âbhidhāne kevalaṃ kleśayiṣyati vācam, ātmanaḥ punar an|akṣaram api Śūrpaṇakhā|mukhaṃ sukham āvedayiṣyati Daśakandharasya.

JĀMBAVĀN: *(sa|smitam)* Śravaṇe, ati|lagh'|ûtthānam anartham utprekṣya pramugdho 'smi.

Aikṣvākeṇa pur" âpi Kauśika|makhād
ārabhya Laṅk"|ēśvaro
dhatte śāśvatikaṃ virodham; adhunā
tv ete hatā bāndhavāḥ.
utsāha|prabhu|mantra|śaktibhir alaṃ|
bhūṣṇuś, chala|jño, balī,
dṛptaḥ Śūrpaṇakhā|nikāram aparaṃ
dṛṣṭvā kathaṃ mṛṣyate?

5.40 śanaiḥ śanair anayor virodha|saṃdhukṣaṇena tulya|vyasana|stho Dāśarathir a|sahāyaḥ Sūrya|sūnunā saṃdhātum īṣat|karaḥ syāt.

ŚRAVAṆĀ: ārya, kim idānīm anuṣṭheyam? mama hi śiṣya|putro niṣāda|cakra|vartī Guho Lakṣmaṇa|mitram. anena sopānena sukh'|âdhiroho Raghu|patir asmākam.

JÁMBAVAN: *(with a smile)* So they also went the same way that Virádha treaded, ready to help Vali.

SHRÁVANA: Of course. 5.35

JÁMBAVAN: Shrávana, the enmity between Rama and Rávana has been well established.

SHRÁVANA: *(laughing)* Sir, I think that if Shurpa·nakha is to speak of the defeat of Cruel, Corrupt and the other demons, she will only cause her tongue to hurt. And, in any case, her mutilated mouth will easily convey her own defeat to ten-headed Rávana even without words.

JÁMBAVAN: *(smiling)* Shrávana, seeing that Rama's misfortune is so imminent, I feel quite surprised.

> Ever since Vishva·mitra's sacrifice, Rama has become the archenemy of the Lord of Lanka. And now even Rávana's relatives have been hurt. Rávana possesses the power of perseverance, he has authority and wit. He knows how to cheat people, he is strong and proud. Now how will he bear to see Shurpa·nakha's being gravely insulted?

As the enmity between these two is slowly kindled, Rama, who is without any help, will easily form an alliance with Sugríva, the son of the Sun, since he is in a similarly difficult situation. 5.40

SHRÁVANA: Sir, what shall I do now? My disciple's son, the King of Nishádas, Guha, is a friend of Lákshmana's. With his help, we can easily approach Rama.

JĀMBAVĀN: *(sa|harṣa|smitam)* Śravaṇe, satyam asi Sugrīva|pakṣa|pātinī. tad gaccha, sa|tvaram upasthāpaya Niṣāda|rājam!

iti ŚRAVAṆĀ *niṣkrāntā.*

JĀMBAVĀN: *(sarvato nirūpya)* aye, purāṇa|priya|suhṛd asmākaṃ dakṣiṇasyāṃ diśi parāpatan Jaṭāyur iva lakṣyate. tad enam anupālayāmi tāvat. dūra|dṛśo hi gṛdhrāḥ. kadā cid eṣa Laṅkā|dvīpa|vṛttāntam apy upalabheta.

5.45 *praviśya.*

JAṬĀYUḤ: prāpt" âiv' êyam asmābhiḥ Pañcavaṭī, yad amūr Godāvarī|taraṅga|sīkara|seka|sukumāra|māṃsala|parisar'|âraṇya|mālinyo Janasthāna|sīmānaḥ. api ca,

dṛśyante madhu|matta|kokila|vadhū|
nirdhūta|cūt'|âṅkura|
prāg|bhāra|prasarat|parāga|sikatā|
durgās taṭī|bhūmayaḥ
yāḥ kṛcchrād atilaṅghya lubdhaka|bhayāt,
tair eva reṇ'|ûtkarair
dhārā|vāhibhir asti lupta|padavī|
niḥśaṅkam eṇī|kulam.

JĀMBAVĀN: *(kiṃ cid upasṛtya)* kutaḥ punar iyatā vegena vayasyaḥ?

JÁMBAVAN: *(smiling happily)* Shrávana, you are indeed biased toward Sugríva. So go and take the King of Nishádas to Rama quickly.

SHRÁVANA *exits.*

JÁMBAVAN: *(looking everywhere)* O, it seems that my good old friend Jatáyus is seen there, flying toward the South. I shall wait for him here. Vultures can see very far; perhaps he learned some news about the island of Lanka at some point.

JATÁYUS *enters.* 5.45

JATÁYUS: At long last I have reached Pancha·vati, for here are the borders of Jana·sthana, adorned with the surrounding forests, which are made thick and tender by the showers of water that originate in the waves of the Godávari River. Moreover,

> The female cuckoos, drunk with honey,* shook the mango buds, from which fell so much sand-like pollen that it now seems to have made the riverbanks difficult to cross. The black deer, scared of hunters, have leaped beyond those dunes somehow, and as their tracks have been recovered by the continuous shower of pollen, they are now staying over there without fear.

JÁMBAVAN: *(approaching him slowly)* Why is my friend in such a hurry?

JAṬĀYUḤ: *(dṛṣṭvā)* katham, Jāmbavān! sakhe, kṣamasva. na sa|bhājayiṣyāmi tāvad bhavantam. mayā hi Malay'|âcala| kulāyād ārya|Saṃpāti|pādān abhivādya nivartamānena, Mārīca|sahāyena saṃcarann imām araṇyānīm abhilakṣito rākṣasa|rājaḥ. tad ati|viṣamam āśaṅkamānaṃ māṃ vatsa|Rāma|bhadra|snehas tvarayati.

5.50 JĀMBAVĀN: *(sva/gatam)* vayam apy etad eva pratipatsāmahe. *(prakāśam)* sakhe, tvarasva!

iti niṣkrāntaḥ.

JAṬĀYUḤ: *(parikramy' âvalokya ca)* iyam agre Pañcavaṭī. *(sa/vitarkam)*

nīto dūraṃ kanaka|hariṇa|
chadmanā Rāma|bhadraḥ.
paścād enaṃ drutam upasaraty
eṣa vatsaḥ kaniṣṭhaḥ.
bibhyad bibhyat praviśati tataḥ
parṇa|śālāṃ ca bhikṣuḥ,
dhik, kaṣṭam bhoḥ, prathayati nijām
ākṛtiṃ: Rāvaṇo 'yam!

ahaha,

5.55 «ārya|putra, ārya|putr' êti» rudantīṃ kurarīm iva
ratham āropya Vaidehīm eṣa pāpaḥ kva gacchati?

s'|āṭopaṃ parikrāman

re re, Rāvaṇa, re re!

vadhūṭīm Ikṣvākor
nija|kara|tala|sparśa|malinām
imāṃ kurvāṇasya
sphurati hṛdi śobh" âiva bhavataḥ.

JATÁYUS: *(seeing him)* O Jámbavan, my friend, please forgive me that I cannot greet you appropriately. I was on my way back from our nest in the Málaya mountain, after I visited the my elder brother, Sampáti, when I noticed the king of demons, accompanied by his friend Marícha, heading for this forest. I suspect some wicked plot is being hatched here, and my love for my dear Rama is urging me to go and see him.

JÁMBAVAN: *(aside)* I should also like to know what is hap- 5.50
pening... *(aloud)* My friend, do not delay!

JÁMBAVAN *exits.*

JATÁYUS: *(goes around the stage and watches something)* Here is the Pancha·vati in front of me. *(reflecting)*

> Rama got lured far away by Marícha disguised as a golden deer, and then his young brother, Lákshmana, followed him quickly. Now here is a mendicant entering timidly their hut made of leaves. Fie, now he discloses his real form—this is Rávana!

Ah,

> Sita is crying out for her husband like a *kúrari*,* but 5.55
> that wicked demon has put her on his chariot—where is he going with her?

He goes around the stage proudly.

Hey, Rávana, hey,

> You have defiled Rama's wife, whom he has just married, by touching her with your hand—and your heart throbs with joy! But how come you have not even considered those in whose dynasty

kule yeṣāṃ kiṃ ca
tvam asi, gaṇitās te 'pi guravo
na sapta brahmāṇaḥ
katham iva Pulastya|prabhṛtayaḥ?

(punar ākāśe) alīk'|âṭṭa|hāsa|dhūma|dhūsarita|daśa|vaktra|valmīka! kim āttha, re, rākṣas'|âpaśada? kim āttha?

5.60 «jagad|vilobhi|Sīt"|ākhyam āmiṣaṃ harato mama
ayaṃ kila jarad|gṛdhraḥ karād ācchidya neṣyati?»

iti? āḥ, pāpa, katham evam abhidadhāsi? tiṣṭha tiṣṭha!

bhuja|viṭapa|madena vyartham andhaṃ|bhaviṣṇur,
dhig, apasarasi cauraṃ|kāram ākruśyamānaḥ.
tvad|urasi vidadhātu svām avaskāra|keliṃ
kuṭila|karaja|koṭi|krūra|karmā Jaṭāyuḥ.

iti niṣkrāntaḥ.

śuddha|viṣkambhaḥ.

you were born: your elders, the seven sages, Pulástya and the others?*

(again, in the air) Your ten swollen heads are covered with smoke from your false laughter! What did you say, you wretched demon? What did you say?

"I am taking Sita, coveted by the whole world, with me. Now, could this old vulture take her out of my hands, like it would grab a piece of meat for prey?" 5.60

O wicked demon, how can you say that? Stop, stop!

You are blinded by your pride without reason, thinking that your arms are very strong—fie, you are escaping from those who have declared you a thief. But Jatáyus, who is cruel with his sharp and crooked nails, shall play a game of scratching with you.

JATÁYUS *exits.*

End of the Sanskrit prelude.

ACT V
SUGRÍVA'S CONSECRATION

tataḥ praviśati LAKṢMAṆAḤ.

LAKṢMAṆAḤ: aho, dur|nivāra|dāruṇa|krodha|śoka|lajjā|gahano viṣamo 'yaṃ daśā|vivartaḥ, yasminn iti|kartavyat"| âbhidhānam apy asmākam an|aupayikam. tathā hi,

tat|tādṛg|Daśa|kaṇṭha|vañcana|ruṣā
    dhūmāyamāno giraṃ
  n' ârdh'|ôkti|pravilīna|varṇa|vidhurām
    āryaḥ samāpnoti me,
cāpe tāta|Jaṭāyu|jīvita|kathā|
    paryanta|dhūmāyita|
  krodh'|ôtpīḍa|nipīta|śoka|jaḍimā
    dṛṣṭis tu viśrāmyati.

(nepathy'|âbhimukhaḥ) ita ita ārya Mārīca|mathana, dṛśyantām amūr avācīṃ kakubham abhivardhamānā Vindhya|vana|vīthayaḥ.

praviśya.

RĀMAḤ: *(ākāśe lakṣyaṃ baddhvā)*

kule vā śaurye vā
    bhuja|samudaye vā tapasi vā
  babhūvur na prāñcas
    tvam iva bhavitāro na carame;
aho, diṅ|mohas te
    samajani cirād, eṣa na khalu
  pravīrāṇāṃ panthā,
    Daśa|vadana, yen' âsi calitaḥ.

Then LÁKSHMANA *enters.* 5.65

LÁKSHMANA: This turn of our fate is terrible and is pervaded by our anger, dejection and shame, which are harsh and difficult to control. In this plight we are at a loss even to tell ourselves what we should do:

> His voice is overwhelmed with grief and the sounds he makes melt away as he pronounces only half the words, being enraged by that trick of ten-headed Rávana—my brother cannot finish what he started saying to me. But the numbness of dispair disappears from his eyes at the sharp feeling of wrath he experiences when he learns everything about how our good old Jatáyus's life ended, and his glance is now fixed on his bow.

(toward the rear of the stage) Come over here, killer of Marícha. Look, here are the forests in the Vindhya mountain stretching toward the southern direction.

RAMA *enters.*

RAMA: *(looking at something in the air)* 5.70

> No one has been and no one will ever be comparable to you in breed, courage, strength or asceticism. But, alas, you lost your sense of direction a long time ago; for the path you follow is not that of heroes, o ten-headed Rávana.

(vimṛśya, sa|kheda|smitam) aho Paulastya,

siddha|śrotra|paramparā|parigatair
ebhiḥ prapautrasya te
vṛttair adya Pulastya|varjam abhitaḥ
smereṣu deva'|rṣiṣu,
viṣvag|vṛttir a|saṃgatā namayituṃ
durvāra|lajjā|bhara|
mlāna|śrīs tu catur|mukhī bhagavato
Dhātuḥ kathaṃ vartate?

(kṣaṇam anudhyāya) hā priye, Videha|rāja|putri! *(iti saṃvaraṇaṃ nāṭayati)*

5.75 LAKṢMAṆAḤ: *(upasṛtya)* ārya, ko 'yam abhiṣaṅgo nāma bhavā|dṛśān apy āspadī|karoti?

patati vyasane daivād dāruṇe dāraṇ'|ātmani
saṃvarmayati vajreṇa dhairyaṃ hi mahatāṃ manaḥ.

RĀMAḤ: *(dīrgham uṣṇaṃ ca niḥśvasya)* vatsa,

sahaja|dhairya|vaśaṃ|vada|vṛttayo
hṛdi rūṣaś ca śucaś ca niyantritāḥ.
iha tu kiṃ karavai, yad apatrapā
kim api mām avamatya vijṛmbhate?

LAKṢMAṆAḤ: *(puro 'valokya)* ārya, ayam agre tāta|Jaṭāyuṣo vīra|loka|sādhana|siddha|kṣetram araṇyanī|saṃniveśaḥ. paśya,

(reflecting, smiling with fatigue) Hey, Rávana, descendant of Pulástya,

When the divine sages learn about your deeds, transmitted to them by a series of *siddhas*,* they will all laugh, except Pulástya, since you are his great-grandson. And then the four heads of Brahma, the venerable Creator, which are turned to the different directions and thus make it impossible for the god to bend them down at once, will lose their luster because of the great and unbearable shame—but what else can they do?*

(thinking for a moment) Alas, my dear princess of Vidéha! *(He mimes that he conceals his feelings.)*

LÁKSHMANA: *(approaching him)* My brother, what is this despair that can affect even someone like you? 5.75

When a terrible and great disaster that can tear one apart happens, then great people's hearts build a diamond shield out of their courage.

RAMA: *(heaving a deep sigh of despair)* My little brother,

Anger and sorrow can be kept in the heart, for they are under the control of one's natural fortitude. But what can I do if the shame that has somehow overcome me is so manifest?

LÁKSHMANA: *(looking ahead)* My brother, here is the part of the forest that has become a site of holy power, because our old Jatáyus ascended to the heaven of heroes in this very place. Look,

5.80 bhagno 'yaṃ katham asti Rāvaṇa|rathas
tātena vajr'|âṅkura|
krūr'|âpaskiramāṇa|bhaṅgura|nakha|
troṭi|truṭad|bandhanaḥ?

RĀMAḤ: *(sa|karuṇam)*

hā Sīradhvaja|rāja|putri, sa tadā
dṛṣṭas tvayā dhanyayā
Pakṣ"|îndro Daśa|kaṇṭha|kuñjara|śiraḥ|
saṃcāri|pañcānanaḥ.

iti LAKṢMAṆAM *avaṣṭabhya dhyānaṃ nāṭayati.*

LAKṢMAṆAḤ: *(sva|gatam)* mahān doṣaḥ khalv ayam atiprasajyamāno mānasaḥ śok'|ākhyo vikāraḥ. tad anyataḥ prasārayāmi. *(prakāśam)* ārya, paśya paśya!

5.85 Vindhya|giri|rāja|kany"|
ântaḥ|puram etās taraṅga|mālinyaḥ
vetasvatībhir adbhis
taurya|trika|guṇanikāṃ dadhate.

RĀMAḤ: *(unmīlya cakṣuṣī, dīrgham uṣṇaṃ ca niḥśvasya)* vatsa, darśanīyam etat.

kumuda|vana|viśāya|jāgrad|ambho-
ruha|kṛta|yāmika|vibhramā ramante
mada|kala|kari|karṇa|tāla|nṛtyan|
mukhara|mayūra|manoramās taṭinyaḥ.

Why, he was able to break Rávana's chariot, when he tore its rope with his bent claws and beak, which cruelly scratch anything like sharp pieces of diamond. 5.80

RAMA: *(with compassion)*

Alas, daughter of King Jánaka, you were lucky enough to see this King of Birds, who was attacking Rávana's heads like a lion would attack the head of an elephant.

Turning toward LÁKSHMANA, *he mimes to be in deep thought.*

LÁKSHMANA: *(aside)* When this mental illness called sorrow lasts long, it is very harmful. I shall go somewhere else. *(aloud)* My brother, look, look,

These rivers garlanded by their waves form the harem of the royal Vindhya mountain. With their waters full of reeds, they practice music, singing and dancing. 5.85

RAMA: *(opening his eyes and heaving a deep sigh)* My little brother, look how wonderful this is—

The rivers are gracefully enjoying themselves as the day-lotuses take their turn to act as sentinels, while the night-lotuses go to sleep; and on the beautiful riverbanks the peacocks are noisily dancing to the rhythm beaten by the flapping ears of elephants in rut.*

iti parikrāmataḥ

LAKṢMAṆAḤ: ārya, ayam ito girir Mālyavān.

5.90 iha mahiṣa|viṣāṇa|vyasta|pāṣāṇa|pīṭha|
skhalana|sulabha|rohid|garbhiṇī|bhrūṇa|hatyāḥ,
kuhara|viharamāṇa|prauḍha|bhallūka|hikkā|
caya|cakita|kirāta|srasta|śastrā van'|ântāḥ.

RĀMAḤ: *(ciraṃ dṛṣṭvā, sa|karuṇ'|âsram)*

pratiparisaraṃ bhūyān arghaḥ
śikhaṇḍa|bhṛtāṃ, yathā|
militam alibhiḥ saṃbhujyante
kadamba|vibhūtayaḥ;
abhinava|ghana|vyūḍh'|ôraskaḥ
pravarṣati Mālyavān
viṣadhara|vadhū|garbh'|ādhāna|
priyaṃ|karaṇīr apaḥ.

vatsa Lakṣmaṇa, dhāraya mām. na śaknomi stambhayitum ātmānam.

iyam a|virala|śvāsā
śuṣyan|mukhī bhidura|svarā
tanur avayavaiḥ śrānta|
srastair upaiti vivarṇatām.
sphurati jaḍatā, bāṣpā-
yete dṛśau, galati smṛtir,
mayi rasatayā śoko
bhāvaś cireṇa vipacyate.

5.95 *iti* LAKṢMAṆENA *dhāryamāṇo nimīlit'|âkṣa eva*

hā priye, Daṇḍak'|âraṇya|vihāra|sa|brahma|cāriṇi!

They both walk around the stage.

LÁKSHMANA: My brother, here is the Mályavan mountain.

> Here, at the edge of the forest, buffaloes split the rocks into pieces with their horns, and as pregnant deer stumble on those stones they often lose their fetuses; and here huge bears living in the caves frighten the hunters with their grunts so that they drop their weapons. 5.90

RAMA: *(staring, then with compassion and in tears)*

> The peacocks are having a great feast everywhere, and the bees are enjoying the rich blossoms of the *kadámba** trees wherever they find them.* The chest of the Mályavan mountain is covered with newly formed rainclouds—it is now showering down the waters, which please the cobra wives and make them conceive.

My little brother, Lákshmana, hold me now. I cannot keep myself upright.

> I can hardly breathe, my mouth is parched and my voice trembles, my limbs are tired and hang down loosely while my body becomes all pale; my apathy increases, tears appear in my eyes and my memory fails—my state of sorrow is slowly being tranformed into a dominant sentiment.

As he is being held by LÁKSHMANA, *he closes his eyes.* 5.95

O my beloved! You spent your time in ascetic chastity with me in the Dándaka forest.

iti punaḥ saṃvṛṇute.

LAKṢMAṆAḤ: *(sa|khedam, ātma|gatam)* kena punar eṣa raso ras'|ântareṇa tiras|kriyate?

NEPATHYE: āḥ pāpa, Kabandha|hataka, ayaṃ na bhavasi!

5.100 RĀMAḤ: *(ākarṇya, sa|saṃbhramam)* vatsa Lakṣmaṇa, dur|ātmanā Danukabandhena kalahāyamāno vayasyas te Guha iva śrūyate. bahu|chalāni rakṣāṃsi. tat tvaritataram abhyupapadyasva.

LAKṢMAṆAḤ: tathā.

iti niṣkrāntaḥ.

RĀMAḤ: *(sa|karuṇam)* devi vāmaśīle, Sīradhvaja|rāja|nandini, iyaṃ te viśva|visrambha|vimarda|vedinī nicula|nikuñja|rekhā. iha hi,

«sva|vapuṣi nakha|lakṣma svena kṛtvā ‹bhavatyā
kṛtam› iti caturāṇāṃ darśayiṣye sakhīnām.»
iti rahasi mayā te bhīṣitāyāḥ smarāmi
smara|parimala|mudrā|bhaṅga|sarvaṃ|sahāyāḥ.

5.105 *iti dhanur avaṣṭabhya* LAKṢMAṆA*/vṛttānta/datta/cetās tath" âiv' āste.*

tataḥ praviśati LAKṢMAṆAḤ, GUHAḤ *ca.*

GUHAḤ: jayatu devaḥ.

He faints again.

LÁKSHMANA: *(with sorrow, aside)* Which other sentiment could possibly override this one?

BEHIND THE SCENES: O wicked one, wretched Kabándha, you will not get away this time!

RAMA: *(hearing, with alarm)* My dear Lákshmana, I think I 5.100
hear your friend Guha fighting with Danu·kabándha.* Demons play many tricks. So go and help him quickly.

LÁKSHMANA: I will.

LÁKSHMANA *exits.*

RAMA: *(with compassion)* My cross-tempered queen, daughter of Jánaka! Here is the line of thickly grown *níchula* reeds that have experienced a most intimate contact with you. For here,

> I said to you in secret that I had made a nail mark on my body and would show it to your clever friends saying that it was you.* Then you got frightened of this plan of mine and were ready to endure anything to erase that sweet seal of love—this is how I remember you now.

Leaning on his bow, he sits there thinking about what LÁKSH- 5.105
MANA *has told him.*

LÁKSHMANA *and* GUHA *enter.*

GUHA: Long live Prince Lákshmana.

vinetā dṛptānām
ayam a|bhaya|durgaṃ divi|ṣadām,
kaniṣṭhaḥ Kākutstho
jayati jagad|āścarya|caritaḥ,
yad|astraiḥ pāpmānam
rajanicara|janma|graha|sṛjaṃ
vijitya svar|lokān
a|vikalam upātiṣṭhata Danuḥ.

RĀMAḤ: sādhu vṛttam. śivās tasya deva|yānāḥ panthānaḥ. vatsa Guha, viyati vartamānaḥ kaś cid acala iva lakṣitaḥ, kim asau ten' âiva Yojana|bāhunā praharaṇī|kṛtaḥ?

5.110 GUHAḤ:

Dundubhiṃ nāma daity'|êndram niṣpipeṣa kap'|īśvaraḥ.
tasya kaṅkāla|kūṭo 'yaṃ kumāreṇa viloḍitaḥ.

tatas tan|nimitta|janmā saṃprati Vālino mahān abhiyogaḥ saṃbhāvyate.

LAKṢMAṆAḤ: tataḥ kim?

RĀMAḤ: vatsa, mā m" âivam. mānanīyaḥ khalv asau purāṇa|vīro mah"|Êndra|sūnuḥ. (GUHAṂ *prati)* kutaḥ punar āgacchato vatsasya Yojana|bāhur antar|āyaḥ saṃvṛttaḥ?

5.115 GUHAḤ: deva, vyoma|yānena sa|tvaram atikrāmati Rāvaṇe Sītā|devyāḥ—

You chastise those who are vain, you ensure the safety of the gods when they are in danger and you surprise the world with your exploits; you are ever victorious, the youngest descendant of the solar dynasty. Thanks to your arrows, Danu·kabándha has overcome the curse by which he was incarnated in the race of demons and he has reached heaven without fail.*

RAMA: Well done. May his path to heaven be auspicious. My dear Guha, I see some mountain-looking object moving in the air. Was that also transformed into a weapon by Danu·kabándha, with his eight-mile-long arm?*

GUHA: 5.110

The king of monkeys, Vali, tore the demon chief, Dúndubhi, to pieces. It is that demon's heap of bones that Prince Lákshmana has just turned over.

Now, because of this, Vali will launch a big attack on us.

LÁKSHMANA: So what?

RAMA: My brother, you should not speak like this. We should respect this famous hero, who is the son of the great Indra. *(to* GUHA*)* For what purpose were you on your way here when you stumbled into the long-armed Danu·kabándha?

GUHA: Your Majesty, when Rávana was quickly flying away 5.115
in the air, in his chariot, and queen Sita's. . .

RĀMAḤ: *(s'|āśaṅkam, ātma|gatam)* tataḥ kiṃ syāt?

GUHAḤ: yad uttarīyaṃ patad utplutya Hanūmān agrahīt, tad etad deva|guṇ'|ânurāgiṇā kumāra|Sugrīveṇa sa|bhājayitum upasthitavato mama haste devasya prābhṛtī|kṛtam.

iti RĀMASYA *arpayati.*

RĀMAḤ: *(gṛhītvā, hṛdaye nidhāya, s'|âsram)* hā devi, Videha|nandini, katham uttarīya|śeṣā dṛśyase. *(iti nimīlit'|âkṣo* LAKṢMAṆAM *avalambate.)*

5.120 LAKṢMAṆAḤ: *(niḥśvasya)* sakhe Niṣāda|rāja, kuśalaṃ Sugrīvasya?

GUHAḤ: adya tvayi vārttam anuyuñjāne.

RĀMAḤ: *(sva|gatam)*

jānann eva Daś'|ânano 'paharate
naḥ preyasīm, astu vā
Candr'|āpīḍam upāsitaṃ sa hi śiro|
dāma svayaṃ kṛttavān.
daṇḍo 'nyo Daśa|kandharasya na punaḥ
kaṇṭh'|âṭavī|kartanād,
dhig, bāṇair mama Candrahāsa|hataka|
kṣuṇṇo 'yam adhvā vṛtaḥ.

LAKṢMAṆAḤ: ārya, katham asmāsu van'|âukaso 'pi saujanyam anurudhyante?

RAMA: *(with apprehension)* Then what happened?

GUHA: . . . and queen Sita's upper garment flew away, Hánuman caught it in the air. And when I left to come and pay homage to you, then Prince Sugríva, who takes your side in this matter, gave it to me as a present for you.

Thus he gives the garment to RAMA.

RAMA: *(takes it and presses it against his heart, with tears in his eyes)* O my queen, Princess of Vidéha, I can see only a piece of your clothes now. *(He closes his eyes and leans on* LÁKSHMANA.*)*

LÁKSHMANA: *(with a sigh)* My friend, King of the Nishádas, is Sugríva in good health? 5.120

GUHA: Yes, and he thanks you for your kind inquiry.

RAMA: *(aside)*

> Ten-headed Rávana took away my beloved, although he knew well the consequences of his act. Once he cut his garland of heads himself to worship Shiva—still, there is no other punishment for him than cutting his numerous heads. And thus, no matter how terrible it is, my arrows will have to follow the path trod by that wretched sword of Rávana called Chandra·hasa.*

LÁKSHMANA: My brother, how come even these animals are so generous toward us?

5.125 RĀMAḤ: kim ucyate. Sugrīvaḥ sa|nābhir asmākam. asya hi prabhavo bhagavān aikṣvākasya rāja'|rṣi|vaṃśasya prasavitā Sahasra|dīdhitiḥ. *(hṛdaya/stham uttarīyaṃ dṛṣṭvā)* vatsa Guha, spṛhayāmi Sugrīva|Hanūmator darśanāya. tad Ṛṣyamūka|gāminaṃ mārgam ādarśaya.

GUHAḤ: *(sa/harṣam, ātma/gatam)* katham, a|cirād eva phalavatī Jāmbavato mantra|śaktiḥ! *(prakāśam.)* ita ito Mataṅg'|āśrama|vartmanā devaḥ.

iti sarve parikrāmanti.

GUHAḤ: deva, paśya, paśya!

vidadhati mudam akṣṇor nūtan'|ânūpa|nīpa|
prahasana|saha|caryā|nitya|nṛtyan|mayūrāḥ
phala|pulakita|jambū|kuñja|kūjat|kapota|
priya|śabara|purandhrī|bandhavo Vindhya|rekhāḥ.

5.130 RĀMAḤ: *(sarvato nirūpya, sa/khedam)*

samantād unmīlad|
bahala|laharī|laṅghana|kalā|
laghu|preṅkhat|pamp"|â-
nila|vidalad|elā|surabhayaḥ
a|vidyā|Vaidehī|
śata|lipi|karīṇāṃ mama dhiyām
amī hast'|ālambaṃ
vipina|viniveśā vidadhate.

RAMA: Of course they are very generous! Sugríva comes from the same family as we do, for his father is also the ancestor of our family of royal sages, descending from Ikshváku: the thousand-rayed Sun. *(looking at the garment pressed against his heart)* My friend Guha, I should like to see Sugríva and Hánuman. So please show me the way to the Rishya·muka mountain. 5.125

GUHA: *(happily, aside)* How quickly Jámbavan's clever plan bears its fruit! *(aloud)* Come this way, Your Majesty, follow the way to the sage Matánga's hermitage.

They all walk around the stage.

GUHA: Your Majesty, look here,

> Peacocks on this mountain are incessantly dancing to accompany the cheerful blossoming* of the new *kadámba* flowers on the trees surrounded with water.* And the wives of hunters here love the cooing doves* in the woods, where rose-apple trees laden with their fruit look thrilled.* Thus do the ranges of the Vindhya mountain, the friends of these hunter wives, fill our eyes with joy.

RAMA: *(looking everywhere, dejectedly)* 5.130

> These forest grounds smell good with the cardamoms that are being opened up by the breeze over the Pampa lake; the wind is blowing gently as it jumps over the many rising waves everywhere skillfully. While my mind pictures hundreds of imaginary Sitas, these places give it a helping hand.

LAKṢMAṆAḤ: ārya, itas tāvat,

bhaya|bhraṣṭa|preyo|
viraha|nirahaṅkāra|hariṇī|
mukh'|ālok'|ônmīlad|
guru|karuṇa|rugṇāṃ sahacarīm
vilokya mlecchantīm
«alam, alam» iti prāk praṇihitaṃ
śaravyāl lubdhānāṃ
hṛdayam aparāddhaṃ na tu śarāḥ.

RĀMAḤ: *(s'|âsram)* hā devi,

5.135 Mārīca|mṛgayā|vyagre mayi, prāpte ca Rāvaṇe
āsām iva kuraṅgīṇāṃ tav' ôtpaśyāmi locane.

LAKṢMAṆAḤ: *(sva|gatam)* kaḥ punar upāyo yena vinodyate hṛdayam āryasya?

NEPATHYE: bho bho van'|âukasaḥ! kathayantu bhavantaḥ, ken' âsmat|kīrti|kāminī|caṅkramaṇa|keli|parvato vivartito Danu|rāja|kaṅkāla|kūṭaḥ?

GUHAḤ: *(dṛṣṭvā, sa|saṃbhramam)* deva, paśya paśya! kanaka|maya|sahasrapattra|vaikakṣyaka|prabhā|maṇḍalena, Dundubhi|karaṅka|vyatikara|janmanā roṣa|rāgeṇa svabhāva|piṅgalatayā ca tri|guṇa|piśaṅgīṃ tanum ādadhānaḥ plavaga|rājo 'yam ita ev' âbhivartate.

LÁKSHMANA: My brother, come over here,

> When the selflessly devoted female deer was left behind by her beloved who had escaped in fright, the hunter's wife, seeing her face, was overwhelmed by deep compassion and prayed in confusion to her husband, "Please, stop this, stop." And although the hunter's heart turned away from his target at this sight, the arrows he had already sent away did not.

RAMA: *(in tears)* O my queen,

> When I was busy chasing Marícha, and Rávana arrived here, then your eyes must have been like the eyes of these deer—or so I imagine them. 5.135

LÁKSHMANA: *(aside)* With what means could I divert my brother's mind?

BEHIND THE SCENES: Hey, inhabitants of the forest! Tell me, who turned upside down the heap of Danu·kabándha's bones, which had served as the playground of my beloved Fame to roam there.*

GUHA: *(seeing him, with alarm)* Your Majesty, look, he has a bright golden lotus garland on his chest; his anger is flaming because this heap of Dúndubhi's bones has been turned over and he is also naturally reddish brown—thus, the king of monkeys has taken on a form that is thrice reddish for these three reasons, and he is now approaching us.

Paulasty'|âvayav'|âugha|saṅkaṭa|bhujā|
mūla|kṣaṇ'|ônmūlita|
dvai|rājyām Amarāvatīṃ kṛtavate
vīrāya yasmai Hariḥ
nity'|ālokana|kautuka|vyasaninīḥ,
śaṅke, sahasraṃ dṛśaḥ
piṇḍī|kṛtya dala|chalena kanak'|âm-
bho|ja|srajaṃ dattavān.

5.140 kṣaṇaṃ ca devasya mahā|vīro 'yam Ṛṣyamūka|yātrām antarayiṣyati. tad aham agrato gatvā, diṣṭyā vardhayāmi Sūrya|tanayam.

RĀMAḤ: evam astu.

GUHAḤ: vācikaṃ punar etāvat kumāra|Sugrīvasya yad: «mitra|paryāy'|ântaritaṃ devasya dāsyam icchām' îti.»

RĀMAḤ: *(apavārya)* vatsa Lakṣmaṇa, evam āha vayasyas te Guhaḥ. kiṃ ca, mantr'|ôtsāha|śakti|sampannānām api prabhu|śaktim apekṣante siddhayaḥ. tad ahaṃ Vāli|sthāne Sugrīvam ādiśya, tat|kośa|daṇḍābhyāṃ samagra|śaktir vaira|pāraṃ gantum icchāmi.

LAKṢMAṆAḤ: *(sa|smitam)* yady evam, upayujyamānam Indra|sūnum upekṣya, Sugrīveṇ' ôpayokṣyamāṇena sandhir iti vakraḥ khalv ayam panthāḥ.

> This hero managed to save the celestial city of Amarávati in a moment from being ruled by two kings at the same time when he squeezed Rávana's limbs under his armpits.* It appears that Indra then transformed his own thousand eyes, which were constantly observing everything with great interest, into a thousand-petaled lotus, and had given it to him as a reward, in the form of a golden lotus necklace.

In an instant, this great hero shall obstruct you on your way to Rishya·muka. I shall go before you and give my best wishes to Sugríva. 5.140

RAMA: Let it be so.

GUHA: Prince Sugríva has also sent the following message to you: "What is only alluded to in friendship is servantship, and it is your servant that I should like to be."

RAMA: *(aside)* My brother, Lákshmana, this is what your friend, Guha, says to me. Moreover, even for those who possess the gifts of cleverness and perseverance, success depends on one's power to rule. Therefore I shall put Sugríva on Vali's throne, and thus obtain all the conditions for power, as I shall be supported by his royal fortune and scepter.*

LÁKSHMANA: *(smiling)* If it is so, then instead of turning to Indra's son, Vali, who could help us at present, we shall form an alliance with Sugríva, who will be able to help us later—we have a rather crooked way of doing things, indeed.

5.145 RĀMAḤ: *(sa|smitam)* vatsa, sādhv evaṃ bravīṣi. kiṃ tu,

dṛpyat|Paulastya|kaṇḍū|bhidura|bhuja|bhar'|ôṣ-
māyamāṇaḥ Kap'|îndro
n' âyaṃ naḥ sandadhīta, kva cid api hi vidhau
n' âiva sāhāyya|kāmaḥ.
so 'haṃ Sugrīvam etad|damana|dṛḍhataraṃ
mitram icchāmi kartuṃ;
pāra|straiṇeya|putra|vyaya|śithila|śucaṃ
Śakram ārādhayāmi.

LAKṢMAṆAḤ: sādhu|darśinī buddhir āryasya. kiṃ ca, vidhūta|śāpen' âpi Danunā deva|bhūyaṃ gatim upalambhitena sandiṣṭam āryasya yathā: «asya Niṣāda|pater vacasi deven' âvadhātavyam» iti.

RĀMAḤ: tad Guho 'pi pratidūtyam arhati.

LAKṢMAṆAḤ: (GUHAṂ *prati)* evam asmad|girā Sugrīvo vaktavyaḥ:

5.150 «pitā 'yaṃ reto|dhās
tava taraṇir asmat|kula|gurur,
Manur vaimātreyas
tad api sahajaṃ mitram asi naḥ.
ath' âpi jñāteyaṃ
śithilayasi kāpeya|taralaḥ,
śarās tan me Vāli|
kṣataja|rasa|lolāḥ pratibhuvaḥ.»

RAMA: *(smiling)* My brother, you are perfectly right. However, 5.145

The monkey-king, Vali, whose heavy arms put an end to the itch of the conceited Rávana to fight, is glowing with his power and will not form an alliance with us; he does not want to help us in any matter. Therefore I should like to be the ally of Sugríva, who is more determined to tame his adversary. And if Indra then becomes somewhat upset to lose the son he had from someone else's wife,* I shall duly propitiate him.*

LÁKSHMANA: You are clever to foresee everything so well. Moreover, the demon Kabándha, who was liberated from his curse* and reached the celestial realms as a god, also warned you that you should listen to what the Lord of Nishádas tells you.

RAMA: So Guha should be sent back as a messenger.

LÁKSHMANA: *(to* GUHA*)* Our message should be transmitted to Sugríva as follows:

"The father who begot you is the ancestor of our family: the Sun; and Manu, the first man, is your stepmother's son*—therefore you are our natural ally. But if, true to your fickle monkey character, you betray us, your relatives, then these arrows of mine, which will be restless after tasting Vali's blood, shall make sure to look after your fate." 5.150

RĀMAḤ: *(vihasya)* vatsa Guha! eṣa khalu Paulastya|gaten' âmarṣeṇa dhūmāyamāno yayā kayā cid vācā Saumitrir abhidadhātu nāma. satata|samidhyamāna|Jānakī|viraha|vaiśvānareṇa Rāma|cetasā punar agni|sākṣikam eva Sugrīvo mitram abhyupagataḥ.

GUHAḤ: *(sa/harṣam)* param anugṛhīto devena vikartana|tanayaḥ. *(sa/parihāsa/smitam)*

Sugrīve yadi pakṣa|pāta|madhuraṃ,
deva, tvadīyaṃ manaḥ,
kiṃ nas tena? vidāṃ|karotu bhagavān
ambhojinī|vallabhaḥ,
navyen' ātmaja|rājya|lābha|rabhas'|ôd-
bhūtena yas tejasā
pūrvasmād adhikena duḥ|sahataro
lokeṣu vartiṣyate.

LAKṢMAṆAḤ: *(vihasya)* kathaṃ, Tapana|tanayasya rājya|pradānam apy aṅgī|kāritā vayaṃ vayasyena.

5.155 RĀMAḤ: *(sa/smitam)* vatsa Guha, na tāvat prakāśam evaṃ pratiśuśrūṣati me hṛdayam.

GUHAḤ: *(sa/praśraya/smitam)* svāmin, iyam eva mahatāṃ śailī:

santo manasi|kṛty' âiva pravṛttāḥ kṛtya|vastuni;
kasya pratiśṛṇoti sma kamalebhyaḥ śriyaṃ Raviḥ?

NEPATHYE: bho bhoḥ, saṃnihitā van'|âukasaḥ! kathayantu bhavantaḥ: Dundubhi|karaṅka|vikṣepa|saṃbhāvyamā-

RAMA: *(smiling)* My friend, Guha, let Lákshmana say whatever he wants to, he is fuming with rage against Rávana. I accept Sugríva as friend in front of the fire burning my heart, the fire constantly maintained by the separation from Sita, which shall witness our alliance.

GUHA: *(happily)* Sugríva, the son of the Sun, has been greatly honored by you. *(smiling jokingly)*

> Your Majesty, if your heart is so biased in Sugríva's favor, what are we to do? It is the Sun, the beloved of the day-lotuses, that should be informed about it—then, upon learning that his son is to obtain a kingdom, with renewed delight and vigor he shall shine in this world even stronger, with more unbearable force than before.

LÁKSHMANA: *(smiling)* So our friend seems to have concluded that we would agree to give the kingdom to the son of the Burning Sun.

RAMA: *(with a smile)* My dear Guha, it is just that my heart 5.155
did not want to make a promise in such explicit terms.

GUHA: *(smiling politely)* My lord, such is the conduct of noble people,

> The noble fulfill their duties from their hearts. To whom would the Sun need to promise to bestow beauty upon the lotuses?

FROM BEHIND THE SCENES: Hey, animals in the vicinity! My arms have long been itching to fight, so please tell me who is the person that feels himself so fully and deeply

na|gambhīr'|âvaṣṭambha|nirbhareṇa ken' âsmākam iyaṃ cirasya bhuja|kāṇḍa|kaṇḍūtir apaneṣyate?

GUHAḤ: *(sva|gatam)*

5.160 manye, darp'|āmayāvibhyāṃ
nityaṃ dorbhyām amarṣaṇaḥ
Jāmbavat|preraṇād dīptaḥ
prāpto 'yaṃ plavag'|ēśvaraḥ.

tad aham api vīra|yātrā|darśana|sukhaṃ muhūrtam anubhavāmi.

praviśya.

VĀLĪ: *(puro 'valokya ca.)* aye, prasann'|ôjjval'|ākṛtī kāv etau? niyatam ābhyām eva dānava|nātha|kaṅkāl'|ôtkṣepa|nimittena bhavitavyam. *(smṛtim abhinīya, sa|vitarkam)* saṃdiṣṭam asmāsu priya|su|hṛdā Laṅk"|ēśvareṇa:

«prakḷpta|kāntāra|kumāra|bhuktir,
daurbhāgineyo, janakena muktaḥ,
manuṣya|sāmanta|suto, niṣaṅgī,
sah'|ânujas tiṣṭhati Daṇḍakāyām.

5.165 tau c' âsmākaṃ tatra vihāriṣu niśā|careṣu pāṭaccarīṃ vṛttim ātiṣṭhamānau bhavadbhiḥ pratikartavyau.» iti. tat kim ayam ayaṃ ca etau syātām?

RĀMAḤ: vatsa Lakṣmaṇa, śṛṇu, kim ayaṃ bravīti mahā|vīraḥ?

confident to remedy this itch that he scattered around the bones of the demon Dúndubhi!

GUHA: *(aside)*

> This is he who is always flaming in wrath, as his arms are afflicted by that great disease called pride; and I think he has been urged by the minister Jámbavan—here he comes, the monkey-king. 5.160

I, too, shall now be privileged to see the fight of heroes in a moment.

VALI *enters.*

VALI: *(looking ahead)* Now, who are these two, looking so calm and resplendent. They must be the ones that came to scatter around the bones of the demon king. *(He acts that he remembers something, and then, reflecting.)* My dear friend, the Lord of Lanka, has told me this.

> "He is the son of an unfortunate mother, a mere human sibling who was abandoned by his father, a neighboring king, and he has been made to live on what forest animals eat. Armed with a quiver, he is now in the Dándaka forest, accompanied by his brother.

And while some of us, demons, are amusing ourselves, they 5.165
plan to rob us—therefore, you should take some action against them." So are these two the ones to look for?

RAMA: My brother, listen. What is this great hero saying?

LAKṢMAṆAḤ: *(kiṃ cid upasṛtya)* ita āvām. ito bhavān.

VĀLĪ: bhoḥ, kāv etau yuvām?

LAKṢMAṆAḤ: mahā|bhāga, Rāghavau kṣatriyāv āvām.

5.170 VĀLĪ: āyuṣman, ākāra|viśeṣa ev' âvagamayati jāti|viśeṣam. tad viśeṣaṃ brūhi!

LAKṢMAṆAḤ: nan' ûktam eva: Rāghavāv āvām.

VĀLĪ: *(s'|âbhyasūyam iva)* āḥ,

vapur api vivṛṇoti kṣatratām; ko viśeṣo
Raghuṣu yad abhidhatse «Rāghavāv» ity abhīkṣṇam?
parikalayitum iṣṭaṃ nāma sāṃskārikaṃ vām,
ahaha, katham apatya|pratyayān niścinomi?

LAKṢMAṆAḤ: *(sa|dhairya|saṃrambham)* bhoḥ! āvāṃ tau Rāma|Lakṣmaṇau.

5.175 VĀLĪ: *(sa|vimarśam, ātma|gatam)* kathaṃ «tau» iti sarva|nāma|padena prasiddhāv ity āha. tat kim anayor ev' ânyataraḥ Pinākasya dhanuṣo damayitā? so 'pi Rāma|bhadro Rāmaḥ syāt. bhavatv evaṃ tāvat. *(prakāśaṃ vihasya)*

eko veṣa|parigrahaḥ, parikaraḥ
sādhāraṇaḥ karmaṇām,
ākṛtyor madhuratvam eva sa|dṛśaṃ,
tuly" âiva gambhīratā;
tad draṣṭuṃ ciram utsuko 'smi: kataro

LÁKSHMANA: *(approaching him slowly)* Here we are. Please, come over here.

VALI: Now, who are you two?

LÁKSHMANA: Sir, we are warriors, descendants of Raghu.

VALI: Sir, your appearance already betrays your social status. 5.170
So tell me your particulars.

LÁKSHMANA: As I have said, we are descendants of Raghu.

VALI: *(seems to be irritated)* Ah,

> Your appearance reveals already that you are warriors. What is so special about being the descendants of Raghu that you keep repeating it? I wish to know your given names; for heaven's sake, how can I determine who you are from knowing just in which family you were born?

LÁKSHMANA: *(firmly and proudly)* We are those two, Rama and Lákshmana.

VALI: *(reflecting, aside)* Here it is, he is saying "those two," 5.175
apparently meaning to indicate with this pronoun that they are well known. Isn't it one of them who bent Shiva's bow, the Pináka? Yes, and that one must be Rama·bhadra, the one called Rama. All right, then. *(laughing aloud)*

> You wear the same clothes and the instruments you carry are also the same; you both have an equally agreeable appearance and you are both sincere in the same way. So I am still curious to know which of you is Rama·bhadra, who made to break

vāṃ Rāma|bhadraḥ punaḥ
sarva|kṣatra|vadha|vratī Bhṛgu|patir
yen' âvakīrṇī kṛtaḥ?

LAKṢMAṆAḤ: *(sa|vinayam iva)* ārya, Saṃkrandana|nandana, Lakṣmaṇas tāvad aham.

VĀLĪ: ayam apy aparo Dāśarathiḥ Kauśik'|ânte|vāsī Rāmaḥ.

LAKṢMAṆAḤ: atha kim.

5.180 VĀLĪ: *(sa|harṣ'|ôllāsaṃ, kiṃ cid uccaiḥ)* bho Rāma|bhadra,

eṣa trai|varṇya|mātra|vyavasita|jagato
Bhārgavasy' âstra|garbhād
ākṛṣṭa|kṣatra|jātis tvam asi pathi girām
adya naḥ su|prabhātam;
kakṣ"|ôṣma|sveda|sadyaḥ|śamita|Daśa|mukh'|ā-
sphoṭa|kaṇḍū|vikāro
vīra|śrāddho bhujas tvāṃ paricaratu, ciraṃ
cakṣuṣī nandatāṃ ca.

RĀMAḤ: *(dṛṣṭvā sa|harṣam)* sa eṣa mahā|bāhuḥ Saṃkrandana|sūnuḥ,

yena vīreṇa guptāyāṃ Kiṣkindhāyām iyaṃ mahī
Rāvaṇ'|âbhibhava|klāntā śaśvad ucchvāsam aśnute.

iti parikrāmati.

5.185 LAKṢMAṆAḤ: mahā|bhāga! ayam āryaḥ. ita ito bhavān.

the oath of Párashu·rama, the sworn enemy of all warriors.

LÁKSHMANA: *(courteously)* My lord, son of Indra, I am Lákshmana.

VALI: And he is the other son of Dasha·ratha, disciple of Vishva·mitra: Rama.

LÁKSHMANA: Indeed.

VALI: *(with joy and delight, somewhat loudly)* O Rama·bhadra, 5.180

You have given new birth to the warrior class, saving it from Párashu·rama's weapon, who had recreated the world as made up of the other three classes—a great day has dawned upon me that I have the chance to talk to you now. My arms, which place their trust in heroes, quickly healed Rávana from his sick itch for a fight, with the hot sweat of my armpits*—may these arms encircle you and may my eyes take pleasure in seeing you for a long time.*

RAMA: *(noticing him, with delight)* So here he is, the strong-armed son of Indra,

who bravely protects the territory of Kishkíndha, where the earth, exhausted by Rávana's assaults, can still breathe.

He walks around the stage.

LÁKSHMANA: Sir, my elder brother is here, this way. 5.185

VĀLĪ: *(upasṛtya)* Rāma|bhadra,

sur'|âsurāṇām asubhir dīvyatāṃ sabhiko muniḥ,
adya me Nāradas tuṣṭo yen' âsi bhuja|gocaraḥ.

RĀMAḤ: mahā|vīra, kim ucyate. mūrdh'|âbhiṣikto 'si samara|śauṇḍānām.

devaḥ sa tvām asūta dviṣad|upamṛdita|
svar|vadhū|veṇi|bandha|
prekṣā|dhārāla|vaira|prasṛmara|samar'|ôḍ-
ḍāmar'|âujā Biḍaujāḥ,
yo viddh'|ôtkhāta|bāṇa|vraṇa|nivaha|nibhaṃ
nirbhar'|ôdbhaṅgura|bhrū|
bhīmaṃ bhrāmyadbhir aṅgair udavahata ruṣā
rajyad|akṣṇāṃ sahasram.

5.190 api ca,

vandī|kṛtya jagad|vijitvara|bhuja|
stambh'|âugha|duḥ|saṃcaraṃ
Rakṣo|rājam api tvayā vidadhatā
saṃdhyā|samādhi|vratam,
pratyakṣī|kṛta|Kārtavīrya|caritām
unmucya Revāṃ samaṃ
sarvābhir mahiṣībhir ambu|nidhayo
viśve 'pi vismāpitāḥ.

VALI: *(approaching him)* Rama·bhadra,

> Today the sage Nárada, the umpire of gods and demons playing with lives, shall be satisfied with me, for you have come in the reach of my arms.*

RAMA: Great hero, indeed so; you have been consecrated as the foremost of the heroes addicted to fight.

> It is the god Indra who begot you. When he saw his enemies pulling the braided hair of his celestial wives, he grew very hostile and his uncontrollable energy to fight became manifest. Then the thousand eyes he carries on his whirling limbs became red, like wounds from which the piercing arrows have been plucked out, terrifying with the tightly knit eyebrows, and they were glowing with wrath.*

Moreover, 5.190

> While you were fulfilling your vow of performing penance at the junctures of the day on the seashore, you managed to imprison* even the king of demons, known to be difficult to overcome, since his many colossal arms were famous for having subjugated the world. Thus did you astonish all the oceans together with their river queens, except for* the river Reva, who had already experienced the famous act of Árjuna Kartavírya.*

VĀLĪ: *(vihasya)*

cirāya rātriṃcara|vīra|cakra|
mār'|âṅka|vaijñānika, paśyatas tvām
sudhā|sa|dharmāṇam imāṃ ca vācaṃ
na śṛṇvatas tṛpyati mānasaṃ me.

kiṃ tu,

5.195 yen' ācchidya samasta|pārthiva|kula|
prāṇ'|ântakaṃ kārmukaṃ
Rāmaḥ saṃprati lambhito Bhṛgu|bhuvām
utsarga|siddhāṃ srucam,
draṣṭuṃ, vīra, cirāya dhāma bhavatas
tad bhūr|bhuvaḥ|svas|trayī|
hṛn|marma|vraṇa|ropaṇ'|âuṣadham imau
bāhū bah' ûttāmyataḥ.

RĀMAḤ: *(sa|smitam)*

nanv etad adhimaurvīkaṃ yuddha|sarvasva|dakṣiṇam,
sajjam asty eva me rakṣo|lakṣmī|mūla|haraṃ dhanuḥ.

tan mahā|bhāgo 'pi śastram ādattām.

VĀLĪ: *(vihasya)* sādhu, bho mahā|kṣatriya, yathā|dharmam abhidadhāsi. kiṃ punaḥ,

5.200 nayo hi sāṃgrāmika eṣa doṣmatāṃ,
yad ātma|jāti|pratirūpam āyudham.
ayaḥ|kuśībhiḥ kapayo na śastriṇah,
talaṃ ca muṣṭiś ca nakhāś ca santi naḥ.

VALI: *(smiling)*

You are known to be skillful in killing demon heroes; now that I can see you at last and can hear your voice, which is like ambrosia, my heart still does not rejoice.

However,

Thanks to your power, you neutralized the bow that killed all the kings and you made Párashu·rama take up the sacrificial ladle, which was what members of his family have always done.* O hero, it is this power of yours that my arms would, at long last, like to experience so much, your power to heal the fatal wounds of the hearts in the three worlds: on the earth, in the intermediary space and in heaven. 5.195

RAMA: *(with a smile)*

As you wish: my bow is strung and is prepared to receive a full-scale donation in the form of a battle; here it is, ready to destroy the source of the demons' good fortune.

So may Your Honor also take up his weapon.

VALI: *(smiling)* All right, great kshatriya, you speak as a warrior should. Yet,

It is the rule of warfare between the powerful that everybody employs the weapon appropriate for his birth and status. Monkeys do not use arms of wrought iron—we have our soles, palms,* fists and nails to fight with. 5.200

LAKṢMAṆAḤ: ārya, sādh' ûktaṃ mahā|bhāgena. nity'|ôpana-ta|svāṅga|śastr" âiva tiraścī jātiḥ.

RĀMAḤ: *(vihasya)*

sarv'|âugha|prasareṇa Rāvaṇir asau
yad dur|yaśo|bhāginaṃ
cakre Gautama|śāpa|yantrita|bhuja|
sthemānam Ākhaṇḍalam,
kakṣā|garta|kulīratāṃ gamayatā,
vīra, tvayā Rāvaṇaṃ
tat saṃmṛṣṭam; aho, viśalya|karaṇī
jāgarti sat|putratā.

so 'pi tvam asmākam adhunā daivena śaravyaṃ kṛto 'si.

5.205 VĀLĪ: *(sa|roṣam)* āḥ, Kākutstha,

asmad|dor|mūla|kūlaṃkaṣa|viṣama|bhuja|
granthi|bhaṅga|prasaṅga|
krośal|Laṅk"|êśa|datta|tri|bhuvana|vijaya|
khyāti|sarvasva|dāyaḥ
yaḥ kaś cid vikramo 'yaṃ, sa khalu Khalacurī|
kṣatra|sādhāraṇatvād
antar mandāyamāno vijita|Bhṛgu|patiṃ
tvām a|jitvā dunoti.

tad ehi, vimarda|kṣamāṃ bhūmim avatarāvaḥ.

iti niṣkrāntau.

GUHAḤ: *(sva|gatam)* diṣṭyā phalitam asmad|mano|rathena.

LÁKSHMANA: My brother, His Honor has spoken well. Animals fight with their body parts, which are always at hand.

RAMA: *(smiling)*

> With an attack using all his might, Rávana's brother destroyed Indra's reputation, whose power to fight back was blocked by Gáutama's curse.* But you restored Indra's fame when you reduced Rávana to a crab nesting in the cavity of your armpit, o hero. Such is a real son, who destroys all bad things in his father's way.*

Yet today fate commands that you should be the target of my arrow.

VALI: *(angrily)* Ah, offspring of Kakútstha, 5.205

> Squeezed under my arms, fearing that the joints of his terrible arms should be destroyed, the King of Lanka cried out and offered all his possessions: the reputation he obtained by conquering the three worlds. But this was a victory that Árjuna Kartavírya from Khala·churi had also achieved.* Therefore my heroism is still lagging behind, tormenting my heart until I can conquer you, who have defeated the Lord of Bhrigus, Párashu·rama.*

So come, let us go to a ground that shall bear our fight.

Both exit.

GUHA: *(aside)* Thank god, our desire is being fulfilled.

5.210 LAKṢMAṆAḤ: *(nepathy'|âbhimukham avalokya)* idam anyato vānara|dvayam āryasya pārṣṇi|grāham iva saṃbhramād anuplavate. tad aham api dhanur āropayāmi.

GUHAḤ: *(dṛṣṭvā, sa|harṣam)* kumāra Lakṣmaṇa, alam āvegena. nanv ayaṃ Sugrīvo Rāma|deva|guṇ'|ânurāgeṇa Vāli|matsareṇa ca dvi|guṇit'|ôtsāhaḥ samara|sīmānam āpatati.

LAKṢMAṆAḤ: diṣṭyā sa eṣa Vaikartaniḥ. ath' âparaḥ kaḥ?

GUHAḤ: ayam api Kiṣkindh"|ēśvara|skandh'|āvār'|âika|vīro bhagavataḥ Prabhañjanasya pāra|straiṇeyaḥ putro Hanūmān.

LAKṢMAṆAḤ: *(sa|harṣam)* katham, ayam asāv Āñjaneyaḥ! ayaṃ hi,

5.215 Brahma|śāpa|parāmṛṣṭa|sva|vīrya|jñāna|yantritaḥ,
anyair api bhuvaṃ vīraiḥ kīryamāṇām upekṣate.

niyatam anena kauśaly" âsmākaṃ hṛdaya|śalyam uddhariṣyate. idaṃ tu vartamānam eka|tulā|dyūtam. āryasya jaya|Lakṣmī|parigraha|yautake yaśasi vayam anye Sugrīvo vā na kiṃ cid aṃś'|âdhikāriṇaḥ.

LÁKSHMANA: *(looking toward the rear of the stage)* Here come two monkeys in haste from somewhere else; they seem to be trying to attack my brother from behind. So I shall also string my bow. 5.210

GUHA: *(looking, with delight)* Prince Lákshmana, do not worry. This is Sugríva, who is not only loyal to Rama·bhadra and his values but also envies Vali. With his courage thus redoubled, he is approaching the battlefield to help us.

LÁKSHMANA: Fortunately, this is the son of the Sun, Sugríva. And who is the other one?

GUHA: He is the foremost hero in the army of the Lord of Kishkíndha, the son of the Wind God from another's wife: Hánuman.

LÁKSHMANA: *(with delight)* How good that this son of the Wind is here! For he

> was disciplined by Brahma, who cursed him to 5.215
> forget about his own valor.* Thus he thinks that
> this world must be dominated by heroes other than
> he.

Luckily, this friend of ours shall surely relieve the pain of our hearts. But now is the time for the duel. It is about the reputation of my brother, and, reputation being the exclusive possession of him who obtains the Goddess of Victory, neither me, nor others, nor Sugríva can take part in the fight in any way.

GUHAḤ: *(sa|saṃbhramam)* kumāra, paśya paśya,

sapta tālān ayaṃ bhittvā Vāli|praharaṇī|kṛtān
hatvā ca Vālinaṃ bāṇaḥ Rāma|tūṇīram āgataḥ.

ahaha,

5.220 prāṇaiḥ samaṃ kanaka|puṣkara|kaṇṭha|mālā|
sūtreṇa Dāśarathaye vihit'|ātiyeyaḥ,
dik|kūlam udvaha|yaśaḥ|sarid|ādi|śailaḥ
śete sa vīra|śayane kapi|cakra|vartī.

LAKṢMAṆAḤ: *(sa|khedam)* hā deva Saṃkrandana, kva punar īdṛśaṃ mahā|vīra|prakāṇḍam ātmajaṃ sahasreṇ' âpi locanair ālokayiṣyasi?

nepathye dundubhi|dhvaniḥ, maṅgala|gītiś ca

GUHAḤ: *(sa|harṣam)* katham, ayam ārya|Jāmbavad|ādibhir abhimantritaiḥ śāta|kumbha|kalaśair Nīlaḥ kumāra|Sugrīvam abhiṣiñcati. svayaṃ c' âsya devo Dāśarathiḥ kārtasvara|puṇḍarīka|mālayā kaṇṭham alaṃ|karoti.

LAKṢMAṆAḤ: priyaṃ naḥ, priyaṃ naḥ.

5.225 NEPATHYE: bho bho, vānar'|âcchabhalla|golāṅgūla|yūtha|patayaḥ! sarvān eṣa vo mahā|rājaḥ Sugrīvaḥ samājñāpayati—«sajjayantu bhavantaḥ sarvāṇi yauva|rājy'|ôpakaraṇāni. ayam aham api Sītā|devyāḥ pravṛttim anveṣṭuṃ

GUHA: *(with excitement)* Prince Lákshmana, look,

> Piercing the seven palm trees that were used by Vali as weapons, the arrow killed Vali and returned to Rama's quiver.

Alas,

> Together with his garland of golden lotuses, he has offered his life to Rama, as a gift duly offered to a guest. Just like the first of all mountains, from which the rivers of fame flow all the way to the seashore, in the directions of the compass, the Ruler of Monkeys is lying spread out, motionless, in the battlefield. 5.220

LÁKSHMANA: *(troubled)* Alas, god Indra, even if you have a thousand eyes, where will you find a son who would become such a great hero, in your likeness?

The beating of drums and songs of victory are heard from the rear of the stage.

GUHA: *(with delight)* Lo, here is Nila—he is consecrating Prince Sugríva with golden water pots, whose water has been empowered with mantras by Jámbavan and others. And here arrives His Majesty, son of Dasha·ratha, to adorn Sugríva's neck with a garland of golden lotuses.

LÁKSHMANA: How happy I am!

FROM BEHIND THE SCENES: Hey, leaders of monkeys, bears and dark apes! Sugríva, your king, commands you as follows: "Prepare all the insignia of the heir apparent, while I send Hánuman to learn what has happened to 5.225

prahitya Hanūmantam, ūrdhva|mauhūrttike lagne kumāram Aṅgadam abhiṣekṣyāmi.» iti.

LAKṢMAṆAḤ:

utsavaḥ so 'yam asmākaṃ sarvathā hṛdayaṃ|gamaḥ.
kiṃ tu Vālī vilīno 'yaṃ vyathayiṣyati Vāsavam.

(antarikṣe puṣpa/vṛṣṭy/anantaram) jaya, jaya jagat|pate Rāma|bhadra!

Lakṣmyā Vāli|nibarhaṇa|praśamita|
dvai|rājya|vairāgyayā
Kiṣkindh"|āyatan'|âika|daivatam ayaṃ
Tārā|patir dīpyate.
naptāraṃ yuva|rājam Aṅgadam api
śrutv" âtiharṣād abhūd
asr'|âmbhaḥ|pṛṣat'|âugha|mauktika|mayo
gumphaḥ Sahasr'|ēkṣaṇaḥ.

5.230 LAKṢMAṆAḤ: priyāt priyaṃ naḥ. vayasya, tad ehi. āvām api mah"|ôtsava|saṃvibhāginau bhavāvaḥ.

iti niṣkrāntau.

Her Majesty Sita, and consecrate Prince Ángada in the next auspicious minute."

LÁKSHMANA:

This great festivity is delightful in every way for us; only the death of Vali shall torment Indra.

(after a shower of flowers in the air) Long live the Lord of this World, Rama·bhadra!

The Goddess of Fortune is not fond of kingdoms with two kings. But now that the situation has been remedied by Vali's death, she is here with Sugríva, the unique lord of the sacred territory of Kishkíndha, the illustrious husband of Tara.* And hearing that his grandson, Ángada, has become the heir apparent, the thousand-eyed Indra, shedding many a teardrop out of joy, seems to have become a bracelet of pearls.*

LÁKSHMANA: This is the best that could happen to us. Come, my friend, let us go and take part in the festivities. 5.230

Both exit.

PRELUDE TO ACT VI
SANSKRIT PRELUDE

tataḥ praviśati MĀLYAVĀN.

MĀLYAVĀN: *(sarvato 'valokya, sa|khedam)* ahaha, kaṣṭam!

dagdhāḥ pradīpta|pāvaka|pari-
caya|piṇḍa|stha|hema|veśmānaḥ
kṣaṇam utpucchayamāne
Hanūmati Laṅkā|pur'|ôddeśāḥ.

api ca,

6.5 nija|kiraṇ'|âugha|pramuṣita|
nimn'|ônnata|rūpa|karma|bhedeṣu
maṇi|bhavaneṣu kṛśānu|
jvālāḥ phalato 'numīyante.

(vimṛśya) aho, durnivāratā bhavitavyatāyāḥ.

doḥ|saṃdoha|vaśaṃ|vada|tri|bhuvana|
śrī|garva|sarvaṃkaṣaḥ
Kailās'|ôddharaṇa|pracaṇḍa|carito
vīraḥ Kuber'|ânujaḥ
yatr' âyaṃ svayam asti, s" êyam Amarā-
vaty" âpi vandyā purī
nītā markaṭakena kām api daśāṃ.
dhig, daivam āvaśyakam.

na kiṃ cid etad vā Rāvaṇa|dur|nayena. *(sa|khedam ākāśe)* āḥ, Paulastya,

vidyāś catur|daśa caturṣu nij'|ānaneṣu
saṃbādha|duḥ|sthitavatīr avalokya Vedhāḥ,
tābhyo 'parāṇi niyatam daśa te mukhāni

MÁLYAVAN *enters.*

MÁLYAVAN: *(looking in every direction, anxiously)* Alas,

> When Hánuman raised his tail, he immediately set the whole city of Lanka on fire, reducing all the golden mansions into small lumps as they came into contact with the blazing flames.*

Furthermore,

> As the radiant flames seemed to compete with the various forms and colors of the bejeweled palaces from top to bottom, the presence of fire could be deduced only by the destruction it had caused in those buildings. 6.5

(reflecting) Alas, it is impossible to act against fate.

> Empowered by his pride upon obtaining the riches of the three worlds, which he had subjugated with his many arms, this hero, Rávana, Kubéra's brother, performed the terrible act of lifting up Mount Kailása.* The place where he lives is a city that was even more admired than the celestial capital, Amarávati—but it has been reduced to a horrible state by a wretched monkey; how terrible is our inevitable fate!

And all of this is due to Rávana's bad behavior. *(with dejection, in the air)* Ah, son of Pulástya,

> Surely, Brahma, seeing that the fourteen branches of knowledge* were painfully squeezed in his own four heads, in order to accommodate them well,

svasya praṇaptur akarot sa, kathaṃ jaḍo 'si.

6.10 *(kṣaṇaṃ ca dhyātvā, sa|vyatham)* katham, evaṃ viśīryat' îva naḥ kulam idam.

Khar'|ādīn avadhīd Rāmo, vatsam Akṣaṃ ca Mārutiḥ.
svayaṃ niṣkrāmayām āsa Daś'|āsyaś ca Vibhīṣaṇam.

alaṃ vā durvihitam atītam upālabhya. saṃprati, sindhor udīci tīre niveśita|skandhāvāro Dāśarathiḥ kim ārabhate iti katham pratīmaḥ? *(puro dṛṣṭvā.)* kathaṃ Rāghava|caritāni caritum prahitayoḥ Śuka|Sāraṇayoḥ Sāraṇaḥ prāptaḥ.

praviśya.

SĀRAṆAḤ: jayatu, jayatu kaniṣṭha|mātā|mahaḥ!

6.15 MĀLYAVĀN: *(abhinandya, samīpe upaveśya ca)* vatsa Sāraṇa, kac cid amun" âiva padena Sugrīva|kaṭakād āgato 'si?

SĀRAṆAḤ: atha kiṃ.

MĀLYAVĀN: tad yath"|ânubhavam abhidhīyatām.

SARAṆAḤ: Rāghava|saṃkhyaṃ van'|âukasām asman|mukhen' âiva śataśaḥ pratītaṃ mātā|mahena. adhunā tu setu|grathanāya militeṣu vānara|sainikeṣu, vānara|mūrti|dharo 'py ahaṃ mahā|rāja|Vibhīṣaṇena... *(ity ardh'|ôkte sa|bhayam)* ārya, cira|saṃvāsena Rāma|rājadhānī|pravādo mām anubadhnāti.

created ten other heads for you, Rávana, his great-grandson. So how can you be so stupid?

(reflecting for a moment, with pain) Alas, it seems that our family is being torn apart. 6.10

Rama has killed Cruel and other demons; Hánuman, son of the Wind, has murdered Rávana's son, Aksha; and it is Rávana himself who has sent away Vibhíshana.

But why bother with past faults? Now, how could we learn what Rama and his army, which has been ordered to come to the northern seashore, are up to? *(looking ahead)* Look, of Shuka and Sárana, who were sent to learn about Rama's moves, Sárana has just come back.

SÁRANA *enters.*

SÁRANA: Hail, our youngest grandfather!*

MÁLYAVAN: *(rejoicing, sitting down near him)* My dear Sárana, have you just come back from Sugríva's camp? 6.15

SÁRANA: Yes, indeed.

MÁLYAVAN: Then please tell me what you have seen.

SÁRANA: You have already heard a hundred times from us how many monkeys are in Rama's army. Now, while the monkey-soldiers joined forces to build a bridge, I took up the form of a monkey, but Maharaja Vibhíshana... *(interrupting his speech, with fear)* Sir, it is because I have lived in Rama's camp for a long time that I got used to such expressions.*

MĀLYAVĀN: *(s'|ākūtam)* kim abhiṣiktaḥ kaniṣṭha|vatso Rāghaveṇa?

6.20 SĀRAṆAḤ: atha kim.

MĀLYAVĀN: *(kṣaṇam iva stabdhaṃ sthitvā, niḥśvasya)* vatsa, niḥśaṅkam abhidhehi.

SĀRAṆAḤ: kumāra|Vibhīṣaṇena jñātvā, saṃyamya c' âhaṃ Rāmasya darśitaḥ.

MĀLYAVĀN: *(s'|āśaṅkam)* tatas tataḥ?

SĀRAṆAḤ: tataś ca, Rāghaveṇa nija|saciva|nirviśeṣam upagṛhya puras|kṛtya ca prahito 'smi.

6.25 MĀLYAVĀN: *(sa|harṣam)* kim ucyate. yāvad|dravya|bhāvī guṇo hi vijigīṣūṇām udāttatā. viśeṣeṇa punar ayaṃ Rāma|bhadraḥ. yataḥ,

a|bheden' ôpāste
kumudam udare vā sthitavato
vipakṣād ambhojād
upagatavato vā madhulihaḥ.
a|paryāptaḥ ko 'pi
sva|para|paricaryā|paricaya|
prabandhaḥ sādhūnām
ayam an|abhisaṃdhāna|madhuraḥ.

atha Śukaḥ kim āsīt?

SĀRAṆAḤ: aham api na jānāmi.

MĀLYAVĀN: *(vimṛśya)* vatsa|Vibhīṣaṇasya Rām'|ôpaśleṣeṇa sva|kulyaṃ vyasanam iti pramugdho 'smi.

MÁLYAVAN: *(anxiously)* Has Rama consecrated Rávana's younger brother, Vibhíshana, as a king?

SÁRANA: Indeed, sir. 6.20

MÁLYAVAN: *(paralyzed for a moment, then, with a sigh)* My son, tell me everything without fear.

SÁRANA: When Prince Vibhíshana recognized me, I got arrested and they led me before Rama.

MÁLYAVAN: *(with concern)* And then?

SÁRANA: Then Rama received me as if I had been one of his own ministers, paid respect to me and sent me back.

MÁLYAVAN: *(happily)* Of course, those who want to conquer 6.25 their enemies always maintain their respectfulness, just as a substance always maintains its properties, and this is particularly true for Rama. For,

> The night-lotus worships the bees in the same way, whether they were already inside it or they have come from its enemy, the day-lotus. And good people somehow always know how to serve everybody without limit; whether it is their own people or others, they are kind without having any other intention.

And what has happened to Shuka?

SÁRANA: I do not know it myself.

MÁLYAVAN: *(reflecting)* Our Vibhíshana will cause the fall of his own kind through his alliance with Rama—and I am quite dismayed to see this.

6.30 SĀRAṆAḤ: ārya, tathā dharma|dṛṣṭir ārya|saṃtānaś ca kumāraḥ kathaṃ jyāyāṃsaṃ bhrātaram avadhūya pratipakṣavartī saṃvṛttaḥ?

MĀLYAVĀN: vatsa, Daśa|grīvaṃ pṛccha. *(niḥśvasya)* atha vā daivaṃ pṛccha!

SĀRAṆAḤ: ārya, yadi śravaṇ'|ârho 'smi, tadā nivedaya.

MĀLYAVĀN: vatsa, kesari|kalatra|saṃbhavena Prabhañjana|sūnunā viluṇṭhitām aśoka|vanikām avalokya, rājā tav' âyaṃ Vibhīṣaṇam avocad yathā: «vatsa, paśya manuṣya|pota|dvay'|âvaṣṭabdhena dur|ātmanā kapi|kīṭena kathaṃ vijṛmbhitam!» iti.

SĀRAṆAḤ: tatas tataḥ?

6.35 MĀLYAVĀN: tato Vibhīṣaṇaḥ praṇamya vyajijñapat:

«jātiṃ mānaya mānuṣīm: abhimukho
dṛṣṭas tvayā Hehayaḥ;
smṛtvā Vāli|bhujau na sāṃpratam ava-
jñātuṃ ca te vānarāḥ.
tat Paulastya mah"|âgni|hotriṇam ahaṃ
tvām etad abhyarthaye:
Sītām arpaya, muñca ca kratu|bhujaḥ
kārā|kuṭumbī|kṛtān.»

SĀRAṆAḤ: *(sa|bahu|mān'|āścaryam)* ahaha, «Vāli|bhujāv» iti bruvatā mātā|mahena kim api smārito 'smi. ārya,

SÁRANA: Sir, indeed, how is it possible that a noble-minded prince like Vibhíshana, who was born in a good family, deserts his elder brother to take his enemy's side? 6.30

MÁLYAVAN: My son, ask Rávana about it. *(with a sigh)* Or ask Fate itself!

SÁRANA: Sir, if I am worthy of hearing it, please tell me about it.

MÁLYAVAN: My son, when your king Rávana saw that his *ashóka* grove had been messed up by the son of the Wind, Hánuman, born from a monkey-woman, he said to Vibhíshana, "Look, my brother, what that mean and wretched monkey, supported by those two miserable humans,* has done!"

SÁRANA: And then?

MÁLYAVAN: Then Vibhíshana bowed down respectfully and said, 6.35

> "Respect the human race—you have seen Árjuna Kartavírya face to face. And remember Vali's strong arms—it is not appropriate to despise the monkeys, either.* So I beg you, son of Pulástya, performer of sacrifices, to give Sita back to Rama, and release the gods whom you have collectively imprisoned."

SÁRANA: *(with appreciation and surprise)* Alas, now that you have mentioned Vali's arms, this makes me think of something else. Sir,

kim ācakṣe setu|
kṣitidhara|śiraḥ|śreṇi|kaṣaṇaiḥ
prakoṣṭhe nīromṇaḥ
kapi|bhaṭa|bhuja|stambha|nivahān,
Sumeror mātsaryād
an|ati|cira|saṃrūḍha|mṛdubhiḥ
śirobhir Vindhyo yad|
bharam api na soḍhuṃ parivṛḍhaḥ?

(s'|āśaṅkam) tatas tataḥ?

6.40 MĀLYAVĀN: tataś ca, roṣ'|ândha|tāmisre majjatā Rākṣasa|rājena tathā ceṣṭitaṃ, yathā vipakṣam api āśritaḥ kumāraḥ.

SĀRAṆAḤ: *(sa|khedam, ākāśe)* hā deva Pulastya|nandana, katham bhavat" âiva vaidharmya|dṛṣṭ'|ântena siddhād anumānato mūl'|ôcchedana|nimittāt karmaṇo nivartiṣyate lokaḥ!

(s'|âbhyarthanaṃ ca)

ari|ṣaḍ|varga ev' âyam asyās, tāta, padāni ṣaṭ.
teṣām ekam api chindan khañjaya bhramarīm, Śriyam!

(mantriṇaṃ prati) ārya, yat satyam, Rāghaveṇa vyūḍhāṃ vānara|varūthinīm utprekṣya śaṅke, Vibhīṣaṇa eva yady asmākaṃ kula|tantur avaśiṣyeta.

6.45 MĀLYAVĀN: *(niḥśvasya)* vatsa, dvayor api kaṭakayos tattva|jño 'si. tat kim idānīm ucitam?

> How could I describe the colossal arms of the monkey-soldiers, whose forearms have lost their hair as they gathered together many mountain peaks to build a bridge? The Vindhya mountain, which, being jealous of Mount Suméru, has recently developed new and yet tender peaks,* is not strong enough to bear their burden.

(with apprehension) And then what happened?

MÁLYAVAN: Then the king of demons plunged into the blind darkness of wrath and behaved in such a way that he made even his younger brother an enemy. 6.40

SÁRANA: *(dejected, in the air)* Alas, Your Majesty, Rávana, son of Pulástya, it is your example of lawlessness that people shall cite to prove by induction that such a base act always results in one's total destruction; and that is how they shall refuse to behave in this way.

(humbly)

> My lord, the Goddess of Fortune is like a wandering bee, endowed with six feet in the form of the six major faults.* If you manage to chop off just one of them, you have captured her!

(to the minister) Sir, indeed, seeing how Rama is setting up the army of monkeys, I fear that Vibhíshana will be the only person to survive from our lineage.

MÁLYAVAN: *(sighing)* My son, you know very well both camps. What is the best thing to do now? 6.45

SĀRAṆAḤ: ārya, nanv evaṃ bravīmi: rāja|putro 'ṅgado 'sau bālo nava|buddhir, āmam iva pātraṃ yad yad ādhīyate, tat tad ācūṣayati.

MĀLYAVĀN: tataḥ kim?

SĀRAṆAḤ: tataś ca, «bhavataḥ pitṛ|vairiṇau Rāma|Sugrīvau vyāpādya, Kiṣkindhāyāṃ bhavantam abhiṣicya, Vāli|sauhṛdasy' ātmānam an|ṛṇam icchāma» iti gūḍha|praṇidhi|mukhena Daśa|kandhar'|ādeśam abhidhāya Sugrīva|śibirād apavāhyate. tasminn apakrānte tu, sva|gṛham ahi|bhay'|ôpajāpa|jarjharam avekṣamāṇo vānara|patiḥ śithilita|Rāma|prayojanaḥ syāt.

MĀLYAVĀN: *(sa|smitam)* vatsa, sādhu samarthayase. kiṃ punaḥ sva|jana|gato garbha|rūpo 'bhinav'|ôjjvala|yauva|rājya|sukh'|ôpalālito dur|apavāha eva. ye ca asya mātā|pitṛ|bāndhavāḥ, te 'pi Sugrīvasy' âiva sambandhinaḥ katham enam uttiṣṭhamānam anujānīyuḥ?

6.50 SĀRAṆAḤ: yathā dṛṣṭam āryeṇa. kiṃ ca, kāl'|āpekṣī daṇḍa|nīti|prayogaḥ. tathā katham api mah"|ôtsāhaiḥ kapibhiḥ setu|karmaṇi pravṛttam, yath" âitāvatā kālena saṃtīrṇa|mah"|ârṇavo Rāmaḥ Suvela|śail'|ôpatyakām adhyāste.

SÁRANA: Sir, what I think is this—Prince Ángada* is still a child, his mind is just awakening. He absorbs whatever you place in him, like an unannealed jar.

MÁLYAVAN: Therefore?

SÁRANA: Then, we could send a spy to Ángada who would tell him the following message as coming from ten-headed Rávana: "I shall kill your father's enemies, Rama and Sugríva, and consecrate you as the king of Kishkíndha, for I should like to pay back my debt to my old friend Vali." Thus, Ángada will be lured away from Sugríva's camp. And once he is taken away, the monkey-king, thinking that his home is infested with backbiters and intriguers, will be less eager to serve Rama's cause.

MÁLYAVAN: *(with a smile)* My son, your advice sounds good. However, Ángada is still like a baby, attached to his own people. And since he is flattered and happy to have just become a glorious heir apparent, he is difficult to lure away. Moreover, his parents and relatives are also Sugríva's relations, so if Ángada rises up against him, how would they give their consent to that?

SÁRANA: You are right, sir. And it is also true that it takes 6.50
time to make political moves. In the meantime, those diligent monkeys got so far in their work of building a bridge that Rama has managed to cross the ocean and is at the foot of Mount Suvéla.

MĀLYAVĀN: *(sa|vimarś'|âdbhutam)* ahaha,

asau manuṣya|mātreṇa laṅghito yadi sāgaraḥ,
pratāpo Daśa|kaṇṭhasya bhuvanair api laṅghitaḥ.

(sa|khedaṃ ca)

Paulastyasya sur'|âsur'|êndra|śirasāṃ
nirmālyam aṅghri|dvayaṃ
kurvāṇena Ragh'|ûdvahena ghaṭite
setau nidhāv ambhasām
ady' ônmudrayati sva|hasta|vidhṛtaṃ
rājīvam iddho Raviḥ,
pratyāvṛtta|rasasya c' âmṛta|bhujām
Indoḥ svadante kalāḥ.

6.55 *(vimṛśya)* vatsa Sāraṇa, Vāli|vadha|viśuddha|pārṣṇin" an|eka| vānar'|ânīka|nāyakena sākṣād upakṛtena sakhyā Sugrīveṇa mahā|pakṣasya, Hanumac|carita|jñāt'|âsmadīya|pravṛtter ayam eva su|vihita|sakal'|âbhiyāsyat|karmaṇas tasy' âbhiyoga|samayaḥ.

SĀRAṆAḤ: ārya, evam ev' âitat. ayam eva «ātma|dravya|prakṛti|saṃpanno nayasy' âdhiṣṭhānaṃ vijigīṣur» ity asya pratham'|ôdāharaṇaṃ Dāśarathiḥ.

MÁLYAVAN: *(reflecting, with astonishment)* Alas,

> If that simple human being has been able to cross the ocean, then the power of ten-headed Rávana will also be crossed out by the world.

(with dejection)

> Rama is about to transform Rávana's lotus-feet into withered flowers, unworthy of being touched by the heads of gods and demons.* Now that he has constructed a bridge over the ocean, the sun shall be radiant enough to open up the lotus it has kept closed in its hands,* and the digits of the moon, whose sweet taste has returned, shall be given to the nectar-eating gods to relish.*

(reflecting) My dear Sárana, by killing Vali, Rama made 6.55
sure he would not be attacked from behind and he openly helped his friend, Sugríva, the leader of numerous monkey-troops. Thus, he has obtained many allies, and, thanks to Hánuman and his adventures,* he has also learned about our activities. Therefore, now would be a good occasion for him to make a move, since he has prepared everything properly to attack us.

SÁRANA: Sir, it is indeed so. As it is said, those who wish to conquer must have the positive inner qualities, material means and ingenuity—this is the basis of statesmanship. And the foremost example of this is Rama himself.

MĀLYAVĀN: *(stambhaṃ nāṭayitvā)*

yat tasmin nihate 'pi Vālini vayaṃ
kṣudrās tath" âiv' āsmahe,
tad yuktaṃ; bhujayor balād api balaṃ
durgasya dur|nigraham.
martyen' âpi jagad|vilakṣaṇa|guṇa|
grāmeṇa Rāmeṇa tu
dve gav|yūti|śate hi nāma kiyatī
tīrṇo 'yam arṇo|nidhiḥ.

(dīrgham uṣṇaṃ ca niḥśvasya, ākāśe)

6.60 tarṣ'|ārti|vyatilelihāna|rasanā|
ravyair mukhair aṣṭabhiḥ
krandantī kramaśaḥ papau daśa|mukhī
vatsasya yasyāḥ stanau,
vatse Naikaṣi, viśva|vīra|jananī|
sīmanta|muktā|maṇiḥ
sā tādṛg bhavatī kathaṃ guṇavataḥ
putrasya kiṃ drakṣyati?

SĀRAṆAḤ: śāntam pāpaṃ, śāntam pāpam. pratihatam a|maṅgalaṃ, pratihatam a|maṅgalam. an|artha|śaṅkīni bandhu|hṛdayāni bhavanti. kiṃ ca, ārya,

bhuja|nivaha|vihaṅgik"|âvalambī
nibiḍa|guṇ'|âugha|dhṛto 'pi rājya|bhāraḥ,
svayam api Daśa|kandhare dhurīṇe
skhalati yadi skhalitaṃ, tad asya rūpam.

MÁLYAVAN: *(mimes he is shocked)*

> That we acted poorly and did not do anything even when Vali was killed was not so inappropriate; for, even if one has strong arms, one cannot easily overcome that rough passage, the sea, lying between us. But that human called Rama, who nevertheless possesses a number of otherworldly qualities, has been able to cross the water measuring some two hundred pastures!

(heaving a deep sigh, then in the air)

> While two of his heads were suckling milk from your breasts, the other eight faces of your ten-headed son were shouting out loudly with flickering tongues, eager to lick up anything in their painful thirst. My child, daughter of Níkasha, mother of the greatest hero, a pearl of a mother worthy to adorn a crown, how will you bear to see your eminent son in his plight?* 6.60

SÁRANA: Oh, no, god forbid such an unlucky event. The hearts of parents and relations are always apprehensive without any reason. Moreover, sir,

> The burden of this kingdom rests on Rávana's many arms as carrying poles and it is kept together with the thick ropes of his qualities;* even if it is the carrier of the burden, Rávana himself, who stumbles, the fall will be due to the unstable nature of kingship.*

MĀLYAVĀN: *(aśrūṇi stambhayan)* vatsa,

vidvān apāvṛttam iva sva|bhāgyaṃ
na tāvad ātmānam ahaṃ bravīmi;
mahā|muner Viśravasas tapobhir
nirvāpa|bījaṃ yadi naḥ kule syāt.

6.65 *praviśya paṭ'|ākṣepeṇa saṃbhrāntaḥ* ŚUKAḤ

ŚUKAḤ:

Prahasta|Dhūmrākṣa|Mahodar'|ādīn
vyāpādya sen"|âdhipatīn amātyān
sa eṣa Laṅkām uparudhya Rāmaḥ
śākhāmṛgair arṇavam ātanoti.

MĀLYAVĀN: *(sa|viṣādam)* purastād eva dṛṣṭam idam asmābhiḥ. deśa|kāla|vyavahitasy' âpi prameya|grāmasya yathā|mukhīnam ādarśa|talaṃ hi sthavira|buddhiḥ. *(vimṛśya, ākāśe)* sādhu Rāma|bhadra, sādhu. vijigīṣor a|dīrgha|sūtratā hi kārya|siddher avaśyaṃ|bhāvaḥ.

SĀRAṆAḤ: kathaya, sakhe Śuka, kiṃ|vidhāno Yātudhān'|ēśvaraḥ?

6.70 ŚUKAḤ: *(sa|kheda|smitam)* sakhe, kiṃ tasya vidhānam?

śrutvā Dāśarathī Suvela|kaṭake
s'|āṭopam ardhe dhanuṣ|
ṭaṃ|kāraiḥ paripūrayanti kakubhaḥ,
proñchanti kaukṣeyakān.
abhyasyanti tath" âiva citra|phalake

MÁLYAVAN: *(withholding his tears)* My child,

> I know about our ill fate but I will not talk about myself here; if there remains someone in our family to perform the funeral offering to his manes, it will be thanks to the penance of the great sage Víshravas, Rávana's father.

SHUKA *enters in haste, throwing the curtain aside.* 6.65

SHUKA:

> Rama has killed many a general and minister, such as Spreaded-Fingers, Smokey-Eyes and Big-Belly; and he has surrounded the island of Lanka with the monkeys: they seem to be covering the ocean.

MÁLYAVAN: *(with desperation)* I have predicted all this. The mind of the elderly is like the surface of a mirror in which all things, even if removed in time and space, are seen as if present in front of us. *(reflecting, in the air)* Well done, Rama, well done: conquerors never delay in action, and that is what ensures that they obtain what they desire.

SÁRANA: My friend, Shuka, tell me what the king of demons is doing now?

SHUKA: *(smiling, with fatigue)* My friend, what could he be 6.70
doing?

> Upon learning that Rama and Lákshmana have reached the foot of Mount Suvéla, half of Rávana's twenty hands proudly filled the directions with the twang of his bowstring while they were also sharpening his swords. And his remaining ten hands were all the same practicing—with the help of a

Laṅkā|pates tat punar
Vaidehī|kuca|patra|valli|racanā|
cāturyam ardhe karāḥ.

MĀLYAVĀN: *(niḥśvasya)* hā, vatsa Rāvaṇa, katham ady' âpi s" âiva hṛdaya|parispanda|mudrā. *(*ŚUKAṂ *prati)* vatsa, atha gopura|gaulmīna|bal'|âdhyakṣeṇa vatsa|Narāntakena kiṃ pratipannam?

ŚUKAḤ: *(niḥśvasya)* ārya, kṛt" âiva kumāreṇa dvāra|maryādā. param Aṅgadena so 'pi... *(ity ardh'|ôkte s'|āsram, adho|mukhas tiṣṭhati.)*

MĀLYAVĀN: hā vatsa, Daśagrīva|nandana! katham idaṃ draṣṭum etāvantaṃ kālam asmākam āyuḥ.

6.75 NEPATHYE: bho bho Mahāpārśva|prabhṛtayaḥ sainikāḥ!

vyāvartadhvam, upādhvam uddhura|śara|
jvālā|mukhīṃ mātaraṃ
devīm astra|mayīṃ; plavaṃga|paśavaḥ
paśyanti pṛṣṭhāni vaḥ.
cetaḥ Śakra|jito 'pi Lakṣmaṇa|vadhe
baddh'|ôtsavam, madhyamaḥ
Paulastyaḥ svayam āyudhaṃ vidhṛtavān;
ady' âpi Rāmād bhayam?

SĀRAṆAḤ: *(śrutvā, sa|harṣam)* ārya, jātaṃ jātam asmad|balānām avalambanam, yad ayaṃ pratibuddhaḥ kumāraḥ Kumbhakarṇo Meghanādaṃ puras|kṛty' âbhy|a|mitrīṇaḥ saṃvṛttaḥ.

MĀLYAVĀN: *(niḥśvasya)* svasti, vijayetāṃ Rāma|Lakṣmaṇau Kumbhakarṇa|Meghanādau.

painting board—how to trace designs skillfully on Sita's breasts.

MÁLYAVAN: *(with a sigh)* Alas, my dear Rávana, why is the determination of your heart's desire still the same?* *(to* SHUKA*)* My child, and what has that young Death-of-Humans done, supervising the army of guardians at the gates?

SHUKA: *(with a sigh)* Sir, Death-of-Humans was on duty at the gates, but Ángada... *(interrupting his speech, he looks down with tears in his eyes)*

MÁLYAVAN: Alas, dear son of the Ten-Headed, why have I lived long enough to witness your death...

BEHIND THE SCENES: Soldiers headed by Maha·parshva! 6.75

Eschew fight and worship the mother-goddess of arms, whose face is in flame with terrifying arrows; the wretched monkeys can see your back; Megha·nada's mind can rejoice only if he kills Lákshmana; and the second son of Pulástya, Kumbha·karna, took up his arms himself. So are you still afraid of Rama?

SÁRANA: *(listening, with delight)* Sir, we have got some relief. For Prince Kumbha·karna has understood the situation and sent Megha·nada in front, and has himself started fighting.

MÁLYAVAN: *(with a sigh)* May there be victory in this fight between the two parties: that of Rama and Lákshmana and that of Kumbha·karna and Megha·nada!

ŚUKAḤ: *(sa|viṣādam, ātma|gatam)* katham, a|viśiṣṭa|kartṛ|karma|bhāvam ubhayatra dvi|vacanaṃ prayuktam āryeṇa!

6.80 MĀLYAVĀN: *(sa|khedam)* vatsau Śuka|Sāraṇau, adya khalv iyaṃ rākṣasa|rāja|lakṣmīḥ sarvathā Kumbha|karṇam avaṣṭabhya vartate. idaṃ tu na vidmaḥ,

agra|jaṃ vā Daśa|grīvam, anu|jaṃ vā Vibhīṣaṇam, anvaya|vyatirekābhyāṃ vīraḥ kam abhiṣekṣyati.

NEPATHYE:

«mā bhaiṣṭam, Kamaṭh'|êndra|Pannaga|patī,
kaś cin na vaiśeṣiko
bhūmer adya bharaḥ»—patiḥ pala|bhujām
ājñāpayaty eṣa vām.

ŚUKAḤ: *(sa|harṣam)* nūnam asmadīyair viśeṣeṇa kim api vikrāntam.

6.85 MĀLYAVĀN *avadhatte.*

PUNAR NEPATHYE:

doḥ|śailau haratā pṛthak pṛthag atho
mūrdhānam utkṣipnunā
Rāmeṇ' âpi laghū|kṛtaṃ patati yat,
tat kaumbhakarṇaṃ vapuḥ.

MĀLYAVĀN: hā vatsa! *(iti mūrcchitaḥ patati.)*

ŚUKA|SĀRAṆAU: *(s'|âsram)* ārya, samāśvasihi, samāśvasihi.

6.90 MĀLYAVĀN: *(āśvasya)* vatsau, jīvato Rāmasya Maithilī|haraṇād etad asmābhir āntareṇa cakṣuṣā viṣayī|kṛtam eva. kim idānīm āśvasitavyam asti?

SHUKA: *(dejected, aside)* God forbid. For it may well be the victory of Rama and Lákshmana over Kumbha·karna and Megha·nada, rather than the other way around.*

MÁLYAVAN: *(with pain)* My dear Shuka and Sárana, the 6.80
destiny of the demons depends entirely on Kumbha·karna now. But we still do not know

> whom this hero, Kumbha·karna, shall make the ruler. If he ensures continuity, it will be his elder brother, Rávana; if he produces discontinuity, it will be his younger brother, Vibhíshana.

BEHIND THE SCENES:

> King of Tortoises and Lord of Snakes! The King of the Meat-Eating Demons tells you not to be afraid: the earth will not need to support any special burden today. . . *

SHUKA: *(happily)* Our side must have excelled in the battle.

MÁLYAVAN *listens attentively.* 6.85

AGAIN, FROM BEHIND THE SCENES:

> . . . For Rama has dissected Kumbha·karna's colossal arms and threw his head up in the air—so he made Kumbha·karna's falling body easy for you to bear.

MÁLYAVAN: Alas, my son. *(He faints and falls on the ground.)*

SHUKA AND SÁRANA: *(both in tears)* Sir, take heart, take heart.

MÁLYAVAN: *(regaining consciousness)* My dear sons, when 6.90
Rávana abducted Sita without killing Rama, I foresaw all this. So how could I take heart now?

ŚUKAḤ: dhik kaṣṭam, «kaumbhakarṇaṃ vapuḥ patati.» ity etad api devena ājñāpayitavyam.

MĀLYAVĀN: vatsa Sāraṇa, ady' âpi Rāvaṇ'|ājñā? nūnam anyonyeṣāṃ vaihāsikāḥ kapayo Daśa|kaṇṭham ulluṇṭhayanti.

SĀRAṆAḤ: āḥ kṣudrāḥ,

yady asti vīryam, asty eva tat karma kathayiṣyati.
Meghanādam a|jitv" âiva dhik prahāsa|vibhīṣikām.

6.95 NEPATHYE: bho bho yūtha|patayaḥ, vilumpantu bhavanto Laṅkā|pura|gopura|prākāra|toraṇāni.

saṃnaddh'|Êndr'|āyudham a|viral'|ā-
rambhi|gīrvāṇa|bāṇa|
śreṇī|varṣaṃ tad avajagṛhe
yena duṣṭa|graheṇa. . .

MĀLYAVĀN: *(s'|ôdvegam)* āḥ, kim anena śrāvayitavyo 'sti? *(iti karṇau pidadhāti)*

PUNAR NEPATHYE:

iṣṭvā kāṃ cit praharaṇa|mayīṃ
vīra|yajvānam iṣṭiṃ,
diṣṭyā so 'yaṃ samupaśamitaḥ
Śakra|jil Lakṣmaṇena.

6.100 MĀLYAVĀN: satyo 'yam: «ati|duḥkho nir|duḥkhaḥ.» iti loka|pravādaḥ, yad asminn api sa|mūla|ghātam abhighnati vyatikare tath" âiva śvasimaḥ.

SHUKA: Alas, it is our lord, Rávana, who had to tell us about Kumbha·karna's death.

MÁLYAVAN: My dear Sárana, were these really Rávana's words? Surely, it must have been the monkeys joking with each other, imitating Rávana's voice.

SÁRANA: O those wretched monkeys.

> If they are heroic, their heroism should be true and demonstrated by acts. As long as Megha·nada has not been captured, mockery shall not intimidate us.*

BEHIND THE SCENES: Hey, troop leaders! Climb up the gates on the walls at the main entrances to the city of Lanka. 6.95

> Once this evil demon, Megha·nada, stopped the shower of celestial arrows falling incessantly from Indra's well-strung bow. . . *

MÁLYAVAN: *(nervously)* Does this need to be told? *(covering his ears)*

AGAIN, FROM BEHIND THE SCENES:

> . . . but now he has performed a sacrifice of weapons with the help of a hero who acted as priest—thank God, Megha·nada has been put to peace by Lákshmana.*

MÁLYAVAN: True is the saying that one feels no more pain when in great pain. For even after this terrible event, which gave us such a crushing blow, we are still alive. 6.100

ŚUKAḤ: *(ūrdhvam avalokya)* yathā samantād amūr ambara|cara|vimāna|vīthayaḥ kakubhāṃ mukhāni paryavaṣṭabhnanti, tathā śaṅke, dur|vāra|dāruṇa|krodha|vaḍav"|ânala|nipīyamāna|śoka|samudro Dāśarathi|vijayāya saṃnahyate devaḥ.

SĀRAṆAḤ: *(sa|viṣādam, ātma|gatam)* kaṣṭam, kathaṃ «Dāśarathi|vijayāy' êty» a|viśiṣṭ'|ôpapattika|kartṛ|karma|kārak'|ârtha|viṣayaṃ vayasya|vacanam.

MĀLYAVĀN: *(utthāya)* tad asmābhir api jarasā dūṣitasy' ātmanaḥ prakṣālanāya prāptavyaṃ khaḍga|dhārā|tīrtham.

*iti sa|*ŚUKA|SĀRAṆO *niṣkrāntaḥ.*

6.105 *śuddha|viṣkambhaḥ.*

SHUKA: *(looking upward)* The rows of celestial chariots are filling the directions everywhere: our lord must be preparing the conquest of Rama; for it seems that his ocean of grief has been dried up by the hidden and indestructible fire of his wrath, which is cruel and hard to stop.

SÁRANA: *(dejected, aside)* Alas, my friend talks about the conquest of Rama—not distinguishing between the subject and the object with terminations, whether Rama conquers Rávana or the other way around.

MÁLYAVAN: *(rising)* Being affected by old age, I am going to purify myself on the blade of a sword, rather than in a sacred place.*

He exits with SHUKA *and* SÁRANA.

End of the Sanskrit prelude. 6.105

ACT VI
RÁVANA'S DEFEAT

tataḥ praviśaty ākāśa|yānena VIDYĀ|DHARA|DVAYAM.

PRATHAMAḤ: aho, bahoḥ kālāt anayā gagana|vīthyā nirātaṅkam iva saṃcarāvahe.

(adho 'valokya)

Devendr'|ôpanivedya|Nandana|vana|
srak|toraṇa|ślāghinī
Laṅk" êyaṃ Daśa|kaṇṭha|vikrama|sakhī,
yasyāṃ samantād imāḥ
yuddh'|ālokana|kautuk'|ônmukha|vadhū|
saṃkīrṇa|karṇī|rathā
rathyāḥ—kiṃ kathayāmi? yānti yad amī
na vyomni vaimānikāḥ.

6.110 *(sa|khed'|âdbhutam)* sakhe Hemāṅgada,

etāḥ paśya palāda|pattana|bhuvaḥ
sautrāmaṇīnāṃ dṛśām
asr'|âmbhobhir a|deva|mātṛka|gṛh'|ā-
rām'|ābhirāma|śriyaḥ.
etāsu pratighāti|vikrama|kath"|ô-
pālambha|vaitaṇḍikaiḥ
kḷpt'|Êndra|dhvajinī|jay'|ânukṛtibhir
ḍimbhair api krīḍitam.

DVITĪYAḤ: sakhe Ratnacūḍa, kim ucyate.

Then TWO VIDYA·DHARAS* *enter on a celestial chariot.*

FIRST VIDYA·DHARA: After a long time, we can again fly this way in the sky without fear.

(looking downward)

> Here is Lanka, famous for its gates decorated with flower garlands from Indra's paradise, garlands that should have been offered to the King of Gods; here is the city that is the heroic ally* of the Ten-Headed. Its streets are filled everywhere with palanquins of demonesses who are looking up in the sky, curious to see the battle fought there. What else can I say? This is why the gods in their celestial chariots do not fly over here in the air.

(with sorrow and surprise) My friend, Hemángada, 6.110

> Look at these parts of the demon city where the gardens are pleasant and beautiful, for they have been irrigated by the tears of Indra's thousand eyes.* Here, even the children are playing a game pretending they have defeated Indra's army and they are blabbering insults to belittle the enemy's heroic fame.

SECOND VIDYA·DHARA: My friend, Ratna·chuda, it is indeed so.

rakṣāṃs' îti pur" âpi saṃśṛṇumahe,
vīras tu kas tādṛśo
jāgarti sma jagat|trayī|vipad|alaṃ|
karmīṇa|dor|vikramaḥ
śaśvad dvāra|bhuvi praśasti|racanā|
varṇāyamān'|ēkṣaṇa|
śreṇī|saṃbhṛta|Gotrabhin|maya|jaya|
stambho yathā Rāvaṇaḥ?

PRATHAMAḤ: sakhe Hemāṅgada, paśya paśya. Paulastya|pattana|pratolīṣu dīyamāne saṃnāha|paṭahe,

6.115 dig|dantāvala|danta|mauktika|maya|
dvās|toraṇa|sragviṇo
gīrvāṇ'|âdhipati|pratīṣṭa|nigaḍ'|ônmṛṣṭ'|ânya|bandī|śucaḥ,
vīra|śrī|saha|pāṃsu|keli|suhṛdo
Mandodarī|bandhutā|
śauṇḍīr'|âsura|sundarī|surabhayaḥ
kṣubhyanti rakṣo|gṛhāḥ.

DVITĪYAḤ: *(vihasya)* nūnam idānīm atra,

dṛṣṭvā Rāghavam eka|rākṣasa|vana|
sva|cchanda|dāv'|ânalaṃ,
Jānakyāṃ nija|vallabhasya paramaṃ
premāṇam ālokya ca,
kāṅkṣantī muhur ātma|pakṣa|vijayaṃ
bhaṅgaṃ ca mugdhā muhur
dhyāyantī dhruvam antarāla|patitā
Mandodarī vartate.

We heard long ago about the demons. But where could one find a hero like Rávana, whose heroic arms have been able to cause calamity in the three worlds? He has erected a pillar of royal victory to stand permanently at his door, a pillar on which the letters of the inscribed poetic eulogy seem to be made of Indra's thousand eyes.

RATNA·CHUDA: Look, my friend, Hemángada. As the drums are being beaten in the streets of Rávana's capital to announce the fight,

The demon houses are being shaken up, together with their doorways, on which instead of flower garlands there are rows of pearls produced by the temples of the elephants of the eight directions, pearls that are inlaid in their own tusks,* while the lamentations of other prisoners stop as they see the chains that the Lord of Gods, Indra, had to accept. In these houses the Goddess of Heroism is a childhood friend and the beautiful demon wives are proud to be related to Queen Mandódari. 6.115

HEMÁNGADA: *(smiling)* But now,

Seeing that Rama is like a unique, inextinguishable fire in the forest of demons and, at the same time, observing that her own beloved Rávana cherishes love toward Sita, Queen Mandódari is of two minds about the situation and is unable to see clearly: one moment she wishes the victory of her own people, the other she cannot help wanting a defeat.*

PRATHAMAḤ: *(sa|karuṇa|smitam)* vayasya, vibudha|rāja|vijaya|vikrama|krīta|cetasā vṛddha|pitā|mahena Parameṣṭinā svayaṃ pratiṣṭhit'|Êndra|jin|nāma|dheya|śeṣasya tādṛśas tanū|jasya śucā viceṣṭamānām arāti|gṛhiṇīm apy etāṃ n' âivam adhikṣeptum arhasi. *(puro 'valokya ca)* hanta, hasta|dakṣiṇena katham ayaṃ dvidhā vibhajyate mahā|janaḥ. *(nirūpya ca sa|bhaya|kautukam)* sakhe, paśya paśya:

nyañcan|nyañcad|dharitrī|dhṛta|caraṇa|bharaś
　　Candrahās'|âika|dṛṣṭir,
vyāvalgad|yaugapady'|ôtsuka|sakala|bhuj'|ā-
　　krānta|dik|cakravālaḥ,
krodha|krūr'|âkṣi|rakt'|ôtpala|racita|viyat|
　　toraṇa|srañji bibhrad
vaktrāṇi pratyanīka|prasara|sarabhaso
　　nirjihīte Daś'|āsyaḥ.

6.120 DVITĪYAḤ: *(nirvarṇya)* aho, dṛṣṭa|caram apy asya sāṅgrāmikam ojāyitam ayāta|yāmam iva bhīṣayate. sakhe Ratnacūḍa,

Marutvad|dambholi|
　　kṣaṇa|ghaṭita|ghora|śvayathunā
nisarg'|ôdagreṇa
　　prasabham uras" āpīta|gaganaḥ,

RATNA·CHUDA: *(smiling, with compassion)* My friend, the only thing left of her son, Megha·nada, is his epithet "Conqueror of Indra," which was given to him by Brahma himself, our ancient Creator, whose heart was bought by that demon's courage to defeat the King of Gods. Now that Mandódari is grieving the loss of her son, it is not appropriate to mock her, even if she is the enemy's wife. *(looking ahead)* Why is the crowd splitting into two on the right? *(seeing what happens, with fear and astonishment)* My friend, look,

> The weight of his steps makes the ground bend again and again, his gaze is fixed on his sword, the Chandra·hasa, the space is being filled with his numerous arms moving in different directions, all restless at once, his heads are like flower garlands in the gateways of the sky, garlands made up of his wrathful and cruel eyes, which form red lotuses. He is ready to march with all his force against any army—here comes ten-headed Rávana, who is about to leave the city.

HEMÁNGADA: *(watching)* Although I have already seen how 6.120
powerfully he marches into battle, this looks like something never witnessed before; the whole scene is very terrifying. My friend, Ratna·chuda,

> When his wide and terrible chest, powerful by nature, was split in two by Indra's thunderbolt in a second, it was so huge it seemed to drink up the sky itself in a moment. He also transformed the Goddess of Fortune, once belonging to the gods,

Śriyaṃ deva|drīcīṃ
nija|bhuja|van'|ôddāma|kariṇīm
ayaṃ kurvan vīraḥ
smarasi katham āsīd Daśa|mukhaḥ.

PRATHAMAḤ: sakhe, kim ucyate. mahatām apy upari kim apy ayaṃ Rāvaṇaḥ.

enaṃ kalpa|tar'|ûdbhavair a|su|kara|
vyājaiḥ sadā bhūṣaṇair
ārādhnoti sur'|âdhipaḥ; kim aparam?
dīno nadīnāṃ patiḥ.
daṇḍ'|ādhikya|bhayāt kathaṃ katham api
skandh'|ôpaneyān maṇīn
apy asmai pariśodhayaty apadiśan
niḥ|saṃpadaḥ sv'|ākarān.

DVITĪYAḤ: *(sa|bhayam)* katham, ayaṃ parāpatita eva samara|harṣa|heṣamāṇa|Vanāyu|ja|vāji|nivaha|vitīrṇa|Kīnāśa|kāsara|karṇa|jvareṇa prajavinā rathena kārmuka|pāṇir mahā|vīraḥ.

6.125 PRATHAMAḤ: *(sa|bhay'|ādbhutam)*

kalp'|ânta|krūra|sūr'|ôtkara|vikaṭa|mukho,
mānuṣa|dvandva|yuddha|
krīḍā|kaṇḍūyad|ūrjasvala|sakala|bhuj'|āloka|bhūyo|vilakṣaḥ,
saṃbhūy'|ôttiṣṭhamāna|sva|para|bala|mahā|
śastra|saṃpāta|bhīmām
urvīṃ gīrvāṇa|goṣṭhī|guru|mada|nikaṣo

into a wild female elephant to roam in the forest of his arms. You, too, remember these acts of heroic Rávana.

RATNA·CHUDA: My friend, it was indeed so. This Rávana has somehow become more powerful than the greatest heroes.

Indra keeps offering him ornaments made from flowers of the wish-fulfilling tree, which are impossible to fake. What else is there to say? The Lord of Rivers, the Ocean, is also in despair. He is so afraid that Rávana should punish him too severely that he takes pains to bring him his precious stones on his shoulders, pointing out that there is nothing else left in the depths of the sea.

HEMÁNGADA: *(with fear)* Look, here comes that great hero with a bow in his hand, riding his swift chariot; his steeds, which come from Vanáyu,* are so happy to go into battle that their neighing hurts the ears of the buffalo that carries the God of Death around.

RATNA·CHUDA: *(with fear and admiration)* 6.125

His faces are terrifying like a multitude of scorching suns at the end of the world. When he looks at his numerous powerful arms so eager to play a duel with a mere human, he becomes quite ashamed.* This demon has already been the touchstone to test the pride of the Lord of Gods, and now, as he arrives, the weapons are rising both on his side and on his enemy's side to meet at the same time,

Naikaṣeyo vidhatte.

DVITĪYAḤ: *(sa|kautukam)* sakhe, dakṣiṇataḥ paśya tāvat.

Agasty'|ājñā|sadyaḥ|
śamita|vikal'|ôcchrāya|viṣamān
udasyantaḥ setāv
a|lagitavato Vindhya|śikharān
śiraḥ|saṃkhyā|satyā|
kṛta|Daśa|mukh'|āloka|rabhasād
upety' âti|trastāś
capalam apasarpanti kapayaḥ.

PRATHAMAḤ: *(dṛṣṭvā, sa|harṣam)*

6.130 śastrī|kṛtān kapibhir āpatato mud" âiva
vikramya candana|tarūn dadhate pal'|âdāḥ.
tat|saṅginas tu bhujagāḥ kṣaṇa|pāśa|bandha|
duḥkh'|āsikām avayaveṣu diśanty amīṣām.

HEMĀṄGADAḤ: *(vihasya)* ito 'pi tāvat.

rakṣaḥ|svayaṃ|vara|viḍamba|parāṅ|mukhībhiḥ
puṣp'|ôtkare sura|vadhūbhir anujjhite 'pi,
śastrī|kṛtena taruṇā hariṇā hato 'sau
naktaṃ|caraḥ svapiti tat|kusum'|âvakīrṇaḥ.

making the battleground frightening.

HEMÁNGADA: *(with interest)* My friend, look to the right.

The monkeys are throwing the peaks of Mount Vindhya in the fight, peaks that were not used for the building of the bridge to Lanka, for they were too uneven after being lowered and made defective in a moment through Agástya's command.* These monkeys, after identifying Rávana by counting his heads, approached him, curious to behold him—but then they got scared and quickly fled.

RATNA·CHUDA: *(looking, with delight)*

The flesh-eating demons easily manage to neutralize and catch the pieces of sandalwood that the monkeys use as missiles and hurl onto them; but the snakes hanging from those pieces of wood form fetters for a moment and tie the limbs of the demons painfully. 6.130

HEMÁNGADA: *(smiling)* And over here,

Although the wives of gods could not have thrown any flowers over here (for they would avoid being misunderstood, as if they were choosing their husbands among the demons), this night-roaming rákshasa, who has been hit by a blossoming tree that a monkey had made into a weapon, is now covered with its flowers everywhere while lying on the ground.*

RATNACŪḌAḤ: *(ciraṃ vibhāvya)* sakhe,

sva|tanu|rucibhir dīrgh'|âhnīṃ dyām
itaḥ sṛjatāṃ nijair
atha vidadhataḥ kāy'|ābhogair
a|kāṇḍa|tamasvinīm,
dadhati nitarām uddīprāṇām
atha chidura|śriyo
hari|hutabhujāṃ dhūma|chāyām
amī rajanī|carāḥ.

6.135 HEMĀṄGADAḤ: *(sa/smitam)* sakhe,

kim api kapayaḥ karm'|āścaryaṃ
mahā|taru|śāstriṇo
vidadhati tathā dik|kūlebhyo
yath" âpasaranty amūḥ
dhruvam avapatad|rakṣaḥ|śreṇī|
vimukta|nabho|'ntara|
pratibharaṇikā|niḥsthemāno
Daś'|ânana|kīrtayaḥ.

RATNACŪḌAḤ: *(sa/saṃbhramam)* ahaha, dāruṇam upasthitam.

rakṣo|nipiṣṭa|kapi|mukta|mahīdhra|cūrṇa|
pūrṇ'|ântarābhir iṣu|vṛṣṭibhir ujjihānaḥ
roṣ'|âṭṭa|hāsa|dahana|prasarais taḍitvā|
Laṅk"|âdhipaḥ kim api saṃtamasaṃ tanoti.

RATNA·CHUDA: *(thinking for a while)* My friend,

> The monkeys, blazing like flames, appear to make the sky bright with their radiant bodies, while the demons, whose fortune is frail, seem to create untimely night with the expanse of their forms—here below, they follow the monkeys like smoke does fire.

HEMÁNGADA: *(smiling)* My friend, 6.135

> The monkeys are performing such a miraculous act with their large trees as weapons that Rávana's fame is now certainly not strong enough to fill the sky, which the falling demons leave perforated all over, and it is retreating from the distant directions.

RATNA·CHUDA: *(with alarm)* Alas, something terrible is about to happen.

> The space left in the midst of showering arrows is filled with pulverized mountains, which the demons turned into dust after the monkeys had hurled them onto their sides. And here comes the King of Lanka, rising above that rain of arrows, like a cloud whose lightning is made up of his spreading laughter burning with wrath—he covers everything with darkness.

HEMĀṄGADAḤ: *(kṣaṇaṃ nirvarṇya)* aho, kṣudrair api saṃbhūya bhūyobhir eko mahān apy a|duṣ|karaḥ kadarthayitum. yataḥ,

6.140 dṛpyad|dik|pāla|dantā-
vala|bahala|mad'|âvagrah'|ôgrābhir akṣṇāṃ
tārābhir dīpyamānaṃ
diśi vidiśi Daśa|grīvam udgrīvayantaḥ,
ete niḥ|śeṣa|setu|
grathana|samadhikaiḥ śastriṇaḥ śaila|pādair
uddāmānaḥ kap'|îndrā
rajanicara|purīm uttareṇa plavante.

RATNACŪḌAḤ: *(sa/viṣādam)* hanta, mahad viṣamam iva paśyāmi, yad amī niṣ|kṛpa|kṛpāṇa|yaṣṭi|pāṭyamāna|pratibhaṭ'|ôraḥ|kapāṭa|kaṇṭakita|kapola|bhittayaḥ saṃtāna|pātinībhir anīka|rudhira|dhārābhiḥ pravṛddha|vīra|pāṇa|goṣṭhī|mah"|ôtsavāḥ samantād abhidravanti yātudhānāḥ plavaṃgama|yūtha|patīn.

HEMĀṄGADAḤ: *(sa/harṣam)* sakhe, kṛtaṃ viṣādena. yad eṣaḥ,

Daśa|mukha|śara|pīḍit'|âpayān'|ôd-
yama|paripucchayamāna|vānarāṇi
sa|rabhasam abhisāntvayan balāni
dviṣam abhiyodhayati plavaṃga|rājaḥ.

HEMÁNGADA: *(contemplating the scene for a moment)* If one great person fights against many others, even if they are insignificant, he is easy to overcome. Look,

These proud monkeys, who fight not with weapons but with rocks left from the mountains after the building of their bridge, are now flying toward the northern part of the City of Demons, making ten-headed Rávana look up in the sky in every direction. His fierce eyeballs are so much aflame that they dry up even the abundant ichor of the elephants who are proudly guarding the edges of the world in the eight directions. 6.140

RATNA·CHUDA: *(with despair)* Alas, I think I see some great danger. For the hair on the demons' cheeks stands on end when they happily behold the wide chests of their enemies being split by their merciless swords; they are having a great collective feast of drinking among proud soldiers, swallowing the enemy's blood, which flows incessantly—and now they are attacking the monkeys' chiefs everywhere.

HEMÁNGADA: *(happily)* My friend, do not despair, for here

The king of monkeys is quickly encouraging his monkey-soldiers, who are moving around their tails in their effort to escape from the pain caused by Rávana's arrows—and now he is here to attack his enemy.

RATNACŪḌAḤ: *(dṛṣṭvā, sa|kheda|hās'|âdbhutam)* ahaha,

6.145 astrāṇi plavag'|âdhipena vihitāḥ
Paulastya|vakṣaḥ|sthalī|
saṃghaṭṭ'|ânala|datta|dāva|vipadaḥ
sīdanti bhūmī|ruhāḥ.
utpāṭya prahitaś ca śaila|śikharo
Laṅk'|êndra|hast'|āvalī|
piṣṭo 'yaṃ nija|kuñja|nirjhara|jalair
jambāla|piṇḍāyate.

HEMĀṄGADAḤ: *(vihasya)* sakhe, Daśa|kandharam adhikṛtya na kiṃ cid etat,

tath" âiten' ôddhṛtya
sphaṭika|śikharī so 'pi vidadhe
samantād āmūla|
truṭita|vasudhā|bandha|vidhuraḥ,
amuṃ yen' âdy' âpi
Tri|pura|hara|nṛtya|vyatikaraḥ
purastād anyeṣām
api śikhariṇām ullalayati.

kiṃ cit tarkayāmi,

śastrī|kṛtas taru|varo hari|puṃgavena
Laṅk"|êndra|vakṣasi mṛṇāla|mṛduḥ papāta.
tatra sthitais tu kusumaiḥ Kusum'|êṣur enaṃ
Sītā|viyoga|vidhuraṃ dṛḍham ājaghāna.

RATNA·CHUDA: *(looking, exhausted, smiling and surprised at once)* Alas,

The trees that the monkey-king has used as weapons have perished in the terrible fire produced by the friction when they hit Rávana's wide chest. The mountain peak that Sugríva tore off and hurled against the King of Lanka has been reduced to dust by the demon king's numerous hands, and with its bushes and waterfalls it has become a piece of mud and moss. 6.145

HEMÁNGADA: *(smiling)* My friend, this is nothing for ten-headed Rávana,

Once, he lifted the crystal-peaked Mount Kailása, tearing off completely all its ties that rooted it in the earth—that is why even today, when Shiva, the Destroyer of the Three Demon Cities, starts his dance, it is the Kailása that starts shaking first, before all the other mountains.

I have an idea :

That beautiful tree that the monkey-king made into his weapon fell on Rávana's chest as if it were tender like a lotus fiber; and the God of Love must have used the flowers of that tree as arrows to pierce Rávana's heart, to make him love-lorn for being separated from Sita.

6.150 RATNACŪḌAḤ: *(vihasya)* sakhe, kim ucyate. mahā|sattvatāyāṃ Rāvaṇaḥ khalv asau. tathā hi:

sveṣ' ûtkṛtya huteṣu mūrdhasu javād
agneḥ sphuṭitvā bahir
vyākīrṇeṣv alikeṣu daiva|lipibhir
dṛṣṭv" âpi Rāmāyaṇam,
citten' â|skhalitena yas tad|adhikaṃ
Brahmāṇam aprīṇayat,
kas tasmai prathamāya māniṣu mahā|
vīrāya vairāyate?

HEMĀṄAGADAḤ: sakhe, paśya paśya. bhayānakam, adbhutaṃ ca vartate.

viśikh'|âugha|vikīrṇa|gaṇḍa|śaile
taru|saṃcūrṇita|śakti|tomare ca
kapi|rākṣasa|rājayor ajasraṃ
tumule bhānti talātali|prapañcāḥ.

nūnam idānīm,

6.155 śvās'|ōrmi|pratibandha|tundila|gala|
pracchinna|hār'|āvalī|
ratnair āpatayālubhiḥ kṛta|phaṇa|
prāg|bhāra|bhaṅga|bhramaḥ,
śrotr'|â|bhāva|nir|antarāla|militaiḥ
stabdhaiḥ śirobhir bhuvaṃ
dhatte vānara|vīra|vikrama|bharād
bhugnair bhujaṃg'|âdhipaḥ.

RATNA·CHUDA: *(smiling)* My friend, indeed everyone knows Rávana to be a noble person, as this story shows: 6.150

He cut off his heads and offered them in the sacred fire; but when they cracked in the quickly burning flames and the bones of his foreheads got scattered all over, they showed him the story of the 'Ramáyana' written upon them by Fate. In spite of seeing this, he continued to propitiate the Creator with an unwavering mind. Who would be able to fight such a great hero, the first among the most respected beings?

HEMÁNGADA: My friend, look, there is something terrifying and miraculous happening here,

In their unending battle, Rávana's arrows have split Sugríva's mountain rocks, while Sugríva's trees have reduced Rávana's spear and club to dust—now their one-on-one wrestling begins.

And right now,

The King of Snakes is bending down with his heads 6.155
in the underworld: his neck gets swollen to withhold his panting, while his necklace is split by the effort; and, as the gems are scattered everywhere, they create the impression that his thousand hoods have been destroyed.* Yet he keeps holding up the earth with his motionless heads, which are stuck together without being separated by the ears—all this effort is made to bear the weight of Sugríva's heavy steps on the ground.*

HEMĀṄGADAḤ: *(sa|viṣādam)* ahaha, bāhu|yantreṇ' āpīḍya Sugrīvaṃ kim āha Rāvaṇaḥ?

«asmad|bhuja|van'|āndola|su|labhaṃ phalam āpnuvan,
niyuddha|lāghava|klānta, śākhāmṛga, sukhī|bhava!»

RATNACŪḌAḤ: *(sa|harṣam)* sakhe, karaṇa|kauśala|mocit'|ātmā vipakṣa|dur|vacana|khidyamāna|hṛdayo hṛdayaṃ|gamam abhidadhāti vānar'|êndraḥ:

«viṃśatyā yugapat kṣamair api bhujair
ākarṣaṇa|chedayor
a|cchinnaṃ daśamaṃ śiraḥ kathayati
chinnāni yāni kramāt.
tāny ārāddha|mah"|ēśvarāṇi bhavataḥ
śīrṣāṇi tulyaṃ daśa
chindāno daśabhir nakhair yadi, punaḥ
śākhāmṛg'|êndraḥ sukhī.

6.160 api ca, re re rākṣasa,

Daśa|mukha|vadha|nāṭya|sūtradhāro
Raghupatir, asya ca pāripārśvako 'ham.
prakaraṇa|phala|bīja|bhāvakānām
amṛta|bhujāṃ samupāsmahe samājam.»

ity abhidadhānen' âiva utplutya nir|dayaṃ śirasi tāḍito ratha|dhvaja|daṇḍ'|âvalambī kathaṃ cid āśvasiti Rāvaṇaḥ.

HEMÁNGADA: *(with dejection)* Alas, what is Rávana saying while he is squeezing Sugríva with his arms as if with fetters?

"Monkey, you have got tired of the art of wrestling, so may you obtain your fruit, which is easy to get from shaking my forest-like arms, and may you then rest in peace."*

RATNA·CHUDA: *(happily)* My friend, the monkey-king has managed to free himself, thanks to his dexterity; as his soul is distressed by his enemy's words, he gives him an appropriate reply:

"Although your twenty arms could have pulled and torn off all your heads at once, they left the tenth untouched to tell that the others had been duly cut off. Now the king of monkeys shall find peace only if he can cut all your ten Shiva-praising heads at the same time with his ten nails.*

And o rákshasa, 6.160

Rama is the stage manager of this play about the killing of Rávana; and I am his assistant. We propitiate the assembly of gods as our public, before whom the story of the play unfolds."

Saying this, he jumped and attacked Rávana on the head, hitting him cruelly, but Rávana leaned against the flagstaff of his chariot and regained his force somehow.

HEMĀṄGADAḤ: *(sarvato 'valokya, sa|harṣam)* sakhe, paśya paśya,

yan|mālya|grathan'|âvaśeṣa|vikalaiḥ
santānakair nākināṃ
bhartre garbhakam eva dāma nibhṛtaṃ
svar|mālikair gumphitam,
tasminn adya Daś'|âsya|mūrdhani nava|
prastāvanām āpadāṃ
paśyanto rabhas'|âugha|bhartsita|bhiyaḥ
krośanti naḥ syandanāḥ.

6.165 HEMĀṄGADAḤ: *(sa|viṣādam)* ahaha, āśvasya Daśa|kaṇṭhen' âpi tāḍito mūrcchitaḥ kap'|îndro Nīla|Hanūmadbhyām āśvāsyamāno 'pasāryate.

RATNACŪḌAḤ: sakhe, prathanasya prathama|parvaṇi śata|kṛtvo vijayante, vijīyante ca mahā|vīrāḥ. tatra ko viṣādaḥ?

HEMĀṄGADAḤ: *(anyato 'valokya)* sakhe Ratnacūḍa, diṣṭyā vardhase, yad ayam anuprāptaḥ,

Kuśika|suta|sa|paryā|dṛṣṭa|divy'|âstra|tantro,
Bhṛgu|pati|saha|yudhvā vīra|bhogīṇa|bāhuḥ,
dinakara|kula|ketuḥ kautuk'|ôttāna|cakṣur,
bahu|mata|ripu|karmā kārmukī Rāma|bhadraḥ.

HEMÁNGADA: *(looking everywhere, happily)* My friend, look,

> The celestial garland-makers had to wreathe Indra's small chaplet* secretly, from imperfect bits of flowers left over after Rávana's crown had been made with the blossoms of the wish-fulfilling tree. But now Rávana's crowned head presents a new prologue of bad fate*—and, seeing this, our chariots curse their fear with great vehemence and cry out.

HEMÁNGADA: *(dejected)* Alas, Rávana has regained his force 6.165
and hit the monkey-king so hard that Sugríva has lost consciousness; he is being fanned and carried away by Nila and Hánuman.

RATNA·CHUDA: My friend, in the first half of the battle, heroes gain and lose hundreds of times in a row. So why should we despair?

HEMÁNGADA: *(looking elsewhere)* My friend, Ratna·chuda, you shall be blessed now that he has come here:

> He who has learned the science of heavenly weapons by serving Vishva·mitra, he who has fought Párashu·rama, with his arms ready to strike, the foremost member of the solar dynasty, he who is respected as a great fighter—here comes Rama with his bow, his eyes wide open in curiosity.

RATNACŪḌAḤ: *(sa|harṣaṃ* RĀMAM *avalokya,* RĀVAṆAṂ *prati)* Rākṣasa|rāja,

6.170 bālen' âpi vilūna|Dhūrjaṭi|dhanuḥ|
stambhena bāh'|ūṣmabhir
yena svedayatā mano|haram ṛjū|
cakre munir Bhārgavaḥ,
saṃprāpto Raghu|nandanaḥ; kim aparam?
ten' âdhunā neṣyate
dhanyo Vāli|samāna|kartṛka|vadha|
ślāgh"|âti|bhūmiṃ bhavān.

HEMĀṄGADAḤ: *(sa|kautukam)* sakhe, tūṣṇīm āsvahe tāvat. śṛṇuvaḥ kim bravīti Rāvaṇaḥ.

RATNACŪḌAḤ: *(karṇaṃ dattvā)* kim evam āha: «sādhu, re kṣatriya|ḍimbha, sādhu,

yat kanyām abhilaṣyatā Nimi|pater
na sthāṇavīyaṃ mayā
dor|līlā|tulit'|âvatārita|Hara|
grāvṇ" âpi rugṇaṃ dhanuḥ,
tad drakṣanty adhunā kiyantam avadhiṃ
‹yāvad bhavān› ity amī
Dev'|êndra|dvipa|dāna|dur|dina|bhido
raudr'|ârciṣo mārgaṇāḥ?»

HEMĀṄGADAḤ: *(sa|vismayam)* katham, ady' âpi tṛṇī|kṛta|jagat|trayaḥ sa ev' âsya tāvān ahaṃkāra|granthiḥ.

6.175 RATNACŪḌAḤ: *(s'|ôtprāsa|smitam)* sakhe, katham idaṃ bhavantaṃ vismāpayate?

RATNA·CHUDA: *(happily beholding* RAMA, *toward* RÁVANA*)* King of Demons,

> Even as a child, he broke Shiva's heavy bow, and chastened Párashu·rama in a sweet manner, while making him perspire with the heat of his strong arms. This son of the Raghu dynasty has arrived—what else is there to say now? You are fortunate to become famous as being killed by the same man who killed Vali. 6.170

HEMÁNGADA: *(eagerly)* My friend, let us be quiet and listen to what Rávana is saying.

RATNA·CHUDA: *(listening)* Look, this is what he is saying: "Well done, wretched son of a warrior,

> Although I had lifted and replaced Shiva's abode easily with my arms, I refused to bend his bow when I asked for the hand of Jánaka's daughter. Therefore, how long will my arrows, whose terrible flames have dried up the ichor of Indra's elephant, bear to see you alive now?"

HEMÁNGADA: *(smiling)* Look how much he, who treated the three worlds with contempt, is still puffed up with pride.

RATNA·CHUDA: *(smiling happily)* My friend, how can such a small thing make you smile? 6.175

mān'|ādhmātaḥ svāṃ kil' ôtkṛtya tāvad
  mūrdha|śreṇīm eka|śeṣ'|ôttam'|âṅgaḥ,
strīm ardh'|âṅge vañcayitvā, mukhena
  prītaḥ Śaṃbhor eva pāde papāta.

(ūrdhvam avalokya ca, sa/vitarkam) bhagavato Divas|pater iva ratho Dāśarathim upatiṣṭhate.

HEMĀṄGADAḤ: *(dṛṣṭvā, sa/harṣam)* sakhe, sa ev' âyam. kiṃ na paśyasi? locana|mārga|sahasra|candraka|stabakita|mah"|Êndra|kavaca|hasto Mātaliḥ.

(kṣaṇaṃ nirvaṇya)

6.180 vividha|maṇi|mayūkha|mañjarībhiḥ
  kṛta|sura|cāpa|sahasra|saṃnipāte
adhisamaram ahārayad vimāne
  nijam api kārmukam atra Deva|rājaḥ.

(karṇaṃ dattvā) kim āha Rāvaṇa|pratihāraḥ? «are re Puruhūta|sūta,

darpo 'yaṃ bhavataḥ sur'|âsura|camū|
    doḥ|kāṇḍa|kaṇḍū|viṣa|
  jvālā|jāṅgulikena jāṅgala|bhujāṃ
    paty" âpi na tyājitaḥ,
yen' āindre ratha|varmaṇī Raghu|śiśor
    asy' ôpanīte tvayā.
  rāja|dviṣṭam idaṃ vidhāya sa kathaṃ
    Śakro 'pi vartiṣyate?»

When full of pride, he cut his row of heads leaving only one intact, then, betraying Shiva's female side,* he bowed down happily to touch only the foot of the male side with his remaining head.

(looking upward, reflecting) The chariot arriving next to Rama looks like that of the sun god.

HEMÁNGADA: *(looking, with joy)* My friend, can't you see what is happening? Here comes Mátali, Indra's charioteer, bringing Indra's shield, which has a thousand moon-shaped holes dotted all over it for the god's thousand eyes.

(watching for a second)

In this celestial chariot, which shines like a thousand rainbows with its various gems pouring their reflections over it, Indra has sent even his bow to the battle. 6.180

(listening) Listen to what Rávana's doorkeeper is saying. "Hey, you, Indra's charioteer,

The lord of the meat-eating *rákshasas* has cured the itching of strong arms in the armies of gods and demons, just as a snake charmer counteracts the effect of the venom. But even he was unable to cure you of your arrogance: you have dared to bring this chariot and shield of Indra's for Rama. After doing this hostile act against our king, how shall Indra be able to survive?"

RATNACŪḌAḤ: *(śrutim abhinīya)* kim āha Rāmaḥ? «satyam idam bhoḥ: yac|chīlaḥ svāmī, tac|chīlāḥ tasya prakṛtayaḥ, yad ete 'pi svāmino mūla|cchedinā dur|nayena vikatthante.»

HEMĀṄGADAḤ: *(ākāśe karṇaṃ dattvā.)* kim āha Rāvaṇaḥ? «are tāpasa|baṭo,

6.185 krodhena jvalitā muhūrtam anu ca
svair eva nirvāpitāḥ
klībair aśru|mah"|ōrmibhir makha|bhujāṃ
patyuḥ sahasraṃ dṛśaḥ
yair dṛṣṭā bhuvana|trayī|vijayibhiḥ
sarvaṃ|kaṣāḥ santy amī,
te saṃpraty api me nay'|âpanayayor
nirvāha|mūlaṃ bhujāḥ.»

RATNACŪḌAḤ: *(karṇaṃ dattvā)* kim āha Rāma|bhadraḥ?

«chittvā mūrdhnaḥ kim iti sa vṛto
Dhūrjaṭir, yady amīṣāṃ
doḥ|stambhānāṃ tri|bhuvana|jaya|
śrīr iyaṃ vāstavī te?
mūrdhāno vā na khalu bhavato
dur|labhāḥ saṃbhaveyur,
yad devasya tvam asi jagatāṃ
śilpino 'pi prapautraḥ?

yat punar bravīṣi ‹saṃpraty api te bhujāḥ sant' îti,› tad adhun" âiva jñāsyate.»

RATNA·CHUDA: *(miming that he hears something)* And this is what Rama replies: "Indeed, a king's subjects are like the king himself: they boast with the same bad manners as their master, causing their own total destruction."

HEMÁNGADA: *(listening to something in the air)* And this is what Rávana says: "You wretched ascetic,

My arms were there when Indra's thousand eyes were first blazing with rage for a moment, but then their fire was extinguished by the abundant flow of tears he shed because he was totally helpless. And these very same all-destructive arms have conquered the three worlds, thus becoming the only source to determine, even for you now, what good or bad manners are." 6.185

RATNA·CHUDA: *(listening)* And Rama retorts:

"If your colossal arms really possessed the Goddess of Victory Over the Three Worlds, then why did you need to propitiate Shiva by cutting off your heads?* Or did you cut them off simply because they were easy for you to put back, since you are the great-grandson of the Creator of the World?

So what you said about your arms will be verified right now."

HEMĀṄGADAḤ: *(karṇaṃ dattvā)* kim āha Rāvaṇaḥ? «are re, rājanya|ḍimbha, bhavataḥ purāṇa|pitā|mahena bahu tāvad Anaraṇyen' âiva jñātam. idānīṃ bhavān api jñāsyati.»

6.190 RATNACŪḌAḤ: *(karṇaṃ dattvā, vihasya)* kim āha Rāmaḥ? «are re, rākṣasī|putra,

na dūye naḥ pūrvaṃ
nṛpatim Anaraṇyam, yad avadhīr.
jayo vā mṛtyur vā
yudhi bhuja|bhṛtāṃ; kaḥ paribhavaḥ?
jitaṃ tu tvāṃ kārā|
gṛha|vinihitaṃ Haihaya|pateḥ
Pulastyo yad bhikṣām
akṛta kṛpaṇas tad vyathayati.»

HEMĀṄGADAḤ: *(karṇaṃ dattvā)* kim āha Rāvaṇaḥ? «āḥ, kṣtriya|vaṭo, vācāṭa, katham a|pūrva|śilpī rajanī|car'|êndra|carita|candre 'pi lakṣma likhasi. tad ayaṃ na bhavasi.» *(sa|saṃbhramam avalokya)* katham, upakrāntam eva śara|sahasra|dur|dinaṃ Mandodarī|dayitena.

RATNACŪḌAḤ: kathaṃ, Maithilī|vallabhen' âpi pratyupakrāntam eva. *(vihasya)*

patanti Rāma|bhadreṇa
khaṇḍitā Rāvaṇ'|êṣavaḥ:
pūrv'|ârdhaiḥ phalibhir vegāt,
paśc'|ârdhaiḥ pakṣibhiś cirāt.

6.195 kiṃ ca,

akṣe ca, ketu|daṇḍe ca, sārathau ca, hayeṣu ca
khelanti Rākṣas'|êndrasya syandane Rāma|pattriṇaḥ.

HEMÁNGADA: *(listening)* And Rávana again: "Hey, you miserable son of a kshatriya, your great-grandfather Anaránya tried them out; now it is your turn."*

RATNA·CHUDA: *(listening, then smiling)* Rama replies then: "You, son of a demoness, 6.190

> I am not dejected because you killed my royal ancestor, Anaránya; for if a warrior wins or dies in battle, it is not to his disgrace. But I feel sorry that your poor grandfather, Pulástya, had to beg for your release when you were conquered and put into prison by Árjuna Kartavírya."*

HEMÁNGADA: *(listening)* And to this, Rávana says: "You blabbering khsatriya, you think you are a modern artist who can draw a spot on the moon of Rávana's fame?* I doubt that you should be able to do so." *(looking, with alarm)* Look, Mandódari's beloved Rávana has started showering his arrows.

RATNA·CHUDA: So has Sita's beloved Rama. *(smiling)*

> As Rávana's arrows are split by Rama, their iron-made tips fall quickly, while their feathered ends reach the ground slowly.

And then, 6.195

> On the axle, on the flagstaff, on the charioteer and on the horses—Rama's arrows are playing their game all over Rávana's chariot.

HEMĀṄGADAḤ: *(sa|bhayam)* ahaha,

andha|kārī|kṛta|vyomnā bāṇa|varṣeṇa Rāvaṇaḥ
Rām'|ārūḍhaṃ tiro|dhatte śat'|âṅgaṃ śātamanyavam.

(ciraṃ dṛṣṭvā, sa|vismayam) sakhe,

6.200 nānā|vidhāni śastrāṇi śastrair nānā|vidhair api
imau hi pratikurvāte, na kaś cid atiricyate.

RATNACŪḌAḤ: evam etat.

yad Rāvaṇo bahubhir eṣa bhujaiḥ karoti,
tad Rāghavaḥ prati|karoti bhuja|dvayena.
karma dvayor yad api tulya|phalaṃ, tath" âpi
rakṣo|bhaṭād daśa|guṇaṃ nara|vīra|śilpam.

HEMĀṄGADAḤ: *(vihasya)* sakhe,

viṃśaty" âpi bhujair eṣa dvau bhujāv abhiyodhayan,
a|dūṣita|dvandva|yuddha|maryādo Daśa|kandharaḥ.

6.205 *(sa|kheda|bhayaṃ ca)* katham, ayaṃ Rāvaṇo mah'|Êndra|syandanāt,

tasy' âri|bala|bhīmasya dhvaja|daṇḍasya lāñchanam
darpa|dīptaḥ kṣurapreṇa māyūraṃ piccham acchinat.

RATNACŪḌAḤ: *(sa|harṣam)* sakhe, paśya paśya, kuliśa|ketu|ketan'|âvamānana|vilakṣa|kruddhena,

HEMÁNGADA: *(with fear)* Alas,

> With his shower of arrows Rávana darkens the space and covers Rama's chariot given by Indra.

(watching for a while, then, with a smile) My friend,

> They both reply to each other with various weapons—neither of them can win over the other. 6.200

RATNA·CHUDA: Indeed.

> What Rávana does with his many arms is counteracted by Rama's two hands. Although the result of their acts is the same, Rama's heroic might as a human is ten times that of this fighting demon's.

HEMÁNGADA: *(smiling)* My friend,

> Fighting with twenty arms against only two, hasn't Rávana violated the laws of what could be called a one-on-one battle?*

(with alarm and fear) Look what has happened to the chariot 6.205
given by Indra.

> The peacock feather that ornated the flagstaff of the chariot ridden by Rama, fear of all enemies, has just been cut off by Rávana, puffed up with pride, with his arrow.

RATNA·CHUDA: *(happily)* My friend, look how the Raghu prince is ashamed and angry to see the flag of thunderbolt-brandishing Indra being so little respected:

dik|pāla|dvipa|darpa|dāna|laharī|
saurabhya|garbh'|ânilaiḥ
pakṣair eva samasta|rākṣasa|kathā|
kalp'|ânta|karṇe|japāḥ
dīyante Raghu|puṃgavena kati cit
Paulastya|mauliṣv amī
Paulomī|nayan'|âmbu|sīkara|kaṇ'|â-
vagrāhiṇo mārgaṇāḥ.

HEMĀṄGADAḤ: *(sa|khed'|âdbhutam)* kathaṃ, kirīṭa|param-parā|paribhavam a|mṛṣyamāṇena bāṇa|varṣ'|â|dvaitam ātanvatā Rākṣasa|rājena,

6.210 Videha|kanyā|kuca|kumbha|koṭi|
kaṭhoratā|sākṣiṇi sāyako 'yam
Rāmasya janm'|ântara|mela|kāra|
Śrī|Kaustubhe vakṣasi, hā, nikhātaḥ.

(samyag avalokya) sakhe,

eken' âiva nivāta|kaṅkaṭa|bhidā
Laṅkā|pateḥ pattriṇā
viddho 'yaṃ yadi nāma ko 'pi jagatām
ullāghano Rāghavaḥ,
cakṣur|vartma|sahasra|niḥsarad|asṛg|
dhār"|âugha|jhāṃ|kāriṇā
māhendreṇa tu varmaṇā vivṛṇute
vīraḥ sahasraṃ vraṇān.

RATNACŪḌAḤ: *(sa|harṣam)* Rāghaveṇ' âpi,

Sītā|stana|stabaka|kuṅkuma|paṅka|lopa|
saṅkalpa|pātakini vakṣasi Rāvaṇasya
nyastaḥ śaro vibudha|kuñjara|danta|ghāta|
rūḍha|vraṇ'|ârbuda|catuṣṭaya|madhya|vartī.

These arrows, whose feathers carry a breeze scented by the abundant ichor of the proud world-guarding elephants,* thus suggesting that this is the end of the history of all rákshasas, are to stop the flow of tears coming from the eyes of Indra's wife*—for Rama is now sending them toward Rávana's heads.

HEMÁNGADA: *(with alarm and surprise)* The king of rákshasas cannot bear this insult of his row of crowns and is showering arrows incessantly toward his enemy.

Rama's chest, which carried the Káustubha gem and the Goddess of Wealth* in another birth and felt the stiff, piercing nipples of Sita's large breasts, has, alas, just been hit by Rávana's arrow. 6.210

(looking straight ahead) My friend,

Look, the noble Raghu prince, who is to rescue the world, has been pierced by one single arrow that Rávana sent to cut through his thick armor. But, as the armor came from Indra, it has a thousand holes for Indra's thousand eyes, from which a thousand streams of bubbling blood are flowing abundantly now—our hero, Rama, thus seems to bleed from a thousand wounds.

RATNA·CHUDA: *(happily)* But the prince

has just sent out an arrow and hit Rávana's chest, which sinned gravely in wanting to wipe off the wet kunkuma marks on Sita's round breasts. The arrow is now staked in Rávana, in the middle of four swollen scars remaining from the wounds that

6.215 HEMĀṄGADAḤ: *(karṇaṃ dattvā, sa|vismayam)* ekena savya|pāṇinā viśikham utkhāya kim āha Rāvaṇaḥ? «sādhu, re manuṣya|ḍimbha, sādhu,

traivikramaḥ sakala|dānava|jīvitavya|
vidyā|samāpti|lipir eṣa Sudarśano me
yasmin nipatya hṛdaye dalit'|âra|jāla|
jyotis|tuṣāra|mayam ābharaṇaṃ babhūva.

tasminn api rudhira|darśanaṃ kurvatā bhavatā darśit" êyaṃ sur'|âsura|vīry'|âtiśāyinī hastavattā.»

RATNACŪḌAḤ: ahaha, dviṣad|girām udgāreṇa sarva|granthi|guruṇā dūraṃ dīpyamānasya,

sva|vinihita|Candrahāsa|
vraṇa|kiṇa|valay'|ôpahasita|hāreṣu
Rāmasya mārgaṇa|gaṇāḥ
patanti Daśa|kaṇṭha|kaṇṭheṣu.

6.220 HEMĀṄGADAḤ: *(sa|camat|kāram)* sakhe, paśya paśya. anurūpa|vīra|saṃvāda|pramoda|bhara|dvi|guṇit'|âvaṣṭambha|saṃkṣobhita|bhuvana|trayasya nirantara|prahīyamāṇa|bāṇa|pañjara|vartinā Rāma|bhadreṇa krīḍā|śakunta|kautukam āpūryate Rākṣasa|rājasya. nūnam idānīm,

the tusks of Indra's elephant once inflicted upon him.*

HEMÁNGADA: *(listening, with a smile)* Drawing out the arrow with one of his left hands,* Rávana says: "Well done, wretched human, 6.215

This is the disk called Sudárshana, belonging to Vishnu of the Three Paces,* which has the death, the end of the magic knowledge of all demons inscribed on it. But, as it falls on my heart, its spokes are broken and it becomes an ornament for me, bright and cool.

Now that you have been able to show some blood coming from my heart, you have shown your exceptional heroic skill to conquer all gods and demons."

RATNA·CHUDA: Alas, Rama has been terribly angered by the words that his enemy belched out, words laden with all kinds of lies.

The strings of scars on Rávana's necks, made by his own sword, the Chandra·hasa, look as if they were mock garlands;* and Rama's arrows are now attacking these oddly adorned necks.

HEMÁNGADA: *(with admiration)* My friend, look, the three worlds are stirred up by Rávana's pride, which has been doubled in his joy to have found a worthy hero to challenge. His arrows are incessantly falling on Rama, who is like a pet bird for Rávana to amuse himself with, playing inside the cage formed by those arrows. And now, 6.220

udañcan|nyañcad|bhū|
vivṛta|nibhṛtānām anuphaṇaṃ
maṇīnāṃ vidyudbhiḥ
kṣaṇa|muṣita|pātāla|timiraḥ
bhuja|krīḍā|valgad|
Daśa|mukha|pada|nyāsa|garima|
pragalbhair niśvāsair
ajani bhujagānām adhipatiḥ.

RATNACŪḌAḤ: *(sa|bhayam avalokya)* sakhe, evam etat.

rakṣo|vikṣobha|veg'|ôcchalita|jalanidhi|
vyakta|mātaṅga|nakra|
krudhyad|diṅ|nāga|mukt'|ôddharaṇa|guru|bharām
adya nāg'|âdhirājaḥ
aṅgair aṅgeṣu magnair a|virala|valinā
vāmanena ati|pīvnā
dehen' âpahnuvānaḥ phaṇa|phalaka|parī-
ṇāham urvīṃ bibharti.

(ūrdhvam avalokya) katham, itas tato vaimānikair apakramyate.

6.225 HEMĀṄGADAḤ: *(sa|camat|kāram)* aho, tri|bhuvana|bhayaṃ|karam upakrāntaṃ mahā|vīrābhyām āyodhanam. tathā hi,

dhyāyaty ayaṃ Gādhi|sutād adhītān
divy'|âstra|mantrān Manu|vaṃśa|vīraḥ.
Brahm'|ôpadiṣṭām iha śastra|vidyām
asau tad" ākāṅkṣati Rākṣas'|êndraḥ.

As the ground is moving up and down under Rávana's heavy steps, while his arms playfully wander in all directions, it keeps revealing and hiding in turn the shining jewels in the hoods of the bravely panting Snake King underneath, jewels whose unveiled light thus illuminates the dark underworld with flashes every other second.

RATNA·CHUDA: *(looking with fear)* My friend, indeed,

As the ocean was stirred up by the heavy movements of the fighting demon, it has released its elephantine sea monsters. At this sight, the elephants who sustain the world in the eight directions have left their posts angrily to fight them—thus, the burden of the whole earth is now being borne by the Snake King: the large surface of his hoods disappears as his various parts are squeezed into each other and his body becomes dwarfed, swollen, with folds all over.

(looking upward) The gods are flying away on their chariots!

HEMÁNGADA: *(with admiration)* Ah, the two heroes have started their real fight, to the horror of the three worlds. See what is happening: 6.225

Prince Rama, hero of the Manu dynasty, is evoking the celestial mantra-weapons he learned from Vishva·mitra, while the King of Demons is trying to apply the science of weapons that Brahma taught to him.*

tad āvām apy apasṛty' āsvahe.

HEMĀṄGADAḤ: *(samantād avalokya)* sakhe, yath" âyaṃ bhuvana|saṃkṣobhas, tathā tarkayāmi: tāmisraṃ bhānavīyena, bhānavīyaṃ ca rāhavīyeṇa, rāhavīyaṃ vaiṣṇavīyena, vaiṣṇavīyaṃ ca pauṣpaketavena, pauṣpaketavaṃ ca pāśupaten' âstreṇ' âstraṃ pratikurvāṇayoḥ Pulastya|Kakutstha|kul'|âika|vīrayos tumulam āyodhanaṃ vartate.

RATNACŪḌAḤ: sakhe, Hemāṅgada, kṛti|pratikṛtīnām a|viśeṣe 'pi, jetavyam iti Rāmasya, martavyam iti Rāvaṇasya nirbharo 'yaṃ sarv'|âstra|mokṣaḥ. viśikha|mukh'|ôpasthāyinīnāṃ ca punar devatānām a|balīyān āṭopaḥ kalpyate. tathā hi,

6.230 yad daivataṃ kṣipati pattriṣu Rākṣas'|êndraḥ,
snehena tad Raghu|pater mṛdu saṃnidhatte.
yāṃ devatām upa|dadhāti ca Rāma|bhadras,
trāsād asau Daśa|mukhasya śanair upaiti.

NEPATHYE:

yat yad kṛttaṃ Daśa|mukha|śiras
tasya tasy' âiva kāntau
saṃkrāmantyām atiśayavatī
śeṣa|vaktreṣu lakṣmīḥ.
yo yaḥ kṛtto Daśa|mukha|bhujas
tasya tasy' âiva vīryaṃ
labdhvā dṛpyanty adhikam adhikaṃ
bāhavaḥ śiṣyamāṇāḥ.

Let us watch them from a distance.

HEMÁNGADA: *(looking in all directions)* My friend, while the world is being shaken, it seems as if the fierce battle between the two heroes, Rávana and Rama, each one unique in his family, were being fought with one divine weapon attacking the other: that of the God of Darkness answered with that of the Sun, the Sun's arm counteracted by that of the Demon of Eclipse, his weapon neutralized by Vishnu's, Vishnu's missile overcome by that of the God of Love, which in turn is destroyed by Shiva's weapon.

RATNA·CHUDA: My friend, Hemángada, although their attacks and counter-attacks are the same, Rama keeps sending out all his arrows to win, and Rávana does the same only to die. And the gods who are directing these arrows do not seem to be particularly aggressive. In other words,

When Rávana invokes a god to empower his arrow, 6.230
that deity makes the weapon approach Rama gently, out of affection for him. And the gods whom Rama places on his arrows reach Rávana slowly, out of their fear of him.

FROM THE REAR OF THE STAGE:

Every time Rama cuts off one of Rávana's heads, its splendor is transferred onto the remaining ones, which then shine even brighter. And each time Rama cuts off one of the Demon King's arms, its force is transmitted to the remaining ones, which thus get prouder and prouder.

UBHAU: *(sa|harṣa|rom'|âñcam ākarṇya)* aye, śabd'|ôpalambha|pravartakena karmaṇā nimittena tri|bhuvanasya ko 'yam indriyāṇi prīṇayati?

nepathye kalakalaḥ

6.235 UBHAU: *(sa|bhay'|âdbhutam)* aye, katham ayaṃ kapaṭa|kaṇṭhī|rava|Vaikuṇṭha|kaṇṭha|kaṭhora|kolāhala|kāhala|mahā|nirghoṣaḥ prajā|koṣṭha|bhaṅgam a|parvaṇi prakramate? nūnaṃ c' êdānīṃ ghana|kāla|kūṭa|digdhair iva kaṇṭha|dhvanibhir eva mūrcchayato bhuvanāni Bhairavasya smarati bhṛśaṃ sa|bhayam adya Parameṣṭhī.

punar NEPATHYE:

divy'|âstrair bhūr|bhuvaḥ|svas|tritaya|ḍamaraṇ'|ôḍḍāmarair yodhayitvā
lūn'|ôtkṣiptaiḥ śirobhir daśabhir abhi|nabho darśit'|âikā|daś'|ârkaḥ
Kākutsthen' âvakīrṇo nija|viśikha|śikhā|yoga|pīṭh'|ôpahūta|
Brahm'|âstreṇ' âdhiśete Rajanicara|pater vīra|śayyāṃ kabandhaḥ.

UBHAU: *(sa|harṣa|saṃbhramam ūrdhvam avalokya, sa|vismayam)* sakhe, paśya paśya, pralaya|kāla|karāla|kāl'|ânala|jvālā|puñja|piñjarāṇi Rāvaṇa|śirāṃsi.

sa|tvaram upasṛtya c' adhastāt paśyataḥ.

6.240 HEMĀṄGADAḤ: *(sa|karuṇam)* hā, mahā|vīra|prakāṇḍa, Laṅkeśvara, paryavasito 'si.

BOTH: *(listening happily, with their hair standing on end)* O, who is this person who delights all the senses of the worlds by creating only the perception of a sound?

Tumult from the rear of the stage.

BOTH: *(with fear and admiration)* It is as if Naráyana, in the guise of a lion, was roaring loudly and harshly with the full strength of his voice, emitting a cry to announce the untimely end of the world. And it is really as if now Brahma was suddenly evoking Bháirava with fear, Bháirava who bewilders the worlds with his deep cries coming from his poison-marked throat.* 6.235

Again, FROM THE REAR OF THE STAGE*:*

> Rávana fought with many a celestial weapon, strong enough to shake earth, heaven and the intermediate space. But, when Rama invoked Brahma's missile on the yogic seat formed by the tip of his arrow, he cut off Rávana's ten heads with it, throwing them up in the air to create eleven suns,* while the demon king's headless body was made to fall down. Here it is now, lying on the battlefield.

BOTH: *(with delight and fear, looking upward, then, with a smile)* My friend, look, Rávana's heads are golden red, like the flames of the terrible fire at the end of the world.

They go closer quickly, and look down below.

HEMÁNGADA: *(with compassion)* Alas, lauded hero, King of Lanka, this is your end. 6.240

bhinn'|Āirāvaṇa|gandha|sindhura|śiraḥ|
sampātibhir mauktikaiḥ
śaśvad|viśva|jaya|praśasti|racanā|
varṇ'|āvalī|śilpine,
nāk'|ântaḥ|purikā|kapola|vilasat|
kāśmīra|pattr'|âṅkura|
śrī|vinyāsa|vināśa|bhīṣaṇa|bhuja|
stambhāya tubhyaṃ namaḥ.

(nirvarṇya) sakhe, Ratnacūḍa,

dhruvaṃ patita|Paṅkti|kandhara|
kabandha|pīḍā|bharān
nij'|âvanamana|kram'|ônnamita|
cakravāl'|âcalam
mahī|valayam ardha|kuṇḍalita|
vigrah'|ādhāraka|
pratīṣṭa|phaṇa|maṇḍalo vahati
Kādravey'|âdhipaḥ.

RATNACŪḌAḤ: sakhe, sarvam atiśāyi Rāvaṇasya. pur" âpi khalu,

6.245 calati jagatī|jaitre yatra
sva|bhogi|camū|bhaṭair
valayita|mahā|deha|stambho
bibharti bhuvas talam,
pracalad|a|khila|kṣmābhṛn|mūl'|ô-
pala|vyatighaṭṭit'|ôl-
baṇa|maṇi|śilā|jalpākībhiḥ
phaṇābhir ah'|īśvaraḥ.

You wrote each letter of your own hymn of praise, to celebrate your eternal victory over the world, with the pearls you obtained when you split the head of Indra's perfect elephant;* and your colossal arms were so frightening that they prevented the wives of the gods from beautifying their faces with their glittering makeup of saffron paste.* Here we are to pay homage to you.

(watching) My friend, Ratna·chuda,

As Rávana's headless body falls on the ground with all its weight, the earth bends down in pain, which in turn lifts the great mountains at the edges of the world higher—and the King of Snakes bears all this underneath, while his body is coiled into half its size to support his many hoods, on which the whole world rests.

RATNA·CHUDA: Rávana has always been excessive in everything. Of yore,

when Rávana was treading on the earth as the con- 6.245
queror of the world, all the snake-soldiers gathered around the colossal body of the King of Snakes to help him, for he had to bear the surface of the world with his large hoods, hoods that seemed to be talking as the bottom rocks of all the shaking mountains were scratching his bright head-jewels.

idānīṃ punar utkrānta|vāyur ati|dur|vaho deha|bandhaḥ.

HEMĀṄGADAḤ: *(anyato 'valokya.)* katham, iyaṃ Daśa|kandhara|kabandh'|âbhimukhī śoka|viklavā Mandodarī niśā|carībhir apakṛṣyate. *(ākāśe karṇaṃ dattvā)* kaṣṭam, kaṣṭam. capala|kapi|kul'|ânukriyamāṇa|karuṇa|kāku|tāra|svarā Mandodarī kim āha mahā|vīra|vara|varṇinī?

«bhūyiṣṭhāni mukhāni cumbati bhujair
bhūyobhir āliṅgyate
cāritra|vrata|devat" âpi bhavatā
kāntena Mandodarī.
hā, lamb'|ôdara|kumbha|mauktika|maṇi|
stomair mama ekāvalī|
śilpe vāg|adhama'|ṛṇakasya bhavato,
Laṅk"|êndra, nidrā|rasaḥ.»

UBHAU: *(sa|khedam)* idam a|śaky'|ânubhavaṃ cakṣuḥ|śrotrasya. pratikṛtānām api vyasanam ati|mātraṃ hṛdayasya marmāṇi chinatti. *(sa|vimarśam)* ahaha, na kiṃ cid an|īṣat|karaṃ nāma Kṛtāntasya.

6.250 vandāru|vṛndāraka|vṛnda|bandī|
mandāra|mālā|makaranda|bindūn
Mandodar" îyaṃ caraṇ'|âravinda|
reṇ'|ûtkaraiḥ karkaratām anaiṣīt.

And, now that life has left Rávana, his body seems to be even heavier.

HEMÁNGADA: *(looking elsewhere)* Ah, his dejected wife, Mandódari, who was about to approach Rávana's body, is being drawn away by the demonesses. *(listening to something)* Alas, the queen of this great hero is saying something. She has a high-pitched voice, a shriek of compassion that sounds like the cry of monkeys flying in the air:

> "Although Mandódari has been a chaste wife, she has kissed many lips and has been embraced by many arms, for she was your beloved.* Alas, you have not kept your promise to string a necklace from the pearls released from Ganésha's temples— how can you, the King of Lanka, enjoy your dream now?"

BOTH: *(with pain)* This is impossible to look at or to listen to. Even if she was our enemy, this extreme pain breaks our hearts. *(reflecting)* Alas, nothing is too hard for the God of Death. . .

> When the wives of the respectful gods made the honey drops of the coral tree flowers adorning their crowns fall down, Mandódari made those drops solid with the pollen-like dust of her lotus-feet.* 6.250

tasy" âp' îyam daśā.

NEPATHYE:

nīyante vana|devatābhir amara|
kṣoṇī|ruho Nandanam;
nīto vallabha|pālakena ca nijām
Uccaiḥśravā mandurām;
rakṣobhiś ca Vibhīṣaṇa|praṇayibhiḥ
kārā|gṛhād mocita|
svar|bandī|vadan'|âvaloka|nibiḍa|
vrīḍo Biḍaujāḥ kṛtaḥ.

RATNACŪḌAḤ: *(sa|harṣam)* sakhe, tad ehi. Laṅk"|êśvara|kārā|gṛha|cira|vāstavyaṃ bandhu|vargam īkṣāvahe.

6.255 *iti parikrāntau, vilokya, sa|harṣam anyonyam.*

sakhe, paśya paśya. prahāra|vihvala|valīmukh'|âcchabhalla|golāṅgūla|grāma|saṃvargaṇa|vyagrita|Sugrīvo Lakṣmaṇa|nihita|dhanvā Vibhīṣaṇa|bhuj'|âvalambī jaya|śriyā kim api pradīpta|ramaṇīyo Rāma|bhadraḥ. ayaṃ hi saṃprati,

Paulastya|nyasta|śakti|vraṇa|kiṇa|kaṇikā|
lakṣmaṇo Lakṣmaṇ'|ôraḥ|
pīṭhād nirmukta|lajjo, vibudha|pura|vadhū|
kḷpta|puṣp'|âbhiṣekaḥ,
sadyo naptāram anyaṃ rajanicara|purī|
bhadra|pīṭha|pratiṣṭhaṃ
dṛṣṭvā tuṣyat|Pulastyo, jagati vijayate

And yet she is in this sad state now.

BEHIND THE SCENES:

> The deities of the forest take the celestial trees back to the garden of paradise; Indra's favorite horse, Long Ears, has been led back to his stable by his groom; and the rákshasas on Vibhíshana's side* have released the wives of gods from their prison—but, looking at their faces, Indra has become rather ashamed.*

RATNA·CHUDA: *(happily)* My friend, come, let us see our friends who have spent a long time in the prison of the King of Lanka.

They both walk around the stage, look around and say to each other happily. 6.255

My friend, look, while the bouncing Sugríva is coming here in great leaps, together with wrinkled monkeys, bears and cow-tailed monkeys* afflicted by the fight, Rama gives his bow to Lákshmana, takes Vibhíshana's hand, and his radiance is strengthened by the Goddess of Victory. For,

> Rama is no longer ashamed now because of the small scar on Lákshmana's chest, remaining from the wound the descendant of Pulástya, Rávana, made with a lance;* and the wives of the gods have performed our hero's royal consecration with flowers. While Pulástya is happy to see that suddenly another of his grandsons, Vibhíshana, is consecrated on the throne of the demon city, the only

Jānakī|jānir ekaḥ.

iti niṣkrāntau.

person to be the real ruler in this world is Sita's husband: Rama.

Both exit.

PRELUDE TO ACT VII
INDICATION OF EVENTS

NEPATHYE:

tamisrā|mūrcchāla|
        tri|jagad|a|gadaṃ|kāra|kiraṇe
    Raghūṇāṃ gotrasya
        prasavitari deve Savitari
purah|sthe dik|pālaiḥ
        saha para|gṛh'|āvāsa|vacanāt
    praviṣṭā Vaidehī
        dahanam, atha śuddhā ca niragāt.

ayam api,

ek'|âikāni śirāṃsi rākṣasa|camū|
        cakrasya hutvā nije
    tejo|'gnau, Daśa|kaṇṭha|mūrdhabhir atho
        nirmāya pūrṇ'|āhutim,
adya svasty|ayanaṃ samāpya jagato,
        Laṅk"|êndra|bandī|kṛtāṃ
    Sītām apy avalokya śoka|rabhasa|
        vrīḍā|jaḍo Rāghavaḥ.

7.5 krameṇa ca,

sah' âiva Sugrīva|Vibhīṣaṇābhyāṃ
    Saumitri|Sītā|paripūrṇa|pārśvaḥ
upaiti Vaivasvata|vaṃśa|vṛtta|
    medhyām Ayodhyām atha Puṣpakeṇa.

cūlikā.

BEHIND THE SCENES:

Before the eyes of the sun god, ancestor of the Raghu dynasty, whose rays heal the three worlds of their nighttime stupor, and in front of the guardians of the directions, Sita, accused of having spent too much time in another man's house, entered the fire to prove her innocence and came out purified.

And here he comes...

after he sacrificed the heads of the fighting demons, one by one, in the fire of his zeal, he crowned his offering with Rávana's ten heads. Thus has Rama obtained prosperity for the world, but now, as he looks at Sita, who was captured by the King of Lanka, he is overwhelmed with sorrow, joy and shame at the same time.

And now, 7.5

Together with Sugríva and Vibhíshana, with Lákshmana and Sita on his sides, he is leaving in the Púshpaka chariot for Ayódhya, the city that is sanctified by Manu's presence.*

End of the indication of events from the rear of the stage.

ACT VII
THE HAPPINESS OF THE HERO

tataḥ praviśati vimānena RĀMAḤ, SĪTĀ|LAKṢMAṆAU, SUGRĪVA| VIBHĪṢAṆAU *ca.*

SUGRĪVAḤ: *(*RĀMAM *prati)* deva,

7.10 kiṃ|kurvāṇa|payodhi|sevita|gṛh'|ôd-
yānā mude sarvataḥ
Laṅk" êyaṃ Daśa|kaṇṭha|vikrama|kathā|
bīja|praroha|sthalī,
deven' âtra Daś'|ânanasya daśabhiś
chinnaiḥ śirobhiḥ kramād
ek'|âikena śataṃ śataṃ Śata|makhasy'
āmoditā dṛṣṭayaḥ.

RĀMAḤ: devi Vaidehi, dṛśyatām ito Laṅkāṃ pūrveṇa, Suvelaṃ paścimena,

tvad|arthīya|kravyāt|
kapi|kula|kabandha|vyatikaraiḥ
karāl" êyaṃ bhūmir
bhuvana|bhayam ady' âpi tanute.
abhūvann ambhodher
iha rudhira|mayyo yuvatayaḥ
sahasraṃ, sāhasrās
tri|diva|yuvatīnāṃ ca patayaḥ.

api ca,

udyamya dṛṣṭa|nija|pannaga|ratna|mātrān
astrāṇi candana|tarūn upari bhramantaḥ,
dyāṃ jyotir|iṅgaṇa|mayīm iva Meghanāda|
māyā|tamo|'palapitāṃ kapayo vitenuḥ.

RAMA *enters with* SITA, LÁKSHMANA, SUGRÍVA *and* VIBHÍSHANA *on a celestial chariot.*

SUGRÍVA: *(to* RAMA*)* Your Majesty,

Here is Lanka, where the sea serves the gardens everywhere as a good servant, for the contentment of all, and where Rávana's heroic fame had grown unparalleled. And it is here that Your Majesty delighted Indra's thousand eyes, hundred by hundred, with the ten heads cut off of Rávana's body. 7.10

RAMA: My queen, Sita, look over here, to the east of Lanka and to the west of the Suvéla mountain:

The ground here became terrifying, covered with the headless bodies of monkeys and demons who had been fighting for the two men who wished to obtain you; and the place continues to frighten everybody here. The ocean received thousands of river maidens of blood, and thousands of heroes found their way to marry nymphs in heaven.

Moreover,

Lifting up their weapons, sandalwood branches in which one could see only the bright jewels of snakes inhabiting them, the monkeys were flying all around above in the air. The sky, which was covered with the demon Megha·nada's magic veil of darkness, thus looked as if it were illuminated by fireflies.

7.15 SĪTĀ: ⌜ayya|utta! avi idha jjevva bhuaṃga|pāsa|bandhaṇaṃ Sīdāe kae tumhe sāhidā?⌟

RĀMAḤ: āṃ maithili, ām.

carvita|pīt'|âhi|gaṇaṣ ṭhaṇ iti
  viniṣṭhyūta|phaṇi|maṇir abhīkṣṇam,
ahi|bandhana|vaidhuryaṃ
  vyadhunod iha nau sa viha|g'|êndraḥ.

(vimṛśya sa|smitam) aho, vaiṣamyam asyā ahi|jāteḥ!

dve tāvat karaṇe rasān rasayituṃ,
    śabdāṃś ca rūpāṇi ca
  śrotuṃ draṣṭum ath' âikam indriyam, uro|
    gatyai nigūḍhaṃ padam.
anyeṣv apy aśaneṣu satsu, jagatāṃ
    prāṇāḥ svadantetarām.
  mātaḥ Kadru, yadi prasauti bhavatī
    bhūyaḥ sutān īdṛśān...

7.20 *sarve hasanti.*

SĪTĀ: *(sa|sneha|smitaṃ* LAKṢMAṆAM *avalokya,* RĀMAṂ *prati)* ⌜ayya|utta! Somitti|kitti|kandalīe uppatti|khettaṃ kadaro uṇa saṃṇiveso?⌟

RĀMAḤ: *(sa|harṣa|rom'|âñcam)* devi Maithili, ayam ito hasta|dakṣiṇena Dāśarathi|Daśa|kandhara|skandh'|āvār'|âika|vīrayor Lakṣmaṇa|Meghanādayor dvandva|yuddha|vyatikar'|âika|sākṣī Suvel'|âcala|pādaḥ.

SITA: My lord, is it here that you had to suffer, entangled 7.15
by a magic noose of snakes, because of Sita?

RAMA: Yes, Princess of Míthila.

> The King of Birds, Gáruda himself, swallowed the snakes with great relish, spitting out their head-jewels from time to time—it was he who released me here from the painfully tight grip of those serpents.

(reflecting, with a smile) O, how unusual is the race of snakes!

> They have a double tongue to relish all tastes, but only one organ, the eye, for both hearing and seeing; their feet are hidden as they advance on their chests. Although there are other edibles in the world, they keep consuming the life-breaths of living beings. O Kadru, Mother of Snakes, if you were to beget more of such sons...

They all laugh. 7.20

SITA: *(smiling affectionately, looking at* LÁKSHMANA*, then, to* RAMA*)* My lord, which is the place where Lákshmana has achieved unparalleled and ever-growing fame?*

RAMA: *(with joy, his hair standing on end)* Princess of Míthila, here, to our right, is where two heroes, one from our army, Lákshmana, and one from Rávana's army, Megha·nada, fought a duel, which was witnessed by the majestic Mount Suvéla.

SĪTĀ: ⌜jahi esā,⌟

⌜aṇurāa|rom'|ṃca|kaṇṭaa|
  sea|jalehiṃ ṇisā|arī kā vi
uddīvia|ṇivvāvia|
  ci"|âṇalā daïaṃ aṇu marei.⌟

RĀMAḤ: āṃ Jānakī, āṃ. idam eva Lakṣmaṇa|vīra|lakṣmī|svayaṃ|vara|kautuk'|āgāram. iha hi,

ānīta|Droṇa|śailena Saumitreḥ śalya|hāriṇā
akriyanta jaganty eva niḥśalyāni Hanūmatā.

SĪTĀ: *(smṛtim abhinīya)* ⌜ayya|utta, Kikkindh'|ēsara|kandh'|āvār'|ekka|dhuraṃ|dharo Rahu|ula|kuḍumba|vihura|bandhū so kahiṃ dāṇiṃ Haṇūmanto?⌟

RĀMAḤ: devi,

kṣuṇṇe niśācara|patau ravi|bimba|vartī
  tāto mayā Daśarathaḥ svayam eva dṛṣṭaḥ.
tasy' ājñayā Raghu|purīṃ prahitaḥ pur" âiva
  rājy'|âbhiṣeka|vidhi|saṃbhṛtaye Hanūmān.

(vimāna|vega|nāṭitakena) devi, praṇamyatām ayam ito mahān ambu|rāśiḥ.

Lakṣmīr asya hi yādo
  Viṣṇ'|ûra|sth" âpi su|bhaṭa|bhuja|vasatiḥ.
induḥ sa ca Mṛḍa|cūḍā|
  maṇir api jagatām alaṃ|kāraḥ.

SITA: Here,

> A demoness kindled the funerary pyre of her beloved with thorns of her hair standing on end and put it out with her tears of compassion*—thus did she die on it after her husband.

RAMA: Indeed, daughter of King Jánaka. Here is the marriage hall where the Goddess of Heroic Fortune chose Lákshmana as her husband. And it was in this place that 7.25

> he who brought the Drona mountain here to relieve Lákshmana's pain with its magic herbs* has consequently also eradicated the pain of the world with it: it was Hánuman.

SITA: *(showing that she remembers something)* My lord, where is Hánuman now, the foremost warrior in Sugríva's army and the most helpful friend of the Raghu dynasty?

RAMA: My queen,

> When I killed the King of Demons, I myself obtained the vision of my father, Dasha·ratha, in the sun-disk. It is on his orders that Hánuman has gone to Ayódhya, in order to prepare my rite of coronation.

(showing the chariot's speed with gestures) My queen, here is the great God of the Ocean. Let us bow down to him. 7.30

> Although the Goddess of Good Fortune, who was born from him, adorns Vishnu's chest, she in fact lives in the arms of good soldiers. And another product of the ocean, the moon, even if it adorns Shiva's head, is also the jewel of our world.

(sa|vimarśaṃ ca)

syād eva toyam amṛta|prakṛtir yadi syāt,
n' âik'|ântato 'dbhutam idaṃ. punar adbhutaṃ naḥ
Lakṣmī|tuṣārakara|Kaustubha|pārijāta|
Dhanvantari|prabhṛtayo yad apāṃ vivartaḥ.

api ca, devi,

7.35 ā|kaṇṭha|dṛṣṭa|śiras" âpy a|vibhāvya|pṛṣṭha|
pārśv'|ôdareṇa ciram ṛgbhir upāsyamānaḥ,
nābhī|saroruha|juṣā Caturānanena
śete kil' âtra bhagavān Aravinda|nābhaḥ.

SĪTĀ *vandate.*

LAKṢMAṆAḤ: yat satyam, utsarpiṇī dharm'|ôttarāṇāṃ siddhiḥ.

jarayatu jagat kalp'|ôcchittau,
piparttu payodharān,
vahatu vaḍavā|vaktra|jyotir,
dadhātu sudhā|bhujaḥ;
bhavatu vapuṣā yāvāṃs, tāvān
Agastya|ruṣā punar
nidhir ayam apām īṣat|pānas;
tapāṃsi namo 'stu vaḥ.

(reflecting)

> That this water was the origin of the nectar of immortality is not something extraordinary.* But what really seems to be a miracle to us is that this water was also transformed into the Goddess of Good Fortune, the cool-rayed moon, the Káustubha gem on Vishnu's chest, the celestial Parijáta tree, the physician of the gods, Dhanvántari, and other extraordinary beings.

Moreover, my queen,

> Lord Vishnu is also resting on these eternal waters, while four-headed Brahma, seated on the lotus coming from Vishnu's navel and thus visible to the Lord only above the neck—without his back, front or side—is constantly worshipping Him with Vedic chants. 7.35

SITA *pays her homage.*

LÁKSHMANA: It is true that virtuous people obtain extraordinary supernatural powers.

> This ocean may be able to consume the world at the end of each aeon in a flood, to fill up the cloud with water, to carry the fire of the submarine mare inside and to nourish the nectar-drinking gods.* But, no matter how huge it is, the sage Agástya's wrath still managed to drink it up easily*—so let us pay our homage to Agástya's ascetic power.

RĀMAḤ: *(sa|bahu|mānam)* vatsa, kim ucyate.

7.40 muneḥ kalaśa|janmano
jayati k" âpi gambhīratā
yayā culukam ambhasām
api nidhiḥ samutpadyate,
amuṣya punar īśmahe
na vivarītum uttuṅgatāṃ
yayā bhavati n' ôccakair,
hahaha, so 'pi Vindhy'|âcalaḥ.

api ca, vatsa, dur|avagāha|gambhīra|madhurāṇi mahatāṃ caritāni. tathā hi,

jagad|vigama|ghasra|gha-
smara|sahasra|bhāsvat|prabhā|
parikvathita|piṇḍito
lavaṇa|kūṭa ev' ârṇavaḥ
ayaṃ kṣaṇam abhūd, atha
jvalati Kāla|rudr'|ânale
caṭac caṭad iti sphuṭan
na bhavati sma yāvat kṣaṇāt.

SĪTĀ: ⌜ayya|utta, jalaṇihi|majjha|vaṭṭiṇo Laṅkā|poassa Jambūdīv'|ôvasaṃjamaṇa|siṅkhalā|bandho va ko eso dīsaï?⌟

RĀMAḤ: devi, Medinī|nandini, patita|Paulastya|jagad|vijaya|ketu|daṇḍ'|ânukārī Kākutstha|kuṭumba|duḥkha|saṃvibhāga|dāyādasya vānara|pateḥ kīrtti|mayo mahā|setuḥ.

7.45 SĪTĀ: *(sa|harṣam)* ⌜diṭṭhiā ayya|utta|daṃsaṇa|paccāsā|taruṇo pacchiṇṇassa parohaṇa|mah"|ōsahī va seu|bandho dīsaï. bhaavaṃ, ṇamo de.⌟

RAMA: *(respectfully)* My brother, it is indeed so.

This sage born from a pot has such unfathomable 7.40
and invincible power that even the ocean becomes
just a handful of water for him. Alas, we are unable
to describe well enough his greatness, by which he
transformed even Mount Vindhya into a dwarf.*

Furthermore, my brother, the acts of great beings can be pleasing but are often too complex and difficult to comprehend... As in this case:

On the last day of this world, the heat of a thousand suns shall eagerly dry up this ocean, which thus shall become a lump of salt in a second. Then, when the fire of the end of the world spreads its flames, these remnants shall make a cracking sound and disappear in a moment.

SITA: My lord, what is this thing that looks like a fetter tying the island of Lanka to India as if it were anchoring a ship floating in the ocean?

RAMA: O Daughter of the Earth, this is the famous great bridge built by the King of Monkeys, who shared the troubles of the Kakútstha family. Now it looks as if it were the fallen flagstaff that was originally meant to celebrate Rávana's victory over the world.

SITA: *(happily)* The fortunate news about the construction 7.45
of this bridge after I lost all hope to see you was for me like a healing herb growing at the foot of a felled tree. Let me pay my homage to this bridge.

RĀMAḤ: devi, Viśvaṃbharā|saṃbhave, paśya paśya,

yathā dūr'|āpātya|
tri|diva|yuvatī|netra|sulabhām
apāṃ bhartā hār'|ā-
vali|valaya|lakṣmīṃ vitanute.
tath" âyaṃ māṇikya|
sphaṭika|kanaka|grāva|śikharair
a|śūny'|ātmā setuḥ
prabhavati mahā|nāyaka iva.

api ca, asmin badhyamāne,

śaila|praveśāt prabalī|bhavadbhiḥ
kallola|kūṭair abhitāḍitānām
āsīn nivṛtty' âcala|gāminīnām
ambhodhir eva prabhavo nadīnām.

7.50 (SUGRĪVAṂ *prati)* sakhe,

tathā setu|śraddh"|ôt-
kalita|kapi|nikṣipta|śikhari|
pratiṣṭhā|vardhiṣṇuḥ
kṣaṇam atha nadībhiḥ prativahan
samutkhāta|kṣoṇī-
dhara|kuhara|pūrta|vyatikara|
pramṛṣṭ'|âhaṃkāraḥ,
smarasi, tad|avastho nidhir apām.

SUGRĪVAḤ: deva, bhavac|carita|citra|phalake 'smākaṃ cetasi kiṃ nāma na likhitam asti. api ca,

set'|ûdyoge sapadi lavaṇād
anyam antas|timibhyaḥ
kālen' apāṃ madhuram api hi

RAMA: Daughter of the Earth, look,

> While the ocean looks like a rich necklace easily visible to the eyes of goddesses coming to behold it from afar, this bridge, abundantly topped with rubies, crystal and gold, appears like its greatest gem.

And when this bridge was being built,

> As mountains were brought here to construct the bridge in the sea,* their volume created huge towers of waves, which, when they hit against the rivers originating from these mountains, turned their course in the opposite direction, making the rivers leave and not flow into the sea.

(to SUGRÍVA*)* My friend, 7.50

> You remember how the ocean was expanding as the monkeys were throwing whole mountains into it enthusiastically to build the bridge. Then, suddenly, with the rivers in it, the ocean started flowing against the shores until the caves of the uprooted mountains swallowed its water and destroyed its pride.

SUGRÍVA: Your Majesty, our heart is a painting of your life, all your acts figure in it. Moreover,

> As we started building the bridge, the ocean, the Lord of Waters, was becoming empty all over because the mountains thrown into it were pushing its waters outside. And, after some time, the river

svādam udbhedayantyaḥ,
śaila|kṣep'|ôcchalita|salila|
vyūha|tucche samantād
Vārāṃ patyau paṭutaram amūr
nimna|gāḥ saṃnipetuḥ.

VIBHĪṢAṆAḤ: deva, Manu|vaṃśa|mauktika,

7.55 sadyaḥ pītvā darībhir jala|dhim atha cirād
dṛṣṭa|Maināka|bandhu|
prīti|prauḍh'|âśru|pūra|dvi|guṇa|mahimabhir
nirjharaiḥ pūrayantaḥ
ye vinyastāḥ purastān, niśi niśi nivahair
oṣadhīnāṃ jvaladbhis
te dṛśyante tadātv'|ôṣita|kapi|śibira|
smāriṇaḥ setu|śailāḥ.

SĪTĀ: *(sa/smitam)* ⌜ayya|utta, Gorī|guruṇo gir'|indassa juva|rāo jalaṇahi|majjha|vaṭṭo Meṇāo jāṇāmi pakkha|ccheaṃ viṇā vi ṭhāvarī|hūdo.⌟

RĀMAḤ: *(vihasya)* āṃ Jānaki, āṃ.

Krauñcaṃ vimucya putraṃ ca pitaraṃ ca Himālayam,
praviśya jala|dhiṃ pakṣau rakṣat" ânena kiṃ kṛtam.

SĪTĀ: *(hasantī, Puṣpakaṃ prati.)* ⌜vimāṇa|rāa, gaaṇa|magga|caṃkamaṇa|kodūhal'|ôppulla|māṇasa mhi. tā uṇṇamehi dāva!⌟

maidens, which flowed together quickly to where the ocean had been, made the sea fish taste their non-salty, sweet water.

VIBHÍSHANA: Your Majesty, jewel in the dynasty of Manu,

After drinking up the ocean with their caves quickly, the mountains that were used to build the bridge were so delighted to see their old friend, Mount Mainráka,* that the abundant flows of their tears shed in happiness refilled the ocean with twice as much water. These same mountains we placed here are illuminated at night by the light of the medicinal herbs that grow on them, and thus they make us remember the time when the monkeys' army camped around here.* 7.55

SITA: *(smiling)* My lord, I know that Maináka, the crown prince of the mountains, son of Gauri's father, remained immovable in the water of the ocean, although he escaped from the clipping of his wings.

RAMA: *(with a smile)* Yes, indeed, daughter of Jánaka.

You see what he did in order to protect his own wings—he entered the ocean, leaving his son, the Krauncha mountain, and his own father, Himálaya, behind.

SITA: *(laughing, to the Púshpaka chariot)* Lord of celestial chariots, I am curious and eager to fly up in the sky, so rise up!

7.60 RĀMAḤ: *(sa|kautuka|smitam)* Vaidehi, paśya paśya.

yathā yathā paraṃ vyoma vimānam adhirohati,
tathā tathā apasarpanti parataḥ parito diśaḥ.

kiṃ ca,

āsanna|tapan'|āśyāna|tvacaḥ puṣpaka|pīḍitāḥ
gagan'|ārṇava|yādāṃsi stimyanti stanayitnavaḥ.

api ca,

7.65 amī te gambhīra|
stanita|rava|raudrā nayanayor
an|āyuṣyaṃ puṣyanty
avatamasam uccair jala|mucaḥ,
visarpadbhir yeṣām
upari param indoḥ parimalair
a|saṃbādha|jyotsnā|
timira|caya|citraṃ viyad abhūt.

SUGRĪVAḤ: *(adho 'valokya, sa|kautukam,* RĀMAṂ *prati)* deva, dūrād avalokaya tāvat,

nihnut'|ônnata|nata|pravibhaktiḥ
sva|sva|varṇa|viniviṣṭa|pad'|ârthā
ambu|rāśi|pariveṣavatī bhūś
citra|kuṭṭimam iva pratibhāti.

api ca, deva,

ayam anena mah"|ôdadhi|bhoginā
valayito vasudhā|phaṇa|maṇḍalaḥ
jagad|an|argham avāpya bhavā|dṛśaṃ
kim api ratnam ahaṃ|kurutetarām.

RAMA: *(with enthusiasm, smiling)* Princess of Vidéha, look, 7.60

As our celestial chariot is flying higher and higher, the edges of the horizon are running away from us in all directions.

Furthermore,

The sun is so close to the clouds it is burning their skin, and they are also hurt by our Púshpaka chariot; as they keep thundering and become wet, they look like sea monsters in the ocean of the sky.*

Moreover,

Those huge rain clouds above, whose deep thundering frightens us, maintain a dim darkness to obstruct our sight; but above them, the moon's strong rays come down to make the sky dotted with masses of unobstructed moonlight between the dark patches. 7.65

SUGRÍVA: *(looking below, with enthusiasm, to* RAMA*)* Your Majesty, look there afar,

The hills and valleys are no longer visible on the earth, which is surrounded by the oceans,* and one can see only the various colors of its elements. Now it looks like a floor inlaid with mosaics.

And look, Your Majesty,

The round earth encircled by the oceans is like the hood of a serpent rimmed with its coiled body*—and it is very proud to possess a unique, priceless head-jewel in your person.

7.70 SĪTĀ: *(puro darśayantī)* ⌜ko eso kapp'|âṇala|jjālā|kalāva|ka-ḍhijjamāṇa|jalaṇihi|pheṇa|tthavaa|ṇimmala|phaliha|si-hara|sahassa|mahuro mahī|haro puro viloijjadi?⌟

VIBHĪṢAṆAḤ: devi,

puraḥ Prāleya|śailo 'yaṃ, yasmin Makara|ketave
mṛta|saṃjīvanī Durgā mah"|âuṣadhir ajāyata.

SĪTĀ: *(sa|kautukam)* ⌜avi idha evva Hara|ṇiḍila|loaṇ'|âṇala āhuī|hūdo bhaavaṃ Vammaho?⌟

VIBHĪṢAṆAḤ: āṃ devi, āṃ. iyam uttareṇa Deva|dāru|vana|rekhā Viṣamaśara|dur|anta|sākṣiṇī.

7.75 purā Purāṃ|bhettur iha tri|netrī|
śṛṅgāṭake tulya|ruṣi sthite 'pi,
dhagaddhag ity ajvalad ekam, anye
tad|dhūma|pīḍām api n' âsahetām.

RĀMAḤ: kim ucyate.

Nīlalohita|lalāṭa|lāñchane
locane jayati ko 'pi pāvakaḥ,
rakṣitasya jagad|anta|hetave
yasya saṃjvalanam Ātma|bhūr abhūt.

SĪTĀ: *(RĀMAṂ prati)* ⌜ayya|utta, taha ṇir|aṇukkoso kahaṃ uṇa paḍiṇivutto Mahādevo Devīe?⌟

SITA: *(showing something in front of her)* What is this mountain in front of us, so beautiful with its thousands of pure crystal peaks, which are white as the foam in the ocean at the time of the world's end, when the fire's flames heat its water? 7.70

VIBHÍSHANA: Your Majesty,

> This is the Himálaya in front of us, where the goddess Durga was born, who was to act like a miraculous medicinal herb and resurrect the God of Love.*

SITA: *(with curiosity)* Was it also here that the God of Love became sacrificed in the fire of Shiva's third eye?

VIBHÍSHANA: Yes, indeed, Your Majesty. And here, further north, starts the Deva·daru forest, which witnessed this ill fate of the God of Love.

> Here, of yore, although all the three eyes of Shiva 7.75
> were equally in wrath, only one of them burst into flames*—the other two could not even bear the smoke of its fire.

RAMA: Indeed,

> Long live the miraculous fire in the eye that adorns Shiva's forehead! It is maintained to burn the world at the end of this aeon—but the God of Love became its fuel.*

SITA: *(to* RAMA*)* My lord, if the great god, Shiva, was so unresponsive to the goddess's love, how did he finally change his mind, then?

RĀMAḤ:

7.80 Smara|paribhava|niḥ|sahāya|dīrghair
atha su|bhagaṃ|karaṇair iyaṃ tapobhiḥ
tad akṛta, yad asau nije 'pi dehe
jayati jagat|patir ātmanā dvitīyaḥ.

VIBHĪṢAṆAḤ: *(sa|parihāsam)*

ciram anayā tapasitvā,
kapāla|vṛṣa|viṣadhar'|âika|cittasya
cakre Harasya mūrtiḥ
phalam ardhaṃ phala|dam ardhaṃ ca.

SĪTĀ: *(vihasya)* ⌜kadarassiṃ uṇa saṃṇivese bhaavadīe savva|maṅgalāe pāṇi|ggahaṇa|maṅgalaṃ āsī?⌟

VIBHĪṢAṆAḤ: idaṃ purastād Oṣadhiprasthaṃ nāma naga|rāja|nagaram. atra hi,

7.85 saṃpradātari mah"|âuṣadhī|maye
bhūdhare sukham uvāha Pārvatīm,
mūḍha|kaṅkaṇa|phaṇ'|îndra|nir|bhayāṃ
Tārak'|ēśvara|kiśora|śekharaḥ.

RĀMAḤ: āṃ devi, ām. ih' âiva,

RAMA:

She practiced austerities that should bring about fulfillment, but which seemed very long after her helping friend, the God of Love, had been defeated and thus disappeared.* Then, as a result of her asceticism, the Lord of the Universe accepted her as half of his own body, to conquer the world in this form.* 7.80

VIBHÍSHANA: *(laughing)*

Thanks to her long-practiced asceticism, she turned half of Shiva's body into her reward and half into the bestower of her reward, for the god as a yogi could have given her nothing but a skull-bowl, a bull and a snake in return.*

SITA: *(smiling)* And where is the place where the lucky goddess got married to him?

VIBHÍSHANA: Here in front of us, in this city in the Himalayas called Óshadhi·prastha. For here,

As the father who gave his daughter away was Himálaya, full of healing herbs, the snake that formed Shiva's armlet was at a loss and could not scare the goddess Párvati, whose hand was thus easily taken by the Lord Whose Head Is Adorned with the Crescent Moon. 7.85

RAMA: Yes, indeed, and it was here that

pitari nija|tuhina|saṃpat|
kalpita|hemanta|vibhrame, Gaurī
nir|mada|bhujaṃga|bhūṣaṇam
a|bhīṣaṇaṃ priya|karaṃ bheje.

SĪTĀ: *(sa|smitam)* ⌜ayya|utta, avi edassiṃ evva Maaṇa|taṇu| dahaṇa|vvaïara|ṇir|appa|māṇāe puṇo vi a|vīsandīe Gorīe Canda|cūḍo saṃghaḍido ṇia|sarīreṇa?⌟

RĀMAḤ: *(vihasya)* ām, devi,

7.90 etasyāṃ hi Tuṣāra|bhū|dhara|śiraḥ|
sīmni priy'|ârdhena ca
sven' ârdhena ca tādṛśe Paśupatau
vṛtte ardha|nār"|īśvare,
śeṣeṇ' ârdha|yugena sa|prahasanaṃ
Gaurī|sakhībhis tadā
cakre dakṣiṇa|vāmayor vinimayād
anyo 'rdha|nār"|īśvaraḥ.

api ca,

saṃbhog'|ân|atiricyamāna|vibhavo
yad vipralambho rasas
tad divyaṃ mithunaṃ paras|para|pari-
ṣyūtaṃ namas|kurmahe.
ekasyāḥ pratibimba|saṃbhṛta|vipary-
āse muhur darpaṇe
savy'|âṅga|sthiti|kautukaṃ śamayati
svāmī sa yatr' âparaḥ.

As Himálaya, the goddess's father, brought about the beautiful winter season with his abundant snow, Shiva's snake-bracelet lost its venom in the cold, and the goddess could hold the hand of her beloved without fear.*

SITA: *(smiling)* My lord, was it here that the goddess, who lost her pride after Shiva burned the body of the God of Love, but who still could not trust him, joined her own body to Shiva?*

RAMA: *(smiling)* Yes, my queen,

Here, at the very top of the Himálaya, when Shi- 7.90
va took up that form of half man, half woman, with half of his own body and half of the body of his beloved, then, as a joke, the goddess's friends created another half man, half woman from the remaining two half bodies—a mirror image of the original.

And now,

Homage to the divine couple embracing each other in uninterrupted union, for whom the sentiment of separation in love could never overcome fulfillment. In the mirror, their reflections suddenly change places; so when the goddess's side longs to be united with Shiva's left, the other Lord in their mirror image can easily comfort her.*

VIBHĪṢAṆAḤ: devi,

sva|cchand'|âika|stana|śrīr, ubhaya|mata|milan|
mauli|candraḥ phaṇ'|îndra|
prācīn'|āvīta|vāhī sukhayatu bhagavān
ardha|nār"|īśvaro vaḥ,
yasy' ârdhe viśva|dāha|vyasana|visṛmara|
jyotir, ardhe kṛp"|ôdyad|
bāṣpaṃ c' ânyonya|vega|prahati|simasimā|
kāri cakṣus tṛtīyam!

7.95 api ca,

sved'|ârdra|vāma|kuca|maṇḍala|pattra|bhaṅga|
saṃśoṣi|dakṣiṇa|kar'|âṅguli|bhasma|reṇuḥ,
strī|puṃ|napuṃsaka|pada|vyatilaṅghanī vaḥ
Śambhos tanuḥ sukhayatu prakṛtiś caturthī.

(anyataś ca darśayan)

ādhatte Danu|sūnu|sūdana|bhujā|
keyūra|vajr'|âṅkura|
vyūh'|ôllekha|pad'|āvalī|vali|mayair
aṅgair mudaṃ Mandaraḥ.
ādhārī|kṛta|kūrma|pṛṣṭha|kaṣaṇa|
prakṣīṇa|mūlo 'dhunā
jānīmaḥ parataḥ payodhi|mathanād
uccaistaro 'yaṃ giriḥ.

VIBHÍSHANA: Your Majesty,

> He has one beautiful breast in this form expressing his freedom,* he wears the crescent moon as a crown belonging to both of his halves, while the snake forming his sacred thread glides on his right shoulder—may the Lord as half man, half woman bring you happiness! His third eye emits the glowing fire that destroys the world on one side, on the other it sheds tears of compassion, seeing the burning of the universe; thus do its fire and water neutralize each other's power.

Moreover, 7.95

> The ashes on the fingers of his right hand dry up the sweat drops on the design of the round left breast. May this form of Shiva, which has a fourth gender, ignoring the common categories of male, female and neuter, bring you happiness!

(showing something elsewhere)

> The Mándara mountain was scratched by the pointed jewels of the armlet that adorns the Demon-Killer, but the scratch lines have become the charming folds on its body. We also know that when it was used as a stick to churn the ocean, its base was reduced as it kept rubbing against the back of the tortoise on which the churning was performed—which means that it had been even higher before!*

RĀMAḤ: *(nirvarṇya, sa|smitam)*

7.100 tat|tādṛk|phaṇi|rāja|rajju|kaṣaṇaṃ
samrūḍha|pakṣa|chidā|
ghāt'|âruṃ|tudam apy, aho, katham ayaṃ
Manth'|âcalaḥ soḍhavān?
eten' âiva dur|ātmanā jala|nidher
utthāpya vāmām imāṃ
Lakṣmīm īśvara|durgata|vyavahṛti|
vyastaṃ jagan nirmitam.

SĪTĀ: *(s'|ôdvegam)* ⌜imiṇā evva maṇḍa|sesī|kida|duddha|sāareṇa candaṃ uddharia vippaütta|bhattaassa itthiā|jaṇassa uvari cārahaḍī āraddhā.⌟

sarve hasanti.

VIBHĪṢAṆAḤ: *(tad eva* RĀMA*|s'|ûktaṃ bhāvayan)* ahaha,

prakṣeptum udadhau Lakṣmīṃ bhūyo 'pi valate manaḥ,
kiṃ tu prakṣipta ev' âyaṃ punar āyāti candramāḥ.

7.105 *(vimṛśya)*

kasmai cit kapaṭāya Kaiṭabha|rip'|û-
raḥ|pīṭha|dīrgh'|ālayāṃ,
devi, tvām abhivādya, kupyasi na cet,
tat kiṃ cid ācakṣmahe:
yat te mandiram ambu|janma, kim idaṃ
vidyā|gṛhaṃ? yac ca te
nīcān nīcatar'|ôpasarpaṇam apām,
etat kim ācāryakam?

LAKṢMAṆAḤ: *(sa|hāsam)* hanta, sur'|âsura|mall'|ārabhaṭī|tūrya|tāla|nartakī, sakala|rāja|kula|khalī|kāra|kharjūrī, sāhasika|sahasra|śastr'|ândhakāra|khelana|khadyotī, madhu|

RAMA: *(observing, with a smile)*

> How could this mountain, which was aching after 7.100
> its wings had been cut off, bear the rubbing of the King of Snakes as churning rope against it? It was wicked of him to produce that cruel woman, the Goddess of Fortune, from the ocean, for she upset the harmony of the world with the contrast between the rich and the poor.*

SITA: *(with agitation)* It was also this mountain which, while skimming the cream off the milk-ocean, churned out the moon, to give confidence to women who are far from their beloved.

They all laugh.

VIBHÍSHANA: *(thinking of what* RAMA *said)* Alas,

> One would indeed wish to throw the Goddess of Fortune back into the sea, but you see, the moon, when thrown back there, keeps returning. . . *

(reflecting) 7.105

> O Goddess of Fortune, if you do not mind, I shall ask you a question, after paying homage to you who stay resting on Vishnu's wide chest to play tricks on us. Is your water-lotus seat your house of learning? And is it the water that teaches you to go lower and lower?*

LÁKSHMANA: *(laughing)* Is it the Goddess of Fortune you blame, because she dances to the rhythm of the tabor of fighting gods and demons,* intoxicates and destroys all royal dynasties like wine, plays like a firefly in the

mathana|jīmūta|vilāsa|vidyul|latā Lakṣmīḥ kim evam upālabhyate? iyaṃ hi,

guṇavadbhiḥ saha saṃgamam
uccaiḥ|padam āptum utsukā Lakṣmīḥ
vīra|karavāla|vasatir
dhruvam asi|dhārā|vrataṃ carati.

SĪTĀ: *(s'|âbhyasūyam iva)* ⌜ṇia|devva|duv|vilās'|âlaso loo Lacchīe duj|jasa|vaaṇāṇi gāaï.⌟ *(puro darśayantī)* ⌜ko eso diasa|koḍī|kada|joṇhā|vicchadda|paḍirūvo girī?⌟

7.110 VIBHĪṢAṆAḤ: devi,

so 'yaṃ Kailāsa|śailaḥ, sphaṭika|maṇi|bhuvām
aṃśu|jālair jvaladbhiś
chāyā pīt" âpi yatra pratikṛtibhir upa-
sthāpyate pāda|pānām,
yatr' ôpānt'|ôpasarpat|tapana|kara|dhṛtasy' â-
pi padmasya mudrām
uddāmāno diśanti Tri|pura|hara|śiraś|
candra|lekhā|mayūkhāḥ.

RĀMAḤ: hanta, śatadhā dṛśyamāno 'pi cakṣur an|ati|kautukaṃ naḥ karoti,

giriḥ Kailāso 'yaṃ,
Daśa|vadana|keyūra|vilasad|
maṇi|śreṇī|pattr'|âṅ-
kura|makara|mudr"|âṅkita|śilaḥ,

darkness created by thousands of arrows that our heroes send out and is like a flash of fickle lightning in the dark rain cloud while enjoying herself with Vishnu?* This is how she is. . .

> The Goddess of Fortune, eager to attain heaven and be in the company of virtuous people,* performs, it seems, her own version of the "sword blade observance," by living in the sword of heroes.*

SITA: *(grumbling)* People who are tired of all the bad turns of their fate keep blaming the Goddess of Fortune. *(showing something in front of her)* What is this mountain called? It looks like a heap of moonlight embraced by the daylight.

VIBHÍSHANA: Your Majesty, 7.110

> This is Mount Kailása, where the trees grow on a ground of crystal whose bright light makes their shadows invisible, perceptible only when the trees are reflected from below. Here, although the sun rises at the edges of the mountain and opens up the day-lotuses with its beams, the rays of white light pouring down from Shiva's crescent moon closes them again.

RAMA: Even if one looks at it a hundred times, it does not satisfy the curiosity of our eyes.

> The rocks of Mount Kailása have been marked like women's bodies with crocodile patterns by the shining gems that adorned Rávana's armlet.* And when *yakshas** climb up here, they can see even

amuṣmin āruhya
sphaṭika|maya|sarv'|âṅga|vimale
nirīkṣante yakṣāḥ
phaṇi|pati|purasy' âpi caritam.

api ca,

7.115 Daśa|mukha|bhuja|daṇḍa|maṇḍalīnāṃ
dṛḍha|paripīḍita|līna|mekhalo 'yam,
jala|gṛhaka|vitardikā|sukhāni
sphaṭika|girir Giriśasya nirmimīte.

VIBHĪṢAṆAḤ: *(SĪTĀṂ prati)* devi, dṛśyantām amī:

Kailās'|âdri|taṭīṣu Dhūrjaṭi|jaṭ"|â-
laṃ|kāra|candr'|âṅkura|
jyotsnā|kandalitābhir indu|dṛṣa|dām
adbhir nadī|mātṛkāḥ
Gaurī|hasta|guṇa|pravṛddha|vapuṣaḥ
puṣyanti dhātreyaka|
bhrātṛ|sneha|sah'|ōḍha|Ṣaṇ|mukha|śiśu|
krīḍā|sukhāḥ śākhinaḥ.

api c' âsya nityam adhityak"|âdhivāsī Parameśvaraḥ,

sahasr'|âkṣair aṅgair
namasitari nīl'|ôtpala|mayīm
iv' ātmānaṃ mālām
upanayati Patyau Makha|bhujām,
jighṛkṣau ca krīḍā|
rabhasini Kumāre, saha gaṇair
hasan vo bhadrāṇi
draḍhayatu Mṛḍānī|parivṛḍhaḥ.

what happens down in the underworld of snakes, so transparent is this place everywhere, made of pure crystal.

Moreover,

When Rávana's colossal arms squeezed the slopes of Kailása so tightly they almost disappeared, then this crystal mountain provided its lord with the pleasures of a dais.* 7.115

VIBHÍSHANA: *(to* SITA*)* Your Majesty, look...

On the slopes of Mount Kailása, the trees are nourished by their mothers, the water streams of the moonstones that melt as the light from the crescent moon adorning Shiva's head shines forth in the midst of his ascetic locks. These trees have grown in the care of the Goddess's hands and now they are blossoming, happy to play with six-headed Skanda, whom they love as their brother, son of their foster mother.

And it is the supreme god, Shiva, who lives on the highlands of this mountain.

As the King of Gods, the thousand-eyed Indra, pays his homage to him with all his body, offering himself as a garland of a thousand lotuses, whom the playful Skanda tries to grab thinking he is indeed made of flowers,* Shiva bursts out in laughter together with his attendants—may he bless you all.

7.120 kiṃ ca,

yan|nāṭya|bhrami|ghūrṇamāna|vasudhā|
cakr'|âdhirūḍhe bhṛśaṃ
Merau pārśva|nivāsi|vāsara|niśā|
citre paribhrāmyati,
taijasyas taḍito bhavantu śataśo
dṛṣṭā hi jātāḥ, kathaṃ,
tāmasyo 'pi? sa vaḥ punātu, jagatām
antyeṣṭi|yajvā vibhuḥ!

LAKṢMAṆAḤ:

jayati parimuṣita|lakṣmā
bhayād anupasarpat" êva hariṇena
iha kesari|karaj'|âṅkura|
kuṭilā Hara|mauli|vidhu|lekhā.

SĪTĀ: *(sa/parihāsam)* ⌜eassa dandasūa|ṇara|karoḍi|muṇḍa|mālā|maṇḍaṇassa masāṇa|vāsiṇo bhūa|ṇāhassa bhūsaṇadā|viḍaṃbaṇaṃ evva Rohiṇī|vallahassa kalaṃko. kiṃ uṇa tavassiṇā kuraṅgeṇa?⌟

7.125 VIBHĪṢAṆAḤ: *(vihasya)* śaṅke, bhagavān api na mṛg'|âṅkam alaṃ|kāra|kāmaḥ kalayati.

sahacara|piśāca|pariṣat|
prasattaye kāma|cārato rajanīṃ
kārayitum iva Kapālī
śirasi niśā|karam ayaṃ vahati.

sarve hasanti.

RĀMAḤ: *(sa/bahumānam)*

Śrīkaṇṭhasya kaparda|bandhana|pari-
śrānt'|ôraga|grāmaṇī|

Moreover, 7.120

While he dances, the whole earth is shaking and moving about together with Mount Meru in its middle, which is variously colored by the day and the night on its two sides, producing hundreds of bright lightnings and, to our surprise, hundreds of dark ones. May this lord who sacrifices the world at the end of each aeon purify you all!

LÁKSHMANA:

The crescent moon that adorns Shiva's head has the curved shape of the lion's sharp claws, so the deer we usually see in the moon got so frightened that he escaped without leaving his mark thereon.* May this crescent moon be victorious!

SITA: *(with a smile)* Shiva, the Lord of Ghosts living in the cremation-ground, is adorned with a snake, a skull and a garland of severed heads; and the spot on the moon is his mock jewelry. Why talk of that miserable deer?

VIBHÍSHANA: *(smiling)* I suspect that the Lord does not wear 7.125
the deer-marked moon just to have a piece of jewelry.

It seems that the skull-bearing Lord wears the moon on his head in order to re-create the nighttime whenever he wishes, for the benefit of his attendants, the imps.

All laugh.

RAMA: *(with respect)*

The crescent moon that adorns Shiva's head was squeezed by the Lord of Snakes, who was tired of

saṃdaṣṭāṃ mukuṭ'|âvataṃsa|kalikāṃ
vande kalām aindavīm,
yā bimba|pratipūraṇāya parito
niṣpīḍya saṃdaṃśikā|
yantreṇ' êva lalāṭa|locana|śikhi|
jvālābhir āvartyate.

7.130 *(Puṣpakaṃ prati)* vimāna|rāja, manāg unnamyatām. ālokayatu Maithilī Sumeru|śṛṅgāṇi.

VIBHĪṢAṆAḤ: (SĪTĀṂ *prati)* devi, paśya paśya,

Meror medurayanti saṃmadam adhaḥ|
saṃpātibhir jyotiṣām
āṭopair viṭap'|ôpari|sthita|taru|
chāyā|bhṛto 'dhityakāḥ
niṣpītāsu ca māsi māsi vibudhair
indoḥ kalāsu kramād
uddāma|plavamāna|lāñchana|mṛga|
chinn'|âgra|darbh'|âṅkurāḥ.

api ca,

bhūmeḥ svarṇatayā phal'|ôttara|taru|
smerasya Meros taṭī|
sīmanto 'yam Anūru|sārathi|ratha|
prasthāna|ghaṇṭā|pathaḥ,
yasminn uddhriyate kathaṃ cana hayair
uddāma|caṇḍ'|ātapa|
jvālā|jāla|vilīna|kāñcana|śilā|
jambāla|magnaḥ pradhiḥ.

being stuck in the god's hair to tie it—I praise this crescent, which was pressed on both sides as if with an iron bill to obtain a round shape, while burning in the flames of the fire emitted by the Lord's third eye.*

(to the Púshpaka chariot) Lord of celestial chariots, rise a little higher, so that the queen may see the peaks of Mount Meru. 7.130

VIBHÍSHANA: *(to* SITA*)* Your Majesty, look,

On Mount Meru, the shadows of the trees fall upward, on the highlands of the mountain, since all the planets go around *below* its peaks—thus does Meru increase its attraction. And each month, as the gods consume the digits of the moon, the freely roaming deer released from there come over to these highlands to graze on the tips of the grass shoots.

Moreover,

As the earth has put on a golden color, the chains of Mount Meru, which is happy to carry its trees laden with fruit, form a royal path for the course of the Sun's chariot. But the Sun's horses can hardly drag the chariot wheels upward, for they are sunken—as if in mud—into the golden peaks melting in the flames of the harsh and piercing sunbeams.

7.135 LAKṢMAṆAḤ: (SĪTĀṂ *prati)*

etāsu parvata|nitamba|taṭīṣu, paśya,
madhyan|dine 'pi hari|candana|vāṭik" êyam
pakṣa|sthita|dyumaṇi|bimbatay" âti|dīrgha|
chāyā|vitāna|madhurā mudam ādadhāti.

(nirūpya, sa|harṣa|smitam) katham, upary upari puṣkalāvartakān Abhramu|vallabhaḥ. *(vimṛśya)*

ady' âyaṃ vibudh'|êndra|bāndhava|vadhū|
saṃbhukta|saṃtānaka|
srag|dāmnīm Amarāvatīṃ viharate
nir|vairam Airāvaṇaḥ,
yaṃ dor|mātra|paricchado yudhi mud" ôt-
kṣipya pratīcchan muhuḥ
saṃtene daśabhir nijair api mukhaiḥ
sāṃrāviṇaṃ Rāvaṇaḥ.

SUGRĪVAḤ: satyam. a|gocare girāṃ Daśa|kaṇṭha|krīḍitāni.

7.140 ek'|âike nivasanti te bhuja|bhṛtaḥ,
kasmai nigṛhṇāmahe?
vīra|kṣetram iyaṃ punar vasumatī
Paulastyam ābibhratī,
Vālī tv āhvayamānam enam api yac
cakre, kṛte cakṣuṣī
paśyāmaḥ, śravasī kṛte ca śṛṇumas,
tad vaktum alpe vayam.

RĀMAḤ: *(sa|bahumānam)*

sa kiṃ vācyo Vālī
bhuja|kuliśa|mūlena daśato
Daśa|grīvaṃ yasya

LÁKSHMANA: *(to* SITA*)* 7.135

Look at this beautiful deodar forest on the slopes of the mountain, where, to our delight, the large shadows of the trees are long even at midday, for the sun reaches only up to their sides.

(looking, smiling happily) Above the clouds, there goes Indra's elephant. *(reflecting)*

Today, Indra's elephant roams without any hindrance in the celestial city of Amarávati, where the wives of gods wear garlands of *santánaka* flowers. However, in the battle he was easily thrown up by Rávana's bare arms in the air, who then caught him again and again and made a terrible roar with his ten heads.

SUGRÍVA: Indeed, Rávana's deeds are impossible to put into words.

All sorts of famous heroes have lived in this 7.140
world—how could we distinguish the one who is the best? But this earth chose to nourish Rávana as a hero, whom then Vali challenged to a battle—and what he did to him was witnessed by our eyes and heard with our ears created for such purposes;* but how could we put that into words?

RAMA: *(with respect)*

Is it possible to describe Vali, who squeezed ten-headed Rávana under his thunderbolt-like arms while performing his evening prayer at each of the

prati|jaladhi saṃdhyā|vidhir abhūt?
kathaṃ vā nirvācyaḥ
sa ca Daśa|mukho, yasya damane
manāg āsīd Vāli|
vyaya|caritam ev' ôpakaraṇam?

SĪTĀ: (RĀMAṂ *prati*) ⌜ayya|utta, kiṃ uṇa edaṃ dalia|kappūra|silā|guccha|goraṃ gagan'|âṅgaṇaṃ dīsaï?⌟

VIBHĪṢAṆAḤ: (SĪTĀṂ *prati*) devi, candra|lok'|ôpakaṇṭham adhirūḍho vimāna|rājaḥ. dṛśyatāṃ ca bhagavān ayam,

7.145 yaṃ prāk|pratyag|avāg|udañci kakubhāṃ
nāmāni saṃbibhrataṃ,
jyotsnā|jāla|jhalañjhalābhir abhito
lumpantam andhaṃ tamaḥ,
prācīnād acalād itas tri|jagatām
āloka|bījād bahir
niryāntaṃ hariṇ'|âṅkam aṅkuram iva
draṣṭuṃ jano jīvati.

api ca,

sa Śrīkaṇṭha|kirīṭa|kuṭṭima|pariṣ-
kāra|pradīp'|âṅkuro,
devaḥ kairava|bandhur, andha|tamasa|
prāg|bhāra|kukṣiṃ|bhariḥ,
saṃskartā nija|kānti|mauktika|maṇi|
śreṇībhir eṇī|dṛśāṃ
gīrvāṇ'|âdhipateḥ sudhā|rasavatī|
pauro|gavaḥ prodagāt.

api ca,

prāṇāyām'|ôpadeṣṭā sarasi|ruha|muner,

seven seas? And how could we depict Rávana, for whose defeat Vali's death was only a small episode?

SITA: *(to* RAMA*)* My lord, why does this part of the sky look so white, like a heap of beautiful crystal stones?

VIBHÍSHANA: *(to* SITA*)* Your Majesty, our celestial chariot has climbed up near the sphere of the moon. And look at the majestic Moon:

> He gives the names to the eastern, western, southern and northern directions* and destroys the blind darkness everywhere with the dazzling luster of his rays. He comes from the Eastern Mountain, which is the source of the world's light,* like a shoot comes out of a seed; and people live only to catch sight of him.* 7.145

Furthermore,

> The Moon is the god whose delicate light illuminates Shiva's matted locks to make them look like a floor inlaid with precious stones; he is a friend of white lotuses of the night, for he devours masses of blind darkness. He adorns the gazelle-eyed women with his pearl-like radiance and oversees the preparation of the nectar of immortality for the Lord of Gods*—here he is rising.

Moreover,

> He teaches the right breathing technique to the wise day-lotus, he helps those who are entangled

yauvan'|ônmāda|līlā|
goṣṭhīnāṃ pīṭhamardas, tri|bhuvana|vanitā|
netrayoḥ prātar|āśaḥ,
kām'|āyuṣṭoma|yajvā, śamita|kumudinī|
mauna|mudr"|ânurāgaḥ,
śṛṅgār'|â|dvaita|vādī vibhavati bhagavān
eṣa pīyūṣa|bhānuḥ.

LAKṢMAṆAḤ: *(vilokya, sa|kautukam)*

karṇ'|ôttaṃsa|yav'|âṅkuraṃ kara|tale
kṛtvā hasitvā mithaḥ
saṃhūtaḥ Puruhūta|paura|yuvatī|
vargeṇa kautūhalāt,
grās'|ārti|kṣubhito 'yam aṅka|hariṇaḥ
kurvīta kiṃ kiṃ kalā|
kanthām indu|mayīm ajasra|ghaṭan"|ôd-
ghāṭa|ślath"|âvasthitām?

SUGRĪVAḤ:

romantha|pracal'|âuṣṭha|saṃpuṭa|sukh'|ā-
sīnaś ciraṃ kautukād
dṛṣṭvā siddha|vadhūbhir aṅka|hariṇas
tālair ath' ôttrāsitaḥ,
mā bhāṅkṣīd anu|māsa|navya|ghaṭanā|
niḥsaṃdhi|bandhaṃ vapuḥ
śīt'|âṃśoḥ, kṣubhitas tu śalyavad ayaṃ
duḥkhāya vartiṣyate.

api ca,

etasya kalām ekām
amṛta|mayūkhasya Pārvatī|ramaṇaḥ
varṇ'|āvalim iva vahati

in the foolishness of youth, he is breakfast for the eyes of all the women of the world, he acts as a priest in the sacrifice to obtain long life for the God of Love, he breaks the seal of silence of night-lotuses* and proclaims the philosophy that there is nothing else but love—thus does the nectar-rayed moon prevail.

LÁKSHMANA: *(looking, with curiosity)* 7.150

If Indra's celestial wives were to put on their hands a shoot of barley that they had used as an ear ornament, and, smiling at each other, were to call for the deer on the moon to see what happens, then what would that deer, trembling with hunger, do to the digits of the moon held together as a bunch of rags,* already loosened at the seams by the deer's incessant* movements?

SUGRÍVA:

That deer on the moon has long been comfortably spending its time, his lips moving while ruminating. Now, if the wives of celestial sages see it and frighten it with the clapping of their hands in surprise, then it should not break the moon's body, which is constructed without any joints and is rebuilt every month. But, in its excitement, that deer would cause pain to the moon, like a sharp thorn.

Furthermore,

Párvati's beloved Shiva wears a digit of the moon, 7.155
which reconstructs itself every month, like a string of letters.*

pratimāsaṃ ghaṭyamānasya.

RĀMAḤ: *(s'|ādaram praṇamya)*

tvaṃ gīrvāṇa|gaṇāya nityam amṛta|
śrāddhaṃ bhavad|dīdhitir
dhātrī|karma ca vīrudhāṃ vidadhatī
dhatte jagaj|jīvitam.
soma, tvām a|nidhāya mūrdhani bhavet
kaḥ kāla|kūṭaṃ giran
kaṇṭhe tac|chala|kāla|pāśa|valay'|ā-
līḍho 'pi mṛtyuṃ|jayaḥ?

(SĪTĀṂ prati)

netrāṇāṃ madhu|parka|sattram, udadheḥ
sarv'|âṅga|medas|karaḥ,
śṛṅgārasya rasāyanaṃ, makha|bhujāṃ
pīyūṣa|gañjā|patiḥ,
devaḥ kiṃ stumahe Maheśvara|śiro|
nepathya|ratn'|âṅkuraḥ,
kṣīrod'|ârṇava|śukti|mauktika|maṇir,
dākṣāyaṇī|nāyakaḥ?

7.160 SĪTĀ: *(hasantī)* ⌜ayya|utta, samāṇa|kula|rūva|jovvaṇāṇaṃ vi sa|vattīṇaṃ sīse diṇṇo dhaṇṇāe Dakkha|gotta|kaṇṇāe caaṇo, jeṇa Rohiṇī|ramaṇo tti evva bhaavaṃ cando suṇīe.⌟

RĀMAḤ: *(vihasya)* āṃ Jānaki,

priy'|ôpabhoga|taulye 'pi tārāṇāṃ sapta|viṃśateḥ,
dhatte kim api saubhāgya|saurabhyam iha Rohiṇī.

RAMA: *(bowing down respectfully)*

> You always provide sacrificial ambrosia for the gods; and your rays, which nourish the creepers, maintain life on the earth. O moon, how could Shiva have conquered death without putting you on his head when he swallowed the terrible poison and was to be caught by the noose of death because of this trick?*

(to SITA*)*

> His Majesty the Moon is like an offering of honey and milk to our eyes; he can also make the body of the sea grow, he is the elixir of love and the treasurer of ambrosia for the gods. He forms a tiny jewel on the headdress of Shiva, a piece of pearl produced from the milk-ocean.* He is the lord of the twenty-seven lunar mansions, daughters of Daksha. How could we sing his praise?

SITA: *(smiling)* My lord, although all these twenty-seven co- 7.160
wives are equally young and beautiful, and they come from the same good family, there is one fair daughter of Daksha who is lucky enough to be privileged among them. And that is why the Moon is also called Róhini's beloved.*

RAMA: *(with a smile)* Indeed, Jánaki,

> Although the twenty-seven stars equally enjoy the company of their beloved Moon, Róhini is somehow particularly lucky and charming.

(sparśaṃ ca nirūpayan)

dalita|kumuda|koś'|ôdañcad|ūṣm'|ôpacāra|
kṣaṇa|śamita|cakorī|candrikā|pāna|jāḍyāḥ
abhisṛmara|mṛg'|âkṣī|mūka|dūtyaḥ svadante
śaśi|maṇi|makarand'|ôt|kandalāś candra|bhāsaḥ.

7.165 api ca, jagatām anugrahāya,

udayati kala|mandraiḥ kaṇṭha|tālair alīnāṃ
kumuda|mukulakeṣu vyañjayann aṅga|hārān,
mada|mukhara|cakorī|toṣa|karm'|ântiko 'yaṃ
tuhina|rucira|dhāmā dakṣiṇaṃ loka|cakṣuḥ.

taiḥ sarva|jñī|bhavad|abhisṛtā|
netra|siddh'|âñjanair vā
nīrandhrair vā tri|bhuvana|dṛśām
andha|paṭṭais tamobhiḥ
vyāptaṃ pṛthvī|valayam a|khilaṃ
kṣālayann ucchaladbhir
jyotsnā|jālair ayam udayate
śarvarī|sārva|bhaumaḥ.

RĀMAḤ: *(sa|harṣa|smitam)* priye, priya|vādini,

candra|lokād api paraṃ padam āropayanti mām
amūr amṛta|bindūnām anuprāsās tav' ôktayaḥ.

(showing that he touches something)

The frozenness of moonbeams as they are being drunk by the female *chakóras* is remedied for a moment when the steam starts rising from inside the blooming night-lotuses; the moon's rays delight everyone, they serve as silent messengers of gazelle-eyed women longing for their beloved and they have new shoots as they bathe in the water of the melting moonstones.*

And in order to bestow his grace upon the world, 7.165

The moon rises, and while the bees are humming sweetly to a rhythm, he dances on the blossoms of the night-lotuses.* He looks after the well-being of female *chakóras*,* noisy in their drunkenness; here comes he whose heat is pleasant and ice-cool, the right eye of the world.

While the whole wide earth is covered with darkness as if with a perfect blindfold for our eyes, a blindfold that serves, however, as a magic ointment for the eyes of clever women hastening secretly to their tryst, the moon's far-reaching rays throw down their light—he is rising as the unrivaled Lord of the Night.

RAMA: *(smiling happily)* My beloved, your words are sweet,

It feels as if I were reaching higher than the realm of the moon as I hear your melodious words, rhyming as it were with ambrosia.

7.170 VIBHĪṢAṆAḤ: *(s'|ânurāgam)*

adyʼ ôrvī|tala|mūla|gharṣaṇa|vaśād
unmṛṣṭa|cūḍā|maṇi|
śreṇi|śrī|paripīta|pīvara|tamaḥ|
pūre pure bhoginām
karṇʼ|â|bhāva|nirasta|kuṇḍala|rava|
vyāsaṅgam ādhunvatā
mūrdhnaḥ pannaga|puṃgavena su|bhagaṃ
tvat|kīrtir ākarṇyate.

(vihasya)

bhogʼ|îndraḥ pramadʼ|ôttaraṅgam uragī|
saṃgīta|goṣṭhīṣu te
kīrtiṃ, deva, śṛṇoti viṃśati|śatī
yac cakṣuṣāṃ vartate,
raktābhiḥ sura|sundarībhir abhito
gītaṃ tu karṇa|dvayī|
duḥ|sthaḥ śroṣyati nāma kiṃ sa hi sahasrʼ|
âkṣo na cakṣuḥ|śravāḥ.

RĀMAḤ: *(sa/vilakṣa/smitaṃ* VIBHĪṢAṆA*/s'/ûktam anugṛhya, candraṃ* SĪTĀ*/mukhaṃ ca kṣaṇaṃ dṛṣṭvā, sva/gatam)*

7.175 ārabdhe dayitā|mukha|pratibhaṭe
nirmātum, asminn api
vyaktaṃ janma|samāna|kāla|militām
aṃśu|chaṭāṃ varṣati,
ātma|drohiṇi Rohiṇī|parivṛḍhe
paryaṅka|paṅke|ruhaḥ
saṃkocād, ati|duḥ|sthitasya na Vidhes
tac|chilpam unmīlitam.

VIBHÍSHANA: *(affectionately)* 7.170

Today, in the city of snakes, the thick darkness was destroyed by the radiance of the head-jewels, as they became polished from being rubbed against the lower surface of the earth; for there the King of Snakes, undisturbed by jingling earrings, since he has no ears, is nodding easily while listening to the stories of your heroic acts.*

(smiling)

Your Majesty, the Lord of Snakes shall be able to listen to your story, sung by the snake-damsels with eagerness and joy, for he has two thousand eyes functioning as ears; but how shall Indra, less privileged with his two ears, hear your adventures so passionately sung by the celestial maidens? He has a thousand eyes, but they cannot be used as ears.

RAMA: *(smiling in embarrassment at* VIBHÍSHANA*'s praise, then, looking at the moon and at* SITA*'s face, aside)*

When the Creator started fashioning the moon to form a rival to my beloved's face, and the moon spread out the bright light it possessed as soon as it was born, it became the Creator's enemy by making his lotus-seat close its petals—in such plight, the Creator refused to reveal its form in full.* 7.175

(SĪTĀṂ *prati)*

anena, rambh"|ôru, bhavan|mukhena
tuṣāra|bhānos tula|yoddhṛtasya
ūnasya nūnaṃ paripūraṇāya
tārā sphuranti pratimāna|khaṇḍāḥ.

kiṃ c' âitāny api,

gotre sākṣād ajani bhagavān
eṣa yat Padma|yoniḥ,
śayy"|ôtthāyaṃ yad akhilam ahaḥ
prīṇayanti dvi|rephān,
ek'|âgrāṃ yad dadhati bhagavaty
uṣṇa|bhānau ca bhaktiṃ,
tat prāpus te, su|tanu, vadan'|âu-
pamyam ambhoruhāṇi.

7.180 SĪTĀ: *(smer'|âvanata|mukhī)* ⌜ayya|utta, kahaṃ uṇa saṃpuṇṇa|maṇḍalaṃ erisaṃ candam avamaṇṇia kalā|mettaṃ bhaavaā Bhūa|ṇāheṇa cūḍā|maṇī|kaaṃ?⌟

RĀMAḤ: aṅga, trayāṇām api jagatām upajīvyo 'yam amṛta|dīdhitiḥ. yadi punaḥ samagram enaṃ maulinā Pināka|pāṇir adhāsyad, aṅga, śiva|nirmālyam an|upabhogyam ev' âyam abhaviṣyat.

sarve hasanti.

kiṃ ca, bhagavati māsa|pramite, ayam eva dṛśyate,

pīyūṣ'|āgrayaṇaṃ jagat|traya|dṛśām,
ālāta|lekhā|lavo
viśv'|ônmāthi|hutāśanasya, kakubhām
udghāṭanī kuñcikā,
vīreṣu prathamā ca Puṣpa|dhanuṣo

(to SITA*)*

> You whose thighs are like the interior of a plantain tree, if your face were to be compared to the moon, the moon's radiance would need to be completed—that is why the stars are there, as the moon's small accessories.*

And these,

> Since they come from the same family as the lotus-born Lord Brahma, since they delight the bees all day from daybreak, and since they are exclusively devoted to the sun, the lotuses have deserved to become comparable to your face, my beautiful beloved.

SITA: *(smiling, bending down her face)* My lord, how come Lord Shiva lacked appreciation for the full moon so much that he chose to make his head-jewel from only a part of it, the crescent moon? 7.180

RAMA: All the three worlds need the nectar-rayed moon. If Shiva put the full moon on his head, then, alas, its nectar would become unfit for consumption as unclean remains of an offering to the god.

They all laugh.

Moreover, when the moon starts a new month,

> it is the first Soma offering for the eyes of the three worlds, a piece of firebrand of the flaming passion that torments separated people, the key that opens up the directions illuminating them at night, the first* among heroes in service of the God of Love, it

lekhā, mṛg'|âkṣī|mukha|
śrīṇāṃ ca pratirāja|bījam, adhik'|ā-
nandī navaś candramāḥ.

7.185 SĪTĀ: *(anumodamānā)* ⌜ayya|utta, paripuṇṇā guṇiṇo jahiṃ kahiṃ vi sohandi. khīṇā uṇa sīsam āruhandi tti Hara|cūḍā|cando eva puḍhama|ṇidaṃsaṇam.⌟

RĀMAḤ: *(vihasya)* devi, mahā|kṣatriya|kula|saṃbhave, evam etat.

set'|ûpakrama|saṃbhram'|āhṛta|giri|
prakṣepa|veg'|ôcchalan|
niḥśeṣ'|âmbu|parisphuṭ'|ôdara|darī|
gambhīrimā sāgaraḥ
cakre goṣ|padavad vilaṅghitavato 'py
antar bhayaṃ Māruteḥ;
pūrṇatvād atiricyate hi mahatas
tucchasya dur|laṅghatā.

idaṃ c' âsya,

prācīn'|âcala|cūḍa|candra|maṇibhir
nirvyūḍha|pādyaṃ nijair
niryāsair, uḍubhir nijena vapuṣā
datt'|ârgha|lāj'|âñjali,
antaḥ|prauḍha|kalaṅka|tuccham abhitaḥ
sāndraṃ paristīryate
bimbād aṅkura|bhagna|naiśika|tamaḥ|
saṃdoham indor mahaḥ.

is the source of what reflects the beauty of gazelle-eyed women,* a cause of delight for all—this is the new moon.

SITA: *(happily)* My lord, the perfect and virtuous can distinguish themselves everywhere; but the weak need to go to the top to be seen—the best example of this is the crescent moon in Shiva's hair.* 7.185

RAMA: *(smiling)* My queen, born in the family of great warriors, you speak well.

When the monkeys started building the bridge to reach Lanka, vigorously throwing mountains they had brought there into the water, all the water was squeezed out and revealed the depths of the sea. Its cave-like interior frightened even Hánuman, although he had managed to jump over it before as if it had been just a puddle—but it is much more difficult to jump over a deep void than something full.*

Furthermore,

The moonstones at the top of the Eastern Mountain pay homage to his splendor, oozing to become water and wash his feet; the stars give him their own bodies as an offering of a handful of grains;* his large internal mark is diminished, and even when he is like a shoot, he can tear up the veil of darkness at night—such is the moon's infinite power that spreads out everywhere from his disk.

7.190 mṛga|rāja|karaja|bhaṅgura|
kiṃśuka|kalik"|âvataṃsikāḥ su|dṛśaḥ
bhaya|saṃkucad|aṅka|hariṇa|
bahal'|ôjjvalam indum īkṣante.

VIBHĪṢAṆAḤ:

indor eka|kalāyā Rudreṇ'
ôddhṛtya mūrdhani dhṛtāyāḥ
sthānam iva tuccham etat
kalaṅka|rūpeṇa pariṇamate.

(vihasya, RĀMAṂ *prati)*

rodasī|kūpa|maṇḍūkaḥ kiyad eṣa prakāśate?
candramā yad ayaṃ, deva, tvat|kīrtiṃ pratigarjati.

7.195 SĪTĀ: *(sa|smitam)* ⌜jāṇāmi ayya|utta|kitti|kantīe paḍisiddhaṃ kadua parājieṇa saṃpadi bhaavaā hariṇ'|aṅkeṇa kalaṅka|saṃghaṭṭanā vihaā.⌟

sarve hasanti. RĀMAḤ *smayate.*

SĪTĀ: (RĀMAṂ *prati)*

⌜sārambhaṃ Siri|vaccha|lañchaṇa|bhuā|
pallattha|manth'|âala|
kkhoh'|uccālia|duddha|sindhu|laharī|
gabbha|cchavī|sacchāaṃ,
ko gāyedi ṇa de, Rahūṇaṃ pahuṇo,
andhāra|pakkh'|ândarā|
saṃtuṭṭanta|miaṅka|maṇḍala|maūh'|
ôggāra|goraṃ jasaṃ?⌟

NEPATHYE: deva, tvaryatāṃ tvaryatām! saṃnidhatte khalu bhagavad|Vasiṣṭha|gṛhīto maṅgal'|âbhiṣeka|muhūrtaḥ.

While beautiful women are looking at the moon, its light gets brighter as the deer forming the spot on it contracts its body in fear of those women's earrings of red *kínshuka* shoots, which are curved like a lion's claws. 7.190

VIBHÍSHANA:

The crescent that Shiva has decided to wear on his head has left a hole-like place on the moon—that is what has become of its so-called spot.

(smiling, to RAMA*)*

Your Majesty, the moon, which is like a frog in the well formed by the earth and the sky, shines forth strong enough to croak at your fame.

SITA: *(smiling)* As I understand, it is because the moon tried to compete with the radiance of your fame and got defeated that it has acquired its spot. 7.195

All laugh. RAMA *smiles.*

SITA: *(to* RAMA*)*

It has the color of the rising waves in the middle of the milk-ocean, when it was churned with a mountain for a churning stick handled by Vishnu's arms, at the beginning of our time. It is as white as the rays of the moon disk splitting up the night in the dark fortnight. Such is your fame, o Lord of the Raghus, whose praise is sung by all.

BEHIND THE SCENES: Your Majesty, please make haste. The auspicious moment for your coronation, determined by the venerable Vasíshtha, is near.

7.200 RĀMAḤ: *(ākarṇya)* katham, Ayodhyāyāḥ pratinivṛtto Mārutir asmān tvarayati.

SĪTĀ: *(sa|harṣam)* ⌜kahaṃ, Aṃjaṇā|ṇandaṇo tuvarāvei. tā bhaavaṃ Poppha, oṇama. āsaṇṇa|meīṇī|maggeṇa gacchamha.⌟ *(adho 'valokya* RĀMAṂ *prati)* ⌜ayya|utta, kiṃ uṇa eaṃ taluṇa|jīmūda|sāmale mahī|valaammi Mahu|mahaṇa|vakkha|tthale Kotthuha|kiraṇa|tthabaaṃ via jalantaṃ lakkhīaï?⌟

RĀMAḤ-: *(dṛṣṭvā,* VIBHĪṢAṆAṂ *prati)*

tarku|ṭaṅka|likhit'|ârka|maṇḍala|
  procchalat|kaṇa|kadamba|bhāsuram
śilpa|śālam iva Viśvakarmaṇaḥ,
  kiṃ vibhāti mṛga|tṛṣṇikā|mayam?

VIBHĪṢAṆAḤ: deva, sa eṣa

7.205 jyeṣṭhā|mūlīya|yātrā|sa|rabhasa|karabhī|
    kāmya|kāntāra|vartmā
  dūre 'pi jyotir akṣṇor apalapati marur
    jājvalaj|jāṅgala|śrīḥ;
viṣvadrīcībhir asmin nibiḍam uḍu|pateḥ
    kāntibhiḥ prasnuvānāḥ
  phenāyante nij'|ôṣma|kvathana|pariṇamad|
    budbudāś candra|kāntāḥ.

sarve vimān'|âvarohaṇaṃ nāṭayanti.

RĀMAḤ: *(vilokya,* SĪTĀṂ *prati)* devi, dakṣiṇena,

Siṃhala|dvīpam ambhodhi|saṃbhūtam idam utpalam,
Māṇiky'|âcala|kiṃjalka|ramaṇīyam udīkṣyate.

RAMA: *(listening)* Why, this is Hánuman who has returned from Ayódhya and is urging me. 7.200

SITA: *(happily)* Look, Hánuman is urging you. So, dear Púshpaka chariot, do descend. Let us go near the ground. *(looking down, turning to* RAMA*)* My lord, on the ground, which is black like a fresh rain cloud, dark as the rays of the Káustubha gem on Vishnu's chest, something is burning—what is it?

RAMA: *(seeing it, then to* VIBHÍSHANA*)*

What is that thing made of mirages? It shines forth as if it were the workshop of the Architect of the Gods, which is bright with the particles flying up from the sun-disk while it is being chiseled.*

VIBHÍSHANA: Your Majesty,

This beautifully burning desert, whose difficult pathways are the favorite of female camels happily marching there in the autumn months, blinds our eyes even from this distance. Here the moonstones are constantly melting in the all-pervading moonlight, making a bubbling sound as they are boiling and foaming in the heat of the desert. 7.205

They all show with gestures that the celestial chariot is descending.

RAMA: *(watching, to* SITA*)* My beloved, on the right

this wonderful island of Lanka looks like a lotus born in the sea, and its blossom is the Ruby Mountain.

SĪTĀ: ⌜jassiṃ kāsa|kusuma|saṃkāso Agatthi|haṃso caraï.⌟

7.210 RĀMAḤ: *(smitvā)* āṃ maithili, ām. ih' âiva Rohaṇa|girer upatyakāyāṃ dvitīyam āyatanaṃ muner Lopāmudrā|vallabhasya. tathā hi, sa tatra|bhavān,

bṛhat|pātra|prāptyā
vitata|jalam ambhodhim udare
dadhāv īṣad|gāḍhaṃ
kila kalaśa|janmā kula|patiḥ,
yam ārādhyaṃ Vindhy'|â-
cala|śikhara|śoph'|âika|bhiṣajaṃ
Vivasvān āśvīnaṃ
gaganam adhirohan kalayati.

api ca,

nipīte yen' âb|dhau
stimita|gurubhiḥ pakṣa|paṭalaiḥ
prayatnād uḍḍīya
pratipadam apavyasta|patitāḥ,
viśantaḥ kaulīraṃ
kuharam a|śaraṇyāḥ śikhariṇaḥ
kṣaṇaṃ dṛṣṭās; tasya
stutiṣu na girāṃ sāhasa|rasaḥ.

api c' âtra, śṛṅgāra|sārva|bhaumasya ratna|siṃh'|āsane Siṃhala|dvīpa|nāmni pradoṣ'|ārambheṣu,

SITA: There roams sage Agástya's swan, which looks like a white Kasha flower.

RAMA: *(smiling)* Indeed, Máithili. It is here, at the foot of the Róhana mountain, that the second home of this sage, Lopa·mudra's beloved, is situated. 7.210

> This master of numerous disciples, this sage born from a jar, easily drank up the ocean, whose abundant water thus filled just another large vessel, Agástya's stomach. Then, after he alone managed to remedy the overgrowth of Mount Vindhya's peaks, he was praised by the Sun himself, who was enabled to pursue his daily course in the sky thanks to him.*

Moreover,

> When he drank up the water of the sea, the mountains that had been hiding there lost their shelter, and although they were trying to fly away with their wings heavily soaked, they fell back awkwardly at each movement; then, when eventually they decided to enter some crab holes, he immediately saw them.* How could one dare to sing the praise of someone so powerful?*

And here is the bejeweled throne of the King of Love, which is called the island of Lanka. Here, at twilight,

7.215 udeṣyat|pīyūṣa-
dyuti|kara|kaṇ'|ārdrāḥ śaśi|maṇi|
sthalīnāṃ panthāno
ghana|caraṇa|lākṣā|lipi|bhṛtaḥ
cakorair uḍḍīnair
jhaṭ|iti kṛta|śaṅkāḥ pratipadaṃ
parācaḥ saṃcārān
a|vinayavatīnāṃ vivṛṇate.

(anyato darśayan) iyam ito mauktikīyānām apām ādhāras, Tāmraparṇī.

śuktikā|garbha|saṃbandha|stambhitās toya|bindavaḥ
bhramanti su|bhruvām aṅkād aṅkam asyāḥ prasūtayaḥ.

api ca,

yuvati|kuca|bhoga|karmabhir
udbhūtaiḥ śukti|saṃpuṭa|dhṛtāni
dadhat' îha Tāmraparṇyāṃ
sthira|karaka|bhāvam ambhāṃsi.

7.220 SĪTĀ: ⌜ayya|utta, jeṭṭh" êti dāhiṇṇa|metteṇa evva bhaavado sāarassa Bhāīrahī|pakkha|vāo. pemma|savvassa|ṇīsando uṇa sahaa|savv'|aṅga|motti'|āhalaṇa|ramaṇīāe Tambavaṇṇīe evva vaṇṇīaï.⌟

RĀMAḤ: *(vilokya, vihasya, anyato darśayan)*

ramayati Malay'|âcalo 'yam; asmād
upanamatā pavanena māninīnām
dayita|vinaya|kūṭa|sākṣiṇībhiḥ

> The pathways, which are wet with moonstones that have melted in the scattered rays of the rising moon, bear the deep lac traces of footsteps and give away these wanton women when, rushing to their tryst, suddenly scared by the *chakóras*' flying up,* they take some steps backward every now and again. 7.215

(looking elsewhere) Here is the river Tamra·parni, whose water produces so many pearls.

> The pearls born in this river, which are water drops hardened by the contact with the inside of conch shells, go around in the laps of women of beautiful eyebrows.*

Moreover,

> Here, the water drops in the Tamra·parni, thanks to their good *karma* of enjoying the breasts of young women, were kept inside conch shells until they hardened into hail-like pearls.*

SITA: My lord, it is only out of courtesy that Lord Ocean appears to be biased in favor of the Ganga, who is the eldest of the river goddesses. But the object of his true affection seems to be the beautiful river Tamra·parni, who is naturally adorned with pearls on her whole body. 7.220

RAMA: *(looking, smiling, then showing something else)*

> This Málaya mountain is delightful. Thanks to the soothing breeze coming from it, it is easy for the maids to make their jealous mistresses well dis-

sa khalu sakhībhir a|duṣ|karaḥ prabodhaḥ.

LAKṢAMAṆAḤ: *(agrato darśayan)*

sva|pāṇi|prāgbhāga|
prabala|vitat'|ôttāna|salila|
svayaṃ|dṛṣṭa|krīḍat|
timi|nivaha|lagnām iva ghṛṇām
dadhānasy' āpīt'|ôj-
jhita|jalanidher etad aparaṃ
puro Lopāmudrā|
sahacara|muner āśrama|padam.

7.225 api ca,

catur|abdhi|pāna|ceṣṭā|
dṛṣṭa|pipāse munāv udayamāne
pāyayitum iv' ātmānaṃ
viśodhya sajjī|bhavanty āpaḥ.

SUGRĪVAḤ: *(sa|smitam)*

dhruvam iva catur|ambhonidhi|
racit'|āpo|'śāna|karmaṇi mun'|îndre,
bhakṣyaṃ|manyāni kim api
cakampire sapta bhuvanāni.

(sarvato 'valokya, sa|harṣ'|âdbhutam) aho, cireṇ' âdya catur|daśa|lok'|âika|daṇḍa|dhāre dharm'|āsan'|âdhikāriṇi Rāma|deve Daṇḍak'|âraṇya|gṛha|medhinām ṛṣīṇāṃ tapo|dhanānām ṛddhayaḥ.

posed to their beloved, by telling them lies about how properly those lovers behaved.

LÁKSHMANA: *(showing something in front of him)*

> When the sage Agástya drank up the ocean held on the palms of his hands, on which the water was so stretched out it became shallow, he must have seen the groups of fish playing there, and, taking pity on them, he re-emitted all the ocean after swallowing it. Here we have arrived in front of his second hermitage, where he lives with his companion, Lopámudra.

And here, 7.225

> The waters have seen how he quenched his thirst by drinking up the four oceans, and now, when this sage rises, they purify themselves as if in preparation to offer themselves as a drink.

SUGRÍVA: *(with a smile)*

> When the sage swallowed the four oceans to rinse his mouth,* the seven worlds, certainly thinking that they themselves were to be consumed as a meal next, started trembling without reason.

(looking everywhere, with delight and astonishment) Ah, at long last, now that His Majesty Rama has become the righteous ruler to reign alone over the fourteen worlds, the ascetic sages live in great prosperity together with their wives in the Dándaka forest.

7.230 RĀMAḤ: *(sa|lajja|smitaṃ, vimāna|vega|nāṭitaken' âdho 'valokya)* kathaṃ, hiraṇya|mṛga|vihāra|kāntāra|sthalīnām upari pratiṣṭhāmahe.

SUGRĪVAḤ: *(s'|ôpahāsam)* iyaṃ sā Mārīca|śarīr'|ôpahāra|rakṣit'|ātmano Daśa|kaṇṭhasya kapaṭa|bhikṣu|veṣa|viḍamba|ḍambar'|âika|marma|jñā Pañcavaṭī. *(s'|ādaraṃ ca)*

Viśvāmitra|makha|dviṣe ca, vapuṣā
  citreṇa patyur mukhād
apy ākṛṣṭa|Videha|rāja|tanayā|
  netr'|âravindāya ca,
Mārīcāya namo namaḥ; kim aparam?
  yasmai kule rakṣasāṃ
dvau vārau vibhun" âpi Dāśarathinā
  cakre tata|jyaṃ dhanuḥ.

SĪTĀ *lajjate.*

RĀMAḤ: *(*PRASRAVAṆ*'|âcalaṃ darśayan,* SĪTĀM *apavārya)* devi,

7.235 naktaṃ ratna|mayūkha|pāṭava|milat|
  kākola|kolāhala|
trasyat|kauśika|bhukta|kandara|tamāḥ
  so 'yaṃ giriḥ smaryate,
yatr' ākṛṣṭa|kuc'|âṃśuke mayi ruṣā
  vastrāya pattrāṇi te
cinvatyā vana|devatās taru|latām
  uccair vyadhuḥ kautukāt?

SĪTĀ: *(smayamānā, kapota|hastaṃ kṛtvā)* ⌜bhaavadīo Jaṇaṭṭhāṇa|vāsiṇīo devadāo, esā vo paricāriā Jāṇaī paṇamadi.⌟

RAMA: *(smiling timidly, miming that the chariot is moving fast, looking downward)* Look, we are flying over the forest where the golden deer roams. 7.230

SUGRÍVA: *(laughing)* Here is the Pancha·vati forest, the only witness to the tricks of Rávana disguised as a mendicant. He managed to escape only thanks to Marícha's offering of his own body. *(then, with respect)*

> Marícha, born in the family of rákshasas, threatened Vishva·mitra's sacrifice and, taking up a miraculous form, he lured even Sita's lotus-eyes away from her husband's face. Who could do more than this? Thus, because of him, Lord Rama was forced to string his bow twice.* Let us pay homage to this demon.

SITA *is ashamed.*

RAMA: *(showing the Prásravana mountain, turning to* SITA*)* My queen,

> Do you remember this mountain where the owls hide themselves in the dark caves at night, for they are scared by the noisy ravens that gather together near the light of brightly shining gems?* Here, when I took away the clothes from your breasts, you angrily tried to cover them with leaves, but the deities of the forest,* curious to see you, lifted up the branches of the trees. 7.235

SITA: *(smiling, folding her hands)* Deities living in Jana·sthana, I am your servant, homage to you all.

RĀMAḤ: *(anyato darśayan)* devi, vandasva bhagavatīm ito Godāvarīm. *(jan'|ântikam)*

etasyāḥ pulin'|ôpakaṇṭha|phalinī|
kuñj'|ôdareṣu srajaṃ
kṛtvā kiṃśuka|korakair, a|karaja|
krīḍā|sahiṣṇu|stane
dattvā vakṣasi te, mayi prahasati
prauḍh'|âparādhe tadā
kaumāra|vrata|bhaṅga|kopitam api
smeraṃ tav' āsīd mukham.

SĪTĀ *sa|lajja|smitaṃ mukham avanamayantī Godāvarīṃ praṇamati.*

7.240 RĀMAḤ: *(parivṛty' âvalokitakena sa|khedam)* devi,

asmin Mālyavatas taṭī|parisare
kādambinī|ḍambaraḥ
sa sthūlaṃ|karaṇo mad|aśru|payasām
āsīd a|varṣann api,
yad|dhārā|lulitair na śākhibhir api
tvat|pālitair māṃ tathā
dṛṣṭvā kandalitaṃ, na kekibhir api
prārambhi saṃgītakam.

SĪTĀ: *(many'|ûtpīḍa|gadgada|kaṇṭha|granthila|svarā Puṣpakaṃ prati.)* ⌜vimāṇa|rāa, pasīda! jalaï, ṇa dalaï evva vajja|maaṃ me hiaaṃ. taha tuvarehi, jadhā esā antarīadu Daṇḍa'|âraṇṇa|vicchoḷī.⌟

RAMA: *(showing something elsewhere)* My queen, please salute the river goddess, Godávari, over here. *(Aside.)*

In the middle of a thicket of *priyángu* creepers near the bank of this river, I made a garland of red *kínshuka* buds to adorn your breasts, which could not have yet supported the nail marks of love. And when I laughed, then, although you were angry that I had thus committed the sin of depriving you of your chastity, your face smiled.*

SITA, *smiling in embarrassement, bends down her head, and bows down to the river Godávari.*

RAMA: *(roams around watching, then with dejection)* My queen, 7.240

Here, near the foot of the Málavan mountain, although the dark clouds first did not rain at all, they seemed to make my tears flow more and more. And even after the rain started pouring heavily, shaking up the vegetation, the trees you had looked after did not flower when they saw me crying, nor did the peacocks begin their dance.

SITA: *(her voice choking and faltering, pained with sorrow, to the Púshpaka chariot)* Lord of Chariots, do not worry. My heart, hard as a diamond, is just burning but not breaking. Make haste, so that the trees of the Dándaka forest be quickly out of our sight.

RĀMAḤ: *(vimāna|vega|nāṭitakena vilokya,* SĪTĀṂ *prati)* idam agre Mahārāṣṭra|maṇḍal'|âika|maṇḍanaṃ Kuṇḍinaṃ nāma nagaram. iha hi,

an|anya|kṣuṇṇa|śrīr
    Malaya|vana|janm" 'yam anilo
  nipīya sved'|âmbu
    smara|makara|saṃbhukta|vibhavam,
vidarbhīṇāṃ bhūri|
    priyatama|parīrambha|rabhasa|
  prasaṅgād aṅgāni
    dvi|guṇa|pulaka|srañji tanute.

7.245 kiṃ ca,

bibhratīṃ kaiśikī|vṛtti|saurabh'|ôdgāriṇīr giraḥ,
dūr'|âdhvāno 'pi kavayo yasya rītim upāsate.

VIBHĪṢAṆAḤ: *(dakṣiṇato darśayan)* deva, praṇamyatām ayam Andhra|viṣaya|lakṣmyāḥ sapta|godā|vara|hāra|kalāp'|âika|nāyako bhagavān Bhīmeśvaraḥ. ayaṃ hi,

tat|kāl'|ārabhaṭī|vijṛmbhaṇa|pari-
    trāsād iva bhraśyatā
  vām'|ârdhena tad|eka|śeṣa|caraṇaṃ
    bibhrad vapur Bhairavam
tulyaṃ c' âsthi|bhujaṃga|bhūṣaṇam asau
    bhog'|îndra|kaṅkālakair
  bibhrāṇaḥ Param'|ēśvaro vijayate
    kalp'|ânta|karm'|ântikaḥ.

RAMA: *(mimes that the chariot is moving fast, looking, then to* SITA*)* Here in front of us is the unique jewel of Maha·rashtra, the city called Kúndina. For here,

> The breeze coming from the forests in the Málaya mountain, incomparable to any other, drinks up the sweat drops whose abundant flow has been enjoyed by the *mákaras* of love drawn on the breasts of women here,* while it also doubles the goosebumps* on their skin as they enjoy the many wild embraces of their lovers.

Moreover, 7.245

> This is the place of origin of the Vaidárbhi mode of composition,* in which the words are as sweet as in the Káushiki style of drama*—even poets of distant regions make use of it.

VIBHÍSHANA: *(showing something on the right)* Your Majesty, here is the central gem of the sevenfold necklace formed by the Godávari River, worn by the Goddess of Wealth in the region of Andhra: the terrifying god Shiva. Let us bow down to him. For,

> His female half is gone during his last violent dance, for it seems to be frightened by how much he grows when he starts his performance. Thus, his terrifying body, wearing bones of skeletons and the King of Snakes as ornaments, is left with only one leg. May this great lord who withdraws the world at the end of each aeon be victorious!

RĀMAḤ: *(kṛt'|âñjaliḥ)*

7.250 nṛtt'|ārambha|rasa|trasad|Giri|sutā|
rikt'|ârdha|saṃpūrtaye
nirvyūḍha|bhrami|vibhramāya, jagatām
īśāya, tubhyaṃ namaḥ,
yaś cūḍā|bhujag'|ēśvara|prabhṛtibhis
tādṛg bhramantīr diśaḥ
paśyadbhir bhrama|ghūrṇamāna|nayanaiḥ
śānto 'pi na śrad|dadhe.

api ca,

krīḍā|naṭasya pralay'|ândha|kāraiḥ
kaṇṭhe nipīte tava, Kāla|kaṇṭha,
pṛthak kabandhaṃ, pṛthag uttam'|âṅgaṃ
nṛtyad bhayād aikṣata Kāla|rātriḥ.

sarve namasyanti.

RĀMAḤ: *(anyato darśayan)* devi, Drāviḍa|maṇḍala|mauli|māṇikya|maṇi|stabakam idaṃ Kāñcī|nāma|dheyam āyatanaṃ Mīna|ketanasya. *(SĪTĀM apavārya)* iha hi,

7.255 sveda|jala|picchilābhir tanubhir
yūnāṃ ca śithilam āśleṣam,
vipulaṃ pulaka|śalākā|
paṭalaṃ jhaṭ|iti pratikaroti.

RAMA: *(folding his hands in respect)*

When Párvati left your half, as she was frightened by the style* of the beginning of your dance, you accelerated your spinning performance to fill up that void by revolving. Homage to you, Lord of the World. Then, although you were no longer dancing, the Lord of the Snakes on your head and other ornaments you wore could not believe you had stopped, as their eyes kept rolling around, following the directions that still seemed to be revolving. 7.250

Furthermore,

O Shiva, your black neck was hidden by the darkness of the end of the world when you took up your dancer form, and your wife, the Night of Universal Destruction, was terrified at the sight of your separately dancing head and body.

They all bow down.

RAMA: *(showing something elsewhere)* My queen, this is an abode of the God of Love, the city called Kanchi. It is like a row of rubies in the crown of the Dravida country. *(aside to* SITA*)* For here,

the embrace of young couples would not be so strong, for their bodies are slippery with sweat drops; but this slipperiness is immediately compensated by the bristle-like goosebumps that spread all over them.* 7.255

api ca,

abhimukha|patayālubhir lalāṭa|
śrama|salilair avadhūta|pattra|lekhaḥ
kathayati puruṣāyitaṃ vadhūnāṃ
mṛdita|himadyuti|nirmalaḥ kapolaḥ.

SUGRĪVAḤ: *(anyato darśayan)* iyam iha śṛṅgāra|devatā|garbha|gṛham Avantī|viṣaya|sīmanta|mauktikam, Ujjayinī nāma rājadhānī. iha hi,

kamitur abhisṛtvarīṇāṃ
gaur'|âṅgīṇām ih' êndu|gaurīṣu
uḍḍayamānānām iva
rajanīṣu param īkṣyate chāyā.

7.260 api ca,

adhastāt saudhānām
iha hi caratām indu|kiraṇān
ghan'|ôdañcac|cañcū|
puṭa|nihita|netrā yuvatayaḥ
cakorāṇāṃ jyotsnā|
rasa|kutupa|kautūhala|kṛtām
udīkṣante naśyat|
timira|viśad'|ābhogam udaram.

api ca,

iha yuvati|vadana|kāntibhir
āpyāyitas tunda|parimṛjaḥ śete,
bhukt'|â|bhukta|himadyuti|
marīcir antaḥpura|cara|cakoraḥ.

VIBHĪṢAṆAḤ: ih' âiv' âyam Alakāyāḥ śākhā|nagara|gaurava|bhāji Tri|pura|dahan'|âdhiṣṭhāne pratiṣṭho bhagavān

Moreover,

> Musk design on women's cheeks are washed away by the sweat drops falling from their foreheads onto their faces; their cheeks, now purer white than the moon, betray that they took the man's role when making love.

SUGRÍVA: *(looking elsewhere)* This is the capital called Újjayini, the sanctum sanctorum of the God of Love, a pearl in the crown of the Avánti country. For here,

> As the fair-bodied women go to meet their beloved during the moonlit night, they seem to be flying—one can see only their shadows.

Moreover, 7.260

> In this city, young women in their palaces are looking down at the *chakóra* birds, who are constantly lifting up their open beaks to drink the rays of the moon. These birds are so busy swallowing gobletfuls of moonlight nectar that the inside of their bellies becomes clearly visible as the darkness is destroyed there by the moonbeams.

Moreover,

> Here, the *chakóra* bird of the harem sleeps rubbing his belly lazily, munching on the moonlight only every now and then, for he is fed well enough with the radiance of women's faces.*

VIBHÍSHANA: This city of Újjayini is as famous as if it were a suburb of the celestial city of Álaka, presided over by Shiva as the destroyer of the three demon cities. Here

Mahā|kāla|nātha|devaḥ. ayaṃ hi,

7.265 uddāma|bhrami|vega|vistṛta|jaṭā|
vallī|praṇālī|patat|
svar|Gaṅgā|jala|daṇḍikā|valayitaṃ
nirmāya tat pañjaram,
saṃbhrāmyad|bhuja|ṣaṇḍa|pakṣa|paṭala|
dvandvena haṃsāyitaḥ
trai|lokya|vyaya|nāṭikā|naya|naṭaḥ
svāmī jagat trāyatām.

RĀMAḤ: *(prāñjaliḥ)*

namas tubhyaṃ dev'|â-
sura|makuṭa|māṇikya|kiraṇa|
praṇālī|saṃbheda|
snapita|caraṇāya Smara|jite,
mahā|kalpa|svāhā|
kṛta|bhuvana|cakre 'pi nayane
niroddhuṃ bhūyas tat|
prasaram iva Kāmaṃ hutavate.

kiṃ ca,

vegād agād, deva, tava, Tri|netra,
yugm'|êtarasmān nayanāt Kṛśānuḥ.
Kāme tu saṃmohana|śastra|haste
Svāhām anudhyāya ciraṃ jaḍo 'bhūt.

is established one of his forms, called Lord Maha·kala.* For,

> As he whirls around in a frightening way, his matted locks, disheveled, spread out to form channels in which the celestial Ganga's water can fall down in streams all around him—thus he builds a bird's cage around himself, in which he spreads out his many arms as a swan would its veil-like wings. He is the dancer that plays the hero in the spectacle staging the end of the three worlds, he is our Lord—may he protect the universe. 7.265

RAMA: *(folding his hands in respect)*

> Homage to Shiva, the conqueror of the God of Love, Shiva whose feet have been washed in the streams of light that radiate from the jewels in the crowns of gods and demons while they bow down to him. He prevented his third eye, which could have burned up the three worlds as it does at the end of each aeon, from bringing about destruction once again, and offered the God of Love into its fire instead.*

Furthermore,

> Lord Shiva, you sent out the fire from your third eye very fast; but when he reached the God of Love, who was holding the arrow of infatuation in his hand, then the fire started remembering his own beloved, Svaha,* and remained paralyzed for some time.

7.270 *sarve namanti.*

SĪTĀ: *(vihasya)* ⌜aho, tatta|bhaavado Sasa|hara|seharassa kavalia|caü|ddaha|loavassa vi ṇa palāidā acchi|bubhukkhā jeṇa Maaṇo vi gāsī|kio.⌟

sarve hasanti.

RĀMAḤ: *(sa|vimarśam)* asya hi purāṃ bhagavataḥ,

bāṇī|bhūta|Purāṇa|pūruṣa|dhṛti|
  pratyāśayā dhāvite
vidrāt' īkṣaṇaj'|āśu|śukṣaṇi|kaṇa|
  klānte Śakunt'|ēśvare,
namr'|ônnamra|bhujaṃga|puṃgava|guṇa|
  vyākṛṣṭa|bāṇ'|âsana|
kṣipt'|âstrasya Pura|druho vijayate
  saṃdhāna|sīmā śramaḥ.

7.275 *(anyato darśayan)* iyaṃ ca Khalacurī|kula|nar'|êndra|sādhāraṇ'|âgra|mahiṣī Māhiṣmatī nāma Cedi|maṇḍala|muṇḍa|mālā nagarī. iha hi,

āśleṣa|cumbana|rat'|ôtsava|kautuk'|ādi|
  krīḍā|durodara|paṇa|pratibhūr Anaṅgaḥ;
bhogas tu yady api jaye ca parā|jaye ca
  yūnor manas tad api vāñchati jetum eva.

All of them bow down. 7.270

SITA: *(smiling)* The third eye of the Lord Adorned with the Crescent Moon was not satisfied even after consuming the fourteen worlds—it had to devour even the God of Love.

They all laugh.

RAMA: *(reflecting)* Of yore,

> when Naráyana became an arrow for Shiva's bow, his animal vehicle, the Lord of Birds, first rushed there hoping to hold him, but recoiled when the fire sparkles from Shiva's third eye hurt him. As the bird approached and then left, the King of Snakes, who formed the string on Shiva's bow, first bent himself in fear and then straightened up, thus drawing the bow, which sent out its arrow. May Shiva's effort, which was only to put the arrow on the bow to destroy the demon cities, be fruitful.

(showing something elsewhere) Here is the city of Mahíshmati, 7.275
the crown of the Chedi country, the shared queen of the kings in the family of the Khala·churis. Here,

> embraces, kisses, feasts of pleasure and joy—all these are wagers in a playful game, in which the bail is the God of Love. And although enjoyment is the prize of both the winner and the loser, young men and women are such that their hearts desire to win.

(vimāna|vegaṃ rūpayitvā) devi,

devyā Bhūmer mṛga|mada|maṣī|
 maṇḍanaṃ, Siddha|sindhoḥ
sadhrīc" îyaṃ jayati Yamunā,
 yā taṭ'|âik'|âgra|vṛttīn
prem'|ôtkarṣād iva Pitṛ|pater
 bhrātur ācchidya hastād
ast'|ābādhaṃ gamayati pitur
 maṇḍalaṃ Caṇḍa|bhānoḥ.

LAKṢMAṆAḤ: *(dūram aṅgulyā darśayan)*

7.280 Tri|pura|hara|kirīṭa|krīḍitaiḥ prīṇayadbhir
 bhuvanam Amṛta|bhānor bāla|mitraiḥ payobhiḥ
Sagara|suta|citāyāḥ pāvanī, toyarāśer
 iyam iyam agham agre Jāhnavī nihnute naḥ.

RĀMAḤ: *(sa|harṣam)*

Gaurī|vibhajyamān'|ârdha|saṃkīrṇa|Hara|mūrdhani,
amba, dvi|guṇa|gambhīre, Bhāgīrathi, namo 'stu te.

(SĪTĀṂ prati) vandasva, devi,

devasy' Âmbuja|saṃbhavasya bhavanād
 ambhodhim āgāmukā,
s" êyaṃ mauli|vibhūṣaṇaṃ bhagavato
 Bhargasya Bhāgīrathī.
udyātān apahāya vigraham itaḥ

(demonstrating that the chariot is moving fast) My queen,

> This is the victorious river goddess, Yámuna, friend of celestial Ganga; she is like an ink-black musk mark decorating the goddess Earth. Out of great affection, she saves those who come devotedly to her banks, grabbing them from the hands of her brother, Yama, the Lord of the Manes, and sends them up to the pain-free realm of her father, the Sun.

LÁKSHMANA: *(pointing at something further with his finger)*

> Her streams are the childhood friends of the moon; 7.280
> they played in Shiva's hair and then came down to amuse the earth. With them, she purified the ashes of Ságara's sons. Here she is in front of us, the river goddess Ganga, the Ocean's wife—may she purify our sins!

RAMA: *(with delight)*

> Goddess Ganga, as you can spread out on only half of Shiva's head when his other half is formed by Párvati, you become twice as deep there—let us pay our homage to you.

(to SITA*)* My queen, please do greet her,

> The river Ganga, who adorns Lord Shiva's head, comes from the home of lotus-born Brahma, and flows until she reaches the sea. People who abandon their bodies at her banks go up all the way to the World of Brahma immediately with her help,

srotaḥ|pratīpān api
srotas|tīvratara|tvarā gamayati
drāg Brahma|lokaṃ janān.

7.285 SĪTĀ: *(kṛt'|âñjaliḥ)* ⌜esā ṇia|sotta|saṃdāṇia|tti|huaṇā Mandāiṇī vandaï.⌟

LAKṢMAṆAḤ: *(anyato darśayan)*

Dhan'|âdhinātha|praṇay'|ânurodhād
a|bhagna|Kailāsa|niketanasya
devasya kalp'|ânta|kapāla|pāṇer
Vārāṇasī nāma purī purastāt.

RĀMAḤ: *(sa|harṣam avalokya)*

plavamānair a|pāro 'yaṃ janaiḥ saṃsāra|sāgaraḥ;
dvīpe Vārāṇasī|nāmni viśrāntair iha tīryate.

7.290 api c' âināṃ nityam adhyāste bhagavān,

kaṇṭha|chāya|nipīta|pannaga|phaṇā|
ratn'|âugha|mātra|sthite
hāre nir|bhaya|Pārvatī|bhuja|latā|
bandh'|ôllasat|kandharaḥ,
tat|sarv'|âṅga|virāma|vāmanatarair
ebhiḥ svaraiḥ Sāma|gaṃ
bibhrad Brahma|śiraḥ, śivāya jagatām
Eṇ'|âṅka|cūḍā|maṇiḥ.

as she lifts them quicker than the flow of her water,
although she has to take them against her current.

SITA: *(with folded hands)* Homage to the river Ganga, who connects the three worlds with her flow. 7.285

LÁKSHMANA: *(showing something elsewhere)*

To fulfill the request of the King of Treasures, Lord Shiva did not leave his abode, Mount Kailása. But this, in front of us, is really the city of* Shiva who carries a skull for a begging bowl at the end of each aeon: it is Benares.

RAMA: *(watching happily)*

This ocean of transmigration is difficult to cross by those who want to swim through it; but if they have a rest here, in this island called Benares, they can reach the other shore.

And Lord Shiva always dwells here, 7.290

As the shadow of his dark-blue throat conceals the black snake that forms his garland, so that only the shining head-jewel in its hood remains visible, Párvati is no longer scared and puts her liana-like arms around his neck, much to his delight. He carries Brahma's head, which sings the *Sama·veda* with faltering voice, for Brahma is deprived of all the other parts of his body—may He Who Is Adorned with the Moon on His Head be well-disposed to everyone.

(anyato darśayan, SĪTĀṂ *prati)* devi, dṛśyatām itaḥ,

nav'|ônmīlan|maurvī|
kiṇa|nikara|kārkaśya|sadaya|
pravṛttas tvat|pāṇau
kim api nibiḍaṃ pīḍayati me
kṛt'|ârtho yatr' âyaṃ
samajani karaḥ, s" âiva purataḥ
purī pūrveṣāṃ te,
nayanam iyam ālānayati naḥ.

SĪTĀ: *(sa|smit'|ânurāgaṃ* RĀMAṂ *prati paśyantī, purīṃ prati)* ⌜amba Mihile, vandīasi, guru|aṇe vi vandaṇaṃ me viṇṇavehi.⌟

7.295 RĀMAḤ: *(*SUGRĪVA|VIBHĪṢAṆAU *prati)* vayasyau, paśyatām, iyaṃ sā Jānakīṃ prajāyamānāyā bhagavatyā Bhūmer ariṣṭa|mandiraṃ Mithilā nāma nagarī.

SUGRĪVA|VIBHĪṢAṆAU: *(sa|kautukam)* yatra bhagavataḥ Pārvatī|jīvit'|ēśvarasya dhanur|dhanur|ante|vāsināv Ajagava|Bhārgavau bhaṅgam abhajatām, yatra ca saha|pāṃsu|krīḍā|sakh" îyaṃ Vīra|lakṣmīḥ.

RĀMAḤ: *(sa|lajja|smitam anyato darśayan)* devi! iyaṃ punas tato 'pi purastāc Champā nāma Gauḍānāṃ vinaya|madhura|śṛṅgāra|vilāsa|ramaṇīyā Makara|ketana|kaumāra|vrata|caryā|tapo|vanam iva rājadhānī. (SĪTĀM *apavārya.)*

rom'|âñc'|ôcchvasad|aṅga|sandhi|nibiḍair
āliṅganair yāminīṃ
śeṣī|kṛtya vivṛṇvate nija|rahaś|
cāturyam eṇī|dṛśaḥ

(showing something elsewhere, to SITA*)* My queen, look over here,

My hand, which had become hard with newly acquired calluses caused by Shiva's bowstring,* was to act gently with you—but your hand squeezed it very strongly, and thus fulfilled its desire. It all happened here, in the city in front of us, the capital of your ancestors, which attracts our eyes.

SITA: *(smiling affectionately while looking at* RAMA, *then, to the city)* Homage to you, the city of Míthila. And please convey my respectful greetings to my elders.

RAMA: *(to* SUGRÍVA *and* VIBHÍSHANA*)* Look over here, this is 7.295
the "delivery room" where the goddess Earth gave birth to Sita: the city of Míthila.

SUGRÍVA AND VIBHÍSHANA: *(with curiosity)* And this is where you broke Shiva's bow called Ájagava, and defeated Shiva's disciple, Párashu·rama, in archery. It is here that the Goddess of Heroes became your childhood friend.

RAMA: *(smiling timidly, showing something elsewhere)* My queen, here in front of us is the city called Champa, the capital of the Gaudas, which is enjoyable with its pleasant and courteous love games—a true ashram where one could practice observances, devoted solely to the service of the God of Love. *(aside to* SITA*)*

Here the gazelle-eyed women pass the greater part of the night tightly embracing their lovers, pressing their bodies with the hair standing on end closely

yaṣṭi|sthe sapadi pradīpa|mukule
dagdhvā daśāṃ mallikā|
taile prajvalati stṛṇāti vasatīr
yan nābhi|daghnaṃ tamaḥ.

LAKṢMAṆAḤ: *(agrato darśayan)* ete bhagavatyau bhūmi|devānāṃ mūl'|āyatanam Antarvediṃ pūrveṇa kṛṣṇ'|âguru|malayaja|mayam aṅga|rāgam iv' ânyonyasya kurvāṇe Kalinda|kanyā|Mandākinyau saṃgacchete.

7.300 Himālay'|ôtsaṅga|sad"|âdhivāsato
jāt" êva pāṇḍuḥ pratibhāti Jāhnavī,
Nidāgha|bhānoḥ pitur aṅka|lālanāt
kṛt" êva kālī Yamun" âpi dṛśyate.

VIBHĪṢAṆA: *(vibhāvya ca)*

Bali|dviṣaḥ pāda|nakh'|âṃśu|rājibhiḥ,
Smar'|âri|maul'|îndu|marīci|vīcibhiḥ,
Himādri|niṣyanda|rasaiḥ, pade pade
vivardhate vaibudha|saindhavī ruciḥ

api ca,

Prayāgaḥ sarva|tīrthebhyas tīrtham uccaistarām ayam.
saṃsār'|âbdheḥ paraṃ pāram iha|sthair avalokyate.

to theirs.* They demonstrate their secret skills until the wick of a bud-like lamp perched on a high pole burns out, while the jasmine oil keeps burning and the darkness hides their mansions up to the navel.

LÁKSHMANA: *(showing something in front of him)* Here, to the east of the Antar·vedi region,* which is the principal seat of brahmanas, is where the two river goddesses, the Ganga and the Yámuna, meet. They look as if they were anointing each other with black aloe cream and with sandalwood paste.*

It seems that the Ganga, since she was born and raised in the lap of the Himálaya, is white; while the Yámuna, who was fondled in the lap of her father, the Sun of burning rays, has become black. 7.300

VIBHÍSHANA: *(thinking)*

The goddess of the Ganges first obtained radiance from Vishnu's toenail, then she received the light of the moon on Shiva's head, to finish her course in the streams of the Himalayas—thus, at every step she made, her magnificence became greater.*

Moreover,

Prayága* is the most prestigious of all sacred places: those who live here can see the other shore of the ocean of transmigration.

7.305 RĀMAḤ: *(s'|ādaram)* kim ucyate.

satyam eva Prayāgo 'yaṃ mokṣa|dvāram udīryate,
devyau yasy' âbhito Gaṅgā|Yamune vahataḥ śriyam.

*(*SĪTĀṂ *prati)* Vaidehi, praṇamyatām itaḥ,

Śyāmo nāma vaṭaḥ so 'yam etasy' âdbhuta|karmaṇaḥ,
chāyām apy adhivāstavyaiḥ paraṃ jyotir niṣevyate.

sarve praṇamanti.

7.310 *(vimāna|vegam abhinīya, sa|harṣam)*

yūp'|âṅkura|prakara|dantura|tīra|lekhā|
saṃkhyāyamāna|manu|saṃtati|saptatantuḥ,
Ikṣvāku|rāja|mahiṣī|pada|paṭṭa|lakṣmīr
devyā Bhuvo, bhagavatī Sarayūr iyaṃ naḥ.

iyaṃ hi bhagavaty Ayodhyā,

gagana|tal'|âsmad|udīkṣaṇa|
kutūhal'|ôttāna|pṛthula|niṣpandaiḥ
unnāla|sthala|kuvalaya|
vanam iva jana|locanaiḥ kriyate.

RAMA: *(with respect)* Indeed, 7.305

> It is true that the city of Prayága is said to be the door to final liberation, a door to which the two river goddesses flowing around it, the Ganga and the Yámuna, add their beauty.*

(to SITA*)* Princess of Vidéha, you can pay your homage here.

> Here is that well-known fig tree called *Shyama* (Black), which performs miracles. Even if one merely stays in its shade, one shall obtain the supreme Light.

They all bow down.

*(*RAMA *mimes that the chariot is moving fast. Then, with delight.)* 7.310

> The way to count the number of royal sacrifices here is to look at this riverbank, along which pointed sacrificial posts are scattered in a ragged line. This river is radiant, like the silk veil used for the consecration of the Ikshváku queens, in the dynasty belonging to the goddess Earth—this is our holy river, the Sárayu.*

And this is the venerable city of Ayódhya,

> As people are looking up in the sky to see us, with their motionless eyes wide open and turned upward, the city seems to be transformed into a forest of land-grown lotuses with upright stalks.*

sarve namasyanti.

7.315 SUGRĪVA|VIBHĪṢAṆAU: *(nirvarṇya)*

vṛntair iva kratu|sahasra|bhuvāṃ phalānām
ālokya yūpa|nikarair madhurām Ayodhyām,
rājñām iha prabhavatāṃ ca vicintya siddhiṃ,
devaḥ Śacī|sahacaro 'pi na rocate naḥ.

RĀMAḤ: *(tau prati)* vayasyau,

tādṛśāḥ prāg ajāyanta rājāno yad ih' ânvaye,
tad Vasiṣṭha|caror aindrā|bārhaspatyasya vaibhavam.

(puro 'valokya, sa|harṣ'|ôllāsam) kathaṃ, sa ev' âyaṃ bhagavān upakalpit'|âsmad|abhiṣeka|saṃbhāro Bharata|Śatrughnābhyāṃ saha Vasiṣṭho māṃ pratīkṣamāṇas tiṣṭhati. *(Puṣpakaṃ prati)* vimāna|rāja! avatīryatāṃ Kakutstha|kul'|ôpakārikāyām.

7.320 *sarve vimān'|âvataraṇaṃ nāṭayanti.*

tataḥ praviśati paṭ'|ākṣepeṇa VASIṢṬHO BHARATA|ŚATRUGHNAU *ca.*

VASIṢṬHAḤ:

cakre Laṅk"|ēśvara|paribhava|
cheda|niṣṇāta|doṣṇā
yad vatsena tri|jagad|a|bhayaṃ,
tan na citrīyate naḥ.
bālen' ājau vigalitavato
vīrya|niryāsa|rāśer
yat piṇyākaḥ sa munir amunā
nirmito Jāmadagnyaḥ.

All of them bow down.

SUGRÍVA AND VIBHÍSHANA: *(watching)* 7.315

> Seeing the beautiful city of Ayódhya, where the sacrificial posts are the stalks of the fruit that thousands of sacrifices yield, and thinking of the success that the kings living here obtain, even Lord Indra, Shachi's husband, seems to lose his splendor in our eyes.

RAMA: *(to both of them)* My friends,

> That such extraordinary kings have been born in this dynasty shows how powerful is the offering that Vasíshtha made to Indra and Brihas·pati.

(looking in front of himself and happily rejoicing) What? Here is the venerable Vasíshtha with Bharata and Shatrúghna, carrying all that is necessary for the consecration and waiting for me. *(to the* PÚSHPAKA *chariot)* King of chariots, please descend to the palace of the Kakútstha dynasty here.

All of them show with gestures that the chariot is descending. 7.320

VASÍSHTHA *enters, tossing the curtain away suddenly, accompanied by* BHARATA *and* SHATRÚGHNA.

VASÍSHTHA:

> It does not surprise me that this prince's arms were able to defeat and kill Rávana to ensure peace in the three worlds, for even as a small child he extracted Párashu·rama's heroic essence in a battle, and left him there like an oilless seed.

(RĀMAM *avalokya, sa|harṣam)*

7.325 bhall”|âvalūna|Daśa|kandhara|kaṇṭha|pīṭha|
sīmā|samāpta|bhuja|vikrama|karma|kāṇḍaḥ,
diṣṭyā jagad|vijaya|māṅgalikair yaśobhiḥ
so ’yaṃ punar nayana|vartmani Rāma|candraḥ.

RĀMAḤ: *(sa|saṃbhramam upasṛtya,* VASIṢṬHA*|pādāv upagṛhya ca)*

Raghu|brahma|kriy”|ācāryaṃ,
purāṇa|brahma|vādinam,
brahma’|rṣiṃ, Brahma|janmānam
eṣa Rāmo ’bhivādaye.

VASIṢṬHAḤ: (RĀMAM *āliṅgya)* vatsa Rāma|bhadra, kā tubhyam āśīḥ?

ādāya pratipakṣa|kīrti|nivahaṃ
Brahm’|âṇḍa|mūṣ”|ântare
nirvighnaṃ dhamatā nitāntam uditaiḥ
svair eva tejo|’gnibhiḥ,
tat|tādṛk puṭa|pāka|śodhitam iva
prāptaṃ guṇ’|ôtkarṣiṇā
piṇḍa|sthaṃ ca mahattaraṃ ca bhavatā
niḥ|kṣāra|tāraṃ yaśaḥ.

7.330 api ca,

tri|jagad|aṅgaṇa|laṅghana|jāṅghikais
tava yaśobhir atīva pavitritāḥ
prathama|pārthiva|puṃgava|kīrtayo
Vibudha|sindhu|jalair iva sindhavaḥ.

(looking at RAMA, *happily)*

> Rama performed a final demonstration of how strong his arms were in the art of battle by cutting through the napes of ten-headed Rávana with his missile. Thus he has become famous* as conqueror of the world; and now, fortunately, here he is before our eyes. 7.325

RAMA: *(approaching quickly, touching* VASÍSHTHA*'s feet in respect)*

> Master of Vedic ritual for the Raghu dynasty, knower of the ancient sacred word, brahmanic sage, son of Brahma—here is Rama to salute you.

VASÍSHTHA: *(embracing him respectfully)* My dear Rama, how could I bless you?

> You took the fame of your enemies in a bunch and put it inside the Egg of Brahma, which served as an air hole. Then, blowing heavily the rising fire of your energy without being hindered, you obtained a pure mixture, thanks to your exceptional qualities: the result has become your spotlessly shining fame, enormous and solid.

Moreover, 7.330

> As your fame is spreading, running fast to every corner in the three worlds, it purifies that of previous kings completely, just as the water of the Ganga does the sea.

tath" âp' îdam astu.

jagad|āloka|dhaureyau sūryā|candramasāv iva,
putrau gotrasya goptārau janaya sva|bhujāv iva.

SĪTĀ *muniṃ vandate.*

7.335 VASIṢṬHAḤ: vatse Janaka|vaṃśa|suvāsini, yuvayoḥ sādhāraṇīm eva Rāma|bhadrasya vayam āśiṣam avocāma.

SĪTĀ: *(sa|harṣam ātma|gatam)* ⌜ammahe, ṇī|sāvattaṃ me ayya|uttassa gharaṇittaṇaṃ havissadi.⌟

LAKṢMAṆAḤ: Sagara|gotra|guro, Maitrā|varuṇe, Saumitrir abhivādayate.

VASIṢṬHAḤ: vatsa Lakṣmaṇa! āśiṣāṃ viṣayam atikramya vartase.

vīram Indra|jitaṃ jitvā diṣṭyā vardhayato jagat,
a|bhaye dakṣiṇīyas te Gīrvāṇa|grāmaṇīr api.

7.340 tath" âpi yūyaṃ sarve 'pi dvau dvau janayat' ātmajau,
yair ādi|rāja|vaṃśo 'yam aṣṭa|śākhaḥ prarohati.

RĀMAḤ: *(sa|harṣaṃ, kṛt'|âñjaliḥ)* bhagavan, param anugṛhītam Ikṣvāku|kulam.

BHARATAḤ: *(*RĀMAṂ *prati)* ārya, śūnya|bhavana|prakoṣṭh'|âika|rakṣā|padātir Bharataḥ praṇamati.

And may it be this way.

> May you beget two sons who will be the foremost to illuminate the world, just as the sun and the moon, and who will protect your family, as your own two arms.

SITA *pays her homage to the sage.*

VASÍSHTHA: My dear child, daughter of Jánaka, the blessing I have given to Rama also applies to you. 7.335

SITA: *(happily, to herself)* Thank god, then I shall be the only wife of my husband.

LÁKSHMANA: Master of the Ságara family, son of Mitra and Váruna! Lákshmana salutes you.

VASÍSHTHA: My dear Lákshmana, you are beyond all blessings.

> Luckily, you have defeated heroic Índrajit* and made the world prosper—thus even the Lord of Gods, Indra, himself is obliged to you for his safety.

> May you all, in the same way, beget two sons each, thanks to whom this family tree of Manu, the first king on earth, shall prosper in eight different branches. 7.340

RAMA: *(happily, with folded hands)* My master, the family of Ikshvákus is grateful for your blessings.

BHARATA: *(to* RAMA*)* My brother, the soldier who has been in charge of guarding the foreground of the palace while you were away, Bharata, has come to salute you.

RĀMAḤ: *(sa|harṣam āliṅgya)* vatsa Bharata,

ātmānam indu|kara|medura|candra|kānta|
stambh'|ôjjvalaṃ vitara me hṛdi, nirvṛṇomi.
na bhrātṛ|saṃgama|sukh'|āsikayā jahāti
Viṣṇoḥ sa|Kaustubham uraś capal" âpi Lakṣmīḥ.

7.345 BHARATAḤ: *(SĪTĀṂ prati)* devi, praṇamāmi.

SĪTĀ: ⌜vaccha Bharaa! uṇha|kara|kiraṇa|ṇiurumba|cumbiaṃ| kamala|khaṇḍaṃ via ciraṃ āṇaṃdaṃ uvvaha.⌟

LAKṢMAṆO BHARATAṂ *vandate.*

BHARATAḤ:

vatsa Lakṣmaṇa, s'|ôtkaṇṭhaṃ cirāt parirabhasva mām.
śraddhālur bhrātur aṅgeṣu candaneṣv apy a|rocakī.

7.350 *(nirbharaṃ parirabhya)* hanta, Raghu|vaṃśa|taṭāka|yūpa|daṇḍena Lakṣmaṇa|bāhunā parirabhyamāṇaś cireṇa śītalī|kṛto 'smi.

indoḥ kalā|kalāpena paṅkti|krama|niveśinā
sarva|duḥkh'|âpanodāya s'|ôdarāṇāṃ bhujāḥ kṛtāḥ

ŚATRUGHNAḤ: ārya, pādukā|bhṛty'|ânubhṛtyaḥ praṇamati.

RAMA: *(embracing him happily)* My little brother, Bharata,

> You are like a radiant column of moonstones, melting softly in the rays of the moon*—come to my bosom and I shall be satisfied. The Goddess of Fortune, although she is fickle, does not abandon Vishnu's chest, for she is happy to find her brother, the Káustubha stone there.*

BHARATA: *(to* SITA*)* I also salute the queen. 7.345

SITA: Dear Bharata, your presence gives me great happiness after a long time; it feels like when lotuses are kissed by the rays of the sun. Come over here.

Then LÁKSHMANA *also salutes* BHARATA.

BHARATA:

> Dear Lákshmana, I have been waiting for this moment for a long time. Embrace me! One who is devoted to his brother does not need to hold sandal-anointed arms.

(tightly embracing him) Lákshmana's arms are like sacrificial 7.350 columns in the sacred pond of the Raghu family. Now that they have embraced me, I feel calm and satisfied at last.

> It is of the digits of the moon, arranged in an orderly row, that the arms of brothers have been fashioned, so that they destroy all sufferings.

SHATRÚGHNA: *(to* RAMA*)* My brother, here I am, Shatrúghna, the servant of him who served your sandals. I salute you.*

RĀMAḤ: *(gāḍham āliṅgya)* katham, ākṛtyā Lakṣmaṇam anubhavāmi. *(apavārya,* SĪTĀYAI *darśayan)*

etat tad eva mukham a|kṣata|candra|bimba|
saṃvāvadūkam ava|lokaya Lakṣmaṇasya.
gīrvāṇa|vāraṇa|kar'|ârgala|karkaśau māṃ
tāv eva Lakṣmaṇa|bhujau nu pariṣvajete.

7.355 ŚATRUGHNAḤ SĪTĀṂ *praṇamati.*

SĪTĀ: ⌜vaccha, savva|loa|soa|sall'|uddharaṇa|goravillehiṃ caridehiṃ Lakkhaṇa|sariso hohi. vaccha Sattuhaṇa! ajjā|jaṇo kahiṃ?⌟

ŚATRUGHNAḤ: kṛta|maṅgal'|ôpacāro madhyam'|âmbā|bhavane bhavatīṃ pratīkṣate.

upasṛtya, LAKṢMAṆAṂ *praṇamati.*

LAKṢMAṆAḤ: *(sa|harṣam āliṅgya)* vatsa, diṣṭyā dīrgh'|āyuṣi tvayi dīpyamāne na vayam ekākinam ārya|Bharataṃ parityajya gatāḥ.

7.360 RĀMAḤ: *(muniṃ prati)* bhagavan, etau Laṅkā|Kiṣkindhayor adhipatī Vibhīṣaṇa|Sugrīvau bhagavantam praṇamataḥ.

VASIṢṬHAḤ: vikartana|kula|kīrti|mālā|toraṇa|stambhāv imau cirasya bhūyāstām.

RĀMAḤ: (BHARATA|ŚATRUGHNAU *prati)* vatsau, vandethāṃ mah"|ātmānāv etau Paulastya|Sāvitrau.

RAMA: *(embracing him strongly)* It is as if I were seeing Lákshmana. *(aside, showing him to* SITA*)*

> Look at his face, it is like Lákshmana's, resembling the perfectly round disk of the full moon. And these two arms, also those of Lákshmana, which embrace me, are as hard as the colossal trunk of Indra's elephant.

SHATRÚGHNA *bows down to* SITA. 7.355

SITA: May you be like Lákshmana and perform glorious acts to relieve the suffering that torments the world. Dear Shatrúghna, where are my in-laws?

SHATRÚGHNA: They have performed the auspicious ceremonies and are waiting for you now in the quarters of the king's second wife.

He approaches LÁKSHMANA *and bows down to him.*

LÁKSHMANA: *(embracing him with delight)* My dear brother, thankfully you stayed here to be company for Bharata, whom we did not have to leave all alone.

RAMA: *(to the sage)* My master, here is the King of Lanka, 7.360
Vibhíshana, and the Emperor of Kishkíndha, Sugríva, to greet you.

VASÍSHTHA: They are like two garlanded columns of a gate erected to celebrate the glory of the Sun's dynasty. May they live long.

RAMA: *(to* BHARATA *and* SHATRÚGHNA*)* My dear brothers, please pay homage to these two great persons, from the families of Pulástya and Sávitri.

BHARATA|ŚATRUGHNAU VIBHĪṢAṆA|SUGRĪVAU *ca yath"|ôcitam ācaranti.*

VASIṢṬHAḤ: *(sa|harṣam)* diṣṭyā catur|daśabhiḥ parivatsaraiḥ punar udayamānaṃ Daśaratha | kuṭumbam īkṣāmahe. *(sa|vimarśa|smitam)*

7.365 jetāraṃ Daśa|kandharasya jitavān
ev' Ârjunaṃ Bhārgavas;
taṃ Rāmo yadi kāka|pakṣaka|dharas
tat pūrit" êyaṃ kathā.
ūrdhvaṃ kalpayatas tu bāla|caritāt
tat|prakriyā|gauravād
any" êyaṃ kavitā tath" âpi jagatas
toṣāya vartiṣyate.

*(*RĀMAṂ *prati)* vatsa, māṅgalika|lagnam atikrāmati.

tad ehi Raghu|siṃhānāṃ siṃh'|āsanam alaṃ|kuru!
rājanvantaḥ pratanvantu mudam Uttara|kośalāḥ.

RĀMAS *tathā karoti.* VASIṢṬHO *mantra|pūtābhir adbhir abhiṣiñcati. anye t' ûcc'|âvacam abhiṣekaṃ nāṭayitvā pañc'|âṅga|cumbita|bhūmayaḥ praṇamanti. nepathye maṅgala|nāndī|vādyāni ca.*

BHARATA *and* SHATRÚGHNA *honor* VIBHÍSHANA *and* SUGRÍVA *as is customary.*

VASÍSHTHA: *(happily)* Thankfully, after fourteen long years we can witness the rise of Dasha·ratha's family again. *(smiling and reflecting)*

> Párashu·rama defeated Árjuna Kartavírya, who had defeated Rávana; and Rama, already as a young boy, won against Párashu·rama—this shows clearly enough the outcome of our story. And the poet who writes his poem about what happened to Rama after his childhood tells a different tale, one about the glory of his exploits, only to delight the whole world.* 7.365

(to RAMA*)* My child, the auspicious moment for the consecration should not be missed.

> Come and adorn the throne of powerful Raghus with your presence. And may the kingdom of Úttara·kóshala rejoice to have a good king in your person.

RAMA *follows him.* VASÍSHTHA *consecrates him with water purified by the appropriate mantras. The others show with various gestures that the consecration takes place and perform full prostration touching the ground with their whole body. Words of auspicious greetings and benediction from the rear of the stage.*

VASIṢṬHAḤ: *(sa|harṣam)* vatsa Rāma|bhadra, saṃprati,

7.370 udayad|udayad|dharma|skandhe
dhuraṃ tvayi bibhrati
kva nu paribhavau dṛṣṭ'|âdṛṣṭau
prajāḥ paricinvate.
api khalu yathā jīv'|ātmanaḥ
prabhoḥ param'|ātmano
diśi diśi diśām aṣṭau nāthās
tav' âiva vibhīṣikāḥ.

RĀMO *lajjate.*

VIBHĪṢAṆAḤ: *(kṛt'|âñjalir, jānubhyāṃ praṇipatya)* deva,

Laṅkā ca Puṣpakam idaṃ ca vimānam āryād
yakṣ'|ēśvarād apahṛtaṃ Daśa|kandhareṇa;
ekāṃ bhavān adita mahyam, ath' êdam anyad
ājñāpaya: drutam upaitu patiṃ nidhīnām.

RĀMAḤ: (VASIṢṬHEN' *anujñātaḥ, Puṣpakaṃ prati)* vimāna|rāja, prathama|svāminaṃ prathama|Paulastyam upatiṣṭhasva.

7.375 VASIṢṬHAḤ: *(sa|harṣam)* Rāma|bhadra, kiṃ te bhūyaḥ priyam upaharāmi?

RĀMAḤ: bhagavan, itaḥ param api kiṃ priyam asti bhagavat|prasādāt?

tāt'|ājñām adhimauli|mauktika|maṇiṃ
kṛtvā, Mahā|potriṇo
daṃṣṭrā|Vindhya|vilāsa|pattra|śabarī

VASÍSHTHA: *(happily)* My dear Rama,

> Now that you have become the support of righteousness that shall continue to increase, and you have taken up the burden of royalty, your subjects need not fear any harm, whether visible or invisible.* Just as the individual souls are various outposts of the supreme soul, the eight guardians of the directions are your own outposts to protect your kingdom. 7.370

RAMA *is embarrassed.*

VIBHÍSHANA: *(falling on his knees, with folded hands)* Your Majesty,

> The island of Lanka and this celestial chariot, the Púshpaka, were taken away by Rávana, from the venerable Lord of the Spirits, the god Kubéra. You have given me the former, now please give an order to return the latter quickly to the Lord of Treasures.

RAMA: *(with* VASÍSHTHA*'s approval, to the* PÚSHPAKA *chariot)* Lord of celestial chariots, return to your first owner, the eldest of Pulástya's sons.

VASÍSHTHA: *(happily)* Dear Rama, what else can I do for you? 7.375

RAMA: Venerable Vasíshtha, there is nothing else that your grace could bestow upon me. Thanks to you,

> I listened to my father's command, precious to me as a pearl in a crown, and went away to see the earth as an untouchable barbarian woman dressed in

dṛṣṭā bhṛśaṃ medinī.
setur dakṣiṇa|paścimau jala|nidhī
sīmantayann arpitaḥ
kalp'|ântaṃ ca, kṛtaṃ ca viśvam a|Daśa|
grīv'|ôpasargaṃ jagat.

tath" âp' îdam astu Bharata|vākyam:

samunmīlat|sūkta|
stabaka|makarandaiḥ śravaṇayor
a|viśramyad|dhārā|
snapanam upacinvantu kavayaḥ.
na śabda|brahm'|ôtthaṃ
parimalam an|āghrāya ca janaḥ
kavīnāṃ gambhīre
vacasi guṇa|doṣau racayatu.

7.380 api ca,

devasy' Ātma|bhuvaḥ kamaṇḍalu|jala|
srotāṃsi Mandākinī|
Gaṅgā|Bhogavatī|mayāni punate
yāvat tri|lokīm imām,
tāvad vīra|yaśo|rasāyana|madhu|
syandaḥ kavīnām ayaṃ
jāgartu śruti|śuṣkalī|valayita|
vyom'|âvagāhī guṇaḥ.

iti niṣkrāntāḥ sarve.

leaves and roaming in the Vindhya, in the mountain that is like Varáha's tusk.* And also thanks to you I had a bridge built to divide the southern and the western oceans, a bridge to last until the end of this aeon, and I have freed the whole world of Rávana's rule.

And may this be the final benediction of this play:

May poets incessantly shower their audience with the honey of their poems, which are like blossoming flowers. And may people refrain from judging the merits and faults of poets' profound verses without having smelled the scent of the Surpeme Spirit, who is the Word.

Moreover, 7.380

As long as the god Brahma purifies the three worlds with the water of his pot, which flows down in the three streams of the Ganga in heaven, earth and the underworld, may poets' merits remain to sing in sweetly flowing magic words* about heroic fame, and may their merits be perceived.*

All exit.

CHĀYĀ

The following is a Sanskrit paraphrase (chāyā) *of the Prakrit passages (marked with* ⌜corner brackets⌟*) in the play. References are to chapter and paragraph.*

1.35 dinakara|kiraṇ'|ôtkaraḥ priya|kāraḥ ko 'pi jīva|lokasya / kamala|mukul'|âṅka|pālī|gata|madhukara|karṣaṇa|vidagdhaḥ.

2.17 ārya Śunaḥśepa! kim apy āścaryam bhīṣaṇam ca vartate.

2.19 adya «Rāma iti ko 'pi kṣattriya|kumāra āgata» iti śrutvā kautūhalena dhāvataḥ sā tapo|vana|prānta|pratiṣṭhitā prastara|putrikā satya|mānuṣī bhūtvā mam' âiva saṃmukham parāpatitā. tāṃ prekṣy' ôttar'|āsaṅga|valkalam apy ujjhitvā palāyito 'smi.

2.21 tad rakṣatu mām āryo 'syāḥ duṣṭa|rākṣasyā mukhāt.

2.24 śṛṇomi, yā Janaka|vaṃśa|purohitasya Śatānandasya jananī. tatas tataḥ.

2.26 aho! āryasya prasādena jīva|loke pratiṣṭhito 'smi. tath" âpi śaṅkā|jvaro 'dy' âpi māṃ na parityajati. tad, muhūrtaṃ viśramyatāṃ.

2.29 kathaṃ viṣaya|mṛga|tṛṣṇā|jhalaṃ|jhalyāṃ bhagavatā Hariṇ" âpi hariṇatā viḍambyate?

2.31 manye, etasyā muni|gṛhiṇyāḥ puṇya|paripāko atra Rāma|bhadrasya pravāse kāraṇaṃ.

2.33 ārya, dvitīyam api śrotum anena te vacanena paryutsuko 'smi.

2.35 tatas tataḥ.

2.38 aho! sthavira|bhallūkasya mantr'|ôpanyāsaḥ parihāsa|kuśalatā ca. tatas tataḥ.

2.40 ārya! yaḥ sa Mārutis «trailokya|malla» iti śrūyate

2.42 ārya! yathā tathā vā bhavatu, svāmī svāmy eva. taṃ parityajya na sadṛśas tādṛśasya mahā|bhāvasya pratikūla|parigrahaḥ.

2.44 huṃ. tad ucitam eva yad guru|putraḥ sa|brahmacārī v" ânuvartyate. tatas tataḥ.

2.46 katham a|parihīṇa|mitra|dharmo 'pi sa rākṣasaḥ!

2.49 tatas tataḥ.

2.51 «nāga|sahasra|balā str" îty» a|śruta|pūrvam etat! tatas tataḥ.

2.53 jāne Rāmabhadra iti rākṣasānām upary avatīrṇaḥ khalv eṣaḥ.

2.55 manye mantra|mayībhir astra|devatābhiḥ samaṃ bal"|âtibale śaktī api Rāme saṃkramiṣyata iti.

2.57 ārya! nanu bhaṇāmi: yadi nija eva śaktī, nijā eva astra|vidyāḥ, tat kim ity ātmano vighn'|ôpaśame Rāghavasya gauravam arpayati tatra|bhavān Kauśikaḥ?

2.57 atha vā prāhuṇika|hastena sarpa|māraṇaṃ khalv etat?

2.60 ārya! śobhanaṃ mantrayase. anyat kim api praṣṭu|kāmo 'smi.

2.62 sarvathā nigūḍham api vānarāṇāṃ ṣāḍguṇyam āryeṇa katham pratipannam?

2.72 aham api kṣatriya|kumārayor darśana utkaṇṭhito 'smi. tat kathaya, tau kutra paśyāmi?

3.6 ārya! praṇamāmi!

3.8 ārya, cireṇa kuto yūyam?

3.10 atha kim. ārya, prabhavaṃ nāmadheyaṃ ca tayoḥ śrotum asti me kautūhalam.

3.14 yath" âsmākaṃ gṛhe bhartṛ|dārikā Sītā, Ūrmilā ca, Māṇḍavī, Śrutakīrtiś ca.

3.14 kathaṃ, mahā|kula|prasūtāḥ khalv ete kumārāḥ.

3.14 kuto 'smākam īdṛśaṃ bhāga|dheyam?

3.16 tatas tataḥ.

3.18 ārya sarva|jana|manīṣit'|ânukūlam iva tatra|bhavataḥ Śatānandasya vacanam.

3.20 tat kiṃ manyadhve? Śaṃkara|śar'|âsan'|āropaṇa|vyavasāyena rāja'|ṛṣer Janakasya pratijñā|sāhasaṃ nirvahati Rāghavaḥ?

3.23 ārya! pravṛtti|viśeṣa|lābhena dur|manāyamānam ātmānaṃ pāñcālikā|keli|vyāpāreṇa vinodayantīṃ bhartṛ|dārikāṃ prekṣya, pratipattum āgatay" āryasya darśanena mayā vismṛtam. etena punas te rākṣasa|nāma|grahaṇena smārit" âsmi.

3.25 yathā kila Sītā|devīṃ prārthayituṃ Daśa|grīva|purohita parāgata iti.

3.27 ārya! evaṃ nv etat. ārya iti śithilī|kṛta|lajjā saṃpraty ev' ânubhūtaṃ kim iti nivedayāmi.

3.30 tataś ca tābhir ṛjvībhir nirbadhyamānā lajjitum api lajjate.

3.33 ārya! śobhanaṃ mantrayase. sarvasy' âpy anubhava|saṃvādinī te vācā.

3.36 bhavatu! na kim api yuṣmābhiḥ śrutam!

3.38 hat'|āśo Rāvaṇo devīṃ pariṇayati!

3.42 evaṃ bhavatu! ārya! samprati kutra tau Rāma|Lakṣmaṇau?

4.24 aho, saumya|sundara|vivāha|nepathya|lakṣmī|vistārita|kānti|prāg|bhārāṇi Raghu|kula|kumārāṇāṃ mukha|puṇḍarīkāṇi paśyantī, jugupsiten' âpi māyā|mānuṣī|bhāvena, kṛt'|ârth" âsmi. aho, sā tādṛśī guṇānāṃ prakṛtir, yad vipakṣa|hasta|patit" âpi sukhayati.

4.26 katham, ih' âiv' âṭṭālaka|śikhara|varti|pragrīve mātā|mahaḥ. aho, duḥ|śliṣṭatā duṣṭa|karmaṇāṃ, yad idānīṃ prajāgara|klinna|locanaḥ pratikṣaṇaṃ jṛmbhikā|prasārita|mukha|kuhara|dṛṣṭa|hṛdaya|sthita|kaṭhina|kārya|bhāro 'nya iva ko 'pi dṛśyate.

atha vā sāmānyasy' âpi garīyān khalu mantri|bhāvo, viśeṣeṇa punaḥ sāhasa|ras'|âika|vyavasāya|caṇḍa|caritasy' âsmat|svāmino Rāvaṇasya. jānāmi mām eva pratipālayan tiṣṭhati. yāvad enam upasarpāmi.

4.26 ārya, vande!

4.28 ārya, Daśaratha āgate kumārāṇāṃ godāna|maṅgale ca saṃvṛtte mayā praviṣṭaṃ Mithilā|nagaraṃ.

4.30 atha kiṃ.

4.33 ārya! evaṃ nv etat. sa tu mayā brāhmaṇo Vasiṣṭha|maha"|êṣiṇo api pura|sphuran dṛṣṭaḥ.

4.37 ārya, na khalu balāt|kāram parihṛtya ko 'py anya upāyas tarkyate.

4.41 yathā nirūpitaṃ mātā|mahena. aho, kālasya māh"|ātmyaṃ, yad idānīṃ tri|bhuvana|jaya|lakṣmī|līlā|bandī|kāre mahā|rāje Rāvaṇe 'py evaṃ mantryate.

4.44 kaḥ saṃdehaḥ. tasmiṃ vivāha|mah"|ôtsave sarvaṃ mayā pratyakṣī|kṛtaṃ.

4.46 ārya, kim idānīṃ yuktaṃ?

4.48 kathaṃ kṣatriya|poto Vāli|nigrahe 'pi sahāyaḥ samīkṣyate? tatas tataḥ.

4.50 ārya, kiṃ punas tat saṃvidhānakaṃ?

4.52 aho, vṛddha|ṛkṣasya kuṭilatā kārya|kuśalatā ca!

4.54 ārya! ôpanatasy' âivaṃ kriyate?

4.56 anyad bhaṇāmi. apy evaṃ kariṣyati Rāma|bhadraḥ?

4.58 kiṃ c' ânyad apy an|arth'|ântaraṃ tatra bhaviṣyat' îti tarkayāmi.

4.60 mayā Janaka|nagarān niṣkrāntayā śrutam, yathā khaṇḍita|Śrīkaṇṭha|śar'|âsanasya Dāśarather matsareṇa sakala|kṣatriya|kṛt'|ântaḥ Paraśurāmaḥ parāgata iti.

4.64 dugdha|mukhe 'py etasmin kṣatriya|vaṭuka evaṃ saṃbhāvayati mātā|mahaḥ!

7.15 ārya|putra! ap' îh' âiva bhujaṃga|pāśa|bandhanaṃ Sītāyāḥ kṛte yūyaṃ sāhitāḥ?

7.21 ārya|putra! Saumitri|kīrtti|kandalyā utpatti|kṣetraṃ kataraḥ punaḥ saṃniveśaḥ?

7.23 yatr' âiṣā,

7.24 anurāga|rom'|âñca|kaṇṭaka|sveda|jalābhyāṃ niśā|carī k" âpi / uddīpita|nirvāpita|cit"|ânalā dayitam anumriyate.

7.27 ārya|putra, Kiṣkindh'|ēśvara|skandh'|āvār'|âika|dhuraṃ|dharo Raghu|kula|kuṭumba|vidhura|bandhuḥ sa kutr' êdānīṃ Hanūmān?

7.43 ārya|putra, jalanidhi|madhya|varttino Laṅkā|potasya Jambūdvīp'|ôpasaṃyamana|śṛṅkhalā|bandha iva ka eṣa dṛśyate?

7.45 diṣṭy" ārya|putra|darśana|pratyāśā|taroḥ pracchinnasya prarohaṇa|mah"|âuṣadhir iva setu|bandho dṛśyate. bhagavan, namas te.

7.56 ārya|putra, Gaurī|guror gir'|îndrasya yuva|rājo jalanidhi|madhya|varttī Maināko jānāmi pakṣa|chedaṃ vin" âpi sthāvarī|bhūtaḥ.

7.59 vimāna|rāja, gagana|mārga|caṅkramaṇa|kautūhal'|ôtphulla|mānas" âsmi. tad unnama tāvat!

7.70 ka eṣa kalp'|ânala|jvālā|kalāpa|kvathyamāna|jalanidhi|phena|stabaka|nirmala|sphaṭika|śikhara|sahasra|madhuro mahī|dharaḥ puro vilokyate?

7.73 ap' îh' âiva Hara|niṭila|locan'|ânala āhutī|bhūto bhagavān Manmathaḥ?

7.78 ārya|putra, tathā nir|anukrośaḥ katham punaḥ pratinivṛtto Mahādevo Devyai?

7.83 katarasmiṃ punaḥ saṃniveśe bhagavatyāḥ sarva|maṅgalāyāḥ pāṇi|grahaṇa|maṅgalam āsīt?

7.88 ārya|putra, apy etasminn eva Madana|tanu|dahana|vyatikara|nir|ātma|mānayā punar apy a|viśvasantyā Gauryā Candra|cūḍaḥ saṃghaṭito nija|śarīreṇa?

7.101 anen' âiva maṇḍa|śeṣī|kṛta|dugdha|sāgareṇa candram uddhṛtya viprayukta|bhartṛkasya strī|janasy' ôpari cārabhaṭy ārabdhā.

7.109 nija|daiva|dur|vilās'|âlaso loko Lakṣmyā dur|yaśo|vacanāni gāyati. ka eṣa divasa|kroḍī|kṛta|jyotsnā|viccharda|pratirūpo giriḥ?

7.124 etasya dandaśūka|nara|karoṭi|muṇḍa|mālā|maṇḍanasya śmaśāna|vāsino bhūta|nāthasya bhūṣaṇatā|viḍambanam eva Rohiṇī|vallabhasya kalaṅkaḥ. kiṃ punas tapasvinā kuraṅgena?

7.143 ārya|putra, kiṃ punar etad dalita|karpūra|śilā|guccha|gauraṃ gagan'|âṅgaṇaṃ dṛśyate?

7.160 ārya|putra, samāna|kula|rūpa|yauvanānām api sa|patnīnāṃ śīrṣe datto dhanyayā Dakṣa|gotra|kanyayā caraṇo, yena Rohiṇī|ramaṇa ity eva bhagavāṃś candraḥ śrūyate.

7.180 ārya|putra, kathaṃ punaḥ saṃpūrṇa|maṇḍalam īdṛśaṃ candram avamatya kalā|mātraṃ bhagavatā Bhūta|nāthena cūḍā|maṇī|kṛtam?

7.185 ārya|putra, paripūrṇā guṇino yatra kutr' âpi śobhante. kṣīṇāḥ punaḥ śīrṣam ārohant' îti Hara|cūḍā|candra eva prathama|nidarśanam.

7.195 jānāmy ārya|putra|kīrti|kāntyā pratispardhāṃ kṛtvā parājitena saṃprati bhagavatā hariṇ'|âṅkena kalaṅka|saṃghaṭṭanā vidhṛtā.

7.198 sārambhaṃ Śrī|vatsa|lāñchana|bhujā|paryasta|manth'|âcala|kṣobh'|ôccalita|dugdha|sindhu|laharī|garbha|chavī|sacchāyam, ko gāyati na te, Raghūṇām prabhor, andha|kāra|pakṣ'|ântarā|saṃtuṭyan|mṛgāṅka|maṇḍala|mayūkh'|ôdgāra|gauraṃ yaśaḥ?

7.201 katham, Añjanā|nandanas tvarayati. tad bhagavat Puṣpaka, avanama. āsanna|medinī|mārgeṇa gacchāmaḥ.

7.201 ārya|putra, kiṃ punar etat taruṇa|jīmūta|śyāmale mahī|valaye Madhu|mathana|vakṣaḥ|sthale Kaustubha|kiraṇa|stabaka iva jvalal lakṣyate?

7.209 yatra kāśa|kusuma|saṃkāśo 'gastya|haṃsaś carati.

7.220 ārya|putra, jyeṣṭh" êti dākṣiṇya|mātreṇ' âiva bhagavataḥ sāgarasya Bhāgīrathī|pakṣa|pātaḥ. prema|sarvasva|niṣyandaḥ punaḥ sahaja|sarv'|âṅga|mauktik'|ābharaṇa|ramaṇīyāyāṃ Tāmraparṇyām eva varṇyate

7.236 bhagavatyo Janasthāna|vāsinyo devatāḥ, eṣā vaḥ paricārikā, Jānakī praṇamati.

7.242 vimāna|rāja, prasīda! jvalati, na dalaty eva vajra|mayaṃ me hṛdayaṃ. tathā tvarayasva, yathā êṣ" ântarīyatāṃ Daṇḍak'|âraṇya|viñjoliḥ.

7.271 aho, tatra|bhavataḥ Śaśa|dhara|śekharasya kavalita|catur|daśa|lokasy' âpi na palāyit" âkṣi|bubhukṣā yena Madano 'pi grāsī|kṛtaḥ.

7.285 eṣā nija|srotaḥ|sandānita|tri|bhuvanā Mandākinī vandate.

7.294 amba Mithile, vandyase, guru|jane 'pi vandanaṃ me vijñāpaya.

7.336 diṣṭyā niḥ|sāpatnyaṃ ma ārya|putrasya gṛhiṇītvaṃ bhaviṣyati.

7.346 vatsa Bharata! uṣṇa|kara|kiraṇa|nikurumba|cumbitaṃ|kamala|khaṇḍam iva ciram ānandam udvaha.

7.356 vatsa, sarva|loka|śoka|śaly'|ôddharaṇa|gauravavadbhiś caritair Lakṣmaṇa|sadṛśo bhava. vatsa Śatrughna! ārya|janaḥ kutra?

NOTES

Bold *references are to the English text;* ***bold italic*** *references are to the Sanskrit text. An asterisk (*) in the body of the text marks the word or passage being annotated.*

1.1 The invocatory stanza describes Vishnu at the beginning of creation, lying on the serpent Shesha in the primeval waters. The **sheldrake** is said to be united to his mate only during daytime, and that is why one of **Vishnu's eyes**, the sun, delights him. It is also a common belief in Sanskrit literature that the ***cha-kóra*** partridge feeds on moonbeams. The **lotus**, from which the demiurge Brahma is to be born, is not yet fully open, because it blossoms in sunshine, but the moon is still there as Vishnu's other eye. Because of the similarities of color and form, the opening white lotus bud is compared to Vishnu's other attribute, the **conch shell.**

1.5 Or "Quarrel and Controversy" (***Kalahakandala***).

1.5 **Bahu·rupa**: "Multiform."

1.6 The sentence is aimed at the rival troupe of Kálaha·kándala in the first place, whose performances do not serve the aesthetic pleasure of the public. But there may be a double meaning here, as Rucipati clarifies, and the sentence could also be translated as follows: "The delight of those who assist in the sacrifice is the beloved wife (Sita) of the warrior. After defeating her kidnapper (Rávana), I shall bring her back." It must be remembered that the stage manager is to play Rama.

1.8 This verse also alludes to the story to be enacted, for Rama shall be helped by the monkeys in the siege of Lanka, and the demon king, Rávana, shall be forsaken by his own brother, Vibhíshana.

1.17 Lit. "Valmíki's capital / stock of fine speech."

1.19 Lit. "This is the ripening of virtues for all poets." Or, with the variant reading: "All this is the ripening of virtues for poets." Viṣṇubhaṭṭa understands ***katham*** in the sense of "why."

1.24 Lit. "the weavings of words."

1.27 Lit. "whose word power manifests itself as sweet and profound owing to the importance of his various qualities."

1.27 Lit. "help themselves." The expression is ambiguous, possibly implying poetic as well as spiritual advancement or perfection. Viṣṇubhaṭṭa takes it in the spiritual sense.

1.33 Lit. "filled with the depth of qualities." As Viṣṇubhaṭṭa points out, the word *saurabha* can mean "importance or depth of qualities" (*guṇa/gaurava*). As he explains, *saurabha* can also refer to the scent that the fame of the Kakútsthas confers on the poet.

1.35 As the stage manager explains, this verse announces the entry of Vishva·mitra, who will take away Rama from Dasha·ratha's lap. The construction of the last compound is problematic; for a discussion, see STEINER's note 45 on p. 86.

1.36 The stage manager and his assistant will appear in two principal roles later, as Rama and Lákshmana, for which they can prepare while the first half of the first act is performed.

1.43 Note the play on the word ***guru***, meaning "master" and "excessive" (bias), and the irony it conveys.

1.44 Lit. "a friendship of the stars," spontaneous or unaccountable love.

1.45 Because it opens at moonrise. The parallel between Vasíshtha and the moon, on the one hand, and between Dasha·ratha and the night-lotus, on the other, is quite obvious.

1.51 Lit. "I have well taken the word of my teacher on my head." The expression refers to a solemn promise with a gesture of touching the head; see also 2.242 and 4.216.

1.54 I take the plural ***vayam*** to refer to Vama·deva and Vasíshtha, in the sense of "we, brahmins, only teach you / give you advice." But the sentence could also be translated in the singular, Vama·deva referring to himself.

1.55 The comparison is somewhat elliptical, in order to praise both Dasha·ratha and Vasíshtha. In the context of Vama·deva's previous words, it can mean that Dasha·ratha needs little instruction from Vasíshtha to follow the path of virtue, just as the night-lotuses need only a little of the moon's rays to open up. But, in view of the second line, it can also be praise for Vasíshtha, suggesting that his influence, even if it is not fully felt, just as with the rays of the moon on a cloudy night, is enough to determine the course of things.

1.57 For the story about Ságara and his sons, see "Recurring mythological references and divine attributes" in the Introduction.

1.57 This is again a praise of the king and his ancestors ending as a praise of Vasíshtha.

1.59 King Tri·shanku wanted to reach heaven in his mortal body, but was refused by Vasíshtha as well as the gods. Vishva·mitra nevertheless performed a sacrifice for him, but when his body was propelled toward heaven Indra threw him back. Vishva·mitra managed to prevent his body from falling back, and thus Tri·shanku became suspended between heaven and earth. He is identified with a constellation. See, e.g., *Rāmāyaṇa* 1.59 ff. Note that Vama·deva mentioned Tri·shanku's failure to reach heaven just before Vishva·mitra's entry.

1.66 Vishva·mitra, who was born a kshatriya, a warrior, performed severe penance in order to become a Brahmin. See *Rāmāyaṇa* 1.51 passim.

1.66 With the echoing words ***(agādhaḥ. . . Gādhi/putro)***, the second line emphasizes the contrast between his kshatriya origin (as the son of King Gadhi) and brahminical achievements (his dominant qualities being non-Rajasa, i.e., pure brahminical). The word ***guṇa*** is used in referring to the triad of *Sattva* (Purity), *Rajas* (Activity) and *Tamas* (Darkness), of which Vishva·mitra appropriated the first, brahminical one, although he was originally pervaded by the second one as a kshatriya.

1.68 Lit. "the star Arúndhati," for Vasíshtha's wife is identified with the morning star. Vasíshtha is also identified with one of the stars of the Great Bear.

1.69 I.e., Dasha·ratha's family.

1.73 In the course of the **Ashva·medha** (horse sacrifice), a horse is let loose to wander for a year, and the territory it covers is then considered to belong to the king.

1.75 I follow Viṣṇubhaṭṭa, who takes ***su/bhagam/bhāvuka*** in the sense of "being able to subjugate," while Rucipati (who is followed by STEINER) understands it to mean "become beautiful / charming."

1.75 Dasha·ratha killed several demons in battle to help Indra (see *Rāmāyaṇa* 2.9.9 ff), which is implied here by the humiliation of their wives.

1.77 **Dilípa** is an ancestor of Dasha·ratha.

1.92 Or right arm, implying that Dasha·ratha was sitting to the left of Indra.

1.92 Dasha·ratha felt a thrill in recalling his heroic fights.

1.96 The ***mákara*** is an imaginary animal of the sea, and the vehicle of the God of love (Kama).

1.96 Lit. "female *mákaras* of musk-drawings, made out of play, on the seat of the goddesses' cheeks." The fact that the Ikshvákus have been looking after the drawings on the goddesses' cheeks means that they have been protecting the gods themselves. The implication of the verse is this: members of your dynasty have always performed the protection of the gods, which was considered a common duty by them; now that you have secured the Goddess of Good Fortune for Indra, you simply fulfilled a common duty, and therefore you think it needs no special eulogy.

1.98 "**As the gods bowed down**" is not in the Sanskrit.

1.98 In the story of Tri·shanku (see 1.59), Vishva·mitra thinks of attempting a new creation to give Tri·shanku a heaven.

1.100 "**To arrive so late**" is not in the Sanskrit.

1.101 Lit. "of great affection, to respect you" (a *Tatpuruṣa* compund).

1.103 In Sanskrit, fame is considered to be white. Note the echoing ***yaśobhir aśobhi*** and that the three similes cover the underworld (the abode of snakes), the earth and the sky, thus suggesting that the king's renown reaches everywhere (Viṣṇubhaṭṭa).

1.105 I.e., let the sun still shine, although your splendor would give enough light for the world.

1.109 Each of the first three lines of the poem can be interpreted as describing the various realms in the world and as referring to various problems of royal policy.

1.109 "**Unlike the sky, the sea and the underworld**" is not in the Sanskrit.

1.111 All these mythical animals and the mountains are carriers of the earth, for whose well-being the good king is also responsible.

1.116 I.e., you have learned it to be able to teach the sons of this dynasty.

1.128 For they have not offered protection to Vishva·mitra.

1.130 That is: if you need Rama, it means I am / we are the only ruler(s) of the earth, the only husband(s) of the earth. (According to Viṣṇubhaṭṭa's reading and interpretation.) Or, reading *caratu* with Rucipati: our land shall be a faithful wife and wait for Rama; i.e., Dasha·ratha envisages already that Rama shall be his successor on the throne.

1.140 "**As a new constellation in the sky**" is not in the Sanskrit.

1.140 The path mentioned here is the so-called *Vaiśvānarī*. These seven sages were created by Vishva·mitra in imitation of the seven sages of the constellation of the Great Bear. He then agreed to keep them elsewhere, on the path of the ancestors (*Pitṛ/yāṇa*), in the South. See also Viṣṇubhaṭṭa's commentary. For the story, see, e.g., *Rāmāyaṇa* 1.59.20 ff. and *Vāyupurāṇa* 1.50.208–213.

1.149 The sage **Rishya·shringa** performed a sacrifice for Dasha·ratha that brought about the birth of Rama and his three brothers.

1.150 He did so by performing the sacrifice that brought about the birth of his sons.

1.160 Rama, identified with Vishnu, is praised as the ultimate godhead here. The stanza also foresees all the exploits of Rama enacted in the play.

1.160 For Vishnu lying on the primeval waters before creation starts, see the opening verse of the play. At the beginning of creation, Vishnu takes the form of a boar to bring up the earth from the bottom of the sea, on which men can then perform sacrifices to the gods. Also, this boar form of Vishnu is identified with the sacrifice itself. The four examples illustrate the ways in which Vishnu creates and protects the sacrifice.

1.171 Lit. "mouths filled with their double tongues."

1.178 Lit. "long and hot," which implies pain and sadness.

1.181 For it follows the changes of his son, the Moon. This refers to the story of the churning of the milk-ocean, which produced the moon, among other miraculous objects and beings, before the ambrosia. Therefore, the sea is taken to be the father of the moon here.

1.181 "**By opening up at night**" is not in the Sanskrit. Affection between Rama and Vishva·mitra is due to the fact that they are both noble-minded, but it has nothing to do with the affection of father and son, Dasha·ratha and Rama. Note the use of the grammatical term ***jani/kartṛ***.

1.183 The same myth is referred to here as before: the miraculous **Káustubha gem**, the **ambrosia** and the **coral tree** were also produced from the sea.

1.183 Here Dasha·ratha emphasizes the importance of friendship over family relations, alluding to the friendship of Vishva·mitra and Rama, which is stronger than family ties, he reckons.

2.13 I follow Viṣṇubhaṭṭa in taking ***tarku*** in this sense (*Viśva/karmā*), but the word normally means "spindle." (Note also that Rucipati gives the variant *tvaṣṭṛ* for *tarku.*) STEINER takes *tarku/ṭaṅka* in the sense of "grindstone."

2.36 The following speech by Jámbavan enumerates the various reasons that an alliance with Rávana is undesirable, according to the rules of classical Indian policymaking, the *Arthaśāstra*.'

2.36 Or "if a neighboring king attempts to attack you."

2.36 The technical term ***asura/jayin*** means "he who conquers with demonic / unfair means." The expression is probably deliberately ambiguous.

2.36 Both the demon king Rávana and the Lord of the Riches, Kubéra, are the sons of the sage Pulástya.

2.37 I.e., in the Kailása mountain.

2.48 Lit. "he whose hair stood on end because of the relish of the cutting off of his heads." Rávana was ready to cut off all his heads to prove his devotion to Shiva, but the god stopped him when he was about to cut off the tenth head. The story illustrates that Rávana was ready to offer his head only to delight Shiva, not to obtain anything from him. Thus, he also offers Vali his help out of true friendship, and not to profit from the alliance. (I follow Viṣṇubhaṭṭa's and Jinaharṣagaṇi's reading and interpretation, which is also given by Rucipati as a variant reading and interpretation. If we follow Rucipati's first reading (*tv asmai nava. . .*), it can be understood to mean "he is as thrilled to delight him [Vali] as he was when he relished the cutting off of his nine heads.")

2.62 Six ways of political action are meant here: alliance, war, expedition, halt, seeking shelter and "double dealing" (*sandhi*, *vigraha*, *yāna*, *āsana*, *saṃśraya*, *dvaidhībhāva*).

2.66 It is believed that oysters produce white pearls from white water. In the same way, the lotus buds, which have drunk the darkness of the night, emit black bees for pearls.

2.80 For the story of this incarnation of Vishnu, see the section "Recurring mythological references and divine attributes" in the Introduction.

2.81 These are the study and teaching of the Vedas, sacrifice, worship, donations and acceptance of donations. See, e.g., *Āpastamba-dharmasūtra* 2.5.5 or *Manusmṛti* 10.75. The text has "twice-born," by which brahmins are meant here.

2.83 Various interpretations of this passage are possible. Viṣṇubhaṭṭa's first interpretation is that the yearly animal sacrifice is made more often here (which is an envisaged option in the ritual texts). The second is that because all householders perform this sacrifice at the same time, it seems as if this rite was performed more often than usual. Viṣṇubhaṭṭa also envisages the possibility that not householders but Vedic officiating priests (*adhvaryu*) are understood here. Rucipati seems to take the word ***nitya*** in the non-ritual sense of "always."

2.83 Either in the sense that they invoke Indra, the King of Gods, who thus has to come down to earth, or meaning that because they make these sacrifices they are on the way to reaching heaven. Both interpretations are given by Viṣṇubhaṭṭa.

2.94 The **lines** that these ants form resemble patterns drawn on one's face or body with musk or other fragrant substances. The lines are variagated because ants are black and the rice grains are white (Viṣṇubhaṭṭa).

2.103 As the name shows, this river was originally Vishva·mitra's sister, who changed into a holy river.

2.110 Lit. "devoid of the impure and the dark strains of material creation."

2.110 I follow Viṣṇubhaṭṭa in taking ***āhlādate*** in the causative sense.

2.115 According to Viṣṇubhaṭṭa, this also refers to the fact that a mirage is produced.

2.125 The repetition of the sentence "This is an auspicious day" is prescribed three times at the beginning of most religious ceremonies. In this way, Rama refers to his war against the demons as a holy act.

2.129 Viṣṇubhaṭṭa cites the *Yogavāsiṣṭha* (untraced citation) to show that even those who are liberated in this existence must perform the rites prescribed for them.

2.131 A **garland** of the flowers of the coral tree, one of the trees of Indra's paradise.

2.131 On these stories about Vishva·mitra, see 1.59 and 1.98.

2.144 Through protecting the sacrifice performed for him.

2.151 For this incarnation of Vishnu, see "Recurring mythological references and divine attributes" in the Introduction.

2.162 As STEINER points out, there may be a personification of the world, who puts on her previously scattered garments.

2.166 This implies their suffering during the night, when they cannot meet their mates, owing to a curse.

2.166 If the reading of the northern editions is accepted, the translation of the last clause is as follows: "they look like grains of twilight ground by the violent friction of the day and the night."

2.168 I.e., the sun.

2.170 I.e., the sun has set.

2.171 There is a pun on ***kāṣṭha*** (wood) and ***kāṣṭhā*** (direction), noted by INGALLS and STEINER. STEINER also notes the ambiguity of ***kiraṇa***: dust and ray of light.

2.183 In classical India, law books are believed to be the **words of sages**, therefore Vishva·mitra's command to kill the demoness is not less valid here than the prescription that one should not fight against a woman.

2.185 Viṣṇubhaṭṭa understands this line to mean that, for Rama as a mortal being, there is no reason to be ashamed of this act: *kṣaṇikajīvināṃ kā lajjā—iti bhāvaḥ.*

2.191 Lit. "who is this new shoot of a stain that attacks the solar dynasty?" The word "shoot" also alludes to Rama as offspring.

2.196 As Rucipati and Jinaharṣagaṇi explain, this **arrow** was given by the God of the **Wind**.

2.196 Lit. "while still alive"; the word ***jīvan/maraṇa*** is perhaps meant to allude ironically to *jīvan/mukti*, liberation in life. Viṣṇubhaṭṭa understands that it implies that the demon was trying to escape when hit. Both Marícha and Subáhu are Tádaka's sons, who attempted to obstruct the sacrifice (see *Rāmāyaṇa* 1.18–19). Viṣṇubhaṭṭa seems to take ***tāḍakeya*** to refer to Marícha.

2.198 This refers to Dasha·ratha, who helped Indra in his battle against demons, and thus made him useless as a warrior.

2.207 The **moonlight**, on which the *chakóra*s feed, makes them intoxicated, while the birds make the light thicker with their glances.

2.208 RĀMACANDRA MIŚRA and INGALLS both remark that the image evokes the story of the milk-ocean churned with Mount Mándara and producing foam. According to Viṣṇubhaṭṭa, the whitened mountaintops appear as if they were foam produced by the stirred-up ocean, while the world emerges in the moonlight, just as a pot emerging from a well produces bubbles.

2.210 Lit. "in the front line of the army." As STEINER points out, the image suggested is that of an army of moonbeams marching against the darkness. When the moon as their commander arrives, it can show only its flag or sign, i.e., its spot (a pun on ***lāñchana***, meaning both "sign" and the spot of the moon). For a similar image, see 2.216.

2.212 The **moonstone** is believed to ooze away under the influence of the moon. Here, the moon causes it to overflow.

2.212 The word ***kuraṅga*** means "deer" as well as the spot on the moon pictured as a deer.

2.214 As STEINER points out following Rucipati, the moonbeams are related to Paulómi's **saffron powder**, because both are yellow in color and both the rising moon and Indra's realm are in the East.

2.216 The image evokes again the commander of an army (the moon), who sends forth his soldiers (the moonbeams) to capture prisoners (patches of darkness). Cf. 2.210.

2.218 This **nut** is said to clear muddy water, pushing the mud to the bottom.

2.222 ... **pervade the hearts of the shelduck:** in the form of the burning pain of separation.

2.224 According to Viṣṇubhaṭṭa, the second line means either that the moon makes the moonstones look clustered together although they are dispersed, or that each moonstone looks like a heap of moonstones.

2.226 Rahu (here called lit. "he who afflicts / strikes at the moon") is a demon personifying the ascending node of the moon as well as its eclipse.

2.232 Since the lotuses do not receive the moon who arrives as a guest and thus act against the rules about the obligation of receiving guests, they are punished: the moon transfers his "sin," his dark spot, onto them and takes away their meritorious acts. The word ***agha*** means both "impurity" (i.e., the spot of the moon) and "sin," while ***su/kṛta*** can also denote both "good construction / shape" and "meritorious act."

2.234 This sage and six others represent the stars of the Great Bear. In the Puranas, **Atri** is said to have produced the moon from his eye while he was practicing austerities. In this verse, Vishva·mitra points out that all the things people see as the effects of the moon can in fact happen without it.

2.235 The word ***aṅka*** is used here in the sense of sham fight or military show, *citra/yuddha*, for the fight against Tádaka was not more for a warrior like Rama.

2.236 There is a pun here on a popular name of Rama, Rama·chandra, which means "Rama-Moon."

3.12 Because Dasha·ratha killed the demons.

3.12 For Dasha·ratha did his job for him by killing the demons. Note the use of numbers in the verse: **thirty-three** and thirteen meaning **gods**, "thousand-rayed" meaning the **sun**, "ten-charioted" meaning Dasha·ratha, "hundred-pointed" meaning the **thunderbolt** and "he who has a hundred sacrifices" meaning Indra.

3.20 Lit. "fulfill the promise," for Jánaka took an oath to give his daughter to the man who can bend Shiva's bow.

3.22 The question is rhetorical: Vishva·mitra, a sage who can see the future, has certainly brought Rama here to win Sita's hand.

3.26 As Steiner remarks, the "**blessings**" may not be merely the rite to mark the transition to puberty but the physical transformation itself.

3.35 Lit. "is there a taste / aesthetic pleasure that would be above / outside them?" Note the use of the word ***rasa***, which is probably deliberately chosen to allude to the aesthetic meaning.

3.52 This is an auspicious sign.

3.52 Jánaka implies that Vishva·mitra's arrival promotes prosperity in his kingdom.

3.60 For the story in which Yajnaválkya proves that he is wiser than other brahmins and thus receives a **thousand cows** from the king, see *Bṛhadāraṇyaka Upaniṣad* 3.1.1 and 4.3.33. Note the pun on ***go***, which means both "cow" and "ray."

3.76 For these two attributes, see the section "Recurring mythological references and divine attributes" in the Introduction.

3.79 The **sacrificial horse** covered the whole territory of the earth during its year of wandering, which meant that Dasha·ratha was to become a universal monarch; but, as mentioned here, he then gave the world to the priests. Steiner understands a simile here, "he whose fame reaches everywhere like a swift sacrificial horse. . . "

3.79 In that his four parts became embodied as the four sons whom Dasha·ratha obtained thanks to this sacrifice.

3.89 Lit. "by Indra's [menacing] roar." For the story of Tri·shanku, see 1.59, 1.98, and notes.

3.89 "**By this destruction of his creation**" is not in the Sanskrit.

3.106 Lit. "Rama's deeds have clearly been frightening and profound owing to his innate power."

3.111 Lit. "having you as my protecting Lord."

3.114 Indra's bow is the rainbow. The point is that the kings do Indra's job of protecting the world and therefore Indra does not need to use his weapon.

3.114 Lit. "these kings carried their arms in vain."

3.130 Sháushkala gives an ungrammatical but fitting etymology of the name Vishva·mitra here: enemy (*amitra*) for us all (*viśveṣām asmākam*).

3.133 Viṣṇubhaṭṭa understands that "ritual prescription" (***vidhi***) refers to Rama, while ***mantra*** refers to Lákshmana. But this distribution may not be necessarily so.

3.134 **Anaránya** was killed by Rávana; see, e.g., *Rāmāyaṇa* 7.19.

3.135 Lit. "the blood-wine"; the demon Subáhu, Tádaka's husband, is referred to here.

3.143 Lit. "whose essence of heroism has been devoured by. . . " On the stories referred to, see "Recurring mythological references and divine attributes" in the Introduction.

3.161 In fact, the reference is made to a **cup** full of precious jewels, etc., taken by force on a festive occasion. The image implies that Sita is not "given" by Jánaka but is to be taken by the man who strings the bow (Viṣṇubhaṭṭa, citing Yādava, citation untraced by H. N. Bhat).

3.172 Lit. "may the blackness of calluses caused by the bowstring on their arms take possession of the faces of those who are heated / zealous in their heroism."

3.181 The **King of Snakes** is pictured here as Shiva's ornament and bowstring at the same time. When the upraised bow is strung, the string pulled reaches as far as the ear, therefore the snake becomes the god's earring, while after the arrow is released it becomes Shiva's armlet, curled around his upper arm.

3.186 Brahma has four heads, representing the four Vedas, therefore he has **eight ears**.

3.186 Earth, water, fire, air, ether, the sun, the moon and the sacrificing priest.

3.186 Snakes are supposed to hear with their eyes.

3.189 This sound is uttered by women at weddings, according to the commentators (in the South—according to Rucipati), but it is not clear how exactly women produce it. The Bombay edition and Rucipati (followed by STEINER) read "on the surface of their (temples and) cheeks," but Viṣṇubhaṭṭa and Jinaharṣagaṇi read differently, which could be translated literally as "on the surface of the cavity of their cheeks" (*kapola/kandala/tale*).

3.189 Rucipati envisages the possibility that the voices of the priests and the women are metaphorically identified with that of the breaking bow.

3.192 Or "so that he can fulfill the duties of a householder."

3.204 Lit. "where the wedding feast is starting anew" or "where the wedding feast is bright with new praises" (both interpretations are given by Rucipati).

3.212 As the elephant lost his pride.

3.212 The **bees** were attracted to this elephant because of its particularly sweet ichor (a common topos in poetry), but as it dried up when the elephant saw Rávana, the bees lost interest in him. If they are still around him, it is because he wears a flower garland as decoration.

3.216 Lit. "Rávana who is pure / white due to his good character / fame. . . " **Fame** is considered to be white and good-smelling. There is probably a pun on the word ***saurabhya***, which means "fame" as well as "scent." But note that the word is primarily used here in the sense of "reputation" or "good character" (Rucipati: *khyāti*; Viṣṇubhaṭṭa: *guṇa/gaurava*).

4.3 She curses her domestic life during the night because she meets the male only after sunrise. Both long compounds of the first *pāda* qualify ***kakubhaḥ***.

4.5 The **shelduck** receive the enjoyment for they finally meet after their separation at night, and the **white night-lotuses** (***kumuda***) will be given people's sleep, for they are "awake," i.e., they are open at night.

4.11 According to Rucipati, they are trying to deny the horripilation—caused by remembering the night—as well as the nail marks before each other; according to Viṣṇubhaṭṭa, they are simply talking about the events of the past night. As STEINER remarks, the long compound in the last line could also be adverbial, "while their goosebumps are interspersed with nailmarks."

4.17 Although Rávana has defeated the King of Gods, Indra, and is thus playing with goddesses, he is still not content, for he has not obtained Sita; therefore, he does not make Mályavan fully satisfied, either.

4.21 **Pulástya** was an ancestor of Rávana.

4.21 Lit. "jewels in the couch of the upper room in his palace, formed by Indra's crown / head." The image shows that Indra was subjugated by Rávana and bowed down before the demon, touching Rávana's feet with his head.

4.26 "**Grandfather**" may be a simple honorific appellation.

4.28 *Godāna/maṅgala* must refer to a ceremony of tonsure before marriage.

4.31 **Warrior-brahmin**: because Vishva·mitra was a kshatriya, and through his asceticism he managed to become a brahmin.

4.34 An ironic statement: while all sages are twice-born, for they had a natural birth and one when they were initiated into Vedic studies, Vishva·mitra outdoes them in the number of his births.

4.45 Lit. "It would be the destruction of one piece of clay." This is an expression used in *Arthaśāstra* 1.17.39, where it appears to mean "to break someone like a clod of earth." Viṣṇubhaṭṭa understands that the expression refers to the death of people who quarrel only for a piece of clay. Rucipati understands that one of the two parties must die, or that it refers to many people killing one person with a piece of clay. However, these explanations do not yield much sense in the context.

4.45 A citation from *Arthaśāstra* 7.3.11–12, with two insignificant variants.

4.55 This citation of *Arthaśāstra* 7.16.30 slightly differs from the edited text, which reads as follows: *yas t' ûpanatān hatvā baddhvā vā bhūmi/dravya/putra/dārān abhimanyeta tasy' ôdvignam maṇḍalam abhāvāy' ôttiṣṭhate*—"But he who kills or imprisons kings who have become dependent, desiring the land, possessions, sons or wives of those kings, will provoke the aggrieved countries he has conquered to revolt with the intention to destroy him."

4.62 This refers to the story in which Árjuna Kartavírya stops the flow of the Nármada River while playing with his wives there. Cf., e.g., *Rāmāyaṇa* 7.32.

4.62 By killing Árjuna Kartavírya, Párashu·rama avenged his father's death; now that his preceptor's—i.e., Shiva's—bow has been treated by Rama without respect, he will surely retaliate.

4.73 The **arms** are compared to **columns** (*stambha*, such as those erected to commemorate a king's victory), and the marks of the bowstring to panegyrics (***praśasti***, which is also a term for the beginning portion of inscriptions: the eulogy of the king in power).

4.73 Lit. "the throne of his chest."

4.75 Lit. "to steal."

4.78 Viṣṇubhaṭṭa understands ***nirvyūha*** to be a synonym of *matta/vāraṇā*, probably referring to a decoration with elephant motifs on the couch, instead of ivory. This decoration would then be the filaments of the lotus, the bedroom the pericarp, and the palace the lotus itself.

4.80 Even when Shiva had not yet killed the demons, their wives were already mourning them, which is signaled by the breaking of the bangles. Note the parallels between what happens to Shiva's ears and arm and to the demonesses' earrings and armlets.

4.83 Lit. "from Árjuna's one thousand arm bones." I follow Viṣṇu-bhaṭṭa, who takes the expression to suggest that the arms are shattered to pieces. The battle-axe is pictured here as the God of Fire, Agni, who licks the sacrifice with his tongues, i.e., with its flames.

4.88 The meaning of ***bhasm'/âṅkura*** is "son of an ascetic who has broken his ascetic vow," according to Rucipati as well as to Viṣṇubhaṭṭa's second interpretation, an insult to Skanda, Shiva's son. Viṣṇubhaṭṭa remarks that this refers to the story in which the ascetic Shiva seduced the wives of the sages in the Deva·daru forest.

4.90 Lit. "friend in the payment of the debt of anger over the killing of my father, killing committed through the sin of a wicked ruler." The "wicked ruler" is Árjuna Kartavírya. For the story, see Párashu·rama in the List of Characters.

4.92 Since Skanda has six heads, Párashu·rama had the privilege of seeing half of the god's faces even when Skanda turned his back toward him to escape.

4.98 From here on, the words of Rama can be understood as praise as well as insult (*nindā/stuti*), according to Viṣṇubhaṭṭa. In this sentence, Rama praises Párashu·rama as his elder, agreeing that he is like a lion, while Rama is like a deer. On the other hand, it is also an insult, meaning that, as far as heroic qualities are concerned, there is no difference between them; the difference is only in behavior.

4.99 Meaning that **Bhrigu** was his father as well as his Vedic teacher.

4.99 **Káshyapa**, a grandson of Brahma, is the father of gods, demons and all living beings on the earth.

4.100 If understood as an insult, all this is ironical and is meant to denote the contrary. Alternatively, the three may refer to the three qualities of Párashu·rama, which Rama has just praised.

4.103 I.e., the bow broke.

4.105 There is a pun on the word ***śara***, meaning "arrow," and Skanda's place of birth, which was a *śara/vaṇa*, "thicket of reeds."

Since Párashu·rama did not kill him, the *śara/vaṇa*-born Skanda gained a second ***śara*-birth** thanks to Párashu·rama's arrows (*śara*).

4.107 Viṣṇubhaṭṭa gives the alternative interpretation of this praise as insult. In the insult, ***strīṣu*** can be connected to ***pravīra***, i.e., Rama calls Párashu·rama a hero among women. Then, the compound construes as before, or one can also understand *strīṣu pravīra* as a vocative. Since Párvati is mentioned, it implies that Párashu·rama impressed only her, and not Shiva. Moreover, the name of Skanda, Viśākha, may refer to a weak enemy and therefore the victory over him is nothing to boast about.

4.109 Or: "so fond of amusing itself in war" (Rucipati: *vīra/goṣṭhī* = *yuddham*). The expression refers ironically to the fact that this battle-axe killed all the warriors. STEINER translates ***vinoda*** with "scattering, dispelling" [the assembly of heroes], in which case the expression is not ironical.

4.111 The verse is rather ambiguous and can definitely be interpreted as a praise as well as an insult. A commentator, Viṣṇubhaṭṭa, understands the heroic duty to be the future fight with Párashu·rama if the stanza is a eulogy, and to refer to the breaking of Shiva's bow if it is an insult. The last ambiguity is taken up by Párashu·rama himself.

4.115 According to Vedic texts (e.g., *Ṛgveda* 10.90), warriors were created from the arms of a primordial man who was sacrificed to the gods.

4.117 Because Párashu·rama annihilated all the warriors.

4.125 I.e., tears that would flow to mourn Rama's death.

4.130 Lit. "turned to the highest Brahma."

4.132 Párashu·rama's point is that he will spare King Jánaka, for Jánaka is a sacrificer rather than a fighting king; but he is determined to kill the Raghu warriors, for they are real kshatriyas.

4.135 Note how Murári inserts skillfully yet another grammatical term into the text: ***ākṛti/gaṇa*** (list of specimens of words that belong to a certain grammatical rule). The implication is that, unfortunately, the list of brahmins is not defined as a closed list, and therefore Shatánanda can also regard himself as one.

4.135 If members of the Raghu dynasty consider themselves true warriors and Shatánanda regards himself as a true brahmin, then this battle-axe is of no use, for it has not annihilated such false people.

4.137 Bhrigu is the son of the first Manu, who was created by **Brahma**. Here, this Bhrigu and the sage Bhrigu, otherwise called Jamad·agni, Párashu·rama's father, are identified.

4.137 **"In spite of your hurting words"** is not in the Sanskrit.

4.137 Note that ***kudṛṣṭi***, "evil eye," also means "doctrine opposed to the Vedas" ("bad view"), which is probably a suggested meaning here, in contrast with the first word qualifying Párashu·rama: ***vedavān***. Viṣṇubhaṭṭa glosses it with *durjñānam*.

4.140 Since here Lákshmana is about to kill Párashu·rama, who is a brahmin, he stands up as an individual in order to avoid having his family suffer for his sin of murdering a brahmin.

4.144 Párashu·rama is said to have pierced through the **Krauncha mountain**, being jealous of Skanda, who was the first to do so.

4.158 Viṣṇubhaṭṭa paraphrases the expression with "which spreads its flames in all directions," and remarks that while the flames of ordinary fire go upward, this fire of anger spreads in all directions.

4.159 Párashu·rama cut off the head of **his mother** with his axe at the command of his father, while none of his brothers was willing to do so.

4.159 The **swans** said to reside in the caves are pictured as pieces of bones coming out of the deep wounds of the pierced mountain, the wounds being the caves.

4.170 According to Viṣṇubhaṭṭa, this vocative refers to Jánaka and Vishva·mitra.

4.174 Lit. "fleshy," probably implying similarity with the full moon. Steiner understands it in the sense of [looking] "wrinkled," because of her expression of jealousy. Beautiful faces are often compared to the moon.

4.174 I.e., that by stringing another bow Rama could be awarded a second wife. Viṣṇubhaṭṭa's interpretation has been followed in taking the face in the compound to be Sita's, but it could also be Rama's. Viṣṇubhaṭṭa mentions that, because she has some doubts, she looks up in the sky, reflecting.

4.174 I follow most commentators in interpreting ***gati*** in the sense of **way to heaven**, thus making the passage agree with the story of *Rāmāyaṇa* 1.75, in which Párashu·rama loses the worlds earned through his ascetism. However, the text of the *Rāmāyaṇa* uses the same word in a different meaning.

4.179 As Viṣṇubhaṭṭa remarks, it will attain **relief** because the burden of ruling shall be given to Rama.

4.207 Lit. "from the noble middle-mother," for she was Dasha·ratha's second wife.

4.216 As a sign that he will respect what is written in it.

4.216 Lit. "a fellow-student in gratifying me."

4.224 Lit. "I have only the state of the enjoyer / experiencer"; i.e., without being able to do anything against the events.

4.230 Ill fame is pictured as dark, in contrast with good fame, which is considered white.

4.233 Or perhaps: "wait for me" (as STEINER translates).

5.7 This is the king of the town of Śṛṅgavera. See *Rāmāyaṇa* 2.44 ff.

5.11 Lit. "whose breasts were to be measured (***grāhya***) by the length between the tips of the fingers of either hand when the arms are extended (***vyāma***)." **Shabaras** are mountaineers, and are considered to be barbarians.

5.17 It was because of the request of Bharata's mother, Kaikéyi, that Dasha·ratha had to send Rama into exile.

5.17 Lit. "by touching his body." Commentators (Viṣṇubhaṭṭa and Rucipati) point out that the **gesture** implies the following: "if you keep insisting, it is like touching my body to kill me."

5.17 Thus indicating that the real ruler of the country would be Rama.

5.18 Jámbavan is happy to learn that Rama is now definitely away in exile.

5.21 I follow Viṣṇubhaṭṭa, who understands ***maṅgala/kalaśa*** (lit. "auspicious water pot") in the sense of a pot filled with water and placed near the king to protect the king ritually during his sleep. Here, Agástya protects Vatápi's eternal sleep, i.e. death. For these stories concerning Agástya, see "Recurring mythological references and divine attributes" in the Introduction.

5.24 Viṣṇubhaṭṭa understands that Sita's breast was like the "container of offering for black magic to be used against demons," reasoning that Sita was the cause of the infatuation and death of Rávana and the demons. Jinaharṣagaṇi also mentions this as an allusion. STEINER takes it as a simple container of offering, which usually attracts crows. Note that crows are particularly associated with black magic.

5.24 Following Rucipati, who understands ***carama*** in this sense. The alternative reading is *caturaṃ*, meaning "skillful."

5.31 As Viṣṇubhaṭṭa points out, the word ***rasa*** is ambiguous here: it denotes passion or love, as well as poison. Rucipati understands it only in the latter sense.

5.31 In that she wanted to give poison to Rama, whom she originally imagined or desired as her husband.

5.31 This is a reference to the story of Lákshmana's mutilating Shurpa·nakha.

5.47 Or: "crazy at springtime" (***madhu*** = *vasanta*, according to Rucipati's second interpretation).

5.55 Female osprey, Pandion haliaetus, according to BANERJI (1980).

5.58 I.e., how can you defile your elders' fame with this deed?

5.73 ***siddhas*** are semi-divine holy sages, often associated with celestial bards, the *cāraṇas*.

5.73 Out of shame, Brahma would certainly like to bend his heads down, but it would be impossible for him, given that he has four heads in the four directions (with only one neck to hold them).

5.87 As Viṣṇubhaṭṭa clarifies this common topos, the **peacocks** take the elephant ears for roaring clouds and dance because they expect the rain to come.

5.92 Anthocephalus indicus, according to SYED 149. It has red or orange flowers, and is said to blossom at the roaring of thunderclouds, when the peacocks are also said to start their dance.

5.92 Or: "as they arrive." Or, according to Viṣṇubhaṭṭa, wherever they meet each other, referring to bee couples. Viṣṇubhaṭṭa also takes the peacocks to refer to peacock couples.

5.100 The latter part of the demon's name (***kabandha***) means "headless trunk."

5.104 I follow Viṣṇubhaṭṭa in understanding that Rama did not actually make that mark, that he said all this only to tease Sita. Other commentators take Rama's words to report what he really did.

5.108 There is a reference to the story according to which Danu, who was originally a semi-divine being, was cursed to be reborn as a demon, but then got released from this curse thanks to being killed by Lákshmana and Rama. See *Rāmāyaṇa* 3.65–69. In the *Anargharāghava*, this deed is attributed to Lákshmana alone.

5.109 ***Yojana/bāhu*** ("he with one *yojana* long arms") is another name or epithet of Danu·kabándha.

5.123 Note the relation emphasized between Shiva and Rávana: Shiva is called "he who wears the moon as a crown" (***Candr'/āpīḍa***) and the name of Rávana's sword is also mentioned (***Candrahā-sa***).

5.129 The word that expresses the **blossoming** literally means "comedy, farce, laughter."

5.129 Viṣṇubhaṭṭa explains that, because of the presence of **water**, the *kadámba* blossoms, which the peacocks take to be the sign of the coming rain, and that is why they are dancing.

5.129 Viṣṇubhaṭṭa adds here that the hunter wives love the doves because their cooing sounds like the murmuring uttered during lovemaking (*maṇitam*). It is for the same reason that the rose-apple trees seem thrilled.

5.129 Lit. "rose-apple trees that have their hair standing on end with their fruit." The image with erotic undertones is that the fruit of the rose-apple trees are pictured as having their hair standing on end.

5.137 **Fame** (***kīrti***) is personalized here as a lady, who has a small hill in her pleasure garden to roam around and play with, which is pictured here as the **heap of Danu·kabándha's bones**.

5.139 When Vali squeezed Rávana under his armpit, the celestial throne Rávana usurped was freed for a moment and given back to Indra, thus Vali saved the city from being under two rulers (Rávana and Indra).

5.143 These two, financial supply from the treasury (***kośa***) and the authority to punish, symbolized by the scepter (***daṇḍa***), are the prerequisites to possessing royal authority (*prabhutva*), which is what Rama now desires to obtain through the alliance with Sugríva. He already possesses the other two powers, wit or cleverness (***mantra/śakti***) and perseverance (***utsāha/śakti***).

5.146 Vali is Indra's son, born from Áruna (the red color of dawn, personified as the Sun's charioteer), who took the form of a beautiful woman.

5.146 According to Viṣṇubhaṭṭa, Rama alludes to his plan to propitiate Indra by consecrating Vali's son, Ángada, as the king of monkeys.

5.147 Because he was killed by Lákshmana's arrows, and, leaving his demonic body, ascended to heaven.

5.150 **Manu** is also the ancestor of Rama's dynasty.

5.181 This refers to the story in which Vali squeezed Rávana under his armpits. See "Recurring mythological references and divine attributes" in the Introduction.

5.181 Both Rucipati and Viṣṇubhaṭṭa take this to mean the announcement of the fight. However, the "**encircling**" is probably intended in a double meaning, referring to a greeting as an embrace as well as to a fight.

5.187 And thus Nárada can witness the game, which will be our fight.

5.189 According to Viṣṇubhaṭṭa, it is a praise (*stuti*) of Vali as the son of a great hero, but at the same time an abuse (*nindā*), implying that Indra simply got angry (without taking action).

5.191 What is referred to is that Vali squeezed Rávana under his armpit. (See Jinaharṣagaṇi: *kakṣādarīcārake nikṣipya* = having put him in the prison of the cavity of his armpit; Viṣṇubhaṭṭa's comment implies the same interpretation.) STEINER's interpretation of *vandīkṛtya*, "making him his praising bard," seems wrong.

5.191 This is the right interpretation of ***unmucya***, as is suggested by all the commentaries. STEINER's translation, "freeing the Reva," is wrong (and would require a causative in any case); these two stories of Rávana's defeat are not related anywhere.

5.191 The Reva was not surprised by Vali's victory over Rávana, for it had already seen Árjuna Kartavírya conquer the demon king. On the subjugation of Rávana by Vali and by Árjuna Kartavírya, see "Recurring mythological references and divine attributes" in the Introduction. Viṣṇubhaṭṭa points out that this is again a praise (*stuti*) of Vali's heroism, but it is also an insult (*nindā*), because Árjuna Kartavírya performed a similar act.

5.195 This is a reference to Rama's victory over Párashu·rama, also described in Act 4. The taking up of the **sacrificial ladle** symbolizes that Párashu·rama retires from worldly matters, especially from war, which is appropriate, for he is from a brahmin family.

5.200 Viṣṇubhaṭṭa, who reads the masculine plural, remarks that ***tala*** means "the palms" if in the masculine; but possibly both **soles** and **palms** are intended here.

5.203 This is a reference to the victory of Rávana's brother over Indra's heaven. See "Recurring mythological references and divine attributes" in the Introduction. Indra could not react because he had been cursed by the sage Gáutama to be unmanly.

5.203 Another reference to Vali's victory over Rávana, squeezed under his armpits, and to his being Indra's son.

5.206 This refers again to Árjuna Kartavírya's victory over Rávana. See "Recurring mythological references and divine attributes" in the Introduction.

5.206 Because Párashu·rama conquered Árjuna Kartavírya, but was in turn defeated by Rama. Thus, with a victory over Rama, Vali would prove that he is above all others.

5.215 This refers to the story in which Brahma makes Hánuman forget his heroic qualities because he is afraid of Hánuman's power.

5.229 In addition to the kingdom, Sugríva receives Vali's wife, **Tara**.

5.229 The **teardrops** forming the pearls in it.

6.3 Hánuman burned the city of Lanka with the flame coming from his tail, which had been set on fire by the demons holding him captive, at Rávana's command.

6.7 This refers to the fact that Rávana tried to lift up Shiva's abode and got his fingers crushed by the god. See "Recurring mythological references and divine attributes" in the Introduction.

6.9 As Rucipati and Viṣṇubhaṭṭa point out, these are the four Vedas, the six branches of Vedic studies (*śikṣā*, *kalpa*, *vyākaraṇa*, *nirukta*, *jyotiṣa* and *chandas*) and the *Mīmāṃsā*, *Nyāya*, *Dharmaśāstra* and *Purāṇa*.

6.14 The appellation "**youngest** maternal **grandfather**" may be honorific, without implying any precise relationship.

6.18 I.e., that he calls Vibhíshana respectfully a maharaja. At the same time, this appellation betrays that Vibhíshana has been consecrated by Rama to be the (future) king of Lanka.

6.33 I.e., by Rama and Lákshmana.

6.36 Vibhíshana reminds Rávana that he has been once defeated by a human, Árjuna Kartavírya, and once by a monkey, Vali. For the stories, see "Recurring mythological references and divine attributes" in the Introduction.

6.38 This refers to a myth according to which the Vindhya tried to become the highest mountain. See "Recurring mythological references and divine attributes" in the Introduction.

6.43 These are desire, anger, avidity, pride, delusion and envy (*kāma, krodha, lobha, mada, moha, matsara*).

6.46 Son of Vali, the heir apparent after Sugríva to the throne of the monkey-kingdom.

6.54 Previously, the gods, being subjugated, bowed down before Rávana and touched his lotus-feet with their heads. Now these feet shall be made impure by Rama, i.e., he shall liberate the gods, who will not need to honor Rávana. The feet are metaphorically identified with the impure ***nirmālya***, the flower garland already used in worship, which makes it impure for subsequent use.

6.54 There is perhaps a pun on ***hasta***, which means "hand" but may be used as a synonym of *kara*, "ray." I.e., until Rama's victory over Rávana, the sun withholds its rays, thereby keeping the day-lotuses closed.

6.54 By defeating Rávana, Rama shall give back the sun's powerful radiance and the sweetness of moonbeams. As usual, the moon and its rays are pictured as ambrosia.

6.55 As it is alluded to in the first verse of this act, Hánuman had come to Lanka to explore the demon city before the attack.

6.60 Mályavan already foresees Rávana's defeat and death.

6.62 The word ***guṇa*** has a double meaning here: "rope" or "thread" as well as "quality" or "virtue."

6.62 For he has done everything to protect it well, better than an average king.

6.72 For Rávana still has not given up on possessing Sita.

6.79 Mályavan uses the dual when wishing victory, which creates an ambiguity between the object and the subject, i.e., as to which couple should win. Shuka remarks to himself on the ambiguity of the object and the subject.

6.83 The implied sense, which will be contradicted later, would normally be the following: the tortoises and snakes, i.e., the animals that are supposed to carry the earth, should not be afraid; Kumbha·karna's heavy body will not fall on the ground to create a new burden. This is why Shuka's first reaction is delight.

6.94 Lit. "fie on the mockery scarecrow."

6.96 This refers to Megha·nada's past victory over Indra, who is also the god of rain and whose bow is the rainbow.

6.99 The image is the following: just as a maleficent planet-demon (*graha*) that blocks the rain is propitiated by a priest, so Megha·nada has been pacified in a sacrifice of his weapons, in which Lákshmana acted as the sacrificial priest.

6.103 Instead of going to a **sacred place** to die in a purified state (e.g., to Benares), Mályavan announces that he will go to die in the battle.

6.106 ***Vidya·dhara*s** are semi-divine beings who possess supernatural powers.

6.109 Lit. "girlfriend in heroism," for Lanka is a feminine substantive.

6.111 This is a reference to Indra's defeat by Rávana. See "Recurring mythological references and divine attributes" in the Introduction. What is translated as "**irrigated**" (***a/deva/mātṛka***) is lit. "not having the god [of rain] as mother [to suckle]," i.e., "not rained upon, supplied with water artificially."

6.115 Elephants are supposed to produce **pearls** in the temples, especially when in rut. The **eight directions** of the world are guarded by eight elephants. The fact that their tusks and pearls adorn the doorways indicates that Rávana has conquered the whole world. In the same way, capturing Indra implies the demons' victory over the gods.

6.117 She wants the victory of the demon race, but would prefer that her husband, Rávana, did not obtain Sita.

6.124 A region famous for its good horses (cf. Viṣṇubhaṭṭa).

6.126 Because he has twenty arms to fight against Rama's two arms (according to Viṣṇubhaṭṭa).

6.128 This refers to a myth in which Agástya prevents the Vindhya from becoming too high. See "Recurring mythological references and divine attributes" in the Introduction.

6.132 A dead hero would be showered with flowers by the nymphs. This demon is also covered with flowers, but it is because the flowers of the tree that hit him have fallen on his body.

6.155 For each of his **thousand hoods** carries a jewel.

6.155 The King of Snakes is one of the animals to support the burden of the earth.

6.157 As the commentators explain: just as a monkey, tired of climbing trees, can obtain the fruit of a tree by shaking it, so Sugríva can obtain his death by shaking Rávana's arms.

6.159 For the story of Rávana's offering his heads to Shiva, see "Recurring mythological references and divine attributes" in the Introduction.

6.164 Lit. "garland that is a chaplet of flowers"; but, as the commentators explain, this expresses the fact that Indra could not wear a proper crown, because Rávana was in power. I follow Viṣṇubhaṭṭa's gloss on ***garbhakam***: *svalpam*.

6.164 Because Sugríva has hit it. The word ***prastāvanā*** is a term for the **prologue** at the beginning of a drama, a dialogue between the stage manager and an actor.

6.176 Shiva is pictured here in his Ardha·naríshvara form, of which one side is male and the other is female.

6.187 Why did you need to propitiate Shiva and ask him for a boon, i.e., for the three worlds?

6.189 Rama's ancestor, Anaránya, was overthrown by Rávana in Ayódhya.

6.191 According to Viṣṇubhaṭṭa, Rama feels sorry to fight such a disgraceful warrior.

6.192 **Fame** being white by convention, it is often compared to the **moon**.

6.204 Although there is no rhetorical question in the Sanskrit, the sentence is definitely ironical.

6.208 As Viṣṇubhaṭṭa explains, the **elephants** of the directions had their **ichor** dried up in fear of Rávana, but now they are sure that Rama is to win and are emitting their ichor out of joy.

6.208 Since the arrows shall destroy Rávana, Indra and his wife shall rejoice.

6.210 *Śrī* denotes Vishnu's wife, the **Goddess of Good Fortune and Wealth**. In the form of Vishnu, in a previous birth, Rama had the Káustubha gem (Vishnu's mark) on his chest and was already together with Sita, who is identified with Vishnu's wife.

6.214 **Indra's elephant** is said to have four tusks.

6.215 He has twenty arms, and thus ten **left hands**.

6.216 The epithet refers to Vishnu—here identified again with Rama—who, in his universal form, crossed the three worlds by taking three steps.

6.219 The **scars** were made when he cut his head to prove his devotion to Shiva. For the story, see "Recurring mythological references and divine attributes" in the Introduction.

6.226 As Viṣṇubhaṭṭa remarks, the wording suggests that Rama shall win, for he has actually acquired the knowledge of **mantra-weapons**, while Rávana has simply been taught. The fight seems to be performed here by remembering magical formulas (this being the most probable meaning of both ***mantra*** and ***vidyā*** here), rather than by sending out weapons physically.

6.235 Another reference to the end of the world. On the mark of poison on Bháirava's, i.e., Shiva's, throat, see "Recurring mythological references and divine attributes" in the Introduction.

6.237 The ten radiant heads, together with the real sun. The compound qualifies the "headless body" ***kabandhaḥ*** in the phrase "which made eleven suns visible."

6.241 Elephants of a superior type (***gandha/sindhura***, "scent-elephants") are supposed to emit pearls from their temples when in rut.

6.241 Accepting a variant reading of B (which could explain how the other variants arose), I understand that the wives could not use their makeup because their husbands lost against Rávana, thus there was nothing to celebrate and beautify themselves for.

6.248 For Rávana himself had ten heads and twenty arms.

6.250 I.e., even the wives of gods had to bow down in front of her and touch her feet with their heads to honor her.

6.253 Since Vibhíshana was on the gods' side, his allies followed him.

6.253 For he has also been helpless and imprisoned (cf. Viṣṇubhaṭṭa).

6.256 *Golāṅgūla* is a type of monkey with a dark body, red cheeks and a cow's tail.

6.257 For Rama has killed Rávana, who did this to Lákshmana.

7.6 The seventh **Manu**, the Sun's son, is regarded as the progenitor of all living beings and as the founder of the solar race of kings who ruled Ayódhya.

7.21 Lit. "the place that is the region of birth of Lákshmana's plantain-fame."

7.24 Lit. the goosebumps are also said to be due to her compassion or great affection (*aṇurāa*).

7.26 "**With its magic herbs**" is not in the Sanskrit.

7.33 Because both the water and the ambrosia are liquids.

7.38 With the nectar of immortality that was produced from it.

7.38 Agástya drank up the ocean because it had offended him and also in order to help Indra and the gods in their wars against the Kaleya demons, who had hidden themselves in the waters and oppressed the three worlds.

7.40 On Agástya's story of birth, see "Recurring mythological references and divine attributes" in the Introduction. Lit. the first line describes the sage's "profoundness" and the second his "highness." The first line refers back to the story alluded to in the previous verse, while the second recalls the myth of Agástya and the Vindhya. The Vindhya mountain wanted to rival Mount Meru (the axis mundi) and rose until it obstructed the sun. The gods sent Agástya to solve the problem, and he asked the Vindhya to prostrate itself so that he could be able to go to the South. He also requested the Vindhya to remain in that position until his return. Since he never returned to the North, the Vindhya never attained the height of Meru.

7.49 **"To construct the bridge"** is not in the Sanskrit.

7.55 This mountain, son of Himálaya and Mena, was the only one to retain his wings when Indra clipped those of other mountains, because Mainàka was a friend of the ocean, in which he could hide himself.

7.55 According to Viṣṇubhaṭṭa, the **light of the herbs** reminds one of the fires lit by the camping monkeys; they used the fire either to see the enemy or to cook food on it. According to Rucipati, the place turns reddish because of the light of the medicinal herbs, and it is this reddish color that reminds one of the color of monkeys.

7.63 Lit. "they get wet" (***stimyanti***). According to Viṣṇubhaṭṭa, their skin is scratched and thus they emit their liquid (i.e., as if they were bleeding), which is not only due to the effect of the sun but also because the chariot scratches them.

7.67 According to classical Indian cosmography, the earth is surrounded by seven oceans. Viṣṇubhaṭṭa explains that the oceans surround the earth to protect it, just as an inlaid floor is surrounded with protection so that animals should not trample on it.

7.69 According to Rucipati, the ocean is dark and recalls the color of the black cobra's body.

7.72 **Medicinal herbs** are supposed to grow in mountains. The point of the image is that although Shiva burned up the body of the **God of Love** (Kama), he then still fell in love with Párvati (daughter of Himálaya), thus Párvati resurrected love itself (Viṣṇubhaṭṭa).

7.75 To burn the God of Love, who tried to influence him.

7.77 According to Viṣṇubhaṭṭa, by burning the God of Love he also destroys the universe, for the Self-born Kama is at the origin of the world.

7.80 I.e., he was burned to ashes by Shiva.

7.80 This refers to Shiva's form as half man, half woman, of which the female half is identified with his wife, Párvati.

7.82 My interpretation follows Viṣṇubhaṭṭa's reading and understanding. As Párvati became half of Shiva's body, that was her reward, and the other half, which remained Shiva himself, was the bestower. Shiva figures here as the ascetic who has nothing to give his devotee but his attributes and his own body. If we read ***viṣa*** for *vṛṣa*, the attribute in question is not the bull, Shiva's animal, but the poison he swallowed to save the nectar of immortality for the gods. The word ***eka/cittasya*** in the compound may have a double or triple meaning: that Shiva had only these objects in mind in general (as an ascetic), that he had these objects in mind to give to Párvati, or simply that he is presented in his yogic form here.

7.87 Snake **venom** is supposed to be less effective in the cold season.

7.88 This is another reference to the half man, half woman form of the god, which is pictured here as the goddess joining her body to that of Shiva.

7.92 In the Ardha·naríshvara form, the right side is male and the left side is female, seen here as Párvati's side. In this stanza it is imagined that Párvati also wishes to be united with Shiva's left, and her desire is satisfied in their reflection.

7.94 His **freedom** is to take whatever form he wishes.

7.98 This **mountain**, which was placed on the tortoise avatar of Vishnu during the churning of the milk-ocean to obtain the nectar of immortality, got scratched by Vishnu's arms, which held it and got rubbed on his back as it was used as a churning stick. Thus, as the stanza suggests, although it is considered to be the highest mountain, it was probably even higher before the churning than now. I understand ***mudam ādhatte*** to mean "furnishes joy (to the beholder)," as INGALLS does, but translate it with the adjective "charming."

7.100 Rucipati remarks that the verse is also a general attack on women, which would explain Sita's reply. However, Sita may feel uncomfortable with this remark also because as Vishnu's wife, she is identified with the Goddess of Fortune, Lakshmi. In her reply, she then alludes to Rama's leaving her for a long time.

7.104 This refers to the fact that the moon reappears each night, although it seems to disappear each morning in the sea. Since the Goddess of Fortune is also a product of the sea, she may behave in the same way as the moon.

7.106 The ***kim*** in the questions could be translated as "why." According to Rucipati, the first question implies that this goddess is crooked like the shape of the lotus, and the second that her teacher is something that goes lower and lower (in learning? socially?). The second question follows the first because the water is naturally associated with the lotus, which is Lakshmi's seat according to her iconography. The rhetorical question, lit. "Is it the water that teaches you to approach those who are lower than the low?" may simply refer to the fact that Lakshmi helps mean people.

7.107 Implying that she is on the winner's side, according to Viṣṇu-bhaṭṭa.

7.107 She is compared to lightning, because she is fickle, while Vishnu resembles the rain cloud, with his dark skin.

7.108 According to Viṣṇubhaṭṭa, the line also means "to attain a higher place with those who have the rope [to climb up]"; i.e., there is a wordplay on the two meanings of ***guṇa*** (virtue / thread or rope) and ***uccaiḥ/padaṃ*** (heaven / place above).

7.108 The "**sword blade observance**" is a tantric observance in which erection is maintained without ejaculation. Rucipati wrongly thinks it is walking on a sword blade; Viṣṇubhaṭṭa mentions an observance with a consort toward whom the practitioner should not feel sexual desire, which seems more appropriate. The stanza is again directed at the Goddess of Fortune, and, by extension, at (fickle) women.

7.113 For Rávana lifted it once, to shake Shiva's abode. For the story, see "Recurring mythological references and divine attributes" in the Introduction.

7.113 A class of demigods or spirits, usually dwelling in trees, wells, etc., and guarding hidden treasures.

7.115 "**. . . surrounded with cascading rivers.**" Lit. created the pleasure of the raised seat (***vitardikā***) in the middle of a shower-house. As Ingalls explains, what is meant is that the cascading rivers were like the water flowing outside a shower-house to cool it down.

7.119 "**Thinking he is indeed made of flowers**" is not in the Sanskrit.

7.123 Thus is the explanation of why one does not see the spot on the crescent moon.

7.129 Viṣṇubhaṭṭa explains that the crescent moon resembles silver, while the snake takes the role of the iron bill, to smelt the crescent moon.

7.140 According to Viṣṇubhaṭṭa's second interpretation, the sentence could also mean "Seeing and hearing what he did to him, our eyes and ears were satisfied."

7.145 Because one can have a sense of orientation at night when seeing the moon.

7.145 The **Eastern Mountain** is also where the sun rises.

7.145 The word ***aṅkura***, "shoot," probably also alludes to the pointed shape of the crescent moon. This shoot comes out of what is lit. "the seed of seeing for the world," the Eastern Mountain.

7.147 The moon is associated with this nectar, which is sometimes said to be produced there. The moon's rays are also thought to contain ambrosia.

7.149 I.e., he makes them blossom. Lit. "he takes away the passion of the night-lotuses for the seal of silence."

7.151 The moon is pictured here as a piece of ragged clothing (made up of the digits) that, however, does not tear.

7.151 In the sense that the deer moves there every month, according to Viṣṇubhaṭṭa.

7.155 The meaning of ***varṇ'/āvali*** (and, consequently, the poetic image) is slightly problematic: Rucipati takes the word to mean "a series of letters," i.e., the alphabet; Viṣṇubhaṭṭa understands *varṇ'/āvali* to be a white streak or line (perhaps of chalk, *varṇa/rekhā*). In both cases, the reconstruction takes place by adding another unit to the rest to obtain a full form, just as the moon adds another digit to its body every night, to fill up its disk. If the alphabet is meant here, perhaps there is a reference to the fact that there are sixteen vowels in the Sanskrit alphabet (including the *anusvāra* and the *visarga*), just as the moon has sixteen digits.

7.157 The **trick** was to swallow the poison that was to fall into the milk-ocean and mix with the ambrosia. Thus Shiva saved the ambrosia for the gods. In most accounts, Shiva's wife stops the poison in his throat so that he does not die. Here Murári suggests that it was the moon on Shiva's head that saved him, for the moon itself is supposed to produce ambrosia (and is called ambrosia-rayed, etc).

7.159 Lit. "from the milk-ocean as a seashell."

7.160 **Róhini** is the personification of the fourth lunar mansion.

7.164 The moonbeams have new shoots as they are nourished by the nectar flowing out of **moonstones**, which are melting because of the moonlight.

7.166 I.e., he opens up the petals. The lotus provides the stage on which the moon is the dancer and the bees form the orchestra.

7.166 I.e., he gives his ambrosia-rays to them as food. The Pondicherry edition has *toya* for ***toṣa***, but Viṣṇubhaṭṭa's understanding seems to support *toṣa*.

7.171 Viṣṇubhaṭṭa explains that while moving his heads in appreciation, the head-jewels of the king of snakes rub against the surface of the earth from below (from the netherworld, where snakes are supposed to live), and thus they illuminate the darkness of that realm. According to the conceit of the stanza, although snakes have no ears, they can better listen to Rama's story because they are undisturbed by the sound of their earrings, which would otherwise jingle too loud as they are moving their heads.

7.175 Moonlight makes the day-lotus close. The implication is that if the moon had not made the blunder to close Brahma's lotus-seat, Brahma would have made it as charming as Sita's face.

7.177 Just as one weighs gold on a balance and the larger weight needs to be completed with smaller ones to have the equivalence, the stars need to be added to the moon to have the equivalent of Sita's face (Rucipati).

7.184 Lit. "the first line," which is interpreted by commentators as the first small and crooked line one draws when counting.

7.184 It is the full moon that is compared to the face of women, but the new moon is its source. Each comparison is partly based either on the idea that the new moon represents a beginning or on its shape.

7.185 The crescent moon needs to be in that high position, on Shiva's head, to be seen, while the full moon is visible in any position.

7.187 Rama adds another thought here on the subject of the difference between the full / full moon and the not full / crescent moon.

7.189 Thus, the moonstones and the stars perform the ritual of welcoming a guest. I follow MIŚRA, STEINER and INGALLS in the interpretation of ***nijair niryāsair***. Viṣṇubhaṭṭa and Rucipati take the expression to refer to the light of the stars.

7.203 Lit. "carved out with a spindle-hatchet."

7.211 For the myths alluded to here about Agástya, see "Recurring mythological references and divine attributes" in the Introduction.

7.213 Rucipati understands that they were seen by people. Viṣṇubhaṭṭa seems to say that Agástya himself saw them, and, out of compassion, he re-emitted the water he had drunk. The mountains were hiding in the sea to escape from Indra, who wanted to clip their wings. For the story, see "Recurring mythological references and divine attributes" in the Introduction.

7.213 Lit. "voices have not got the sentiment of courage for [singing] his praises."

7.215 Lit. "the pathways where there is a doubt / fright created by the up-flying *chakóras*."

7.217 Rucipati understands that the **pearls** go from the lap of the river to the laps of women. Viṣṇubhaṭṭa rightly points out that the river is pictured as a woman who receives the semen in the form of water drops. Thus the pearls are the river's children, looked after and entertained by women of beautiful eyebrows, who actually use them as pieces of jewelry.

7.219 The implications in this stanza are not entirely clear. Perhaps the water drops may be in contact with the breasts because women bathe in the river, and therefore they are rewarded with a rebirth as pearls (which perhaps also implies that they will be worn on these women's breasts).

7.228 Lit. the four oceans were the pre-meal water, drunk while reciting prayer. Viṣṇubhaṭṭa has *apo/'śāna*, while Rucipati writes ***āpo/'śāna***, both in the same sense.

7.232 I.e., once when Marícha wanted to destroy the sacrifice and once when he lured Sita away.

7.235 Because of the **shining gems** in the mountain, all the birds think it is daylight, even at night. Thus, the owls hide themselves and the ravens make noise.

7.235 The expression "**deities of the forest**" also means trees. Lit. they lift up the lianas of the trees.

7.238 As the commentators point out, the slightly bent *kínshuka* buds are meant to imitate the nail marks left by a lover; that is why Rama has metaphorically deprived Sita of her chastity, by expressing his desire for her in this way.

7.244 The **sweat drops** (which are produced during lovemaking) are pictured here as forming the water in which the *mákara* designs bathe. (Alternatively, "sweat drops over which the *mákaras* of love enjoy lordship.") The ***mákara***, a mythical aquatic animal often confused with the crocodile, is the vehicle of the God of Love. The stanza is more precisely about women of the Vidárbha region (modern Berar). I follow Rucipati's reading of the feminine. Note that Viṣṇubhaṭṭa may also have read the same; he omits the word in the commentary.

7.244 Lit. the rows or garlands of goosebumps.

7.246 A style (one out of six) devoid of harsh words and sentiments, with short compounds. See, e.g., *Kāvyādarśa* 1.41–53, *Sāhityadarpaṇa* 626 and *Pratāparaudrīya* p. 47, cited by Viṣṇubhaṭṭa.

7.246 A style (one out of four) presenting a delicate subject matter dominated by love and compassion. See, e.g., *Sāhityadarpaṇa* 411 or *Pratāparudrīya* p. 43, cited by Viṣṇubhaṭṭa.

7.250 Lit. the flavor (***rasa***), following the reading of Viṣṇubhaṭṭa, who understands it in the sense of "passion" (*anurāga*). Párvati formed one half of Shiva's half man, half woman body before leaving it.

7.255 Lit. by the "large veil of bristle-like goosebumps." As the commentaries explain, the **goosebumps** compensate for the slipperiness, so finally they do manage to embrace each other strongly; Viṣṇubhaṭṭa remarks that it implies continuous pleasure.

7.263 I.e., their faces are more radiant than the moon.

7.264 The Lord of Time / Death.

7.267 Shiva's burning of Kama is pictured here as a form of his grace to save the world from an untimely destruction.

7.269 **Svaha** is an exclamation used when offering oblations to the gods. It is also the name of such an oblation, and is personified as the wife of Agni, the Fire.

7.287 According to Viṣṇubhaṭṭa, the stanza implies that although Shiva remains in Kailása, his favorite city is still Benares.

7.293 **"Caused by Shiva's bowstring"** is not in the Sanskrit.

7.298 Lit. with embraces tight at the body joints, thickening with goosebumps.

7.299 This is in fact the tract of land between the two rivers.

7.299 Since, according to tradition, the water of the Yámuna is dark and that of the Ganga is fair.

7.302 In mythology, the Ganga is said to originate from **Vishnu's toenail**, when the god took the form of a dwarf. She descended from heaven through Shiva's hair, in which her passage led her near the moon, worn by Shiva. And, lastly, her earthly origin is in the Himalayas, the abode of snow.

7.304 The place where the Ganga and the Yámuna meet, near today's Allahabad.

7.306 There is perhaps an allusion to the fact that these river goddesses are often depicted on the two sides of temple doors.

7.311 The **Sárayu** is the river on whose bank Ayódhya stands.

7.313 As is common in Sanskrit poetry, the eyes are compared to lotuses.

7.325 Lit. obtained auspicious fame.

7.339 This demon named "Conqueror of Indra" here, but otherwise called Megha·nada, son of Rávana, had conquered Indra once but was defeated by Lákshmana later.

7.344 Rama's name, Rama·chandra (lit. "Moon-Rama"), is probably alluded to here.

7.344 Both the goddess Lakshmi (Vishnu's wife) and the Káustubha stone were produced at the churning of the milk-ocean, therefore they are considered brother and sister.

7.352 He who served Rama's sandals is Bharata, who put the sandals on the throne to show that Rama was the real king to govern the country.

7.365 The fact that Rama defeated Párashu·rama implies that he could then easily defeat Rávana—thus the story need not be told to learn about what happened, the outcome of the *Rāmāyaṇa* is evident. If poets sing about Rama's fight against Rávana and his other exploits, it is to delight their audience with the storytelling itself, whose ending is not questionable.

7.370 As the commentators explain, visible harm implies political threat, and invisible harm means such things as natural catastrophes.

7.377 **Varáha** is an avatar of Vishnu in the form of a wild boar. Following Viṣṇubhaṭṭa, both the Vindhya and Varáha's **tusk** are impenetrable, and that is why the metaphor is used. Jinaharṣa-gaṇi has the same understanding of the compound. The image refers to Rama's exile in the forest of the Vindhya.

7.381 Poetic words have a magical power in that they make fame live long (Viṣṇubhaṭṭa).

7.381 Lit. "may it plunge in the space surrounded by the flesh of the ears." Note that Viṣṇubhaṭṭa understands ***guṇa*** not as merit but in the sense of "word / sound" (*śabda*).

INDEX

Sanskrit words are given in the English alphabetical order, according to the accented CSL pronunciation aid. They are followed by the conventional diacritics in brackets.

affliction, 293
Agástya *(Agastya)*, 22, 313, 509, 513, 589, 598, 601, 608
Agni *(Agni)*, 584, 611
Ahálya *(Ahalyā)*, 109, 219
Ájagava *(Ajagava)*, 533
Aksha *(Akṣa)*, 373
Álaka *(Alakā)*, 523
Amarávati *(Amarāvatī)*, 345, 371, 489
ambrosia, 57, 71, 79, 95, 99, 105, 141, 159, 165, 167, 299, 359, 495, 497, 572, 596, 601, 606, 607
  word-, 57
Anaránya *(Anaraṇya)*, 209, 427, 580, 599
ancestor, 65, 67, 89, 201, 267, 299, 303, 341, 347, 427, 451, 533, 568, 569, 571, 582, 593, 599
Andhra *(Āndhra)*, 519
Ángada *(Aṅgada)*, 24, 367, 381, 389, 592
anger, 137, 155, 209, 211, 217, 219, 247, 261, 271, 275, 287, 315, 327, 329, 343, 433, 585, 587, 595
Ángiras *(Aṅgiras)*, 177, 189, 277
Antar·vedi *(Antarvedi)*, 535
archer, 221, 227, 305
archery, 83, 85, 221, 263, 283, 287, 533
Ardha·naríshvara *(Ardhanārīśvara)*, 599, 603
Árjuna Kartavírya *(Arjuna Kārtavīrya)*, 211, 213, 253, 261, 265, 267, 289, 357, 361, 377, 427, 549, 584, 585, 593–595
army, 75, 117, 247, 363, 373, 389, 399, 403, 457, 577
  of demons, 117, 155, 157
  of monkeys, 379, 467
  of Rávana, 457
  of Sugríva, 459
Áruna *(Aruṇā)*, 592
Arúndhati *(Arundhatī)*, 65, 69, 569
ascetic, 65, 67, 73, 87, 89, 91, 93, 97, 111, 113, 131, 135, 143, 155, 157, 191, 251, 263, 295, 311, 333, 425, 483, 585, 603
asceticism, 69, 127, 129, 143, 243, 265, 277, 327, 473, 583
ashram, 533
Ashva·medha *(Aśvamedha)*, 69, 569
assembly, 49, 129, 271, 417, 586
Atri *(Atri)*, 167, 169, 578
autumn, 67, 507
Avánti *(Avanti)*, 523
Ayódhya *(Ayodhyā)*, 22, 25, 121, 249, 311, 451, 459, 507, 537, 539, 599, 601, 611

Bahu·rupa *(Bahurūpa)*, 49
bark, 163
bath, 135, 139, 497, 609, 610
battle, 71, 75, 169, 211, 213, 251, 261, 265, 359, 391, 399, 403, 405, 415, 419, 423, 427, 429, 437, 489, 539, 541, 569, 576, 597
battle-axe, 253, 261, 265, 271, 275, 279, 281, 287, 291, 297, 584, 586, 587
battlefield, 285, 363, 365, 439
beauty, 57, 167, 349, 503, 537
bees, 607
beings, 91, 111, 249, 415, 457, 461, 463, 572, 585, 597, 601
Bháirava *(Bhairava)*, 439
Bharata *(Bharata)*, 21, 22, 177, 225, 241, 249, 301, 305, 311, 313, 539, 543, 545, 547, 549, 612
Bhatta Vardhamána *(Bhaṭṭa Vardhamāna)*, 53
Bhrigu *(Bhṛgu)*, 259, 263, 267, 275, 287, 297, 361, 585, 587
birds, 163, 433, 523, 525, 527, 576, 609
  king of, 331, 457
  lord of, 527
blossom, 127, 333, 419, 497, 507, 592
boat
  of Guha, 309
body, 75, 111, 121, 147, 153, 175, 179, 233, 249, 253, 309, 333, 335, 361, 391, 435, 439, 441, 443, 455, 469, 473, 475, 477, 483, 493, 495, 505, 511, 515, 519, 521, 531, 568, 589, 593, 597, 598, 600–603, 606, 610, 611
  kshátriya, 69
  mortal, 568
boon, 213, 237, 599
bow, 75, 139, 141, 151, 153, 155, 157, 205, 217, 219, 221, 223, 253, 255, 259, 261, 263, 265, 277, 279, 289, 291, 313, 315, 327, 335, 359, 363, 393, 405, 419, 421, 423, 445, 515, 527, 580, 581, 585, 588
  of Indra, 75, 205, 580, 597
  of Shiva, 141, 171, 177, 183, 193, 203, 205, 207, 215, 217, 225, 243, 245, 247, 253, 255, 261, 267, 269, 275, 287, 289, 353, 527, 533, 578, 584, 586
  of Vishnu, 293
  Shiva's, 203
Brahma *(Brahma)*, 89
Brahma *(Brahmā)*, 45, 57, 67, 79, 147, 199, 205, 273, 281, 329, 363, 371, 403, 435, 439, 461, 501, 529, 531, 541, 553, 581, 585–587, 590, 594, 607
Brahman *(Brahman)*, 139
Bráhmana *(Brāhmaṇa)*
  Shata·patha *(Śatapatha)*, 191
brahmin, 111
breast, 93, 157, 181, 235, 313, 385, 389, 477, 511, 515, 517, 519, 609

large, 311, 431
round, 49, 161, 431, 477
bride
newlywed, 235
bridegroom, 195
bride-price, 201, 203, 217
bridge, 463
Brihas·pati *(Bṛhaspati)*, 539
brother, 49, 89, 93, 99, 127, 129, 131, 133, 135, 137, 141, 145, 151, 177, 191, 193, 207, 211, 223, 281, 283, 289, 301, 321, 327, 329, 331, 333, 337, 339, 343, 345, 347, 351, 355, 361, 363, 371, 375, 377, 379, 391, 463, 483, 529, 543, 545, 547, 566, 571, 588, 594, 612
bull, 115, 473, 603
burden, 83, 85, 107, 241, 299, 379, 385, 391, 435, 551, 588, 597, 598
capital, 233, 371, 401, 523, 533, 566
care, 83, 483
cave, 283, 333, 465, 467, 503, 515, 588
chakóra *(cakora)*, 45, 79, 149, 159, 163, 167, 497, 511, 523, 566, 576, 609
Champa *(Campā)*, 533
Chandra·hasa *(Candrahāsa)*, 339, 403, 433
channels, 131
chariot, 79, 115, 137, 321, 331, 337, 395, 399, 405, 417, 419, 423, 427, 429, 435, 451, 455, 459, 467, 469, 487, 491, 507, 515, 517, 519, 529, 537, 539, 551, 578, 602
charioteer, 423, 427, 592
chastity, 259, 333, 517, 609
Chedi *(Chedi)*, 527
Chitra·kuta *(Citrakūṭa)*, 22, 311
Chyávana *(Cyavana)*, 277
city, 169, 237, 241, 253, 309, 345, 371, 393, 399, 403, 411, 445, 451, 473, 489, 499, 519, 521, 523, 527, 531, 533, 537, 539, 592, 595, 596, 611
claw, 133, 283, 331, 485, 505
clothes, 115, 141, 289, 339, 353, 515
clouds, 71, 75, 81, 121, 333, 461, 469, 489, 517, 591
companion, 513
compassion, 151, 155, 333, 335, 343, 439, 443, 459, 601, 608, 610
conch, 45, 95, 511, 566
conduct, 203, 243, 349
consecrated, 253, 357, 375, 445, 595
consecration, 299, 445, 537, 539, 549
coral, 572
country, 169, 251, 305, 521, 523, 527, 589, 612
cow, 191, 289, 579
cream, 479, 535
creator, 45, 107, 165, 237, 329, 403, 425, 499
creature, 229, 285
crocodile, 481, 610
crossroads, 57

crown, 477
curse, 347, 361, 363, 419, 575, 582, 591, 594
Daksha *(Dakṣa)*, 495
dancer, 607
Dándaka *(Daṇḍaka)*, 249, 251, 301, 333, 351, 513, 517
Danu *(Danu)*, 591
Danu·kabándha *(Danukabandha)*, 335, 337, 591
darbha *(darbha)*, 161
Dasha·ratha *(Daśaratha)*, 15, 17, 18, 20–22, 57, 59, 63, 69, 71, 87, 91, 95, 97, 153, 175, 197, 199, 225, 241, 249, 251, 261, 275, 281, 285, 291, 297, 299, 301, 303, 305, 309, 355, 365, 459, 567–569, 571, 572, 576, 578, 579, 589
daughter, 97, 117, 141, 183, 193, 195, 209, 215, 225, 229, 303, 331, 335, 385, 421, 459, 463, 465, 467, 473, 495, 543, 578, 602
dawn, 81, 105, 121, 145, 197, 233, 235, 355, 592
death, 55, 139, 155, 259, 269, 271, 367, 389, 393, 405, 433, 443, 491, 495, 583, 584, 586, 590, 596, 598, 610
deer, 95, 129, 267, 487
  black, 319
  eyes of, 343
  female, 343
  golden, 23, 321, 515
  in the moon, 161, 485, 493, 505
  pregnant, 333
defeat, 401
demon, 15, 17–20, 22–24, 53, 63, 71, 81, 93, 113, 117, 119, 137, 139, 151, 155, 157, 165, 167, 169, 179, 207, 209, 213, 229, 243, 245, 251, 261, 273, 277, 303, 313, 315, 317, 321, 323, 335, 337, 347, 351, 357, 359, 373, 379, 383, 387, 391, 393, 399, 401, 405, 407, 409, 411, 413, 421, 423, 433, 435, 437, 439, 445, 451, 455, 459, 479, 515, 523, 525, 527, 566, 569, 573, 575, 576, 578, 580, 583–585, 590, 591, 593, 595–598, 601
demoness, 18–20, 23, 109, 117, 141, 261, 315, 399, 427, 443, 459, 576, 584
departure, 83
desire, 63, 65, 69, 79, 133, 163, 177, 181, 201, 207, 309, 361, 387, 389, 527, 533, 590, 592, 595, 605, 609
destruction, 379
Deva·daru *(Devadāru)*, 471, 585
devotee, 217, 219, 603
devotion, 573, 600
Dhanvántari *(Dhanvantari)*, 461
Dhara·dhara *(Dhārādhara)*, 22, 313
Dilípa *(Dilīpa)*, 71, 569
disgrace, 283, 427, 599
distress, 73, 201, 211, 275, 417

divine, 53, 55, 119, 197, 247, 261, 329, 437, 475, 590
Drona *(Droṇa)*, 459
drum, 365, 401
duel, 275, 363, 405, 457
Dúndubhi *(Dundubhi)*, 337, 351
Durga *(Durgā)*, 471
dynasty, 51, 57, 69, 71, 73, 77, 83, 85, 87, 91, 93, 153, 157, 177, 195, 197, 237, 249, 263, 275, 279, 281, 283, 285, 289, 293, 299, 321, 337, 419, 421, 435, 451, 459, 467, 537, 539, 541, 547, 570, 571, 576, 587, 593
earth, 63, 65, 69, 75, 81, 85, 87, 93, 135, 147, 161, 171, 197, 227, 261, 269, 271, 273, 279, 287, 291, 303, 355, 359, 391, 413, 415, 435, 439, 441, 463, 465, 469, 485, 487, 489, 495, 497, 499, 505, 529, 533, 537, 543, 551, 553, 568, 570–572, 574, 579, 581, 583, 585, 597, 598, 602, 607
elders, 267, 277, 281, 283, 303, 323, 533, 590
elephant, 63, 83, 93, 95, 107, 115, 117, 119, 133, 229, 259, 261, 267, 283, 331, 401, 405, 411, 421, 431, 433, 435, 441, 489, 547, 581, 582, 584, 591, 597, 599, 600
enemies, 73, 75, 113, 115, 127, 167, 223, 239, 265, 293, 355, 357, 375, 377, 379, 381, 399, 403, 405, 411, 429, 431, 433, 443, 499, 541, 580, 586, 602
exile, 589
fame, 51, 79, 87, 119, 157, 193, 197, 229, 289, 305, 311, 343, 361, 365, 399, 409, 427, 455, 457, 505, 541, 553, 567, 570, 579, 582, 589, 590, 592, 599, 611, 613
family, 53, 57, 65, 67, 69, 71, 83, 85, 87, 91, 175, 177, 209, 217, 277, 279, 281, 283, 285, 301, 305, 341, 347, 353, 359, 373, 377, 387, 437, 463, 495, 501, 503, 515, 527, 543, 545, 549, 569, 572, 587, 594
fate, 205, 327, 347, 361, 371, 377, 387, 415, 471, 481
father, 57, 89, 91, 95, 99, 113, 179, 223, 263, 275, 281, 289, 295, 297, 303, 305, 311, 313, 341, 347, 351, 361, 381, 387, 459, 467, 473, 475, 529, 535, 551, 572, 584, 585, 587, 588
favor, 63, 79, 85, 99, 169, 297, 349, 507, 511, 611
feast, 79, 247, 261, 333, 411, 527
  wedding, 205, 225, 247, 581
feet, 69, 109, 259, 457, 503, 525, 541, 583, 596, 600
  lotus, 77, 383, 443, 596
fetus, 263
  deer, 333
fire, 77, 129, 147, 151, 165, 189, 199, 207, 233, 247, 253, 259, 267, 273, 277, 287, 303, 315, 349, 371, 395, 401, 409, 413,

425, 439, 451, 461, 463, 471, 477, 487, 525, 527, 541, 581, 584, 587, 595, 602, 611
sacrificial, 93, 127, 145, 415
firm, 287, 353
firmness, 181
flame, 145, 147, 149, 189, 261, 273, 275, 371, 389, 409, 415, 421, 439, 463, 471, 487, 584, 587, 595
floor
inlaid, 491
flower, 69, 133, 139, 145, 197, 229, 237, 287, 341, 367, 383, 399, 401, 403, 405, 407, 413, 419, 443, 445, 483, 489, 509, 517, 553, 575, 582, 591, 596, 598
lotus, 57
forehead, 239, 415, 471, 523
forest, 49, 129, 135, 161, 213, 247, 251, 295, 301, 305, 313, 315, 319, 321, 327, 329, 333, 341, 343, 351, 401, 405, 417, 445, 471, 489, 513, 515, 517, 519, 537, 585, 609, 613
forest-dweller, 91
forest-dwelling, 73, 263, 295
fortnight
dark, 79, 505
freedom, 477
friend, 383
fruit, 113, 135, 155, 227, 313, 341, 417, 487, 539, 592, 598
Gadhi *(Gādhi)*, 69, 87, 569
Ganga *(Gaṅgā)*, 511, 529, 531, 535, 537, 541, 553, 611
garden, 399, 455
of paradise, 445
pleasure, 592
garland, 339, 399, 403, 433, 485, 489, 517, 531, 598, 610
flower, 139, 287, 399, 401, 403, 575, 582, 596
jasmine, 197
lotus, 343, 365, 483
of bones, 115
of rays, 105
garment, 259, 303, 339, 341, 575
bark, 109, 135, 157
Gáruda *(Garuḍa)*, 53, 195, 457
Gauda *(Gauḍa)*, 533
Gáutama *(Gautama)*, 18, 109, 219, 279, 594
Gayátri *(Gāyatrī)*, 295
gems, 121, 415, 423, 481, 515, 609
girl, 141, 171, 181, 215, 227, 293
glory, 63, 299, 547, 549
god, 71, 107, 109, 127, 139, 155, 199, 203, 217, 221, 237, 267, 273, 329, 347, 357, 361, 365, 385, 391, 393, 423, 437, 451, 471, 473, 483, 487, 491, 501, 525, 543, 551, 553, 573, 581, 585, 595, 597, 603, 611
of darkness, 437
of death, 139, 259, 269, 271, 405, 443
of fire, 584
of justice, 81
of love, 111, 181, 413, 437, 471, 473, 475, 493, 501, 521, 523,

525, 527, 533, 570, 602, 603, 610
of the ocean, 459
of wind, 363, 576
Godávari *(Godāvarī)*, 319, 517, 519
goddess, 57, 65, 77, 229, 269, 273, 389, 465, 471, 473, 475, 483, 511, 517, 529, 533, 535, 537, 570, 582, 603, 604, 611, 612
of fortune, 93, 211, 213, 227, 245, 261, 305, 367, 379, 403, 459, 461, 479, 481, 545, 570, 599, 604, 605
of heroes, 533
of heroism, 401
of speech, 55
of victory, 265, 363, 425, 445
of wealth, 431
gods, 65, 73, 75, 77, 79, 81, 89, 91, 93, 113, 141, 157, 169, 175, 177, 205, 247, 251, 255, 273, 309, 337, 357, 377, 383, 399, 401, 403, 405, 407, 417, 423, 433, 435, 437, 441, 443, 445, 461, 479, 483, 487, 489, 491, 495, 507, 525, 543, 568, 570, 572, 574, 578, 582, 585, 586, 596, 597, 600, 601, 603, 607, 611
gold, 465, 608
goosebumps, 97, 235, 521
grace, 65, 309, 497, 551, 610
grain, 503
millet, 131
rice, 129, 131, 163, 574
grandfather, 241, 245, 255, 373, 427
great, 427
greeting, 533, 549
grief, 179, 189, 195, 209
ocean of, 395
grove
ashoka, 377
guardians
of the directions, 551
guest, 119, 127, 157, 165, 191, 197, 219, 295, 365, 578, 608
guest-offering, 161
Guha *(Guha)*, 22–24, 309, 311, 317, 335, 337, 341, 345, 347, 349
Háihaya *(Haihaya)*, 265
hair, 71, 113, 237, 411, 487, 503, 529, 533, 611
body, 379
braided, 357
curly, 131
gray, 175
matted, 129, 265
white, 63
half man, half woman, 475, 477, 603, 610
hand, 141, 179, 183, 193, 201, 215, 237, 259, 265, 271, 279, 321, 387, 413, 421, 429, 445, 473, 475, 483, 493, 513, 525, 529, 533, 578
left, 433
lotus-like, 235
right, 477

Hánuman *(Hanumān)*, 18, 21, 24, 115, 117, 249, 309, 339, 341, 363, 365, 371, 373, 377, 383, 419, 459, 503, 507, 594–596
happiness, 57, 189, 299, 467, 477, 545
head, 49, 57, 77, 97, 107, 129, 149, 213, 221, 253, 265, 305, 309, 323, 331, 339, 371, 383, 385, 391, 403, 407, 415, 417, 423, 425, 431, 437, 439, 441, 451, 455, 459, 473, 483, 485, 489, 495, 501, 505, 517, 521, 529, 531, 535, 573, 588, 590, 600, 607, 608
  crowned, 69, 419
head-jewel, 97, 147, 171, 441, 457, 469, 499, 501, 531, 607
headdress, 139, 495
heart, 63, 79, 139, 141, 147, 153, 159, 163, 169, 181, 193, 199, 201, 211, 227, 237, 239, 241, 265, 269, 271, 275, 281, 293, 313, 321, 329, 339, 341, 343, 349, 359, 361, 363, 385, 389, 403, 413, 433, 443, 465, 517, 527
heaven, 51, 55, 67, 111, 127, 139, 153, 183, 197, 261, 311, 337, 359, 439, 455, 481, 553, 568, 570, 574, 593, 611
  kingdom of, 213
  of heroes, 329
  of Indra, 161, 594
Hemángada *(Hemāṅgada)*, 399, 401, 437
herb
  glowing, 467
  healing, 463, 471, 473
  magical, 459
hermitage, 57, 69, 81, 109, 127, 131, 133, 143, 145, 151, 247, 299, 315, 341, 513
hero, 51, 55, 73, 157, 213, 217, 245, 263, 269, 271, 275, 283, 299, 327, 329, 337, 345, 351, 355, 357, 359, 363, 365, 371, 385, 391, 393, 401, 405, 415, 419, 433, 437, 439, 443, 455, 457, 481, 489, 501, 525, 586, 593
  dead, 598
Himálaya *(Himālaya)*, 467, 471, 473, 475, 535, 602
homage, 45, 249, 275, 295, 315, 339, 441, 461, 463, 475, 479, 483, 503, 515, 525, 529, 531, 533, 537, 547
home, 65, 73, 87, 151, 199, 215, 219, 295, 297, 381, 509, 529
honest, 245
horse, 69, 137, 427, 445, 487, 598
  sacrificial, 197
house, 119, 157, 199, 225, 235, 401, 451
  royal, 93, 109, 117, 153, 171, 177, 227, 303
householder, 73, 127, 139, 574, 581
hunter, 319, 333, 341, 343
husband, 65, 111, 193, 251, 263, 289, 303, 367, 407, 447, 459,

515, 539, 543, 571, 580, 598, 600
good, 201
imaginary, 315
hymn, 55, 93, 199, 223, 441
iconography, 604
Ikshváku *(Ikṣvāku)*, 51, 53, 71, 77, 91, 171, 215, 227, 249, 279, 285, 341, 537, 543, 570
illness
mental, 331
Indra *(Indra)*, 16, 18, 65, 71, 73, 75, 77, 99, 107, 111, 113, 143, 177, 199, 211, 219, 251, 337, 345, 347, 355, 357, 365, 367, 401, 403, 405, 423, 429, 431, 445, 483, 499, 539, 543, 569, 570, 574, 576, 578, 580, 582, 592–594, 597–599, 601, 602, 608, 612
Índrajit *(Indrajit)*, 24, 543
induction
proof by, 379
Índumati *(Indumatī)*, 79
íngudi *(iṅgudī)*, 311
instrument, 279, 291, 353
intoxicated, 159, 209, 576
Jamad·agni *(Jamadagni)*, 259, 587
Jámbavan *(Jāmbavān)*, 18, 21–23, 113, 247, 249, 309, 321, 351, 365, 573, 589
Jánaka *(Janaka)*, 19, 20, 22, 109, 171, 175, 177, 183, 189, 191, 193, 195, 197, 201, 203, 205, 207, 209, 211, 213, 215, 217, 221, 225, 227, 229, 253, 273, 277, 295, 297, 299, 305, 331, 335, 459, 467, 543, 578–580, 587, 588
Jánaki *(Jānakī)*, 495
Jana·sthana *(Janasthāna)*, 251, 313, 315, 319, 515
Jatáyus *(Jatāyus)*, 23, 319, 323, 329
jewel, 239, 243, 435, 455, 477, 495, 525
jewelry, 115, 485, 609
journey, 81
joy, 49, 53, 63, 71, 155, 159, 189, 199, 201, 233, 299, 321, 341, 423, 433, 451, 457, 499, 527
feigned, 75
tears of, 367
Kabándha *(Kabandha)*, 23, 335, 347
kadámba *(kadamba)*, 333, 341, 592
Kadru *(Kadrū)*, 457
Kaikéyi *(Kaikeyī)*, 21, 22, 249, 301, 303, 305, 589
Kailása *(Kailāsa)*, 211, 217, 371, 413, 481, 483, 531, 573, 611
Káitabha *(Kaiṭabha)*, 63
Kakútstha *(Kakutstha)*, 57, 195, 225, 237, 361, 463, 539, 567
Kala·hánsika *(Kalahaṃsikā)*, 175
Kama *(Kāma)*, 570, 602, 603, 610
Kanchi *(Kāñcī)*, 521
karma *(karma)*, 511
Káshyapa *(Kaśyapa)*, 267, 585

kátaka *(kataka)*, 161
Kaushálya *(Kauśalyā)*, 18, 101
Káushiki *(Kauśikī)*, 133, 519
Káustubha *(Kaustubha)*, 99, 127, 195, 431, 461, 507, 545, 572, 599, 612
Kékaya *(Kekaya)*, 303, 305, 311
Késarin *(Kesarin)*, 115
Khala·churi *(Khalacurī)*, 361, 527
kindness, 111
king, 63, 67, 69, 71, 81, 83, 91, 93, 139, 171, 175, 177, 183, 191, 195, 197, 201, 203, 205, 211, 215, 217, 219, 225, 227, 229, 237, 239, 243, 249, 251, 253, 255, 259, 267, 275, 279, 281, 287, 289, 291, 303, 305, 309, 311, 313, 317, 319, 331, 339, 345, 351, 359, 361, 365, 367, 375, 377, 381, 409, 413, 423, 425, 431, 439, 443, 445, 451, 459, 527, 539, 543, 547, 570, 579, 580, 583, 584, 587, 595, 596, 601, 612
  demon, 53, 63, 113, 117, 157, 209, 213, 229, 245, 321, 351, 357, 379, 387, 391, 413, 421, 435, 437, 439, 459, 566, 573, 593
  elephant, 93
  good, 81, 549, 571
  monkey, 113, 115, 213, 337, 343, 347, 351, 411, 413, 417, 419, 463, 592
  of love, 509
  of the gods, 81, 89, 157, 399, 403, 483, 574, 582
  of the underworld, 81
  of treasures, 531
  snake, 79, 97, 221, 223, 415, 435, 441, 479, 499, 519, 581, 598, 607
  tortoise, 83, 391
kingdom, 113, 127, 189, 213, 247, 301, 349, 367, 385, 549, 551, 579, 594, 595
kingship, 385
kínshuka *(kiṃśuka)*, 133, 505, 517, 609
Kishkíndha *(Kiṣkindhā)*, 18, 24, 113, 247, 355, 363, 367, 381, 547
Krauncha *(Krauñca)*, 283, 287, 467, 587
Krisháshva *(Kṛśāśva)*, 83, 85
kshatriya, 109
Kubéra *(Kubera)*, 551, 573
Kumbha·karna *(Kumbhakarṇa)*, 24, 389, 391
Kúndina *(Kuṇḍina)*, 519
kúrari *(kurarī)*, 321
kusha *(kuśa)*, 131, 155, 259
Kúshika *(Kuśika)*, 69, 71, 85, 241
Lákshmana *(Lakṣmaṇa)*, 17, 19–25, 89, 91, 93, 95, 97, 101, 119, 127, 141, 145, 155, 167, 171, 177, 183, 189, 197, 199, 207, 209, 211, 219, 221, 223, 281, 283, 289, 301, 309, 321, 327, 331, 333, 335, 337, 339, 345, 349, 353, 355, 363, 365,

387, 389, 391, 393, 445, 451, 455, 457, 459, 543, 545, 547, 567, 580, 587, 591, 595, 597, 601, 612
Lakshmi *(Lakṣmī)*, 49, 604
lament, 205, 401
lamp, 535
Lanka *(Laṅkā)*, 24, 25, 117, 211, 215, 227, 229, 237, 317, 319, 351, 361, 371, 387, 393, 399, 407, 409, 413, 439, 443, 445, 451, 455, 463, 503, 507, 509, 547, 551, 566, 595–597
law, 151, 153, 165, 201, 429
  books of, 576
  of fish, 81
  of warriors, 155
lawful, 109, 299
lawlessness, 379
libation
  midday, 135
life, 87, 139, 233, 249, 299, 305, 327, 365, 443, 465, 495, 576, 582
  long, 175, 237, 493
  previous, 143
  stages of, 181
life-breath, 457
life-force, 73, 155
lightning, 409, 481, 485
lion, 133, 267, 283, 331, 439, 485, 505, 585
Lopámudra *(Lopāmudrā)*, 513
lord, 45, 49, 75, 93, 115, 117, 155, 171, 221, 229, 237, 241, 251, 261, 263, 271, 295, 297, 317, 347, 351, 361, 363, 367, 393, 395, 423, 461, 473, 483, 485, 487, 495, 501, 505, 515, 519, 525, 527, 529, 531, 580
  demon, 245
  of ghosts, 485
  of goblins, 269
  of light, 105, 235, 277
  of riches, 115, 573
  of rivers, 405
  of serpents, 205
  of snakes, 391, 485, 499, 521
  of the gods, 401, 405, 491, 543
  of the luminaries, 201
  of the Manes, 529
  of the mountains, 79
  of the night, 497
  of the spirits, 551
  of the three worlds, 153
  of the universe, 473
  of the waters, 81, 465
  of the winds, 111
  of the world, 367, 521
  of time, 610
  of treasures, 551
lotus, 45, 57, 105, 107, 121, 123, 159, 163, 165, 167, 261, 349, 383, 461, 479, 483, 499, 501, 507, 515, 529, 545, 566, 604, 607
  blue, 105, 127
  day, 77, 83, 107, 149, 159, 235, 331, 349, 375, 481, 491, 596, 607
  golden, 343, 345, 365
  land, 537
  night, 63, 67, 99, 149, 167,

227, 331, 375, 491, 493, 497, 568
red, 403
thousand-petaled, 345
white, 566
love, 111, 131, 181, 219, 321, 335, 341, 401, 413, 437, 471, 473, 475, 483, 493, 495, 501, 509, 517, 519, 521, 523, 525, 527, 533, 570, 602, 603, 610
lovemaking, 523, 592, 610
lover, 235, 513, 519, 533, 609
Madhu *(Madhu)*, 63
Madhu·cchandas *(Madhucchandas)*, 151
magic, 113, 119, 433, 455, 457, 553, 600
black, 313
purificatory, 193
Maha·kala *(Mahākāla)*, 525
Maha·parshva *(Mahāpārśva)*, 389
Maha·rashtra *(Mahārāṣṭra)*, 519
Mahíshmati *(Māhiṣmatī)*, 527
maiden, 233, 237
celestial, 499
river, 455, 467
serpent, 97
Mainâka *(Maināka)*, 467, 602
Máithili *(Maithilī)*, 509
mákara *(makara)*, 77, 233, 253, 519, 570, 610
Málaya *(Malaya)*, 321, 511, 519
Mályavan *(Mālyavat)*, 20, 21, 24, 229, 233, 333, 371, 391, 517, 582, 596, 597
Mándara *(Mandara)*, 477, 576
Mándavi *(Māṇḍavī)*, 177, 225
Mandódari *(Mandodarī)*, 401, 403, 443
mango, 319
Mánthara *(Mantharā)*, 21, 22, 249, 301
mantra *(mantra)*, 119, 135, 251, 295, 580
Manu *(Manu)*, 71, 91, 279, 347, 435, 467, 543, 587, 593, 601
Marícha *(Mārīca)*, 23, 151, 321, 327, 343, 515, 576, 609
Maríchi *(Marīci)*, 215
marriage, 241
marriage hall, 459
master, 509
Mátali *(Mātali)*, 423
Maudgálya *(Maudgalya)*, 53, 55, 57
Megha·nada *(Meghanāda)*, 389, 391, 393, 403, 457, 597, 612
Mena *(Menā)*, 602
Meru *(Meru)*, 147, 485, 487, 601, 602
message, 59, 65, 87, 225, 345, 347, 381
minister, 113, 229, 241, 247, 311, 351, 375, 387
chief, 115, 117
defense, 181
mirror, 475
misfortune, 209, 317
Míthila *(Mithilā)*, 19, 20, 169, 171, 179, 191, 209, 227, 237, 239, 241, 247, 249, 251, 309, 457, 533

Mitra *(Mitra)*, 543
monkeys 15, 18, 24, 113, 115, 117, 121, 213, 337, 343, 347, 351, 359, 363, 365, 371, 373, 377, 379, 381, 383, 387, 389, 393, 407, 409, 411, 413, 417, 419, 443, 445, 455, 463, 465, 467, 503, 566, 592, 595, 602
monkey-king, 18, 23, 24
monsters
  sea, 469
moon, 45, 63, 83, 89, 99, 105, 113, 159, 161, 163, 165, 167, 169, 227, 459, 461, 469, 477, 479, 485, 491, 493, 495, 497, 499, 501, 503, 505, 523, 529, 535, 543, 545, 566, 568, 577, 578, 581, 607, 611
  cool-rayed, 67, 89
  crescent, 171, 473, 481, 483, 485, 501, 503, 527, 605, 606
  digit of the, 79, 383, 487, 493, 545
  full, 501, 547, 588, 608
  new, 503, 608
  rising, 157, 497, 511
  waxing and waning of the, 99
moonlight, 69, 79, 149, 159, 161, 163, 165, 167, 293, 469, 481, 507, 523, 577, 607
moonstone, 161, 163, 483, 497, 503, 507, 511, 545, 608
mother, 109, 219, 263, 269, 287, 351, 385, 483, 588, 589
  of snakes, 457
  step-, 347, 483
mother-of-pearl, 121
mountain, 83, 97, 159, 219, 223, 251, 283, 287, 311, 313, 315, 321, 327, 331, 333, 341, 365, 379, 409, 411, 413, 415, 441, 455, 459, 465, 467, 471, 477, 479, 481, 483, 487, 489, 503, 505, 509, 511, 515, 517, 519, 553, 588, 595, 601, 609
  crystal, 483
  Eastern, 107, 137, 145, 159, 491, 503
  forested, 161
  herbs growing in, 602
  inaccessible, 115
  Ruby, 507
  Western, 105, 137, 149
  white-topped, 576
  winged, 479, 509, 602
Murári *(Murāri)*, 15, 16, 18, 26, 53, 57, 587, 607
music, 331
  festive, 293
musk, 49, 131, 205, 233, 523, 529, 574
Nandi·grama *(Nandigrāma)*, 313
Nárada *(Nārada)*, 357, 593
Narántaka *(Narāntaka)*, 24
Naráyana *(Nārāyana)*, 73, 439, 527
Nármada *(Narmadā)*, 253, 584
níchula *(nicula)*, 335
night, 81, 105, 121, 147, 165, 233, 235, 237, 311, 451, 467, 485, 503, 505, 515, 533, 573, 582, 609

autumn, 67
cloudy, 568
moonlit, 523
untimely, 409
Níkasha *(Nikaṣa)*, 385
Nila *(Nīla)*, 365, 419
Nisháda *(Niṣāda)*, 22, 311, 317, 319, 339, 347
noble, 51, 65, 109, 171, 181, 221, 223, 295, 349, 415, 431
nymph, 91, 161, 455, 598
ocean, 67, 81, 145, 147, 159, 271, 313, 357, 381, 383, 387, 395, 405, 435, 455, 459, 461, 463, 465, 467, 469, 471, 477, 479, 509, 511, 513, 529, 553, 577, 602
milk-, 79, 93, 169, 479, 495, 505, 572, 576, 604, 607, 612
of transmigration, 531, 535
offering, 73, 75, 91, 93, 127, 169, 189, 259, 313, 451, 495, 501, 539
funeral, 387
ritual, 275
Soma, 501
water, 267
oil
jasmine, 535
ointment
magical, 497
orchestra, 607
Óshadhi·prastha *(Oṣadhiprastha)*, 473
outpost, 551
palace, 211, 261, 523, 539, 543, 582
bejeweled, 371
royal, 255
palanquin, 399
Pampa *(Pampā)*, 341
Pancha·vati *(Pañcavaṭī)*, 23, 315, 319, 321, 515
Párashu·rama *(Paraśurāma)*, 21, 22, 221, 253, 255, 259, 263, 265, 267, 269, 271, 273, 277, 281, 283, 285, 287, 289, 291, 293, 299, 355, 359, 361, 419, 421, 533, 549, 584–588, 594, 612
Parijáta *(Pārijāta)*, 461
Párvati *(Pārvatī)*, 269, 273, 473, 521, 529, 531, 586, 602, 603, 610
Pashu·medhra *(Paśumeḍhra)*, 18, 109
peacock, 331, 333, 341, 429, 517, 591, 592
peak, 159
pearl, 283
physician, 461
Pináka *(Pināka)*, 19, 215, 353
pleasure, 233, 279, 355, 483, 527
aesthetic, 566, 579
royal, 253
visual, 111
worldly, 111
poem, 553
power, 111, 119, 135, 157, 189, 193, 203, 205, 207, 229, 263, 267, 293, 317, 345, 347, 359, 361, 383, 463, 503, 584, 594, 598

power
  ascetic, 87, 93, 111, 141, 293, 461
  brahmanic, 91, 119, 279
  holy, 329
  inner, 213
  magical, 613
  meditative, 87
  miraculous, 237
  poetic, 55
  supernatural, 247, 461
Prásravana *(Prasravaṇa)*, 515
Prayága *(Prayāga)*, 535, 537
prayer, 609
  evening, 489
preceptor, 113, 117, 141, 153, 157, 171, 191, 199, 201, 219, 249, 253, 281, 289, 584
priest, 109, 137, 197, 223, 237, 275, 393, 493, 574, 579, 581, 597
  family, 91, 219
  royal, 177, 179, 209
  sacrificial, 57, 207, 215, 291, 581, 597
prince, 83, 85, 93, 95, 123, 177, 179, 195, 197, 201, 203, 205, 209, 237, 239, 241, 247, 305, 311, 313, 315, 377, 429, 431, 539
  crown, 467
princess, 177, 179, 183, 215, 329
priyángu *(priyaṅgu)*, 517
protection, 87, 119, 279, 570, 571, 602
protector, 85
province, 293
Pulástya *(Pulastya)*, 239, 323, 329, 371, 377, 379, 389, 427, 445, 547, 573, 582
Purushóttama *(Puruṣottama)*, 49
Púshpaka *(Puṣpaka)*, 25, 451, 467, 469, 487, 507, 517, 539, 551
pyre, 459
queen, 301, 335, 443, 487, 527, 537, 545
  river, 357
radiance, 205
rage, 77
Raghu *(Raghu)*, 63, 73, 83, 85, 87, 157, 179, 203, 205, 247, 263, 275, 277, 279, 281, 293, 299, 303, 311, 313, 315, 353, 421, 429, 431, 451, 459, 505, 541, 545, 549, 587
Rahu *(Rāhu)*, 165, 578
rain, 69, 481, 507, 517, 591, 592, 597, 605
  of arrows, 409
rainbow, 205, 423
rákshasa *(rākṣasa)*, 113, 407, 417, 423, 431, 445, 515
Rama *(Rāma)*, 15, 17–25, 32, 55, 57, 81, 83, 85, 87, 89, 91, 93, 95, 97, 99, 101, 109, 111, 119, 127, 133, 141, 147, 151, 155, 157, 167, 169, 177, 183, 189, 191, 195, 197, 199, 203, 205, 207, 209, 211, 219, 221, 223, 227, 229, 243, 247, 249, 251, 253, 255, 261, 263, 265, 275, 281, 283, 291, 293, 297, 299,

301, 303, 305, 309, 311, 313, 315, 317, 319, 321, 327, 339, 353, 355, 365, 373, 375, 377, 379, 381, 383, 385, 387, 389, 391, 395, 401, 417, 419, 421, 423, 425, 427, 429, 431, 433, 435, 437, 439, 445, 447, 451, 455, 457, 469, 471, 479, 491, 505, 507, 513, 515, 533, 537, 541, 543, 545, 549, 551, 566, 567, 571, 572, 575, 576, 578, 580, 584–586, 588–592, 594–596, 599–601, 604, 608, 609, 612, 613
Rama·bhadra *(Rāmabhadra)*, 353, 355, 357, 363, 367
Rama·chandra *(Rāmacandra)*, 578, 612
Ratna·chuda *(Ratnacūḍa)*, 399, 403, 419, 441
Rávana *(Rāvaṇa)*, 18, 20, 21, 23–25, 93, 113, 117, 179, 183, 207, 209, 211, 213, 215, 217, 219, 221, 227, 233, 237, 241, 245, 265, 305, 317, 321, 327, 329, 337, 339, 343, 347, 349, 355, 361, 371, 373, 377, 379, 381, 383, 385, 389, 391, 393, 395, 401, 403, 405, 407, 411, 413, 415, 417, 419, 421, 425, 427, 429, 431, 433, 437, 439, 441, 443, 445, 489, 491, 515, 539, 541, 549, 551, 566, 573, 580, 582, 583, 590–601, 605, 612
realm, 529, 607
  celestial, 347
  of Indra, 161
  of the moon, 497
recitation, 93
  Vedic, 147
Rénuka *(Reṇukā)*, 291
respect, 49, 65, 71, 77, 79, 95, 141, 151, 169, 197, 265, 275, 337, 375, 415, 419, 443, 463, 485, 489, 495, 515, 521, 525, 533, 537, 541, 588
  lack of, 584
Reva *(Revā)*, 357, 593
rice, 127
righteousness, 551
Rishya·muka *(Ṛṣyamūka)*, 18, 115, 315, 341, 345
Rishya·shringa *(Ṛṣyaśṛṅga)*, 91, 93, 571
rites, 87, 209, 575
  funerary, 313
ritual, 65, 183
  daily, 255
  fire, 129
  of tonsure, 241
  of welcome, 608
  Vedic, 67, 141, 541
river, 131, 133, 309, 319, 331, 357, 455, 465, 511, 517, 529, 537, 574, 609, 611
  holy, 133, 537
  of the gods, 309
road
  abandoned, 249
Róhana *(Rohaṇa)*, 509
Róhini *(Rohiṇī)*, 495, 607
root, 135, 137, 197

of bad conduct, 243
royalty, 551
rudráksha *(rudrākṣa)*, 265
sacrifice, 65, 67, 69, 73, 75, 81, 85, 87, 93, 97, 107, 139, 141, 153, 157, 169, 175, 179, 197, 199, 207, 209, 243, 261, 273, 277, 279, 287, 291, 317, 377, 493, 515, 539, 566, 568, 571, 572, 574–576, 584, 597, 609
animal, 127, 574
fire, 253, 259
horse, 569
of weapons, 393
royal, 537
Vedic, 119, 151
sacrificer, 67, 167, 587
Ságara *(Sagara)*, 67, 543, 568
sage, 53, 55, 57, 63, 69, 83, 85, 87, 89, 91, 95, 109, 129, 131, 135, 143, 151, 155, 157, 167, 177, 179, 183, 189, 193, 195, 199, 201, 203, 209, 215, 219, 225, 227, 239, 243, 245, 247, 249, 253, 255, 259, 273, 287, 293, 295, 309, 311, 313, 315, 323, 341, 357, 387, 461, 463, 509, 513, 571, 573, 578, 583, 585, 587, 594, 601
ascetic, 513
brahmanic, 541
celestial, 493
divine, 329
of the Anthill, 51
royal, 65, 77, 83, 85, 91, 97, 99, 171, 177, 199, 201, 213, 221, 273, 341
young, 151
sages
seven, 571
Sampáti *(Saṃpāti)*, 321
sandal, 95, 407, 455, 545
paste, 535
sandals, 311, 545, 612
santánaka *(saṃtānaka)*, 489
Sárana *(Sāraṇa)*, 24, 373, 383, 391, 393, 395
Sarásvati *(Sarasvatī)*, 57
Sárayu *(Sarayū)*, 537, 611
Sávitri *(Sāvitrī)*, 135, 547
science
of archery, 85, 283, 287
of grammar, 117
of weapons, 85, 197, 243, 285, 419, 435
seat, 75, 570, 604
lotus, 479, 499, 607
raised, 183, 605
yogic, 439
seer, 191
serpent, 79, 97, 119, 205, 211, 457, 469, 566
servant, 249, 345, 515, 545
good, 455
sesamum, 163
shade, 137, 161, 163, 537
Shara·bhanga *(Śarabhaṅga)*, 311
Shatánanda *(Śatānanda)*, 20, 109, 177, 183, 189, 195, 197, 199, 201, 207, 215, 219, 225, 277, 587
Shata·patha *(Śatapatha)*, 191
Shatrúghna *(Śatrughna)*, 177, 225,

241, 539, 545, 547, 549
Sháushkala *(Śauṣkala)*, 20, 207, 209, 213, 219, 580
sheldrake, 45, 566
shelduck, 163, 233
shell, 51, 121
shelter, 251
Shesha *(Śeṣa)*, 79
Shiva *(Śiva)*, 19–21, 113, 171, 203, 205, 213, 217, 219, 221, 223, 243, 261, 263, 267, 285, 339, 413, 425, 471, 475, 477, 483, 485, 493, 495, 501, 505, 519, 521, 523, 525, 531, 573, 584–586, 598, 599, 602, 603, 607, 611
Shrámana *(Śramaṇā)*, 247, 249
Shrávana *(Śravaṇā)*, 21–23, 309, 311, 317, 319
Shringa·vera·pura *(Śṛṅgaverapura)*, 309
Shri·vatsa *(Śrīvatsa)*, 195
Shruta·kirti *(Śrutakīrtī)*, 177, 225
Shuka *(Śuka)*, 24, 373, 375, 387, 389, 391, 395, 596
Shunah·shepa *(Śunaḥśepa)*, 18, 109, 111, 137, 151
Shurpa·nakha *(Śūrpanakhā)*, 20, 21, 23, 239, 315, 317, 590
Shyama *(Śyāma)*, 537
siddha *(siddha)*, 329, 590
silver, 605
singing, 53, 331
Sira·dhvaja *(Sīradhvaja)*, 169, 171
Sita *(Sītā)*, 19–25, 175, 177, 179, 181, 201, 203, 215, 217, 223, 227, 229, 243, 245, 301, 303, 305, 309, 313, 321, 323, 341, 349, 367, 377, 391, 401, 413, 451, 455, 457, 461, 483, 487, 489, 491, 495, 501, 507, 515, 517, 519, 521, 529, 533, 537, 543, 545, 547, 566, 580, 582, 590, 591, 596, 598, 599, 604, 609
Skanda *(Skanda)*, 263, 265, 269, 483, 585–587
skin, 469, 602
  antelope, 135, 265
  dark, 605
  elephant, 213
sky, 81, 85, 89, 105, 107, 135, 137, 149, 157, 159, 161, 163, 165, 223, 233, 293, 399, 403, 409, 411, 455, 467, 469, 491, 505, 509, 537, 570, 588
snake, 73, 81, 243, 407, 455, 457, 473, 475, 477, 483, 485, 499, 531, 570, 581, 596, 603, 605, 607
  poisonous, 147
  ruler of the, 83
snake charmer, 423
Soma *(Soma)*, 501
son, 53, 83, 85, 87, 91, 93, 101, 115, 117, 141, 143, 151, 155, 167, 169, 197, 243, 263, 275, 281, 285, 295, 297, 299, 305, 309, 317, 347, 349, 351, 365, 375, 377, 379, 381, 385, 391, 403,

421, 457, 467, 483, 543, 571, 572, 579, 583, 585, 587, 593, 602
adopted, 273
dear, 389
dearest, 179
eminent, 385
of a bitch, 279
of a brahmin, 55
of a demoness, 427
of a kshátriya, 427
of Ángiras, 277
of a warrior woman, 279
of ascetics, 131
of Brahma, 541
of Dasha·ratha, 141, 199, 261, 355, 365
of false ascetic, 263
of Gadhi, 69, 87, 569
of Indra, 113, 337, 345, 355, 592, 594
of Índumati, 79
of Jamad·agni, 259
of Kúshika, 69, 71, 241
of Pulástya, 115, 371, 377, 379, 551, 573
of Rávana, 373
of Rénuka, 291
of Ságara, 529, 568
of Shiva, 585
of Sunda, 209
of Tádaka, 155, 576
of the sun, 317, 349, 363, 601
of the wind, 115, 363, 373, 377
of Vali, 592, 595
real, 361
second, 311, 389
spiritual, 151
son-in-law, 189, 195, 239
sorrow, 83, 95, 329, 331, 333, 335, 399, 451, 517
soul, 551
supreme, 551
sound, 97, 145, 149, 223, 439, 463, 581, 613
auspicious, 95
bubbling, 507
of earrings, 607
pleasant, 223
speech, 57, 271, 285, 373, 389, 566, 573
splendor, 79, 123, 437, 503, 539, 570
stage, 607
star, 147, 149, 165, 495, 501, 503, 567, 569, 578, 608
morning, 569
stratagem, 121
stream, 131, 483, 525, 529, 535, 553
of blood, 151, 261, 285, 431
street, 399, 401
student, 117, 119, 121, 157, 588
study, 574
Subáhu *(Subāhu)*, 151, 155, 576, 580
subject, 71, 81, 83, 247, 311, 425, 551
prosperity of, 313
Sudárshana *(Sudarśana)*, 433
Sugríva *(Sugrīva)*, 18, 23–25, 115, 117, 249, 317, 319, 339, 341, 345, 347, 349, 363, 365, 367, 381, 383, 413, 417, 419, 445,

451, 455, 465, 533, 547, 549, 592, 594, 595, 598
Suméru *(Sumeru)*, 379
sun, 45, 57, 77, 79, 81, 85, 95, 105, 107, 123, 135, 137, 145, 157, 199, 23, 235, 249, 273, 277, 281, 299, 347, 349, 383, 405, 437, 439, 451, 463, 469, 481, 487, 489, 501, 509, 529, 535, 543, 545, 547, 566, 570, 575, 578, 581, 592, 596, 600, 601, 602, 606
thousand-rayed, 117, 175, 191, 341
sun god, 171, 303, 423
Sutíkshna *(Sutīkṣṇa)*, 315
Suvéla *(Suvela)*, 381, 387, 455, 457
Svaha *(Svāhā)*, 93, 525, 611
sweat, 97
Tádaka *(Tāḍakā)*, 18, 19, 117, 141, 149, 151, 155, 167, 197, 207, 209, 227, 578
tamála *(tamāla)*, 49, 165, 305
Tamra·parni *(Tāmraparṇī)*, 511
Tántumati *(Tantumatī)*, 53
Tara *(Tāra)*, 367, 594
target, 205, 343, 361
tears, 75, 267, 333, 339, 343, 387, 389, 391, 399, 425, 431, 459, 467, 517, 586
flowing, 97, 275
temple, 63, 183, 261, 267, 401, 443, 581, 597, 600, 611
elephant's, 283
test, 405
text, 574, 583, 587
ritual, 574
sacred, 171
vedic, 189, 586
thought, 57, 87, 237, 331, 606, 608
thunderbolt, 77, 143, 177, 213, 217, 223, 229, 273, 403, 429, 489, 578
time, 83, 87, 97, 111, 137, 245, 275, 333, 363, 381, 387, 451, 467, 471, 493, 505, 574
difficult, 289
long, 63, 69, 71, 143, 171, 175, 185, 189, 193, 203, 293, 295, 299, 327, 355, 373, 399, 445, 545
of festivities, 49
track, 271, 319
tree, 49, 55, 131, 133, 137, 163, 165, 249, 311, 333, 341, 407, 409, 413, 461, 463, 481, 483, 487, 489, 515, 517, 543, 572, 575, 598, 605, 609
celestial, 445
coral, 99, 443, 575
fig, 137, 537
of Sugríva, 415
palm, 365
plantain, 83, 197, 501
rose-apple, 341, 592
sandal, 95
wish-fulfilling, 405, 419
Tri·shanku *(Triśaṅku)*, 67, 77, 139, 199, 570, 579
true nature, 191
of Brahman, 139

truth, 111
  ultimate, 167
twice-born, 574, 583
udúmbara *(udumbara)*, 127
Újjayini *(Ujjayinī)*, 523
underworld, 81, 415, 435, 553, 570
  of serpents, 211
  of snakes, 483
union
  uninterrupted, 475
upright, 333, 537
Úrmila *(Ūrmilā)*, 177, 201, 223
Úttara·kósala *(Uttarakosala)*, 225
Úttara·kóshala *(Uttarakoshala)*, 549
Vaidárbhi *(Vaidarbhī)*, 519
Vali *(Vālī)*, 18, 19, 23, 24, 113, 117, 211, 213, 247, 249, 317, 337, 345, 347, 351, 363, 365, 367, 381, 383, 385, 421, 489, 573, 592–595
Valmíki *(Vālmīki)*, 53, 55, 57
Vama·deva *(Vāmadeva)*, 17, 57, 59, 63, 67, 69, 71, 75, 85, 87, 89, 91, 95, 99, 568
Vanáyu *(Vanāyu)*, 405
Varáha *(Varāha)*, 612
Váruna *(Varuṇa)*, 81, 543
Vasíshtha *(Vasiṣṭha)*, 17, 25, 57, 59, 63, 65, 67, 69, 77, 83, 87, 91, 153, 157, 199, 201, 243, 281, 285, 505, 539, 549, 551, 567–569
Vatápi *(Vātāpi)*, 313
Veda *(Veda)*, 83, 145, 201, 273, 581, 595
verse, 553
Vibhándhaka *(Vibhāṇḍaka)*, 91
Vibhíshana *(Vibhīṣaṇa)*, 24, 25, 373, 375, 377, 379, 391, 445, 451, 455, 507, 533, 547, 549, 566, 595, 600
victory, 401
Vidárbha *(Vidarbha)*, 610
Vidéha *(Videha)*, 169, 183, 215, 225, 261, 277, 291, 329, 339, 469, 537
vidya·dhara *(vidyādhara)*, 25, 399, 597
Vindhya *(Vindhya)*, 251, 313, 327, 331, 341, 379, 407, 463, 553, 595, 598, 601, 602, 612, 613
Virádha *(Virādha)*, 22, 251, 313, 317
virtue, 97, 167, 567, 596, 605
  path of, 49, 568
Vishnu *(Viṣṇu)*, 45, 53, 73, 93, 127, 195, 205, 291, 293, 297, 309, 433, 461, 481, 571, 574, 575, 599, 604, 605, 612
Víshravas *(Viśravas)*, 387
Vishva·mitra *(Viśvāmitra)*, 15, 17–20, 57, 67, 69, 71, 73, 75, 77, 79, 83, 85, 87, 89, 93, 95, 97, 99, 101, 105, 107, 119, 121, 127, 135, 137, 139, 141, 151, 153, 155, 157, 169, 175, 179, 183, 189, 191, 193, 195, 199, 201, 203, 205, 207, 209, 215, 223, 225, 227, 241, 243, 271,

283, 285, 355, 419, 435, 569–572, 575, 578, 580, 583, 588
voice, 95, 149, 175, 233, 327, 333, 359, 439, 517, 581, 609
deep and calm, 273
faltering, 531
harsh, 275
high-pitched, 443
water, 477, 479
weapon, 77, 143, 175, 267, 271, 273, 275, 279, 283, 291, 333, 337, 359, 365, 405, 407, 409, 411, 413, 429, 437, 455, 580, 597, 600
celestial, 439
divine, 119, 247, 437
harsh, 259
heavenly, 419
mantra, 85, 119, 197, 435, 600
of Párashu·rama, 355
powerful, 265
welfare, 189
well-being, 93, 143, 211, 305, 497, 571
wife, 71, 113, 129, 157, 161, 177, 245, 247, 251, 263, 267, 321, 341, 343, 401, 403, 407, 431, 441, 443, 445, 489, 493, 495, 521, 529, 543, 547, 569, 583–585, 588, 592, 594, 599, 600, 603, 607, 611, 612
beloved, 566
celestial, 357
chaste, 443
cobra, 333
dejected, 443
faithful, 87, 571
lawful, 109
of another, 347, 363
pious and devoted, 69
wise, 57, 491, 579
woman, 119, 151, 153, 157, 247, 251, 269, 576, 609
barbarian, 551
beautiful, 167, 592
cruel, 479
monkey, 377
real, 109
warrior, 279
women, 131, 159, 223, 235, 259, 311, 479, 481, 493, 505, 511, 519, 523, 527, 581, 586, 604, 605, 608–610
beautiful, 51, 505
clever, 497
desirous, 145
fair-bodied, 523
gazelle-eyed, 491, 497, 503, 533
lotus-eyed, 159, 235
wanton, 511
young, 183, 511, 523
words, 51, 55, 57, 115, 151, 177, 193, 195, 199, 201, 203, 207, 247, 249, 267, 271, 281, 283, 303, 317, 327, 417, 433, 437, 489, 497, 519, 549, 567–569, 576, 585, 587, 591, 613
ambrosia-like, 79
divine, 53, 55
harsh, 610
magic, 553
melodious, 497

solemn, 55
world, 51, 55, 57, 79, 83, 89, 91, 93, 105, 111, 113, 121, 123, 139, 147, 153, 159, 165, 175, 191, 193, 195, 197, 205, 223, 227, 253, 259, 265, 267, 273, 275, 281, 323, 337, 349, 355, 357, 363, 383, 405, 411, 425, 431, 435, 437, 439, 441, 447, 451, 457, 459, 461, 463, 471, 473, 477, 479, 485, 489, 491, 493, 497, 519, 521, 541, 543, 547, 549, 553, 570, 575, 577, 579, 580, 597, 599, 600, 603, 606, 610
fourteen, 513, 527
human, 55, 237
seven, 513
three, 45, 49, 67, 71, 73, 75, 87, 115, 121, 163, 169, 183, 193, 199, 205, 213, 215, 221, 227, 229, 245, 255, 273, 275, 299, 359, 361, 371, 401, 421, 425, 433, 435, 451, 501, 525, 531, 539, 541, 553, 599, 601
triple, 53, 247, 297
worship, 45, 57, 93, 177, 221, 245, 339, 375, 389, 461, 574, 596
Yajnaválkya *(Yājñavalkya)*, 189, 191, 249, 273, 295, 579
Yajur·veda *(Yajurveda)*, 191, 273
yaksha *(yakṣa)*, 481
Yama *(Yama)*, 529
Yámuna *(Yamunā)*, 529, 535, 537, 611
year, 569, 579
fourteen, 301, 549
thousand, 85
young, 57, 109, 131, 151, 165, 175, 177, 179, 181, 183, 185, 209, 237, 243, 265, 267, 279, 283, 311, 321, 337, 373, 375, 379, 389, 391, 495, 511, 521, 523, 527, 549, 595